EVERYDAY AMERICA

EVERYDAY AMERICA

Cultural Landscape Studies after J. B. Jackson

Edited by
CHRIS WILSON and PAUL GROTH

University of California Press

BERKELEY   LOS ANGELES   LONDON

720, 973
E932

cou

Slightly different versions of chapters 2, 3, 6, and 10 originally appeared in a special issue of *Geographical Review*, vol. 88, no. 4 (October
1998); a slightly different version of chapter 3 also appeared as "Taking
on the Modern Movement: Editor's Introduction," by Helen Lefkowitz
Horowitz, in J. B. Jackson, *Landscape in Sight: Looking at America*
(New Haven: Yale University Press, 1997), pp. ix–xxxi. They are
reprinted here with permission.

University of California Press
Berkeley and Los Angeles, California

University of California Press, Ltd.
London, England

Library of Congress Cataloging-in-Publication Data

Everyday America : cultural landscape studies after J. B. Jackson / edited
by Chris Wilson and Paul Groth.
    p.   cm.
  Includes bibliographical references and index.
  ISBN 0-520-22960-6 (alk. paper)—ISBN 0-520-22961-4 (pbk. : alk.
paper)
    1. Jackson, John Brinckerhoff, 1909–   . 2. Landscape assessment—
United States. 3. Cities and towns—United States. 4. Human
geography—United States. I. Wilson, Chris, 1951 Dec. 23–   .
II. Groth, Paul Erling.
GF91.U6E94 2003
720'.973—dc21   2002011194

Manufactured in the United States of America

12   11   10   09   08   07   06   05   04   03

10   9   8   7   6   5   4   3   2   1

The paper used in this publication meets the minimum requirements of
ANSI/NISO Z39.48–1992 (R 1997) *(Permanence of Paper)*.

CONTENTS

PREFACE

In the 1930s, the maverick writer, philosopher, and publisher John Brinck-erhoff Jackson found the subject of cultural landscape analysis in the specialist academic realm of human geography. Until his death in 1996, he devoted much of his life to broadening cultural landscape study into a popular as well as a professional endeavor that is now an ongoing part of a dozen disciplines. This book is a critical review of Jackson's legacy and a survey of the current creative expansion and redefinition of cultural landscape writing in the United States. The authors collected here start with Jackson's example and with their own work address the question "What next?"

These authors are a representative sample of three generations of cultural landscape interpreters: first, people close to Jackson's own generation, a group that includes a number of people still actively writing, teaching, and designing; second, the generation of scholars and designers who often published in Jackson's journal, *Landscape*, and the students and professors who knew him as a teacher or senior colleague; and a new third generation of cultural landscape interpreters who often have discovered Jackson or the endeavor of cultural landscape studies on their own.

The work in this volume rests on two key premises. First, cultural landscapes—the complex sets of environments that support all human lives and all social groups—provide important and diverse avenues of study for better understanding culture and history. Second, cultural landscape interpretations are essential tools for better design and management of the built environment. These premises help to explain the interest in cultural landscape interpretations as a thread in several disparate disciplines including, in this collection alone, geographers, historians, architects, landscape architects, architectural historians, journalists, and planners.

The introductory chapter surveys the history and diversity of cultural landscape studies. The balance of this collection is organized into four thematic sections, with a brief introduction at the beginning of each. The chapters in the first section focus primarily on the understanding of J. B. Jackson and his work. The next section examines salient methods of teaching and learning visual and spatial literacy. The chapters in the third section interrogate some of the ever expanding theoretical bases of cultural landscape study. The final section provides a chronologically ordered set of case studies that demonstrate fresh insights in cultural landscape study as it enters the twenty-first century.

Just as the pages of *Landscape* magazine presented a variety of writing styles and disciplinary approaches, this collection embraces many different types of voices. The remembrances of the journalist Grady Clay and the practicing architects and planners Denise Scott Brown, Jeffrey Limerick, and James Rojas appear next to chapters by university professors writing within their academic traditions, such as the historian Helen Lefkowitz Horowitz and the landscape architecture historian Louise Mozingo. As diverse as this collection is, it represents just one of several clusters of approaches to cultural landscape study; here, readers will see a set of people who have been influenced by J. B. Jackson.

As a writer and editor, J. B. Jackson did everything he could to keep cultural landscape study in the foreground and himself in the background. Indeed, he resolutely refused to attend any meeting at which he might be featured above any other contributor. In 1998, Stephen Schreiber, director of the architecture program at the University of New Mexico in Albuquerque, initiated the idea of a conference to be held at the UNM campus to honor the contributions of Jackson, who for fifty years had been a resident of New Mexico and a favorite guest lecturer and instructor in the UNM architecture program. That conference, entitled "J. B. Jackson and

American Landscape," was the first large gathering on the subject to be convened after Jackson's death. The planning and paper selection committee (consisting of Schreiber and the editors of this volume) encouraged the eighty speakers not to memorialize Jackson, but rather to evaluate his work as a springboard for new study and as a basis for debate about how that study could be improved. The attendance at the fall 1998 conference—more than three hundred people from throughout North America—gave evidence of a robust continuing interest in cultural landscape studies. The chapters selected for this book, presented here in substantially refined versions, spoke most cogently as original and critical evaluations of Jackson's own work and as creative guides for stretching the boundaries of the field.

Planning for the 1998 conference was already under way when it was learned that J. B. Jackson had bequeathed a substantial endowment to the University of New Mexico "for the betterment of education in the School of Architecture and Planning." This new endowment ultimately supported the conference and the preparation of this book. The support of the J. B. Jackson Endowment was aided by a grant for publication from the Graham Foundation for Advanced Studies in the Fine Arts, of Chicago, Illinois. In addition to Stephen Schreiber, James R. "Ric" Richardson, interim dean of the School of Architecture and Planning, strongly supported the conference, its funding, and the preparation of this edited collection. The subsequent dean at UNM, Roger Schluntz, as well as Donlyn Lyndon and Charles C. Benton, successive chairs of the Department of Architecture at the University of California, Berkeley, also generously provided support. In Albuquerque, David Margolin provided invaluable editorial assistance; Anne Boynton, Anne Tyler, Lynée Busta, and Claudia Smith, research assistance; and Joseph Gallegos, supplemental graphics. At the University of California Press, at every point in the planning and editing process, the project enjoyed the skilled guidance of our editors, Charlene Woodcock, Monica McCormick, and Rose Vekony, and the meticulous contributions of copy editor Jacqueline Volin.

James Borchert, Elizabeth Collins Cromley, and Abigail Van Slyck read the entire manuscript and made helpful suggestions for improvement. Other essential assistance came from Elizabeth Byrne, Thomas Carter, Rita Douthitt, Claudia Farnswick, Helen Lefkowitz Horowitz, Richard Hutson, Lawrence Levine, Richard Longstreth, Margaretta Lovell, Waverly Lowell, Donald McQuade, Kathleen Moran, Louise Mozingo, Carolyn Porter, Christine Rosen, Mary Ryan, William Tydeman, and Dell Upton. We also thank the 1998 conference session chairs and featured plenary speakers—F. Douglas Adams, Daniel Arreola, Joe Bilello, Will Bruder, Julia Czerniak, Dennis Doxtater, Miguel Gandert, Joel Garreau, Edward T. Hall, Kenneth Helphand, Ferdinand Johns, Edith Katz, William Kelly, Andre Larroque, Margaretta Lovell, Bruce MacNelly, Chris Monson, William Least Heat Moon, Baker Morrow, Barton Phelps, Antoine Predock, Robert Riley, Elizabeth Rogers, Virginia Scharff, Darius Sollohub, Marc Treib, and Joseph Wood—and the other conference speakers and participants, whose ideas have actively contributed to this work.

Four of the chapters presented here—Patricia Nelson Limerick, "J.B. Jackson and the Play of the Mind: Inquiry and Assertion as Contact Sports" (chapter 2); Helen Lefkowitz Horowitz, "J.B. Jackson as a Critic of Modern Architecture" (chapter 3); Peirce Lewis, "The Monument and the Bungalow: The Intellectual Legacy of J.B. Jackson" (chapter 6); and Gwendolyn Wright, "Modern Vernaculars and J.B. Jackson" (chapter 10)—were selected by journal editor Paul Starrs to appear in a special issue of the *Geographical Review* dedicated to Jackson's work (88, no. 4, October 1998). These chapters appear here with permission. Starrs also graciously assisted in the preparation of illustrations for Peirce Lewis's chapter.

PAUL GROTH AND CHRIS WILSON

THE POLYPHONY OF CULTURAL LANDSCAPE STUDY

1

An Introduction

In the 1950s, the term *cultural landscape* rarely appeared in print. This was true even when writers needed a term to describe the intricate webs of mental, social, and ecological spaces that help to define human groups and their activities. By the 1990s, however, the term had clearly arrived in professional and literary circles. *Cultural landscape* or, more often, the word *landscape* alone, had come to refer to urban settings, building interiors, and even computer screen images, as well as planted or rural prospects. Between 1950 and 1990, people studying culture, history, and social relations had gradually realized the importance of the built landscape. The scholars who had used the term *cultural landscape* most before 1950—geographers and landscape architects—remained in the lead in the 1990s, with architects and planners not far behind.[1] Even writers for the *New York Times, Preservation* magazine, and National Public Radio now employed the term *landscape* in its cultural landscape sense, without further definition. More surprising, perhaps, was the discovery of everyday built spaces as significant evidence of social groups, power relations, and

1

culture by historians, American studies scholars, literary critics, and a growing number of anthropologists, sociologists, and social theorists.[2]

Indeed, *cultural landscape* is both a useful term and a necessary concept for understanding American environments. It is a way of thinking—one with inherent contradictions and multiple approaches—that people have readily adapted to new questions and social developments. This book surveys the widening conceptions and applications of cultural landscape studies in the United States. It also evaluates the pivotal role of one writer, John Brinckerhoff Jackson, in encouraging the study of cultural landscapes. As participants in a countermovement to the homogenizing forces of architectural and urban modernization, Jackson, his compatriots, and their successors have expanded and deepened the study of common landscapes and, in the process, have revitalized a term in use since the Middle Ages.

EXPANDING THE DEFINITIONS OF LANDSCAPE

The long and varied careers of the word *landscape* in English, and of its cognates in other northern European languages, have centered on the human shaping of space and also on the dynamic interaction of actual places with mental or visual images of place. The conception of landscape has expanded from genres of painting and garden design, through the study of seemingly unchanging agricultural societies, to the entire contemporary American scene, to applications in design and preservation movements and a growing interest in conflicts of race, class, gender, and power.

Old English precursors to *landscape*—*landskipe* and *landscaef*—already contained compound meanings. In the Middle Ages, a *land* was any well-defined portion of the earth, ranging from a plowed field to a kingdom. The original senses of *-skipe, -scipe,* and *-scape* were closely related to *scrape* and *shape,* meaning to cut or create. The related suffix, *-ship,* denotes a quality, condition, or a collection. It yields a word such as *township*—in Old English, *túnscipe*—which primarily meant the inhabitants of a town or village, but, secondarily, the domain or territory controlled by that settlement. Thus, *landskipe* essentially meant a collection or system of human-defined spaces, particularly in a rural or small-town setting.[3]

The Old English sense of landscape, which was social as well as spatial, appears to have faded into disuse by 1600, when artists and their clients introduced a related Dutch word, *landschap,* back into English. A landscape, in this new Dutch sense, was a painting of a rural, agricultural, or natural scene, often accented by a ruin, mill, distant church spire, local inhabitants, or elite spectators. In contrast to the earlier traditions of religious, mythological, and portrait paintings done on commission for the church or nobility, landscapes were painted on speculation for anonymous consumers in emerging mercantile centers such as Antwerp, Amsterdam, and London. As a result, the term *landscape* and the painting genre it described were tied to the rise of a merchant class with the power and leisure to cast their controlling and organizing gaze from the city out onto the countryside. Subsequent painting genres—seascapes, cloudscapes, townscapes—extended this sense of a *scape* as a carefully framed and composed real-life scene.[4]

By the early 1700s, well-to-do English landowners had begun to employ the aesthetics of picturesque landscape painters such as Nicolas Poussin, Claude Lorrain, and Salvator Rosa to record the natural aspects of the lands they visited. A landscape, thereby, became a pleasing view or panorama in seemingly wild or untouched nature. Before long, wealthy landowners also had begun to remake their English country estates to match the artful asymmetries of landscape painting. Interwoven as they were with the European grand tour, picturesque aesthetics, and the Romantic movement, the conceptions of landscape in Europe and the United States by the early nineteenth century involved not only the creation of paintings of natural and rural views, but also a growing interest in naturalistic gardens, vernacular architecture, and picturesque revival buildings (fig. 1.1).[5]

In the United States the popular fascination with the vibrant architecture, communities, and landscapes of everyday America has ranged from Walt Whitman, Mark Twain, and Winslow Homer through early-twentieth-century populism and on to the 1930s regionalism of New Deal writers and painters and the architectural and urban criticism of Lewis Mumford. The concern for environmental degradation caused by human activities was another American theme, spurred particularly by the Vermont writer George Perkins Marsh.[6]

Meanwhile, the growth of universities in the nineteenth century supported the notion among at least a few geographers, anthropologists, and sociologists—all influenced strongly by European colonialism—that everyday surroundings, not just high art, could provide important evidence of social life and cultural values. In Europe, several countries developed a distinct school of thought about the proper questions and methods of cultural landscape study. In Germany, geographers such as Friedrich Ratzel, Alfred Hettner, and Otto Schlüter focused particularly on scientif-

Figure 1.1.   The central campus and campanile of Iowa State University, Ames, Iowa, 1990. The artful, picturesque asymmetry of this site design, by the well-known firm established by Frederick Law Olmsted in Brookline, Massachusetts, embodies late-nineteenth-century picturesque landscape design.

ically categorizing regions and settlements. These German geographers developed close associations with geologists and economic analysts and gained a reputation for emphasizing physical forms. Schlüter, in particular, promoted interest in the idea of the *landschaft,* a discrete area defined by a uniform, harmonious interrelationship of physical elements.[7]

In France, sociologists and philosophers such as Paul Vidal de la Blache, Émile Durkheim, and Frédéric Le Play founded a school of thought that emphasized the interplay between cultural ways of life *(genre de vie)* and relatively small-scale local ecological and social regions *(pays).* While the Germans tended to look for general categories, the French looked for particularities of people and place, defined most of all by day-to-day lives. By World War II, each French region had its own well-written guidebooks to local social and physical landscapes.

In Great Britain, geography tended to emphasize historical approaches. The historian and geographer Halford J. Mackinder emphasized sweeping worldviews and careful descriptions of past landscapes, whose details helped explain surviving elements of the present-day scene. The British emphasis on field observation and map interpretation, even for urban schoolchildren, generated interest in local historical geography, as did the work of the Scottish city and regional planner Patrick Geddes, who applied field study to city and regional planning. After the 1950s, W.G. Hoskins's close documentation of rural landscapes and M.R.G. Conzen's attention to the details of urban streets and buildings inspired new generations of historical geographers and landscape archaeologists who are still active today.[8]

These European approaches found their way in varying proportions to different universities in the United States and became part of the basis for the present-day complexity of landscape study. For instance, by the early 1900s German ideas dominated geography at the University of Chicago, while British geography had more influence at the University of Wisconsin.[9] Beginning in the 1920s, Carl Sauer, who had studied in Germany and at Chicago, became the longtime chair of the geography department at the University of California, Berkeley, where he revised and updated the German *landschaft* idea, using the term *landscape*. Through Sauer, the idea of cultural landscape gained prominence in American geography. In his groundbreaking 1925 essay, "The Morphology of Landscape," Sauer set forth his definition: "The cultural landscape is fashioned from the natural landscape by a cultural group. Culture is the agent, the natural area is the medium, the cultural landscape the result."[10]

Landscape, in this sense, was not a painting, a vista, or a garden, but rather a particular area shaped by a cultural group and strongly influenced by the limits of soil, climate, and plant life. Sauer and the so-called Berkeley School of cultural geography shifted the sense of landscape back from a composed image to the place itself. Like Hoskins and his followers in England, Sauer and his students often equated landscapes with coherent and stable cultures and thus typically left modern, industrialized cities outside their purview. For cultural geographers of the Berkeley School, the historical diffusion of ideas from one region to another became a theme of primary importance. Fred Kniffen was one of several Sauer students who followed vernacular landscape elements—fences, building types, and settlement forms—to identify cultural hearths and migration patterns (fig. 1.2).[11] Thus, by the interwar years of the twentieth century, the study of landscape had several competing and overlapping paradigms in Europe and in the United States.

J.B. JACKSON AS A CATALYST FOR LANDSCAPE STUDIES

The independent writer, editor, and landscape philosopher John Brinckerhoff Jackson played a central role in the maturation of cultural landscape

Figure 1.2.   Farmstead in northeastern Colorado, near Atwood, 1990. The vernacular house, barns, and other outbuildings, as well as the meadow in the foreground and the line of trees shielding the farmstead from the northern winds, are all elements of interest in traditional cultural landscape studies. The abandonment of the house marks recent rural depopulation.

studies in the United States. Although Jackson made his reputation with the study of ordinary, everyday settings, his background was one of wealth and privilege, his education a traditional one in the fine arts. Jackson was born in 1909 in Dinard, France, to American parents. His father, William Brinckerhoff Jackson, was a Washington, D.C., lawyer who had inherited a substantial fortune built in part upon real estate developments in the New Jersey suburbs of New York City. Jackson's mother, Alice Richardson Jackson, was a descendant of another long-established Hudson Valley family. Jackson's parents divorced when he was four years old. His mother subsequently supported herself as a buyer for the Bonwit Teller department store in New York, which often took her to Paris, with her son in tow. The young Jackson attended a series of private boarding schools in the United States and Europe, including two years at Le Rosey in Switzerland, known as the "school of princes," where the future shah of Iran, Mohammed Reza Pahlavi, was a fellow student. Jackson's father provided only for his school expenses; his mother paid for the rest, and her income was more limited. Thus, one assumes Jackson's childhood included having to learn (particularly by close observation) the dress, manners, and speech of people far wealthier than himself.[12]

With such a background, it is hardly surprising that the young Jackson was fascinated by the contrasts of different languages and cultures. By his teenage years, he was fluent in French and German, had traveled widely in Europe, and was already adept at sketching as a method of recording travel impressions. In the mid-1920s, he began spending his summer vacations in Santa Fe with his uncle, Percy Jackson, a Wall Street lawyer who also served as treasurer and legal advisor to the School of American Archeology, head-quartered there. Percy Jackson was well acquainted with the circle of artists and anthropologists then remaking Santa Fe into a tourist center and art colony.[13] In one particularly memorable summer, Jackson accompanied his uncle to Mayan archaeological digs on the Yucatan peninsula, where the Jacksons dined with the senior scholars as they discussed emerging inter-pretations of the Mayan past, based primarily on the physical landscape record, and where Jackson also added Spanish to his linguistic skills.

Jackson finished preparatory school at Deerfield Academy in Massa-chusetts and, at the urging of his headmaster, enrolled in the multidisci-plinary Experimental College of the University of Wisconsin instead of following the family path to Harvard. The program at Wisconsin es-chewed disciplinary boundaries and devoted an entire year to the study of one place during one century. Students were encouraged to examine their surroundings with their own eyes and to consider the importance of reli-gion in understanding culture. A series of visits by Lewis Mumford en-couraged several students to study architecture.[14]

Although the Wisconsin experience greatly influenced Jackson's later work, he was unhappy in Madison, and after one year he transferred to Harvard, completing his bachelor's degree in history and literature in 1932. After studying architecture for one year at MIT and commercial drawing in Vienna, Jackson traveled by motorcycle around Europe for two years. His articles on the rise of fascism for the *American Review* and *Harper's Magazine* led to a 1938 novel, *Saints in Summertime*, which he published under the name of Brinckerhoff Jackson. The *New York Times* called the book "a remarkable piece of work, crafty, witty and original," and the *Saturday Review of Literature* placed Jackson on its cover (fig. 1.3). But instead of immediately pursuing this literary success, Jackson returned to New Mexico to work as a cowboy on an isolated ranch near Wagon Mound.[15]

In 1940, Jackson enlisted in the United States Army. His European ex-perience and his command of Spanish, French, and German led the army

Figure 1.3. J.B. Jackson's cover appearance as Brinckerhoff Jackson in the July 23, 1938, issue of the *Saturday Review of Literature* for his novel, *Saints in Summertime*. Friends who met Jackson before the 1970s knew him by his nickname, "Brinck."

to make him a combat intelligence officer. In northern France during the latter stages of the war, Jackson interrogated German prisoners and pored over aerial photographs, guidebooks, and regional geography studies to form his first comprehensive conceptions of cultural landscapes—the ones where his unit would next fight. Studying the libraries of successive chateaux occupied as military headquarters essentially became Jackson's graduate education in French sociology and geography.

Discharged from the army in early 1946, Jackson drove across the United States in a surplus jeep—sketching, taking notes, and applying the skills he had developed during the war to the American cultural landscape. He ran a ranch in east-central New Mexico until he was thrown and dragged by a horse. During eighteen months of traction, surgery, and convalescence, Jackson decided to go back to writing and to start a magazine inspired by the vivid French regional geographies he had studied during the war, and by a new French journal, *Revue de géographie humaine et d'ethnologie*.[16] At Santa Fe, in the spring of 1951, a forty-one-year-old Jackson began publishing his small magazine, entitled *Landscape*. His first statement of intentions concludes:

> Wherever we go, whatever the nature of our work, we adorn the face of the earth with a living design which changes and is eventually replaced by that of a future generation. How can one tire of looking at this variety, or of marveling at the forces within man and nature that brought it about?
>
> The city is an essential part of this shifting and growing design, but only a part of it. Beyond the last street light, out where the familiar asphalt ends, a whole country waits to be discovered: villages, farmsteads and highways, half-hidden valleys of irrigated gardens, and wide landscapes reaching to the horizon. A rich and beautiful book is always open before us. We have but to learn to read it.[17]

Excerpts from the work of French human geographers in the early issues of *Landscape* indicate Jackson's debt to them.[18] Yet in Jackson's hands, the concepts of *genre de vie* and *pays* became transformed into essays about generic archetypical landscape elements, such as the house, the yard, or the suburb.

Although subscriptions covered some costs, Jackson never accepted any advertising and heavily subsidized the costs of *Landscape* himself. During his seventeen years as publisher and editor, the circulation of *Landscape* magazine never exceeded three thousand individual and library subscribers. Nevertheless, it was read by leading figures in half a dozen fields and by students who would emerge as important scholars and commentators in their own right.[19] Jackson hoped to reach an interested lay audience and typically drafted conversational, wry, and piercing essays of his own in the tradition of Michel Montaigne, Henry Thoreau, and H. L. Mencken.[20] Jackson also contributed to *Landscape* under several pseudonyms, each voice expressing its own style and expertise.[21]

As an editor traveling often to scholarly conventions and universities around the country looking for authors and articles, Jackson consciously wove together a diverse network of geographers, historians, architects, land-

Figure 1.4. The cover of
the autumn 1952 issue of
Landscape magazine, with
an aerial photograph of
contour plowing. Jackson
paid close attention to the
quality of the illustrations
and page design, in part to
attract the interest of visually oriented readers.

scape architects, planners, sociologists, anthropologists, and journalists who
shared his passion for understanding cultural landscapes. *Landscape* articles
on vernacular architecture, ecology, American history, rural and urban planning, the anthropology of space, cultural geography, architectural and landscape design, historic preservation, and tourism were leavened by an extensive book review section, occasionally spirited exchanges about the ideas
surfacing in the journal, and attractive covers and page designs (fig. 1.4).

Jackson's selections of articles and authors, and his occasional pronouncements of editorial policy, reveal his personal expansion of landscape studies. In these changes, Jackson paralleled more official gestures of
inclusiveness following World War II, such as the addition of ethnographic
art to art museum collections and of popular culture topics to academic
research and curriculums. In time, *Landscape's* editor and contributors
covered all manner of human environments: historic and contemporary;
vernacular and architect designed; rural, urban, and suburban. Assessing
Jackson's influence in 1979, the geographer Donald W. Meinig wrote:

> Jackson points the way in his insistence on looking the modern
> scene squarely in the face; and his admonition is not simply for us

to be comprehensive and tolerant, but to see the ordinary land-scapes of the automobile, mobile home, supermarket, and shopping center as legitimately "vernacular"—that is, native to the area, but area now defined more at the national than the local scale.[22]

While he was still publishing *Landscape* magazine, Jackson began a new phase of his career, as a peripatetic university professor and popular guest speaker. After he quoted Carl Sauer approvingly in the second issue of the magazine, a cordial correspondence had ensued, and in 1957, Sauer invited Jackson to visit the Berkeley geography department. Articles soon began to flow from Berkeley to the journal, and Jackson began making ex-tended annual visits to the campus, where he sat in on seminars, gave talks, and finally taught seminar classes of his own. The Berkeley School of cultural geography reinforced Jackson's own impatience with academic fragmentation and specialization and his desire to understand the cultural and physical connectedness of the landscape.

Jackson eventually added the Berkeley architecture and landscape ar-chitecture departments to his annual circuit, and by 1967 he was teaching a course in landscape architecture. Two years later, he began a similar rela-tionship at Harvard. Design faculty at both schools soon became readers and contributors to *Landscape*.

In 1969, Jackson turned over the reins of *Landscape* to a new publisher, Blair Boyd, who, with longtime editor Bonnie Loyd, produced the journal for another twenty-eight years. This freed Jackson to write book-length collections of essays and to teach nearly full time.[23] Jackson was in his late fifties when he began teaching his survey of American cultural landscape history at Harvard in the fall semester of each year, at Berkeley in the winter quarter, and at other universities for one-term rotations. His lec-tures soon were drawing two hundred to three hundred students, with de-sign and architectural history faculty auditing from the back of the room. For these professors and design students, the course was a conversion ex-perience to a new way of looking at the built environment.[24] Jackson's survey lectures, like his earlier writings, took ordinary settings usually overlooked by academic study and made them interesting. Helaine Caplan Prentice observed in *Landscape Architecture*, "His curriculum is as indis-pensable to designers' perceptions today as was once the European grand tour."[25]

In 1978, Jackson retired from regular teaching duties and returned to live full time in his house in La Cienega, a village ten miles southwest of Santa Fe. He continued a voluminous correspondence and hosted a steady stream of academic visitors. Although the income from his family inheritance remained secure, he chose to take a series of manual-labor jobs. Rising early six days a week, he worked successively as a gardener, a trash hauler, and finally, a janitor for Ernie's Auto Repair, a transmission repair shop in Santa Fe owned by a family from La Cienega. Jackson found satisfaction in manual labor: "It is a blessing to be of service," he sometimes explained.[26]

Parallel with these changes in his work life, Jackson also gave up using his nickname, "Brinck," which he felt confused his neighbors and had upper-class pretensions. People who met him after 1978 knew him as John Jackson, as his Hispanic neighbors and fellow members of the local Catholic congregation knew him, or as Brother Jackson, as he was known to the members of the African American church in Albuquerque and an Anglo-Texan Pentecostal mission in Santa Fe that he also enjoyed attending. His jobs and his church visits provided social contacts as well as observations for many of his later essays, which he continued to write each afternoon. Only months before his death in 1996, at the age of eighty-six, he completed a final essay for *Landscape in Sight*, a retrospective of his best writing, edited by Helen Lefkowitz Horowitz.[27]

Much about Jackson's life is contradictory: he was a son of the upper class, educated in fine arts and literary classics, who preferred studying the environments of working-class and middle-class people; a cosmopolitan world traveler who was equally at home in the small towns and factory neighborhoods of the United States; a writer, editor, and popular professor who had no official graduate degrees and who routinely set himself apart from scholars and academic life. Perhaps because of his year in the Wisconsin experimental college, Jackson never claimed any particular academic discipline, preferring "landscape studies" to any of the several disciplines that claimed him as a member. He never attempted to make his speculations seem exhaustive or conclusive on a subject. Instead, his intention was to stimulate other people to take up the challenge, to spur their own seeing, thinking, writing, and designing.

J. B. Jackson also left much work to be done by others. He wrote primarily about the landscapes of men; rarely about those of women and children. Predictable points of view and systematic thinking were not among his many gifts. He often sidestepped political questions and borrowed freely from both conservative and radical sources. Although he avidly read theoretical works (often in their original languages), he took playful, experimental, and often elusive positions on issues of theory, which infuriated doctrinaire followers of any one particular stripe. At the beginning of his formal and informal education, Jackson had found studies of the landscape already in multiple voices and competing schools of thought. His influence was not to create any new, well-defined disciplinary rigor or a single paradigm. Instead, he consciously added still more diversity to the enterprise.

APPLYING LANDSCAPE STUDIES TO DESIGN
AND HISTORIC PRESERVATION

From the beginning of his writing and publishing career, Jackson applied cultural landscape perspectives to contemporary planning, architecture, and landscape architecture, often as part of a personal critique of modernist design and planning. The potential role of designers in making a more meaningful environment was a consistent theme in his writing, and he was vitally interested in the cultural and social meaning of architectural design.[28] Jackson sought out designers as friends, students, and as a reading audience. He and his magazine built important bridges between geography and design. However, Jackson also was exasperated when designers applied landscape study too quickly, looking only at the visible surface of the landscape and not doing the kind of personal observation, research, or reading that lead to deeper analysis. He faulted architectural modernists for neglecting the importance and meaning of popular American settings such as the suburbs, commercial roadsides, office parks, and shopping malls. He also gently chided landscape architects for ignoring the aesthetic qualities and significance of the giant rural grid and ubiquitous parking lots. For Jackson, vernacular landscapes provided indispensable inspiration and context for contemporary design.

In Jackson's writing and teaching, and in other contributions to *Landscape*, designers found inspiration and encouragement for contextualism and regionalism. At Jackson's urging in 1962, four junior Berkeley architecture professors—Donlyn Lyndon, Charles W. Moore, Sim Van der Ryn, and Patrick J. Quinn—wrote an antimodernist manifesto, "Toward Making Places," for *Landscape*. *Learning from Las Vegas*, the path-blazing 1972 book by Robert Venturi, Denise Scott Brown, and Steven Izenour, demonstrated how the study of a new vernacular such as the automobile commercial strip could inform design practice.[29]

Jackson's fascination with commercial architecture did not include a call for its universal preservation, however. His ambivalence about the preservation of historic built environments and the conservation of wilder nature in state and national parks mirrors an ongoing series of debates within the field. Like cultural landscape studies, preservation and environmentalism trace their roots, in part, to the romanticism of the nineteenth century. During the mid-twentieth century, as architectural preservationists broadened their focus from house museums and singular buildings to the protection of urban districts, small towns, and rural landscapes, they drew support from cultural landscape scholars. Academic landscape studies have at times been closely allied with the historic preservation and environmental movements. Following J. B. Jackson's death, *Preservation* (the magazine of the National Trust for Historic Preservation) noted, "Jackson was the first to identify persuasively the elements that make a particular landscape American, and to explain convincingly how commerce, imagination, need, and nature collaborated over time in creating the look of the land."[30] Beginning in the early 1980s, Robert Melnick and Linda McClelland led efforts to systematize the study and nomination of rural historic landscapes to the National Register of Historic Places. The concept was becoming a given within the movement by the time the topic of cultural landscape was adopted as the theme for the 1997 National Trust convention. In a related vein, Elizabeth Barlow Rogers founded the Cityscape Institute in New York to promote high standards for public space design, restoration, and management.[31]

Although Jackson on occasion supported preservation, he also provided ample ammunition for battles *against* preservation and environmentalism. Here is one of the sharp distinctions between Jackson and more preservation-oriented writers such as Hoskins. Like Jackson, other cultural landscape scholars such as David Lowenthal and planners such as Kevin Lynch have voiced serious doubts about the advisability, or even the possibility, of freezing any particular landscape, whether a national park or a trailer park.[32] "The power which an ancient environment possesses to command our affection and respect derives from its having accepted change of function," wrote Jackson. "Its beauty," he continued, "comes from its having been part of the world, not from having been isolated and protected, but from having known various fortunes" (fig. 1.5).[33]

THEORETICAL FOUNDATIONS AND DEBATES

On the questions of method, theory, and philosophy that undergird landscape studies, J. B. Jackson's pronouncements were short, elliptical, and widely scattered.[34] Thus, even the people inspired by Jackson continue to exhibit diverse choices in philosophical underpinnings. Methods and theory have also tended to divide cultural landscape scholars into

Figure 1.5. Downtown commercial building in Zanesville, Ohio, 1985. Strict architectural preservationists might be most attracted to the design of the original 1870s facade, while a cultural landscape approach might find equal interest in the 1960s aluminum refacing of the center section of the building, and in the first-floor storefronts, each from a different decade.

different groups, several of them completely independent of Jackson's influence.

In one way or another, philosophical debates among cultural landscape scholars revolve around the relationship between agency and structure—the ways in which *individual* experience and action become the basis for *shared* social and cultural ideas and actions (and, in a dialectical feedback loop, how social experience influences individual thought and life). This is a basic question of all sociology and social theory. Seeing the landscape as an arena of agency and structure requires a shift from viewing landscape as the somewhat passive result of human activity to landscape as essentially an active influence on social, economic, and political processes. Winston Churchill put it simply when he wrote, "We shape our buildings, and then they shape us."[35] These approaches bring to the foreground the idea that landscapes of the mind (including images of landscape and landscapes only imagined) are inextricably involved in perceptions of and actions within everyday built space.

As the early publication of a "place-making" article suggests, in the 1960s and 1970s, *Landscape* and Jackson himself showed a strong interest in phenomenology and its emphasis on "sense of place" as a way of putting individual experience back into the agency side of the agency-and-structure debate. Jackson published many writers with a phenomenological point of view, including the geographers Yi-Fu Tuan and Anne Buttimer. The notions of place (and its absence, placelessness) remain vital among scholars and designers, and a large literature is now available.[36] Another theoretical foundation of the place literature in cultural landscape study comes from work on individual perception of the environment. Here, again, *Landscape* offered early examples to its readers, including articles by Robert Sommer and Jackson's Santa Fe friend, the anthropologist Edward T. Hall.[37]

In 1975, the folklorist Henry Glassie (a student of Fred Kniffen) made an important advance in this direction in his influential study *Folk Housing in Middle Virginia*. His argument is a direct application of the anthropologist Claude Lévi-Strauss's notion of structuralism: the conviction that deep binary mental structures exist and are expressed and reinforced in ways of thinking about the world and human places within it. For Glassie, seemingly practical decisions—making rooms square rather than oblong, or inserting hallways between rooms to isolate their activities and better specialize their uses—were unself-consciously linked to changing social and cultural ideas. Glassie suggested that at the deepest level of all environmental change and management was the inherent opposition between chaos and control. His example has inspired an entire generation of material culture scholars and vernacular architectural historians.[38]

In the 1980s and 1990s, Marxist and post-Marxist analysis provided a major theoretical realignment in landscape studies and ushered in a greater interest in urban subjects. In the words of the radical geographer Richard Walker, the early cultural landscape concepts of Carl Sauer and J. B. Jackson were "altogether too evasive about systematic forces of political economy in mainstream capitalist America and in answering the question of who and what, in fact, create urban and rural environments."[39] To distance themselves from the rural and bourgeois overtones of traditional concepts of landscape, many recent writers employ the more neutral terms *space* or *social space*. Building on Marxist political economy, theorists such as Henri Lefebvre and David Harvey have posited their own conceptions of the social-spatial dialectic. In Harvey's formulation, "space and time are *constituted by* and *constitutive of*, social relations and practices."[40]

Simultaneously, the meaning and usefulness of the term *culture* have been called into question by Marxist and other writers. James Duncan reminds us that Carl Sauer, like his anthropological contemporaries before World War II, saw culture as independent of, but controlling, individual behavior. Culture was somehow superorganic, responding to laws of its own not related to social action or power.[41] Following from the work of Michel Foucault and Henri Lefebvre, a large number of writers who might—with some protest—be grouped together as postmodernists avoid using the term *culture* altogether and focus on ideology, hegemony, the illusions of representation, and the social construction of knowledge. If they do use the term, they emphasize the contingency and individual acting out of culture, the importance of multiple or hybrid cultures, and opposition to cultural norms as central considerations.[42]

While the Sauerian approach to landscape, like nineteenth-century French and German geography before it, sought evidence of cultural cohesion and continuity, more recent studies of social space have emphasized class conflicts, differing social constructions of identity, and unequal power relationships. One direction of these studies, which we might call the global strategy, has been to situate local landscapes within their worldwide consequences and connections, and to analyze specific landscapes more fully as manifestations of large-scale economic forces and multinational corporate power. In 1984, Anthony King's *The Bungalow: The Production of a Global Culture* showed that the global strategy could be insightfully tied to building types.[43] Another direction of these critical theorists is a focus on locally "contested landscapes"—for instance, the places where ethnicity, race, class, age, or gender are spatially defined, reinforced, and counteracted (fig. 1.6). Here the aim is not only to dissect how spaces have helped to shape (and reproduce) social hierarchies, but also to illuminate how individuals and social movements have opposed those hierarchies. With the contention between field laborers and landowners in California's Central Valley in mind, Don Mitchell usefully extends the definition of landscape: "Landscape is thus best understood as a kind of produced, lived, and represented space constructed out of the struggles, compromises, and temporarily settled relations of competing and cooperating social actors; it is both a thing (or suite of things), as Sauer would have it, and a social process, at once solidly material and ever changing."[44] Dolores Hayden's *The Power of Place: Urban Landscapes as Public History*, published in 1995, and Setha Low's *On the Plaza: The Politics of Public Space and Culture*, published in 2000, are other salient examples of this more local strategy of analysis (fig. 1.7).[45]

Another group of theorists, who sometimes are lumped together as "structurationists," most overtly use the issue of structure and agency as their theme. Applying the ideas of Anthony Giddens, Allan Pred, or Pierre Bourdieu, they trace the relations of power that are often expressed not only in conscious political action but also in common, daily cultural

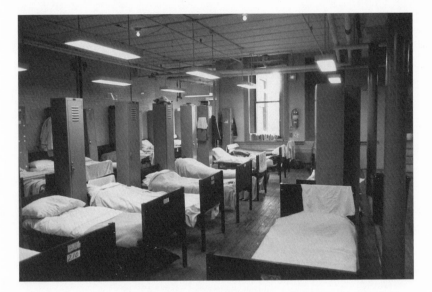

Figure 1.6.   Dormitory-style beds in a men's shelter on the Bowery, New York, 1994. In a space formerly filled with semiprivate cubicle-style rooms, this shelter—now owned and managed by the City of New York—is an official expression of last-resort housing for urban underclass residents.

practices and patterns of consumption that, in turn, interact with cultural landscapes.[46]

Yet another group of theoretically astute landscape analysts primarily use *images* of landscape as their points of departure. Cultural historians such as Raymond Williams and geographers such as Denis Cosgrove have taken an approach closely tied to art history and the Dutch landscape-as-image tradition. Cosgrove, for instance, has argued that the very notion of landscape as a privileged perspectival vision is inextricably linked to the rise of capitalism and the conception of land as a marketable commodity.[47]

The issue of the relationship of humans to wilder nature presents another philosophical focus for cultural landscape study. Even at the end of the twentieth century, the common attitude has been to assume *good* nature and *bad* humankind. The ethnobotanist Edgar Anderson—the most frequent contributor to *Landscape* after J. B. Jackson himself—framed the issues in 1957:

> The Amateur Thoreaus and the professional naturalists have in the United States raised the appreciation of nature to a mass phenomenon, almost a mass religion; yet at the same time they have refused to accept man as part of nature. . . . They are one of the chief ultimate sources of our unwritten axiom, that cities are something to

Figure 1.7. Annual Fiestas, Taos, New Mexico, 1993. A contested landscape, the Spanish colonial main plaza is given over to tourism for most of the year, but is reclaimed by the native Hispanic population during the three-day fiestas of Santiago and Santa Ana each July.

flee from, that the harmonious interaction of man and other organisms can only be achieved out in the country, that the average man is too noisy, too ugly and too vile to be accepted as a close neighbor.[48]

Since the 1970s, environmental historians, led by Donald Worster, Richard White, Carolyn Merchant, and William Cronon, have expanded upon the repercussions of intellectually separating humans and nature, noting that concepts such as nature and wilderness are human constructions. Through nuanced histories of particular regions, they have detailed the intricate interactions of human and environmental forces (fig. 1.8).[49]

Although philosophical underpinnings vary widely within any one field, study of cultural landscape remains strong in the disciplines that first embraced the topic. Historical and cultural geographers such as Michael Conzen, Peirce Lewis, Donald Meinig, Karl Raitz, and Wilbur Zelinsky—and, in turn, their students—have extended both the questions and the methods of landscape study.[50] In American literature and American studies, John Stilgoe and Thomas Schlereth have been influential contributors.[51] The journalist and editor Grady Clay has compiled a lifetime

Figure 1.8.   Grain elevators near Aberdeen, South Dakota, 1978. The historian
William Cronon, in *Nature's Metropolis,* traces the economic and ecological impacts of the invention of the nineteenth-century wooden grain elevator (far left).
The huge, post-1945 concrete additions reflect the expansion and centralization of
the world grain market.

of astute observations of the American city in three books, and two editors—Judy Metro and George Thompson—have developed significant
landscape studies lists.[52] Environmental planners, notably Ervin Zube, and
botanists have also been active contributors; in 1999 the Arnold Arbore-
tum of Harvard University launched an Institute for Cultural Landscape
Studies.[53]

Some landscape writers have faulted politically engaged or highly theoretical scholarship for producing abstract discussion with little or no
grounding in the observation and analysis of actual human places. Meanwhile, theoretically based writers have castigated the work of those who
are spatially specific and interested in the visual realm as being merely descriptive and as confusing surface distractions with the unseen substance
of personal environmental experience and hegemonic discourse. Richard
Walker, who for many years felt himself a pariah in the Berkeley geography department because of his Marxist approach, has characterized this

situation as a "schism between cultural studies and political economy." He suggests the solution may be "the promiscuous mingling and mutual education of cultural geographers and political economists."[54] If cultural landscape scholars need to give more attention to social power relationships, most political economists could better integrate the effects of the physical, spatial world into their analyses. In these exchanges lies an important truth for all landscape study: the lurking, ever-present potential for cunning camouflage and landscape duplicity—that what we *can't* see, what is *not* in view, may be more important than what conscious public relations strategies have made visually obvious.[55]

THE POLYPHONY OF LANDSCAPE STUDIES

Given the variety of impulses that underlie its history and use, cultural landscape study is of necessity a many-voiced endeavor. In the eighteenth century, the conception of landscape first expanded from a genre of painting to the appreciation of natural vistas, then to the design of romantic gardens. In the twentieth century, European schools of geographic thought were refashioned for new American applications. Carl Sauer's Germanic interests in rural societies and ecologies and the French notions of the *pays* were extended by J. B. Jackson to serious consideration of the entire contemporary American landscape. Through Jackson's magazine and his teaching, cultural landscape studies helped invigorate the design professions with a new respect for the vernacular scene. Meanwhile, the sheer number of divergent disciplines, schools of thought, philosophical bases, and professional applications in preservation and design guarantees the continuing expansion of both parallel and divergent approaches to landscape. The recent scholarly interests in race, class, gender, power relations, and world economic exchanges have added still more essential polyphony to the study of cultural landscapes.

Decidedly, we can expect no single, unified, rigidly bounded approach to the study of something so essential and yet so complex as the reciprocal relationships between individuals, groups of people, and their everyday surroundings. Jackson himself required a number of pseudonyms in order to address the different approaches that he personally needed for his journal. The people who have found encouragement and inspiration in Jackson's influence (or who have directly reacted against its limitations) continue to take cultural landscape studies in both old and new directions. And the "Jacksonian" approaches (Jackson would have abhorred the notion of anything named after himself, and especially any single approach) represent only one of several other valid, lively clusters of approaches to understanding and interpreting space, place, and landscape.

Thus, with Jackson's influence and also with the influence of writers not associated with him, landscape has become a common concept in the popular press. As more writers have returned the suffix -scape to its Old English sense of a created or shaped space, people have begun to think and write about cityscapes, townscapes, streetscapes, and the landscapes of tourism, work, automobile travel, and every other human activity. More recently, the trademark Netscape, a major browser for the World Wide Web, is notable because it refers not only to a framed two-dimensional image on a computer screen, not so different from landscape as a painting of scenery, but also to a virtual four-dimensional experience of images and connections changing over time, something more akin to walking or driving down a road than to viewing a painting.

"The indeterminate disciplinary boundaries of Jackson's teaching about the landscape," observed the geographer Michael Conzen soon after Jackson's death, "were its greatest problem and its greatest strength."[56] Yet polyphony is not necessarily cacophony. Many different voices, especially those that can be heard and joined across boundaries, can enrich one another. New approaches can fill in gaps left by other traditions. Whether one opts for "promiscuous mingling and mutual education" between landscape observers and social theorists, more active communication between landscape scholars and design professionals, or bridging disciplinary boundaries to move between description and abstract analysis, the very variety and expansion of approaches and perspectives continue to be the strength of cultural landscape studies—and, we believe, of this collection of essays.

EVALUATING J. B. JACKSON

The historian Patricia Nelson Limerick begins this section of assessments of John Brinckerhoff Jackson. With the kind of humor and accessible language that Jackson himself might have used, she deftly outlines Jackson's rhetorical rules for the "sport" of inquiry and assertion, such as making confident and sometimes outrageous assertions (especially counterintuitive ones), engaging in contradiction, appearing to merge with the opposition, and practicing nonlinear thinking—all of which, Limerick notes, were effective parts of Jackson's campaign to lure specialists away from their cautiously footnoted turfs and toward a more spirited play of the mind.

Helen Lefkowitz Horowitz unlocks some of Jackson's earliest writing and his many pseudonyms in *Landscape* to show how he used his admiration of both baroque design and vernacular architecture to challenge the abstractions of architectural modernism. With an aside to Jackson's wickedly mocking satire, "Living Outdoors with Mrs. Panther," Horowitz traces Jackson's links between the exuberance of the baroque and the par-

allel positive qualities that he found in the flamboyant commercial architecture of the highway strip.

Architect, author, and educator Denise Scott Brown recalls her regular
dinner conversations with Jackson in 1965, when they were both visiting
faculty members at the University of California, Berkeley. She soon discovered that they belonged to a loosely knit international network of intellectuals (including her future husband, the architect Robert Venturi)
who responded to International Style modernism by turning to historic,
vernacular, and popular cultures for inspiration. Here, she draws parallels
between Jackson's and her own experiences growing up among cross-cultural conflicts, and how those tensions helped to form each of their later
perspectives.

The chapter by Timothy Davis, which closes the set of evaluations of
Jackson, traces Jackson's early—and at the time unpopular—embrace of
roads and the roadside architecture of gas stations, motels, and commercial
strips. Davis reminds us that Jackson looked at these landscapes as social
and highly political landscapes, and as arenas for personal expression and
individual experience. Presaging the current academic fascination with
contestation between producers and consumers of cultural space, Jackson
suggested that critics resisted the commercial strip in part because its
bustling, garish heterogeneity underscored the traditional elite's loss of
control over a significant segment of the American public landscape.

J. B. JACKSON AND THE PLAY OF THE MIND

2

Inquiry and Assertion as Contact Sports

The title of this essay and the idea driving it come from the merging of a few impressions. First, J. B. Jackson's use of vision and sight was a lot more vigorous and immediate than my use of vision and sight. When he looked at a landscape, it was a very physical, direct, tactile sort of encounter; in other words, looking at a landscape was, for him, a contact sport. Second, Jackson wrote memorably and vividly about sports and play and had quite a sound understanding of the inner world of sports. Third, Jackson took up the intellectual activities of inquiry and assertion in a manner and with a style that was decidedly different from the ways in which most academics engage in those activities—or at least from the ways in which academics write up the results of their inquiries. In other words, Jackson and academics play the sport of inquiry in quite different ways, and it seemed to me that exploring those differences might be illuminating.

Consider the stance that Jackson took toward universities and academics. Here is an emblematic quotation:

> Like most laymen I had no conception of the Byzantine complexities of the academic world; it seemed a vast tangle of departments, programs, committees, and struggles for promotion and tenure and fellowships and grants, out of which the initiates skillfully wove lifelong shelters for themselves, but which could only bewilder and frustrate the outsiders.[1]

This is a classic statement of distance and outsiderhood from the academic enterprise. But think about it: this man taught at Harvard and Berkeley for years; he was, certifiably, an acute and penetrating observer of the activities of human beings; and we are supposed to believe him when he says he does not understand much about academics? Unless I have missed something important, when it comes to academics, Harvard and Berkeley are the belly of the beast, and for Jackson to say that he doesn't know much about academics is the equivalent of Jonah saying that he doesn't know much about whales.

Jackson's stance, as I understand it, works as a popular and effective strategy for pool-hall hustlers. A fellow walks into a bar, strolls over to the pool table, says to a player, "Just how do you get those little balls to go where you want with that stick?" He then waits until someone is willing to make a bet, before settling in to reveal that he actually knows quite a bit about how to get results from that stick. Jackson, I would say, knew a lot about academics—he knew enough to play us like harps, and one piece of evidence for that proposition is the visible and conspicuous fact that so many of us, certified members of the academic tribe, attended the 1998 University of New Mexico conference in his honor.

My argument thus merges those three opening observations into the idea of inquiry and assertion as activities that Jackson played like contact sports. It was not only that he came into direct and immediate contact with the subjects of his inquiries, but he also played the academic game like a contact sport, strategically colliding with academic postures and positions and generally coming up with plays, steps, spins, and moves that left referees and umpires scratching their heads.

Did Jackson break the rules that govern academics involved in the play of the mind? Or did he discover and demonstrate that the rules, which others have been scrupulously observing, are not actually enforced? I myself think that he brought to intellectual sport some plays and moves that many other players assumed must be prohibited, but which are not. The point of this observation is not that we should all adopt and practice Jackson's plays and moves, but that we could think with a little more freedom and liberation about how we ourselves engage in this sport. Here, then, are eight Jacksonian propositions for the play of the mind.

1. *When in doubt, assert.*

When you confront a question that you could spend the rest of your life investigating, waiting to be certain that your answer is right, do not trouble yourself with doubt. Go ahead and make an assertion and a declaration. When you are struck by the complexity and difficulty of a topic, plow into it anyway. Assert an answer and an explanation, and find out later whether you were right.

This strategy has any number of advantages. It saves time, allowing you to get on to the next project in a prompt fashion. It recruits an informal army of research assistants who are determined to prove you wrong, maybe, but who are still earnestly investigating the subject you found of interest. It entertains: quiet assertion can throw academics into tizzies, which can be quite a bit of fun to watch. Perhaps it also offers a useful opportunity to these academics: they run around looking for a referee to blow the whistle on the play, and that gives them the chance to discover that there is no referee in this sport.

Examples? These are remarks that a quick reader might slide right past, but each is a stunner when you try to think how you would ever go about testing, much less verifying, such claims. "The concept of the home . . ." changed from "the locus of high-minded educational and hygienic endeavor" to "the present concept of the home as a place for recreation and fun."[2] Whose home? Whose concept? Who knows?

Or consider these deeply doubtful generalizations: "In a well-ordered society not much importance is attached to the private religious experience."[3] "The cemetery has lost its meaning both to the individual and to the community."[4] And my favorite: "Historians are in general agreement that sometime in the second half of the eighteenth century, what we call popular or vernacular culture began to lose its vitality and charm."[5] "Historians are in general agreement"? Historians never agree! A decline in "charm"? If the members of the profession have arrived at some sort of shared understanding of when a phenomenon has more charm and when it has less, this breakthrough has been withheld from me.

2. *Confident assertion carries the most satisfaction, and has the most energizing effect on the recipients, when the proposition you assert is counterintuitive.*

Here is Jackson on the subject of commercial aviation and the way in which it introduced a new point of view, which we would have thought was a way of seeing the landscape as a whole:

> Thus the aerial perspective reinforced our modern tendency to
> analyze and reduce phenomena to their smallest components. . . .
> The more extensive our view, the more we concentrate on details. . . .
> Fragments of the whole—studies of microecosystems, isolated
> structures, spaces of little significance—are all that matters.[6]

Once we could see the whole, we looked only at the parts? This seems deeply improbable. And yet, with Jackson's prodding, it does come to mind that the arrival of human access to an aerial view does seem to coincide with an increase in specialization of knowledge. What are we to make of that? Thus the value of these counterintuitive assertions: they provoke the most vigorous play of the mind. The recipient responds in two steps: "That can't be right!" And then, "That may not be entirely right, but it is turning out to be righter than I would have thought."

3. *Recognize consistency as the petty virtue it is, and experience the pleasure that comes from wholehearted contradiction.*

Perhaps the most unsettling example of this rule breaking comes at the end of Jackson's essay "The Movable Dwelling and How It Came to America." Jackson asserts that temporary buildings, easily built, easily abandoned, "always offered . . . a kind of freedom we often undervalue: the freedom from burdensome emotional ties with the environment."[7] One reads this and feels inclined to check the author's name on the title page: J. B. Jackson said that??? The same J. B. Jackson who wrote, on many different occasions, things like "[Activities associated with a landscape] should remind us that we belong . . . to a specific place: a country, a town, a neighborhood. A landscape should establish bonds between people . . . above all a landscape should contain the kind of spatial organization which fosters such experiences and relationships."[8]

One discovers oneself attempting to start up a belated, but still urgent, conversation: "Would you put this together, Mr. Jackson? Declare, if you like, that ties to place burden and entrap us, but please reconcile that statement with the many times you have asserted the value and the benefit of bonds between places and people!" But there is no reconciliation.

The two positions just sit next to each other, evidently indifferent to and unembarrassed by their mutual contradiction.

Self-contradiction makes particular sense—in fact, self-contradiction is logical and appropriate—when you are talking about perceptions, interpretations, and appraisals of change. What could be more intellectually consistent than a changing and shifting attitude toward changes and shifts in landscape behavior? Was Jackson an indulger in and practitioner of nostalgia? Or was he campaigner against nostalgia? He was both, depending on which passage you are reading. When it came to deciding whether the past was preferable to the present or the present was preferable to the past, Jackson felt a perfectly reasonable ambivalence. What could be more ridiculous than a settled, determined, rigid, unchanging appraisal of change?

4. Overstating claims of relatedness and correlation usefully corrects for a long-running imbalance in preference for disconnection, disaggregation, and separation.

There is no question academics have been on a binge of specialization and fragmentation for forty or fifty years. With the pendulum so far gone in its swing toward fragmentation, specialization, and separation, it's no wonder Jackson found it entirely appropriate to put opposite and equal energy into asserting that the world is a place of relatedness and connectedness. Here he ties the seventeenth-century pleasure garden to everything going on in contemporary life; the garden was bound to "a new relationship between theater and actors, and eventually between the city and its inhabitants, the land and the peasants who lived on it."[9] Well, maybe.

But now try this characterization of Americans: "We are all descendants, spiritually speaking, of the peoples of Great Britain and Ireland, of the Low Countries, and to a lesser extent of northern France and western Germany."[10] (Note that phrasing—"to a lesser extent"—as if this were a statement of calculated precision!) Of course, this is a ridiculous statement, given the diversity of the origins of United States citizens, and perhaps especially ridiculous when it comes from an author so committed to life in New Mexico. But then again, people of diverse ethnic origins have lawns, and devote a lot of attention to those lawns, and betray, with every mowing and watering, a certain sentiment for and loyalty to a landscape of northern Europe. In behavior and belief, there may be more to this "relatedness" than genealogy and ancestry alone would tell us.

5. Cultivate an earned reputation for generally clear, down-to-earth ex-pression, and then, from time to time, go cryptic.

Make a pronouncement in the manner of Obi-Wan Kenobi, and then of Yoda, and watch the people in your audience blame themselves for their inability to understand. Since Jackson generally was a lucid and concrete writer, his episodes of crypticness are likely to produce in readers the con-viction that their inability to understand is their own fault. Instead of say-ing to themselves, "J.B. Jackson, who is ordinarily so clear and intelligible as a writer, has slipped up and said something that doesn't make sense," they are much more likely to say, "Since J.B. Jackson is so clear and intel-ligible a writer, my failure to follow what he has just said reveals the weakness of my own mind and imagination."

Here Jackson is discussing the contrast between the landscape of north-ern Mexico and the southwestern United States: "To the south of the Rio Grande, the world of Man is thought of as created in the likeness of a so-cial theory and not, as with us, in the likeness of an economic force."[11] Eh? The United States does have something of a history of behavior in re-sponse to social theory, while in Mexico, poverty qualifies as something of "an economic force" by any definition and has played a big part in shap-ing the landscape. Or take the next example, a discussion of contemporary homes and a peak moment of crypticness, a passage in which I cannot find a single clue as to its meaning.

> There are other forms of energy which the past knew nothing
> about—inexhaustible energy which we are seeking to tap by means
> of spiritual discipline, self-education, and a new experience of
> nature. The contemporary dwelling, for all its cultural impoverish-
> ment, for all its temporary, mobile, rootless qualities, promises to
> capture and utilize more and more of this invisible, inexhaustible
> store of strength. So we can perhaps think of it as a transformer, a
> structure which does more than depend on the energy provided by
> the power company, which transforms for each of its inhabitants
> some of the invisible, spiritual energy we are only now beginning
> to discover.[12]

Am I right to suspect that the author here does not care whether I under-stand this? He has something in his mind, and if it stays in his mind and never gets near ours, then does not every human being, even a writer, have a right to privacy?

6. Calling attention to, and challenging, the unexamined power of middle-class values will throw academics into a particular tizzy.

This strategy works so well because it hits the soft underbelly of the academic stance. In practice, it involves saying to academics, "Look what you missed; look at garages and trailers and trucks and people who do repair work out of their homes; look at how all these things reveal beauty in unexpected places; look at what was under your noses, and so thoroughly taken for granted that you couldn't see how interesting it was." Maybe the most appealing example of Jackson's putting this strategy to work is this: "I am tempted to dwell on the importance of the parking lot. I enjoy it as an austere but beautiful and exciting aspect of the landscape."[13] To middle-class aesthetes, this says, in essence: "You goofy things! You think the world of paintings by Mondrian and Albers, and you are such snobs that you can't see that a parking lot has many of the same charms."

7. Recognize and take advantage of the easy target offered by the lack of self-awareness and critical self-examination of environmentalists.

If you are tired of dealing with subtle and complicated matters, take a break by taking a whack at environmentalists, who will respond by looking alarmed and hurt but who won't have a clue as to how to hit back. Here is Jackson engaged in his play: "I am one of those who believes that our current guilt-ridden worship of the environment is a sign of moral and cultural disarray."[14] Or, on the matter of the wording of his course titles, "Whenever I could I objected to the use of the word *environment*. In the sixties, it will be recalled, the environmental movement was shrill and self-righteous, and I had no wish to be identified with it; and this is still the case."[15]

And yet, in other passages, Jackson offered condemnations of the human determination to master, subdue, and dominate nature, and one would think that these passages had been written by an "environmentalist," if their author had not said so forcefully that he wasn't one. After all, there were important matters at stake here, and in at least one essay, Jackson dropped the kidding and the effort to bait environmentalists. In "To Pity the Plumage and Forget the Dying Bird," Jackson wrote forcefully about the madness of addressing environmental problems without also addressing the human problem of poverty. "Is there really any sense," he asked, "in preaching a 'new land ethic' to men who would promptly wind up on relief if they practiced it?" What is "essential," he declared, "is for every responsible American to add a new social dimension to his definition of landscape beauty."[16] In this essay there is no playfulness, no kidding around, and that is its own indication of why J. B. Jackson, on occasion, hit environmentalism so hard.

8. *Use the pronoun* we *persistently, relentlessly, and with widely varying meanings, until readers become confused and unable to identify the usual boundaries distinguishing the writer's opinions from their own.*

Surely one of the most striking results of looking closely at Jackson's habits and customs as a writer is this recognition: this person whom so many have described as a loner, a stranger, an outsider, a person embracing his marginality, was also one of the heaviest users of the pronoun *we.* This is a study in itself: *we* as we interpreters of the landscape, as we sharers in a certain generational experience, as we Americans in the present moment, as we holders of particular attitudes toward country and city, and as we human beings acting on certain instincts, longings, and yearnings. Jackson uses *we, us,* and *our* as if he were a principal booster and supporter of National Brotherhood Week. It would be easy to say that the heavy use of *we* was evidence of his yearning to belong. Maybe. It was also a very clear contact-sport strategy: Merge with the other team; appear, without invitation and without apology, in the midst of the opposing team's huddle, addressing them as *we.*

We might sum up the overall effect of these strategies and techniques as ways to wake people up, to bring them to alertness, without raising our voice. These are ways to play the sport in a manner in which traditional scholars are not used to seeing it played; ways to break their rules, or what they always thought were their rules. You break their supposed rules, and when no referee or umpire appears to remove you from the game—when, on the contrary, the referees give you prizes and honors and postgame tributes—then, eventually, the other players will have to say to themselves, "How did these rules come to be, and why have we deferred to them for so long?"

I think that one of Jackson's goals was to disrupt the usual operations and systems of academic inquiry and assertion in order to invite academics to reexamine their assumptions, but I suspect that another goal was to take pleasure from watching them get flummoxed, disoriented, agitated, and unsettled. This was a person with an oppositional temperament. Piety invited, asked for, *demanded* his challenge. His irreverent questioning of intellectual habit is so conspicuous that it makes it all the more striking and remarkable to note the areas in which he accepted standing assumptions and submitted to established frameworks of understanding. This anomalous deference was most notable in matters of gender: not only the generic use of *man, men, he,* and *his* but a direct and explicit concentration on the activities of men. His willing acceptance of the conventional forms of excluding women from attention makes for an odd fit with his otherwise hearty intellectual independence.

I did not know J. B. Jackson well, but I do have one personal artifact that strikes me now as very revealing. He wrote a promotional blurb for the cover of my book *The Legacy of Conquest: The Unbroken Past of the American West* (1987). My publisher, W. W. Norton, chose not to put his comment on the book. This souvenir, recently excavated from my files, dated July 15, 1987, seems now an artifact of archetypal Jacksonianism. After a kind appraisal of the book, Jackson then made a reference to the fact that my academic degrees were from an American Studies program, but that I had apparently recovered from this bad start. "American Studies," Jackson said in the midst of the blurb, "can be, and usually is, provincial and antiquarian."

Usually, when writing a promotional blurb, one writes just about the book itself and doesn't pause, mid-blurb, to take a swing at an innocent, or even a not-so-innocent, bystander. I guess it is not particularly surprising that the folks at W. W. Norton chose not to use this blurb. But I am certainly glad they sent me a photocopy of it, because it is so Jacksonian. It is, first of all, nonlinear in content, style, and strategy. As a pathway or trail of thought, it zigs; and, having zigged, then in a very purposeful and deliberate way, it zags. It makes no apology for this somewhat less-than-direct progression of thoughts. And more important for revelations of Jacksonian intellectual style, the blurb is punctuated with one moment in which its author hits a target hard. When Jackson calls American Studies "usually provincial and antiquarian," the message has all the subtlety and indirection of a tackle bringing down a running back. But this is what I also think: the goal of his statement was not to convince people in American Studies that it was time to give up and find a more honorable and productive line of work. The goal was to invite them to stand up, hold their ground, and prove that it wasn't fair to call them and their work "provincial and antiquarian."

Jackson approached his intellectual work of inquiry and assertion in a sporting sort of way. He wrote with a spirit that one could sum up as, "Anything worth saying is worth saying forcefully." He wrote declarative statements where others would have written tentative, cautious, even apologetic speculations. He hit his subjects hard. But that does not mean his goal was to drive opposing opinion from the field. On the contrary: it is a rare and unappealing sports player who wants to play, who prefers to play, against weak and submissive opponents. My feeling is that when Jackson came down hard in favor of one proposition and in opposition to another, he anticipated, expected, and looked forward to having a champion of the temporarily quashed proposition step forward and punch back on its behalf. Successful or not, the individual who pitched in to defend a proposition that had just been flattened by a Jacksonian blast of certainty would, certifiably, be a better person for the exercise.

So that is the J. B. Jackson I would put forward: Jackson as exuberant, innovative, intellectual sports player, but also Jackson as personal trainer, who takes us through calisthenics that trick us into revealing unexpected reservoirs of stamina and agility and who gives us a chance to rethink the rules of the game.

HELEN LEFKOWITZ HOROWITZ

J.B. JACKSON AS A CRITIC OF MODERN ARCHITECTURE

3

John Brinckerhoff Jackson's greatest contribution was to reintroduce Americans to their vernacular landscape, to teach them to see again—and in a new light—the common elements of roads, houses, yards, and towns. Written in a clear and dramatic style, his essays seem artless. They sprang, however, from a highly educated sensibility and careful literary craft. Moreover, they arose from a love of the baroque and an opposition to the Modern movement in architecture and planning (figs. 3.1 and 3.2).[1] Paradoxically, delineating the vernacular landscape of the United States became a way for Jackson to express his distaste for modernism and his love of baroque art, architecture, and planning. An exploration of Jackson's background, education, and antagonism toward modernism is therefore critical to a deeper understanding of the meaning that the American landscape held for him.

J.B. Jackson was a complex, enigmatic man whose writing was inextricably linked to the various roles he assumed. In his later decades he wanted his career to be identified with his defense of the ways of living of

Figure 3.1. Taking pleasure in the baroque. J. B. Jackson's sketch of Pancho Villa's tomb, Chihuahua, Mexico, 1973.

ordinary persons, and he himself took up many of these ways as a common laborer. Yet even as he painted the floor of Ernie's Auto Repair or learned to steam-clean a car, he retained many of the enthusiasms of his earlier life. He loved fine French and Swiss cooking, including chocolate. And he never ceased to love the baroque, or to contrast it with the International Movement in architecture.

Jackson had discovered baroque buildings and art as a boy living abroad much of the time for his education. He was born in 1909 in Dinard, France, of American parents, William Brinckerhoff Jackson and Alice Richardson Jackson.[2] The household, which included a brother and sister by his mother's first marriage, settled for a time outside Washington, D.C., but returned to Europe when he was four. After an interlude in the

Figure 3.2.   The landscape of the Modern movement. J.B.
Jackson sketch, Düsseldorf, Germany, 1959.

United States during World War I, he went to Switzerland at age eleven to
attend Le Rosey, the famed international boarding school, and began the
formal education that would give him a fine classical training. He spent
two years at Le Rosey and one in Paris. These years nourished his deep attachment to French culture, language, and point of view.

He returned to the United States, entered Choate, and then transferred
to the Deerfield Academy. In the summer of 1926, Jackson saw his first
modern building, a house designed by Le Corbusier in the midst of the
Art Deco buildings of the Paris Exposition of Modern Art. In an interview
almost seven decades later, he remembered simply, "I didn't like it." In
1994 he understood his reaction to Le Corbusier as characteristic of the
time: "Everybody was kind of making fun of his houses on stilts and say-

ing it [the architecture] was for chickens. . . . You had to be really intelligent to see that it was novel."[3]

His schooling confirmed his personal reaction, and a freshman year in 1928–29 at the University of Wisconsin's experimental college gave him a full alternative. There, while studying ancient Greece, he read the first volume of Oswald Spengler's *Decline of the West*. "I got a copy of it and it transformed me," Jackson remembered. "It is a fascinating, obsessive book." When Jackson returned to Europe in 1929, he saw the touristic landscape of Gothic cathedrals and baroque churches through the lens that Spengler had given him, opening his eyes to the landscape. His sophomore year took him to Harvard College, where he came under the influence of the conservative literary critic Irving Babbitt. In the course "Rousseau and His Influence," Babbitt mounted a consistent opposition to the original genius of French Romanticism.

Jackson wrote for the *Harvard Advocate*, the undergraduate literary magazine, and served on its editorial board. One of his contributions to the *Advocate*, "Our Architects Discover Rousseau," published in his junior year, stated clearly his guiding aesthetic. In this article he opposed on two grounds the architectural criticism of his day, which lauded the Modern movement as the natural expression of the machine. The first was his judgment that twentieth-century business culture was ruthless and selfish and no proper guide to taste. The second sprang from his understanding that the appreciation of modernism had romantic roots, linking it to the spirit of Rousseau in its insistence on the beauty of nakedness. "Perhaps we are too remote from Nature," he wrote, "but it is hard to understand what is so vile about pretense as long as it represents a sincere effort to be better, and even harder to understand what is so edifying about nakedness."[4]

Proponents of modernism rejected style and history, but to the young Jackson, "baroque was a magnificent style because it typified a magnificent age." To him it was the "last vital style which fulfilled its function of interpreting an age," a style that depended "on man for its growth, not material or method." The baroque era was a time "when man allowed no factors of environment or primitive peculiarities to deter him from becoming what he considered cultured."[5]

And in 1931, high culture was what Jackson valued. In considering architecture, he wrote:

Our attempts to glorify our prosaic edifices may not always be happy, but anything is better than revealing their true nature. Such frankness means that a home is an animal's den, that a railroad station is the assembly place for dirty engines and hurried people, that a dinner is stuffing food into the mouth; whereas it has been the constant endeavor of humanity to dignify itself by dignifying its functions and habitats, making a home the image of the owner's taste, a station a public monument, a dinner a ceremony.[6]

This respect for civilized ceremony is fundamental to Jackson's reverence for the baroque. Paradoxically, his belief that culture and aspiration are the critical links between humankind and nature is also the foundation of his appreciation of the American vernacular landscape.

When he graduated from college in 1932, Jackson was uncertain about his future and tried out a number of career paths: architecture, journalism, and commercial art. In 1934 he went to Europe, first enrolling in a commercial drawing school in Vienna and then embarking on an extended *Wanderjahr* and a period of writing as he attempted to understand the appeal of Nazism. In the course of his travels he went to the 1934 Stuttgart Wissenhof exhibit of modern housing and city planning, which included a hilltop group of white houses and apartment buildings designed by several of Europe's most avant-garde architects. There he took a second look at Le Corbusier, and he had a more wide-ranging view of the work of Bauhaus architects such as Ludwig Mies van der Rohe and Walter Gropius. In 1994 Jackson remembered hating what he saw, judging the houses as "ridiculous, intellectual architecture." However, his writing during this period was focused on politics, not aesthetics. He published a novel, a short story, and an essay, all dealing with political currents in Eastern Europe.[7]

For more than a decade Jackson chose to stay away from the world in which architecture was discussed and criticized, instead ranching in New Mexico and serving as a soldier and later an intelligence officer in World War II. *Landscape* magazine, which Jackson launched in the spring of 1951—when he was in his forties—provided him with a forum for his evolving understanding of landscape, architecture, and planning. *Landscape*'s primary contribution lies in Jackson's own brilliant and evocative essays, beginning with "Chihuahua as We Might Have Been," in the first issue. Secondarily, as outside writers joined its pages, *Landscape* served as an ongoing, lively symposium of new and important ideas and approaches.

From the outset, *Landscape* magazine seemed to have good writers. H. G. West, P. G. Anson, and A. W. Conway appeared in its pages with intelligent commentary. A number of pieces were signed only with initials. But there was, it turns out, only one writer: J. B. Jackson. West, Anson, and Conway were pseudonyms, as were the possible names behind the initials.

In the summer of 1995, I asked Jackson directly about his use of pseudonyms. He stated that he had never used any name but his own outside his own journal. He could not recall the many names he used in *Landscape*, but, yes, his brother Wayne Jackson had been his first contributor. This means that J.B. Jackson wrote all the pieces in the first two issues. My assumption is that he used pseudonyms initially to disguise the fact that the journal began with the writings of a single author. As *Landscape* proceeded, however, I believe that he used fictional names to review books outside his announced interests and to express himself on a wide range of subjects.

At one point I decided to read the pseudonymous articles by J.B. Jackson as a distinct body of work. I was impressed, first of all, with Jackson's ability to write in different voices, a skill enhanced by his earlier work as a writer of fiction. Second, I was struck by what the pseudonymous work revealed about his engagement with significant philosophic, religious, and aesthetic questions. Reading the many pieces allows us to track some of the wide-ranging influences on him during this period. The works of Freud and Jung were helping to shape his understanding of symbol and myth, and Jung's influence was perhaps encouraging Jackson to make the bold statements and sweeping declarative sentences that enliven his essays. Finally, it was here that I discovered—especially in reviews under the names H.G. West and P.G. Anson—the most direct celebration of the baroque and the clearest opposition to the International Style penned by J.B. Jackson in his mature years.

In spring 1952 Jackson laid the groundwork for these positions in a review of a book on the baroque in Latin America. Jackson wrote under the initials H.G.W., which stood for H.G. West, a pseudonym he had used on one previous occasion. Alongside praise of the baroque is his statement about what constitutes an effective understanding of architecture. Critical of the book's illustrations, which showed only the facades of buildings, Jackson/West wrote that architecture exists "not merely in terms of facade treatment: but in terms of plan and location, of the organization of space, of perspective and drama." Jackson believed that architecture was "a three dimensional art, and no collection of photographs of facades can replace the plan, or in the case of a whole city, the map."[8]

With this foundation laid, Jackson addressed modernism in a subsequent 1952 issue of *Landscape*. Writing again as H.G. West, he reviewed *A Decade of New Architecture*, edited by Sigfried Giedion, the important

Zurich writer on modern architecture, and *Early American Architecture*, by Hugh Morrison. Jackson/West lambasted modernism for its emphasis on houses of the rich and its overly intellectual and antiseptic public buildings. It is not that buildings in the International Style are not beautiful, he wrote; they are. Rather, his criticism was that they sprang from an aim not "to improve the lot of Man but a desire to create pure geometrical forms, an autonomous art of cubes and cylinders and two dimensional planes; independent of the past, independent of the earth and of life."[9]

As Jackson/West looked toward the future of architecture, he reflected that those within an architectural movement could not perceive the enemy. Just when the American classicists of the eighteenth century had established clear standards, from an unanticipated quarter had appeared the enemies—"eclecticism and functionalism"—whose proponents "in the matter of a few decades swept the field." Was this about to happen to the International Style? While its aging advocates restated their principles and simplified the design of the house, "all the while there enters through the back door of the modern dwelling a troop of interior decorators, landscape architects, home consultants, psychologists, appliance and television salesmen, each of them bent on making the modern home as complex and irrational and individual as possible."[10]

Modernism, Jackson/West asserted, holds strongly to the tenet "that the architect knows better than the client." In Europe, modern architects thus looked to the state as builder. In the United States, however, building was in the hands of business. "One need not admire flimsy construction, the short-sighted planning, the over-dramatized, over-colored, pseudo-modern ranch houses which are rising all over the country; but one ought to be able to recognize them for what they are: the first grass-roots indication of the dwelling of the future."[11]

Jackson continued his critique in the summer of 1953, again under the pseudonym of H.G. West, with a harsh review of *Built in U.S.A.*, edited by Henry-Russell Hitchcock and Arthur Drexler. By adhering only to architects loyal to the teachings of Gropius, Mies van der Rohe, and Le Corbusier, the editors had missed the vital vernacular buildings of the postwar period, with their profusion of architectural forms: the tract house, the factory, and the drive-ins and businesses lining the highway. The book erred in its focus on suburban private houses, office buildings, and apartment houses, all large and expensive and none of them having to adapt to a neighborhood or the street. These modern monuments were, according to Jackson/West, free to be "works of art." They were undeniably beautiful, but they were not, he argued, works of architecture. Here Jackson/ West insisted that to be architecture, buildings must be "true expressions of domestic or communal life." The landmark buildings of the International Style in the book under review were inspired "less by a desire to accommodate existence as we know it than by an almost fanatic rationalism."[12]

Jackson was hardly the only critic of Modern architecture in the 1950s. What makes his judgment different from that of others is its grounds. He did not argue, as did Henry Hope Reed, for a return to a specific historic style or, as did Carroll Meeks, to a "creative eclecticism"—or to any notion of "style" for that matter.[13] Although he loved seventeenth-century structures, he had been schooled by Spengler to understand that each era has its own spirit and that a person living in the twentieth century must look to engineering and technology rather than to art. What Jackson wanted was not a return to the past but an architecture responsive to the needs of the present. He accepted critical tenets of modernism, such as the need to break with academic principles and the importance of adapting to new materials and methods. What he opposed was an architecture devoted to the beauty of pure geometric forms.

Jackson saw architecture as unlike other art forms, such as painting or sculpture. Architecture's true purpose was to organize space to enhance human existence in structures expressive of domestic and social life. Architects should not limit themselves to buildings that only the rich or the state could afford, structures so large and expensive that no consideration need be given to the neighborhood, the street, or traffic patterns. Jackson protested against an architecture blind to actual construction in the 1950s—housing developments, factories, and drive-ins—and one that ignored the dwellings and structures that ordinary people were choosing for themselves.

One way to challenge modernism was to state the case for its opposite. If discussions of contemporary architecture were ignoring "new vernacular forms," such as the current dwelling, then Jackson himself would write about them. Having proclaimed the primacy of the house, Jackson began to explore the building concerns of ordinary people. This purpose adds an important dimension to a reading of his pathbreaking essay "The Westward-Moving House," shifting focus from the first two sections of the essay to the third, called "Ray's Transformer." This third section deals with house building in the 1950s in a way that casts a negative light on Modern architecture.

"The Westward-Moving House" was actually Jackson's second attempt at looking at the contemporary house in its historic evolution. His first foray, an H.G. West piece called "A Change in Plans: Is the Modern House a Victorian Invention?" in *Landscape*'s first year of publication, discussed the postwar American dwelling as an outgrowth of modern architecture: "It has broken with every tradition, social and esthetic; it recognizes the authority of no other period or class or place. More than any other specimen of the Modern style it has repudiated ancient conventions, and comes close to being what its designers wanted it to be: a shelter, informal and free and hospitable; youthful and capable of taking on any character given it."[14] By the time he wrote "The Westward-Moving House," however, it was clear to Jackson that the dwellings being built did not really belong in the Modern movement.

Writing under his own name in "The Westward-Moving House," Jackson imagined a dwelling being constructed in Bonniview, Texas, in the 1950s, by Ray Tinkham, of concrete block in no architectural style. Its planning was in the hands of Shirley, Ray's wife, a reader of home decorating magazines, who had decided that her goals were informality and efficiency. She would do without ceremonial spaces to save money for the labor-saving devices that would make her life easier. Her design decisions could be best understood as springing from the changing uses of the house. Although Ray worked the soil, the family lived away from the farm, and the house no longer served to process farm products for family use. Nor, in the modern age, was the house a place to educate children or care for the sick. It was not the principal source of social status. The family life of Ray's father in Illinois—"reading out loud together, Bible instruction, games, large holiday dinners, winter evenings in the sitting room, and so forth"—had disappeared, much to Shirley's satisfaction. The house no longer served as a basis of broader culture or family religion.[15]

What were the positive functions of Ray and Shirley's house in Jackson's mind? It was a place of renewal, in this sense a transformer. Jackson was describing the kind of house being built in countless subdivisions in the 1950s, the kind of house that surveys of modern architecture were completely ignoring.

By contrast, the house that architectural critics admired was the house that Jackson wickedly mocked in another piece, "Living Outdoors with Mrs. Panther." Using the pseudonym Ajax, the voice of his playful satires, he pretended to be a reporter visiting Babs Panther, the chic wife of a New York publisher in her expensive suburban dwelling in Connecticut, a house in the International Style. Here Jackson played with the meaning of "natural," a Rousseauian artifice if there ever was one. Jackson let Babs Panther speak for herself, revealing social snobbery, dislike of the real out-of-doors, and pretense. He used the voice of the 1950s shelter magazines to summarize ironically: "the artificialities of city existence are far, far removed from the quiet little eight-room house out here on stilts in the Connecticut woods."[16]

Jackson understood that the new American vernacular was not what Sigfried Giedion valued in his discussions of American architecture, folk functionalism, and efficiency.[17] To Jackson, the essence of contemporary vernacular was extravagance. One might add, a baroque-like extravagance. In "Notes and Comments," his editorial forum in *Landscape*, Jackson spoke boldly and humorously against the International Style. In the winter of 1953–54, using the commemoration of Walter Gropius's seventieth birthday as a foil, he irreverently suggested that it was time for the Bauhaus proponents of modernism to depart from the scene. Real American buildings had a purpose different than that suggested by the theories of modern architects: "They are required to sell goods, to establish social position, to inspire confidence, to impress or elevate or excite. The result is a carnival of extravagant taste, an architectural idiom partaking more of advertising or theater or landscaping than of 'pure space arrangements and the balance of tense contrary forces.' "[18]

It is this notion that Jackson elaborated in 1956 in "Other-Directed Houses," his justly famous celebration of the highway strip.[19] "In all those streamlined facades, in all those flamboyant entrances and deliberately bizarre decorative effects, those cheerfully self-assertive masses of color and light and movement that clash so roughly with the old and traditional there are, I believe, certain underlying characteristics which suggest that we are confronted not by a debased and cheapened art, but by a kind of folk art in mid-twentieth-century garb."[20] On both experiential and aesthetic grounds, Jackson questioned criticism of the American highway and the buildings that lined its path. He analyzed the strip, separating out its leisure functions and those of work, and validated the pleasures of going out for a drive.

As Jackson considered the appeal that a highway establishment had to offer to attract patrons, he noted changes in American notions of pleasure. Jackson was writing at the point when automobiles were flooding the roads and a new idea of leisure was emerging, taking the place of older urban pleasure palaces. Jackson charted buildings along the strip that reflected dreams of the future or of the West and South Pacific. Moreover, he saw that the attractions of the roadside concern had to be conveyed to people in motion. The facades and lights of the strip were designed to please those speeding by in a car at forty miles an hour. Lights and signs erased the workaday world and created in its place one of festivity.[21]

As he considered the strip, Jackson developed more fully the planning ideas that he had been articulating in *Landscape* since 1953. In that year, under the pseudonym P.G. Anson, Jackson explicitly had opposed a number of modern architects in Le Corbusier's circle in a review of their book on urban planning, *The Heart of the City: Towards the Humanisation of Urban Life*, edited by J. Tyrwhitt, J.L. Sert, and E.N. Rogers, for C.I.A.M. (the Congrès Internationaux d'Architecture Moderne), which promoted modern design.[22] In a signed review of Garrett Eckbo's *Landscape for Living*, also from 1953, Jackson addressed other concerns about planning, questioning both practitioners' faith in a central planning authority and their belief that nature could be completely mastered.[23]

"Southeast to Turkey" gives Jackson's fullest response to modern planning principles. In this 1958 essay, in the guise of a travel piece, Jackson explored European urbanism as well as landscape and history, national cultures, and the impact of the Soviet Union on Eastern Europe. His examination of Old World cities also gave him an opportunity to critique modern notions of planning. Jackson elaborated what was so marvelous about Istanbul, a city with every conceivable flaw from a planner's standpoint: narrow streets, filth, dangerous buildings, and rats.

> And yet what marvelous color and variety, what a superabundance of life!... We can study the anatomy of the city, its physical structure until the cows come home; we can design on paper cities which are models of efficiency, comfort, hygiene, even beauty of a sort; but until we learn to study its physiology, to listen to its heartbeat, as it were, to watch its regular breathing, every such project will be dead at birth. For all its sordidness, Istanbul is a city where urban life has created its own forms, and not the other way around.[24]

By the late 1950s, attentive readers of *Landscape* had at hand a fundamental critique of the Modern movement in architecture and planning and a set of new guiding principles, some of which anticipated, in important ways, architectural postmodernism. In his many voices, J.B. Jackson had written that buildings were not to be understood as freestanding works of art, like pieces of sculpture, created by a romantic artistic genius. They were not to be judged, via photographs of beautiful facades, as expressions of pure geometry. Buildings were structures designed for human use. They were three-dimensional compositions, and their interior spaces were as important as their exterior masses. Buildings were intended for actual clients, who held clear notions of what they wanted. Architects may have been creating dwellings in the International Style for the wealthy, but American housing developments reflected the average homeowner's desire for convenience and individuality. Americans chose houses that served to accommodate their families' needs as they defined them, rather than for their reflection of a utopian modernist vision.

Commercial buildings in mid-twentieth-century America had a new purpose, given the universality of automobile travel. Those that lined the strip promised to satisfy contemporary notions of pleasure to those who drove by at high speeds. Thus their extravagant shapes and neon signs were intended to attract attention and offer the delights of places far removed from home and work.

For Jackson, writing in the late 1950s, planners, including landscape architects, could learn nothing from practitioners of the International Style. Houses and corporate structures in the Modern mode failed to respond and interact with their neighbors. Buildings need to be planned in the context of the street, he insisted. Wary of any work coming from centralized, bureaucratic planning, Jackson asked for a reevaluation of the Old World city in all its messiness as an organism overflowing with complexity, intricacy, and abundance of life.

LEARNING FROM BRINCK | 4

During the 1960s and 1970s, J.B. Jackson, Robert Venturi, and I were among a group of academics and professionals who had started to question some core values of the architecture and urban planning of the post–World War II era. Although "Brinck," as we knew him, seemed to dislike designers in print, he maintained friendly associations with many architects and planners, including Bob (then my colleague, later my partner) and me. Our friendship with Brinck, based on a shared interest in the everyday landscape, profoundly influenced our work and perhaps his too.

The parallels in our ideas became public in 1972 with the appearance of our book, *Learning from Las Vegas,* but our lives and his had intertwined earlier.[1] I can't remember when I first met Brinck; it was probably in 1963, at a faculty meeting at the Graduate School of Fine Arts of the University of Pennsylvania. Shortly thereafter, we met again at a planning conference. In 1964, I required students in my "Form, Forces, and Function" studio at Penn to read a book Jackson had recommended, Philip Wagner's *The*

Human Use of the Earth, which became a bible for me on landscape and culture.[2]

In 1965, I moved to California to study the urbanism of the Southwest, largely because colleagues at Penn's planning school had convinced me I could not afford to ignore it. For the spring term, I was a visiting professor at the College of Environmental Design at the University of California, Berkeley. Young and on my own, I felt at times I didn't know who I was or why I was teaching. Brinck helped me feel I must be someone worthwhile, because he invited me to dinner fairly regularly—as I think he did other single ladies. He was a charming host and dinner companion. We always discussed the cultural landscape and how it got to be the way it was.

In the summer of 1966, while teaching at UCLA, I toured New Mexico with two female relatives. Brinck grandly welcomed us to La Cienega and gave us a Brinck-cooked meal in his new house. I had seen the plans of the house at Berkeley and had asked, "Why are your windows so small when you have this wonderful view over the landscape?" He had replied, "I don't like picture windows. I want to feel sheltered in the house. I can go out on the terrace to see the view."[3] He added that the house was to be the most elegant version of the adobe architecture he had chosen, that he had selected a vernacular style but in its grandest form. Then he furnished it with his mother's French antiques. This was the diversity and dichotomy of Brinck. Similar contradictions enveloped his personal life, making him a warm and welcoming friend yet a jealous protector of his background and history. Wandering through the house, I found, on a bureau, a faded photograph of a dowager lady in a big hat. Brinck's mother? I did not ask.

Bob and I were married in 1967, and sometime thereafter I introduced him to Brinck. To define the intellectual landscape we three shared, I will survey several spheres of thought that have influenced Bob and me. Brinck's was one of them. He and we contributed to a pattern of ideas about the world that was evolving in fields ranging from psychiatry to economics, pushed by the civil rights and other social movements of the 1960s. A basic preoccupation in many fields was the increase of complexity in a mass society and the need for a reassessment of the types of planning, social and physical, that would be possible or desirable for that society. Although these themes emerged in parallel from a broad range of disciplines during the two decades after World War II, this was not an organized community or school of thought, but rather an interesting convergence of ideas and influences, one that has continued to reverberate into the 1990s and beyond. Its relevance, for us as for Brinck, had to do with the physical environment, urban and rural, and how it could be understood as a work of art and technology of a multicultural community and society. These lines of thought led us to a critique of the latter-day Modern architecture and urbanism of the 1950s and 1960s and to a search for socially concerned, culturally tuned approaches to design.

My engagement with multiple cultures started early. During my childhood in wartime South Africa, I was influenced by the views of several European refugees. My art teacher in Johannesburg said, "You will not be truly creative unless you are inspired by what is directly around you." At school, our textbooks were English, and England dominated the 1940s South African urban culture, yet this Dutch Jewish refugee told us, "Paint the life of Africans in the streets of Johannesburg." This dichotomy struck me strongly as a child. I became aware quite early that the "is" around me was African, but the "ought" in the textbooks was English, and whereas my grandmother felt this was entirely proper, I considered it ridiculous. It was epitomized in a film I saw of African children in French West Africa reciting lessons about "nos ancêtres, les Gaulois." This, I believe, was Brinck's dilemma too. Perhaps he faced the same need to confront several cultures in his early life.

In England in the 1950s, I discovered the Brutalists and Team 10, groups of young architects in England and Europe who were questioning received architectural values about urbanism and showing that the Corbusierian vision of the future city as skyscrapers rising from parkland did not jibe with the vital street life of the London East End (fig. 4.1). Here was a divergence between "is" and "ought" based on class and culture rather than on colonial dominance.[4]

At the University of Pennsylvania in 1958, I found the urban sociologist Herbert Gans and his colleagues discussing the relation between "is" and "ought" in American city planning, pointing out that urban phenomena, such as commercial strips and suburban sprawl, decried by architects and planners could be considered desirable by others, and discussing the class basis of social and aesthetic value systems. In the late 1950s, as this group and another at Berkeley initiated the American social planning movement, they asked, "Can't you architects hold off your criticism of strips and sprawl just long enough to find out why people use them?"[5]

At the same time, in Penn's planning school, systems thinking—derived from the military and supported in the 1960s by President Kennedy's New Frontier and President Johnson's Great Society—was influencing urban engineers and social scientists. There was a growing interest in computers for their ability to handle complex urban information.

* Concerning the size and
shape of community sub-
division; it must first be
recognized that in modern
urban society there are no
natural groupings above the
level of the family. We must
furthermore recognize that
many recognizable social
entities in existing settlements—say that of the street
in a mining village—have
been created by the built
form. A valid social entity can
result from architectural
decisions. That is, decisions
which include consideration
of plastic organization—the
shape of the community.

Figure 4.1. "Urban Reidentification" and "Close Houses." Diagrams from the
"Team 10 Primer," *Architectural Design* 12 (December 1962): 592, 588. In these
four sketches, Peter and Alison Smithson propose an alternative to Le Corbusier's
vision of a city as skyscrapers set in parks. Here, housing is closely tied to streets,
on the ground (*plan and detail opposite*) or in the air (*above; plan view below*).
In each proposal, continuous linear forms wind across the land, to adapt to topography or to rebuild the unevenly distributed bombed sites and bypass remaining
structures. The Smithsons' texts proclaim the social vision behind these examples
of "active socioplastics" and "a new objectivity."

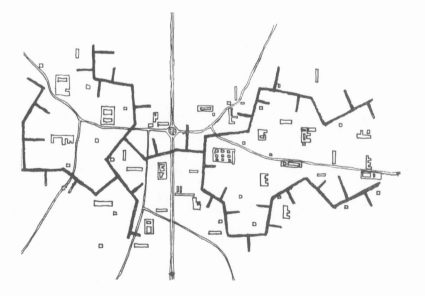

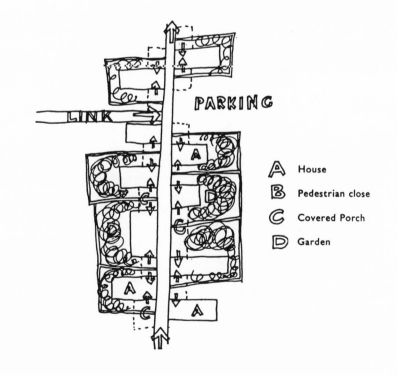

If you think back to the pioneer days of modern architecture you will see that the Hilberseimers and the Le Corbusiers and the Gropius's were producing Ideal Towns in the Renaissance sense, in the sense that their æsthetic was in fact the classical æsthetic, one of fixed formal organization. Now the attitude of Team 10 is that this is an unreal attitude towards towns, and we think that planning is a problem of going on, rather than starting with a clean sheet. We accept as a fixed fact that in any generation we can only do so much work, and we have to select the points at which our action can have the most significant effect on the total city structure, rather than try to envisage its complete reorganization, which is just wishful thinking. Our current æsthetic and ideological aims are not 'castles in the air' but rather a sort of new realism and new objectivity, a sort of radicalism about social and building matters; and (to stress again) a matter of acting in a given situation.
P.D.S.

PARKING

LINK

A House

B Pedestrian close

C Covered Porch

D Garden

For me, how and why systems were distorted was as interesting as the systems themselves. I turned to nonlinear systems and concepts of organized complexity; the saying "Chaos is an order we have not yet discerned" resonated for me. So did the regional scientists' conceptions of the space economy as a mathematical gossamer spread across the landscape. "City physics"—a mix of math and fantasy as intriguing as a Paul Klee painting—was one way of discovering order within the "is" of the city, rather than imposing "oughts" from above. Studying Las Vegas was another.

A further influential encounter was with Charles Seeger, the ethnomusicologist, whom I met in 1963. At that time, Seeger was endeavoring to understand music (he said "musics") as a multicultural language of communication—doing for music what Brinck was doing for the cultural landscape and I was attempting to do for the city in my "Form, Forces, and Function" studio classes. Pop artists, too, helped define my view. Coming from the England of the Independent Group and the Brutalists, I thought the American Pop artists were latecomers, behind the architects.[6] Bob, from the East Coast and Rome, thought they were early. Another thread in the weave was my interest in architectural mannerism—breaking the rules, liking what's shocking—gained from studying historical Mannerist architecture in Italy and England (fig. 4.2).

Given our earlier experiences, Bob and I found we had much in common when we met on the faculty of the Penn School of Fine Arts in 1960. Our professional and academic collaboration dates from that time, when Bob was starting to write *Complexity and Contradiction in Architecture*—which, in this context, can be seen as a creative architect's response to some challenging mid-century conditions and thoughtways, not the "clarion call to Postmodernism" it is now considered to be.[7] Brinck, with his European schooling and love of motels and motorbikes, paralleled us. A similar mixture of influences and enthusiasms defined each of us, conditioning our views of the landscape and our roles in our professions.

So when, in 1965, I stopped in Las Vegas on my way to Berkeley, I was primed to analyze and understand an urban phenomenon intellectually—as an urban planner, social planner, and functionalist architect skeptical of the norms of my field. But on the Strip, my first reaction was an artist's shiver. All those bright and garish signs jostling one another in the brilliant sunshine—did I hate them or love them? I did both. The strength of the emotion was clear, its exact nature puzzling. After my move to UCLA, in August 1965, I set about studying Los Angeles urbanism intensely. In late 1966, I invited Bob to lecture to my students and to visit Las Vegas

Figure 4.2. Michelangelo, Porta Pia, Rome, c. 1561. This gateway through the Roman wall is an ultimate example of Mannerist architecture, breaking the rules of Classical architecture. The central doorway appears to be not one but several different portals superimposed on one another. Above it is a Baroque broken pediment and above that a further piece of arched pediment. Medieval crenelations are included at the cornice line. The scale difference is vast between the central doorway, suited to a monumental entrance, and the windows on either side, which belong in a (somewhat grand) palazzo. These contradictions and juxtapositions produce a building that is both monumental and playful—the essence of Mannerism.

with me. Brinck had come to UCLA to lecture too, arriving, as he often did, by motorbike. Most of my visiting colleagues were happy to stay at my beach cottage in Ocean Park, but Brinck checked in at a 6 Dollar motel before he arrived. Whenever I see a Motel 6, I think of Brinck.

In the late 1960s, when Bob and I wrote the first chapters of *Learning from Las Vegas* and, with Steven Izenour, planned our research studio on the architecture and signs of the Strip, we incorporated ideas we had derived from study, travel, reading, and working as students and young architects. However, we had not read J.B. Jackson's "Other-Directed Houses."[8] When we discovered this great article, predating our work by more than a decade, we wrote to tell him, "Years before we wrote, you wrote, and you wrote better." He was graciously magnanimous and pleased that we liked what he had written. In 1972, Brinck reviewed *Learning from Las Vegas*, but I have not seen the review listed in the best scholarly bibliography of his writings.[9]

And he left me out of the review completely. Bob wrote to him, "You of all people—you know Denise and what she has done. Why?" Brinck apologized and said he didn't know why he did it. But I know why: in the cultural context of the time, as a woman in architecture and planning, I was marginal. I still am. But in some ways, Brinck was marginal too.

This marginality was among the many things Jackson and I shared. When Brinck wrote about "the other," was he also describing himself? There may have been an early component to his marginality: As a child, Brinck had been expensively schooled but in other ways deprived. Perhaps he had formed conflicting allegiances—with the distant parents who paid for his education, and with the paid caregivers who nurtured him day by day. That state of mind—feeling not quite part of several cultures, and maintaining several, even conflicting, loyalties—is what I have called "inner diversity."[10] It is an old dilemma. It was important in my African-Jewish childhood and youth and in Bob's growing up as an Italian-American Quaker. But it has a longer history. When Jesus said, "Give unto Caesar what is Caesar's, and unto God what is God's," he was, I believe, quoting a rabbi. Jews feel the pull between wanting to be part of a community that is global and yet being loyal to the land they live in.

The answer, for me, to feeling caught in such cross-cultural crossfires, is that it's a wonderful problem; we should not hope to solve it but should live with it, using its tension to foster creativity in our work. This, I think, is what Brinck did. The skewed view—the view from a marginal position—can produce useful insights and an unusual vision. Conflict between cultures can lie at the root of artistic creativity. Like Brinck, Bob and I could learn from Las Vegas, perhaps because, like him, we were marginal to our society in many respects.

Other cross-axes we shared with Brinck include a spanning between disciplines: our range is from iconography to regional science; Brinck's was so broad I cannot map it. We shared, as well, a spanning between Europe and the United States. Brinck spoke French, but his French, he claimed, was not particularly useful to him, because it was a child's version. "When children play," he said, "they use strange tenses; they say, 'You be doing such and such.'"

Brinck was an easterner who rode a motorbike across the Southwest. He was a friend and advisor to the working people around him at La Cienega, but he was no pal. His writing reverberates with the tensions between aesthetics and function, the practical and the ornamental, the enjoyment of surface and the excavation of history. He commingled professional and scholarly approaches to learning. I myself am a practitioner, not an academic, and an educator in a profession—two professions. As such, I use scholarly learning for purposes different from those of its academic purveyors—to *do* things. Bob and I are hit-and-run, sometime academics,

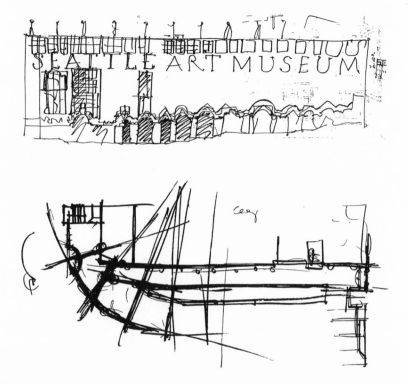

Figure 4.3.   Seattle Art Museum, 1986–91. Sketches by Robert Venturi from *Venturi Scott Brown: Maniera del Moderno,* ed. Carolina Vaccaro (Bari, Italy: Editori Laterza, 2000), p. 20.

sojourners and wanderers across our own intellectual and artistic diaspora. I think Brinck was the same.

Because Bob and I are busy in practice, the writing we do is tense, like a letter from the front lines. So are the drawings we make to communicate with ourselves on the way to a design (figs. 4.3 and 4.4). Brinck drew beautifully. Some of his sketches were made literally within enemy territory, while reconnoitering for an advancing army. Drawn in danger, in less than a minute, the tension in their taut lines is palpable (fig. 4.5). And *Landscape,* too, has the passion and urgency of a little magazine at the firing line in the politics and arts of the cultural landscape.

Yet, in that Brinck was a scholar, he diverged from us. A scholar on a motorbike is not us. That's more like T. E. Lawrence, another luminous, marginal character.[11]

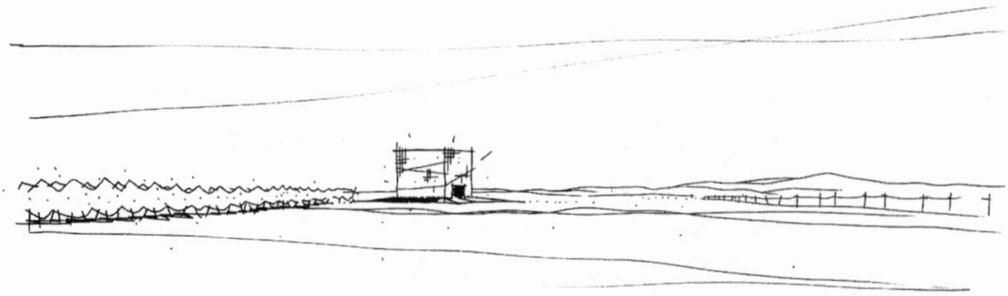

Figure 4.4.   California City, Mojave Desert. Sketch by Robert Venturi of a proposed geometric city hall building, 1970. The structure was to be a cube of gold
mirrored glass, reflecting the desert heat away from the building.

Figure 4.5.   J. B. Jackson, reconnaissance sketch of two towns on the European
front, 1944. From J. B. Jackson, *A Sense of Place, a Sense of Time: An Exhibition
of Drawings by John Brinckerhoff Jackson,* catalog prepared by Eleanor M.
McPeck with Tracy Calvan and Jessica Ingber (New York: The Municipal Art
Society, 1996).

How did we use what we learned from (and with) Brinck? I think we feel his influence most strongly when, as designers, we face a difficult "is"—some hard-to-like given of culture or function—and accept it for, inter alia, aesthetic reasons: because, by sideswiping accepted norms, it skews our view and thereby freshens our eye.

But although we have shared and responded to Brinck's liberating vision, we have diverged from his focus as well. Our reassessment of the everyday landscape has had one further consequence for us: it returned us to the art of architecture, but with an altered view. We learned many lessons from Las Vegas. One of the most important for us artistically was to reassess symbolism and the use of representation and decoration in architecture and urban design. Here the influence was not primarily Brinck's, except where the symbolism related to popular culture. This was the case with a hotel and spa we designed for the Nikko Kirifuri Resort, in central Japan, where we installed a depiction of a Japanese village main street to serve as the lobby.[12] It contained flattened, colored, and illuminated representations of store windows, signs, banners, decorations, street furniture, and a utility wire–scape (fig. 4.6). These elements of the cultural landscape created a setting that was part main street, part museum, part fairy tale. As outsiders in Japan, trying to respond artistically yet respectfully to an enchanting but unfamiliar environment, we needed, and got, a great deal of help in understanding cultural symbols and finding appropriate ways to interpret them.

We have had similar experiences in Europe and the United States, although rarely as directly related to the everyday landscape as at Nikko. The institutional architecture we usually are hired to design limits our opportunity to employ elements of popular culture and the everyday environment symbolically and artistically. When we try, some critics call our work vulgar and ugly and accuse us of slumming—of not really respecting people and of lacking social concern, although social concern was part of what brought us to Las Vegas. All this is difficult for us, and of course we're out of fashion now that the Modernists are back. But they're Neomodernists; we may in fact be the last Modernists. The Neomodernists are no longer ardent functionalists (we still are), and they naively think they can escape symbolism by ignoring it. We feel that to ignore symbolism is merely to become subject to it unconsciously. We continue to place our trust in conventional building, appropriately derived from the cultural landscape—in buildings that look like buildings; that are shelter, not sculpture; that accept social mandates and face difficult problems squarely, yet welcome relevant symbolism and decoration, now perhaps electronic,

Figure 4.6. "Village Street," Hotel Mielparque, Nikko Kiri-furi Resort, Nikko, Japan, 1997. Architecture: Venturi, Scott Brown and Associates.

applied (sparingly) up front. Perhaps this is what architects can learn from Brinck *and* from us.

Brinck was full of strength. His intellectually elegant, artistically driven, emotionally complex human spirit was housed in a lovable, Puck-like persona. The last time we spoke, he said: "You have to change your life when you retire. If you continue trying to do what you have been doing, you'll die young." So he found work on a construction site, where he was employed in cleaning up after the other workers, and he joined an

African American church congregation and told me he was black. I didn't ask why, and he did not respond to my suggestion that many Americans may be part African. He was full of mysteries.

On his last visit (was it in 1980? I can't remember) Brinck had dinner at our house. Our mischievous small son and our housekeeper and cook, a sturdy lady from Trinidad, were there. A letter from Brinck followed, saying, "It was a special visit for me—being in a house with an active little boy, a patient mother in the dining room and a warmhearted cook in the kitchen." It was the nearest to a personal cry I had ever heard from Brinck. "What does he want?" I thought. "What does he need from me?" I wrote a letter, saying, "I think your mother would be very happy with the life you have made for yourself." He did not reply.

Brinck was an artist. He was a lucky artist who found his sources early—found what he wanted to be an artist about. To link his many talents and hold his life together, he cleaved to one major inspiration: the cultural landscape—mainly the landscape of the poor, as it lies down upon the Earth.

LOOKING DOWN THE ROAD | 5

J.B. Jackson and the American Highway Landscape

J.B. Jackson's reputation as the father of landscape studies rests in no small measure on his original and insightful interpretations of the American highway and its attendant culture of mobility. While most contemporary writers condemned the roadside landscape and decried the highway's influence on American life, Jackson sought to understand the modern motorway on its own terms and relate it to broader social and historical patterns. Rather than reject the new highway landscape as an affront to traditional social and aesthetic values, Jackson examined the forces that shaped its development and interpreted its appeal to the motoring masses. Together with a small group of similarly bold and inquisitive writers and artists, he helped transform the common roadside landscape from a target of derision into a valued aspect of America's cultural heritage. Jackson's essays, editorial influence, and personal encouragement played a crucial role in the development of "odology" (his term for the study of roads, from the Greek *hodos,* meaning road or journey) into a respectable scholarly field; a vibrant literary, artistic, and journalistic endeavor; and a rapidly expanding locus of historic-preservation activities.

This essay summarizes Jackson's contributions to road scholarship and then analyzes recent odological developments, some of which would seem to run contrary to Jackson's practices and beliefs. While popular and scholarly interest in the American roadside is at an all-time high, contemporary odology is marked by trends that underscore the tensions and contradictions that develop when highway history—or landscape studies, for that matter—attains the stature of academic orthodoxy and cultural cliché. Historic highways are currently hip, but Jackson might well see their rising popularity as a cause for concern rather than an occasion to celebrate.

Jackson was obviously not the first to write about roads, but he was one of the earliest and most eloquent commentators to defend the mid-twentieth-century roadside landscape against the self-appointed arbiters of good taste and righteous living. These critics objected both to the "tawdry" and "tasteless" visual pyrotechnics of roadside architecture and to the disturbing tendency of the uneducated masses to embrace the automobile and the new American roadside as sources of entertainment, commerce, and social interaction. Before Jackson, much of the landscape contemporary odologists study, celebrate, and labor to preserve was assailed by "experts" and "enlightened citizens" as roadside blight. Typical characterizations of the pre–World War II highway landscape include a "shoestring of sordidness," a "nauseating vulgarity of structural riff-raff," and "the panoramic hodge-podge of hot-dog dispensaries, barbecues, and so-called refreshment stands that unfold in offensive, jazzy patterns along countless miles of our American highways." Popular and professional publications called for limited-access parkways to protect the public from the "ribbon of blight" produced by unregulated roadside commerce.[1]

Similar condemnations continued more or less unabated into the 1960s and have not entirely disappeared today. Critics such as Lewis Mumford, Peter Blake, John Keats, and Bernard De Voto seemed to wish that Americans would simply abandon the automobile and disown the associated landscape of asphalt, unconstrained development, and vulgar commercial display. At the very least, critics insisted, existing highways should be transformed into objects of sanitized and tightly disciplined beauty, with picturesque roadsides protected by tasteful greenswards and strict controls on commercial development, which would be redesigned in conformity with approved architectural fashions. If all highways could be made to look like New York's celebrated Taconic Parkway, if the car could be banished from the city, and if automobile-choked urban districts were redeveloped in the image of charming European cities or, for hard-core Modernists, Rotterdam's Lijnbaan, then the problems of the American landscape would be largely solved.[2] This may be a slight exaggeration of the prevailing point of view, but it reflects the anti-automobile bias, Euro-centric mind-set, and disdain for popular tastes that dominated profes-sional design schools and polite society in the pre-Jackson era. Jackson's tolerant and appreciative views of the commercial strip and other automo-bile-oriented landscapes are widely shared today, but as late as the mid 1960s he was routinely attacked for defending the strip and other aspects of America's love affair with the automobile.[3]

Despite—or rather because of—the controversy they generated, Jack-son's pronouncements about roadside architecture, highways, and the so-cial value and visceral appeal of motoring epitomized his pathbreaking ap-proach to landscape studies. Jackson's interest in ordinary, overlooked landscapes, his emphasis on the experiences of everyday users, his focus on the social function of the built environment, and his willingness to ac-cept and even embrace change were nowhere more evident than in his wide-ranging essays on the road and the effects of the automobile on American culture. Jackson sought to explicate the cultural significance of landscapes that struck many observers as unsightly, insubstantial, and in many cases, threats to traditional norms and values. Rather than judge these landscapes according to conventional canons of taste and decorum, he suggested, critics should try to understand the social forces that shaped them and learn how they reflected the desires of those who built them and used them on a regular basis. A good landscape was not one that im-pressed elite observers as a suitable subject for aesthetic contemplation, but one that answered the myriad needs of its inhabitants.

During the 1950s and 1960s, the ideal target for this temperate and populist approach to landscape studies was the rapidly evolving environ-ment spawned by America's infatuation with the automobile. Many of Jackson's most notable essays were devoted to explaining the commercial roadside and defending it from the forces that sought to eradicate it in the name of efficiency and good taste. Jackson argued that the strip and other manifestations of automobile culture should be interpreted on their own terms, not rejected a priori as ugly, dangerous, or inefficient. He acknowl-edged that such criticisms were not altogether off base, but urged his au-dience to try to understand how and why the strip had evolved, to recog-nize that it served important social functions, and to devote their energy to enhancing its ability to satisfy basic human needs for sociability, economic advancement, and personal expression. Even worse, he suggested that it was perfectly natural and perhaps even commendable that people enjoyed riding around in their cars and experiencing the new landscapes of the automobile age. Jackson also had the temerity to assert that the strip and its garish architecture embodied a new aesthetic attuned to modern needs, modern desires, and modern experiences of space and motion. He maintained that this modern highway landscape and the behaviors people exhibited when they were in it served important social, political, and personal functions.[4]

"Other-Directed Houses" was the first major salvo in this campaign. Written in 1956, just as the Interstate Highway Act was being passed and Detroit's influence on American lives and landscapes was in exuberant bloom, "Other-Directed Houses" was composed as a rebuttal to a De Voto diatribe in *Harper's Magazine* against the impact of automobile-oriented enterprises on the nation's beauty spots.[5] Protesting that it was time to "give these roadside establishments their due," Jackson decried the efforts of landscape reformers who sought to "sterilize" the highway landscape in the misguided pursuit of beauty and efficiency. Jackson admitted that the strip was often "ugly and unwholesome," but he pleaded for its "fleeting beauty" and "occasional usefulness." Conceding that most of the nation's roadways were as "hideous" as the critics contended, he maintained that the American highway landscape harbored enormous and largely uncharted "potentialities for good." In any case, he argued, the reigning climate of knee-jerk condemnation was a dangerous deterrent to serious intellectual engagement with an increasingly significant component of the modern American landscape. "How are we to tame this force," he asked, "unless we understand it and even develop a kind of love for it?"[6]

A closer look at the contemporary highway landscape would reveal that, despite its reputation for "depravity and confusion," the strip was a vibrant social and economic space that fulfilled important civic functions. For better or for worse, the modern motorway had become an indispensable avenue of commerce and consumption. The strip and the broader highway landscape were also becoming the leisure environments of choice for a rapidly growing segment of the American public, replacing the courthouse square, local park, or small-town main street as the common public space where people congregated to engage in spontaneous social intercourse. Jackson illustrated his argument with a vivid evocation of the hotbed of activity encountered on the roadways leading out of a typical American town, where the supposedly sterile and alienating landscape was enlivened by "cars with couples necking, souped-up cars racing the measured mile, cars playing chicken, cars, pickups, motorcycles, scooters, all filled with people driving merely for the sake of driving."[7]

Not only did Jackson contend that the contemporary highway landscape was more complex and socially beneficial than critics maintained, he observed that a good many people delighted in the excesses of roadside architecture and suggested that their affections were not altogether misplaced. More than a decade before Robert Venturi, Denise Scott Brown, and Steven Izenour proclaimed the strip "almost all right," Jackson observed that the visual exuberance of the American roadside heralded the emergence of a new approach to architecture that was more visually stimulating and better attuned to popular tastes than the austere modernism championed by elite critics. Countering the standard criticism that roadside architecture was vacuous and capricious, Jackson pointed out that the seemingly gratuitous excesses of roadside merchants reflected carefully calculated and increasingly sophisticated strategies for engaging the motoring masses. Competition for the consumer's dollar and the need to communicate with motorists passing at forty miles per hour inspired merchants to erect whimsical shapes, dazzling displays of light and color, "crazily tilted facades," and other "deliberately bizarre" decorative effects (fig. 5.1). As a result, the highway strip transcended its utilitarian origins and became a multivalent landscape of leisure and entertainment: a place to escape from the everyday world and indulge in exotic fantasies of wealth, power, and personal freedom. Appropriating a currently fashionable sociological theory, Jackson labeled this emerging style "other-directed architecture," to denote that its creators were not motivated by inherited assumptions of form and propriety but by the unabashed desire to cater to the whims of the audience.[8]

As other-directed architecture, roadside building epitomized the relativistic assumption that merit rested in public use and perception. Jackson pointed out that opinions about the strip were inevitably shaped by the perspective of the viewer, both literally and figuratively. For the teeming hordes roaring gaily up and down brightly lit boulevards, the strip was a "dream environment" of leisure and consumption; for long-distance travelers, the appearance of a few billboards, gas stations, and tourist traps could offer a welcome respite from boredom and isolation; when viewed from an airplane at night, Jackson rhapsodized, the strip was "like the tail of a comet . . . a stream of concentrated, multi-colored brilliance . . . the most beautiful and in a way moving spectacle the western flight can offer" (fig. 5.2). Only when considered as an affront to traditional aesthetic

Figure 5.1.   Roadside architecture. Sketches by J.B. Jackson for Reyner Banham article, "The Missing Motel," *Landscape* 15 (winter 1965–66), pp. 4–6.

Figure 5.2.   "Like the tail of a comet"—the strip as seen from above. Illustration by J.B. Jackson for "Other-Directed Houses," *Landscape* 6 (winter 1956–57), p. 35.

sensibilities, as an innate social menace, or as an insoluble factor in the traffic engineers' equations did the modern highway demand the drastic disciplinary measures proposed by professional designers and elite critics. Rather than dismiss the modern highway landscape out of hand and attempt to impose Eurocentric, antimodern, and antidemocratic landscapes on an unwilling public, Jackson insisted, the design community should aid and abet the exuberant vernacular processes that had created this imperfect yet immensely popular and promising American space.[9]

Espying a broader social dynamic at work, Jackson suggested that a significant source of elite resistance to the commercial strip stemmed from the fact that its garish appearance and bustling heterogeneity underscored the establishment's loss of control over a significant segment of the American landscape. Jackson observed that the rise of automobile ownership had coincided with gains in working- and middle-class leisure time and disposable income, creating a climate in which "a new kind of architecture, popular in the truest sense, was for the first time given an opportunity to evolve." Builders and entrepreneurs with little or no formal training constructed automobile-oriented fantasy lands that Jackson encouraged his readers to view as "a kind of folk art in twentieth-century garb." The guardians of good taste might plead for restrained schemes based on Beaux Arts propriety, nostalgia-infused historicism, or modernist restraint, but Jackson defended the roadside builder's proclivity for exotic decoration aimed at producing lighthearted theatrical effects. The crude pyrotechnics of ordinary roadside architecture could undoubtedly be improved upon, he acknowledged, but professional designers might also learn from the highway merchant's awareness that people liked buildings that were characterful, communicative, accessible, and even fun.[10]

Jackson continued to press the case for understanding and appreciating the new American roadside in various popular and professional forums. In "The Abstract World of the Hot-Rodder," first published in *Landscape* in 1957, he sought to explain why motorists persistently engaged in activities that confounded contemporary planners and sociologists, such as driving around with no apparent goal or destination, jockeying for position in endless lines of traffic, and migrating across the country on gas-guzzling vacations. The answer, simply put, was that people liked to drive. Motoring en masse appeared to fulfill a common human need for recreation and social display. The act of driving and the sense of moving smoothly and effortlessly along the modern highway also allowed ordinary Americans to indulge in formerly elitist experi-

Figure 5.3. Movement in the new landscape. J. B. Jackson illustration for his article "The Abstract World of the Hot-Rodder," *Landscape* 7 (winter 1957–58), p. 25.

ences of mobility that were inherently appealing both physically and psychologically. Along with dramatically expanding the range of personal mobility, the automobile enabled its operator to engage landscapes and social relationships in exhilarating new terms. No longer a static observer or passive passenger, the modern motorist was an active participant in the construction of his or her own individual experience. The motorist sweeping along the curves of the modern highway abandoned conventional perspectives and static relationships to become "the shifting focus of a moving, abstract world." This "new landscape" of movement, Jackson enthused, was composed of constantly changing perceptions experienced "at a rapid, sometimes even a terrifying pace." He suggested that there was a "mystical quality" to this phenomenon, as intellectualized responses to the landscape gave way to a more basic bodily awareness, so that the traditional Western sense of separation from the physical environment was transmuted into a feeling of visceral engagement with the surrounding world (fig. 5.3). Jackson even lamented that modern highways were becoming too standardized and predictable, minimizing the opportunity for creative interaction and prompting the adventurous to seek more intense thrills through hot-rodding, motorcycle riding, and downhill skiing. Jackson's personal predilection for motorcycling undoubtedly figured into these ruminations, but they also reflected contemporary fascinations with existentialist philosophy and Cubist-oriented conceptions of modern design. Jackson admonished that it was hypocritical for elite critics to extol these values when they appeared in the abstruse creations of approved artists and architects, while condemning similar impulses expressed by ordinary citizens through the common medium of the American road and automobile.[11]

Most critics identified the automobile as an antisocial influence, condemning cars for destroying traditional communities and decrying the atomizing effect of far-flung roadside enterprises. Jackson argued that the road and the car were unifying cultural forces. Like the parks and boulevards of an earlier era, automobiles brought people from all realms of society together on common ground, where they intermingled while observing tacitly recognized codes of behavior. Borrowing the concept of territoriality from anthropologist Edward T. Hall, Jackson suggested that a key reason for the automobile's appeal was that it afforded a high degree of public interaction while retaining comfortable levels of physical separation and psychological privacy. The automobile allowed people to cultivate the universal human pleasures of informal communication and gregarious association without becoming unduly intimate or contracting undesirable social obligations. The spaces and enterprises emerging to satisfy the needs of the motoring public, meanwhile, were replacing outmoded community gathering places and creating "new centers of sociability." Jackson explicated these developments in essays such as "The Social Landscape" (1966), "The Public Landscape" (1966), and "Auto Territoriality" (1968), lamenting that the anti-automobile biases of elite critics prevented them from recognizing that the democratic sociability ascribed to traditional pedestrian cities had found its twentieth-century expression in the contemporary roadside landscape.[12]

Despite his obvious enthusiasm for the social possibilities and visual excitement afforded by contemporary automobile culture, Jackson was not an unremitting apologist for the modern highway landscape. For all his spirited defense of the modern roadside's populist ethos and spirited vitality, he maintained that the American highway would be a more attractive and socially beneficial landscape if these impulses could be refined and helped along by professional designers and planners. The challenge lay in finding a middle ground between the democratic chaos of vernacular roadsides and the orderly but highly restrictive environments proposed by highway engineers and scenic beautificationists. Nothing frustrated him more than the tendency of elite critics to focus on superficial aesthetic issues or launch unrealistic attacks on automobile culture in general, when they could be devoting their talents toward more significant and attainable goals. Billboard merchants and roadside stands might spoil the view, Jackson acknowledged, but far greater dangers were posed by the seemingly unlimited authority of highway engineers, whose single-minded pursuit of speed and efficiency threatened to "dehumanize" the public road, "to destroy it as a living and varied aspect of the human landscape."[13] If the professional design community could put aside its condescending prejudices and acknowledge the futility of trying to impose outdated planning concepts on the evolving American landscape, he insisted in essays such as "Limited Access" (1964) and "To Pity the Plumage and Forget the Dying Bird" (1967), it could mediate between inchoate vernacular impulses and inhumane engineering doctrines to help ensure that the modern motorway fulfilled its potential as a unifying, attractive, and socially beneficial institution.[14]

Jackson augmented his own writings on the evolving American roadside by using *Landscape* as a forum for related research and reflective essays. A Grady Clay report on a 1957 conference on the future of the federal interstate highway program reinforced Jackson's contention that the "dictatorship of highway engineers" posed a greater threat to American society than the haphazard activities of roadside merchants.[15] Boris Pushkarev contributed a pathbreaking essay on freeway aesthetics. Reyner Banham extolled the baroque splendor of the commercial strip, castigating the curators of a 1965 Museum of Modern Art exhibition on modern American architecture for neglecting such innovative automobile-oriented structures as parking garages, motels, and shopping centers.[16] *Landscape* also reprinted news items on highway-related topics and reviewed a steady stream of books, ranging from technical treatises on traffic management to more popular offerings, such as George Stewart's *U.S. 40: Cross Section of the United States of America* and Eric Sloane's *Return to Taos*. Jackson's enthusiastic assessment of *U.S. 40* deftly summarized his own approach to landscape studies:

> The author has a sure-fire formula for writing attractive and informative geography: he writes about what he knows at first hand, and he writes about what he loves: in this case the immense and tawdry and beautiful American countryside. He sees its shortcomings more clearly than most of us do; he does not hesitate to point out the esthetic and economic crimes we have committed across the continent. Nevertheless *U.S. 40* is perhaps the best and most original guide book yet produced in this country; a geography that in the best sense is human.[17]

By the time he stepped away from *Landscape* in 1969 to focus on teaching, lecturing, and broader writing projects, Jackson's appreciation of the highway landscape was gaining wider support. A new generation raised among strip malls and drive-ins found these landscapes both less threatening and more interesting than their forbears had. Pop art, meanwhile, had opened the elite's eyes to the visual richness and symbolic appeal of consumer culture. "New Journalists" such as Tom Wolfe and Hunter S. Thompson celebrated American driving habits and the excesses of the commercial strip. The 1960s generation's penchant for sociology, folk culture, and "history from the bottom up" helped fuel the rising interest in common landscapes in general and the highway environment in particular, as did their earnest desire to shock their elders by flouting conventional standards and expectations. Jackson himself relished the role of leather-jacketed rebel and made the rounds of the conference and lecture circuit, titillating the crowds and shocking architectural puritans with his road-warrior persona and eloquent soliloquies on behalf of automobile-oriented landscapes. Geographers, architects, and historians became increasingly willing to accept Jackson's views, incorporate them into their own professional activities, and expound them to students and peers. The publication of *Learning from Las Vegas* in 1972 was a watershed event in this process, reshaping the debate on architectural form and significance by bolstering Jackson's assertions about the visual appeal and cultural complexity of the commercial strip with a more aggressive pop culture sensibility and the institutional authority accorded academically certified architectural theorists.[18] Jackson's own wildly popular classes were so closely identified with the American highway landscape that the Harvard version was nicknamed "Gas Stations," a designation that endured for decades after his retirement. By the late 1970s, when Jackson ended his formal teaching career, the highway, commercial strip, and broader cultural landscape were generally acknowledged as legitimate topics for aesthetic contemplation and academic investigation.

In his later years, Jackson's writing grew more historically focused and philosophical. He traced road-related issues back to Classical and medieval precedents and combined wide-ranging descriptions of development practices and technical details with provocative exegeses of the road's function as a social and political "way"—a term he found more agreeable than "road," which implied a reductive emphasis on physical features. The highway should be studied not just as a physical entity, he maintained, but as a cultural force that shaped and reflected social practices, political relationships, and human perceptions. He urged scholars to extend their inquiries beyond technical matters and relate roads to broader patterns of movement, commerce, social identity, and political authority. It was in this context that he introduced the concept of odology. Emphasizing the importance of the road as a central force in human affairs and underscoring the interdisciplinary scope and sociological underpinnings of his approach, Jackson proclaimed: "Odology is the science or study of roads or journeys and, by extension, the study of streets and superhighways and trails and paths, how they are used, where they lead, and how they come into existence. Odology is part geography, part planning, and part engineering— engineering as in construction, and unhappily as in social engineering as well. That is why the discipline has a brilliant future."[19]

Jackson elucidated his concept of odology in expansive essays that engaged such varied topics as the metaphorical uses of roads as emblems of human life and the evolution of the road itself from a protean vernacular path or abstract "right-of-way" to a permanent physical construction elevating mechanical efficiency over more diverse social goals. He returned repeatedly to the sociopolitical implications of roadways, contrasting the imperial majesty and centralized authority broadcast by French and Roman avenues with the democratic network of public roads that spread across the American national grid in the nineteenth century. Reiterating his emphasis on cultural rather than technical concerns, Jackson concluded, "the best of all landscapes, the best of all roads, are those which foster movement toward a desirable social goal."[20]

Despite his growing fascination with historical perspectives, Jackson kept abreast of contemporary road-related developments. He investigated the expanding influence of long-distance trucking on the American landscape, reexamined the automobile's function as a means of social and economic empowerment, and noted that the strip was no longer geared solely toward the needs of the traveler or recreational motorist, but functioned increasingly as a commercial and manufacturing location for widely varied enterprises (fig. 5.4). The most striking odological development of the twentieth century, he suggested, was that the road had evolved from a means of getting from one place to another into a place in and of itself. It is no coincidence that one of his last substantial essays carried the affirmative title, "The Road Belongs in the Landscape."[21]

Early in his career, Jackson was a voice crying in the putative wilderness of the American highway landscape. By the end of the twentieth century, this wilderness had become crowded with scholars, architects, artists, and preservationists singing the praises of the highway and the commercial strip. On the one hand, there was the academization of odology, most evident in the production of dense scholarly tomes on various aspects of the roadside landscape, the minutiae of which, Jackson noted, were of interest only to a small cadre of codependent historians.[22] At the other extreme lay the popular fetishization of roadside architecture whose

Figure 5.4.   Roadside business. J. B. Jackson, 1973.

charismatic landscape elements were celebrated and preserved to evoke an idealized golden age of American highway culture. Closely allied with both trends was the promotion of highway history by preservation agencies and tourism boards. Jackson would undoubtedly have been pleased to see so many people paying attention to odological issues, but he might also have been perturbed to see the growing interest in the American road expressed in ways that echoed the antiquarian, aesthetic, and academic biases he had labored long and hard to contest.

Popular publications and most preservation activities have focused on the nostalgic associations and kitschy visual appeal of engaging roadside architecture, paying little attention to broader social issues and either ignoring current users or criticizing efforts to adapt aging roadside buildings to evolving social functions. This sentimental embrace of roadside architecture mirrors the narrow artifactual focus Jackson condemned in earlier beautification and preservation movements. Jackson was no fan of historic preservation, whether it was directed at Colonial mansions or charismatic diners. He believed that preserving architectural relics that had outlived their social usefulness was a sign of obsessive traditionalism and cultural rigidity that, while inevitable and perhaps even desirable in small doses, should not be allowed to constrain the vitality of evolving social forces. Not only was Jackson opposed to the antiquarian veneration of individual structures, he was not as much of an aficionado of "classic" roadside architecture as a superficial acquaintance with his writings might suggest. Although Jackson applauded the overall impression of dynamism and gaiety produced by audacious commercial architecture, he rarely focused on individual structures and could actually be quite caustic in his assessment of run-of-the-mill roadside buildings. It was the social function of the strip as a landscape of opportunity and populist expression that he considered important, not its belatedly acclaimed role as a repository of transitory architectural fashions.[23]

At the opposite extreme from the superficial romanticism exuded by roadside architecture buffs lies the academic embrace of odological issues. Professional scholars are hard at work dissecting the twentieth-century automobile-oriented landscape, producing a rapidly expanding corpus of detailed historical studies and trendy theoretical discourses. Sweeping surveys have been followed by exhaustive monographs on specific aspects of the automobile-related landscape, ranging from the evolution of gas stations, motels, and shopping centers to the history of individual roads.[24] While many of these treatises are highly commendable by academic standards, Jackson prided himself on being, as he phrased it, "a virulent opponent of the American academic system."[25] His greatest disappointments with the academization of landscape studies were the substitution of archival research for fieldwork; the emphasis on design, technological, and institutional history over the inhabitant's perspective; and the dearth of speculative inquiries into less tangible social and spatial processes.[26] Jackson also objected to the dismal tone of most academic writing, chastising contemporary landscape interpreters for hiding behind the impersonal facade of academic prose. "Why must landscape studies be so dull," he complained, "so lacking in insight and emotion?"[27]

Jackson was especially frustrated by the tendency of intelligent, well-educated, and clearly impassioned landscape scholars to devote their energies to surveying the "arid terrain" of fashionable theorists. "When will the academy break loose and actually look about itself and forget European philosophers!" he railed after being sent one too many of these derivative discourses.[28] Expressing disgust at the smug tone and scant research underlying critically acclaimed pronouncements about the insidious impact of freeways, shopping malls, and suburbia—most of which, he noted, were essentially "old stuff"—Jackson complained that contemporary scholars were more concerned with impressing fellow academics through solipsistic theoretical performances than with investigating actual landscapes or making their insights palatable to general readers. Much of what passed for cutting-edge landscape analysis was not only ill informed and unintelligible, he maintained, but "written with a sarcastic, condescending attitude toward the public."[29]

A key distinction between Jackson's brand of odology and most recent academic writing on the American road is that he focused on issues of contemporary concern and made a conscious effort to address a popular, or at least middle-brow, audience. In this regard, Jackson would probably sympathize with well-researched journalistic offerings on road-related topics, such as Joel Garreau's *Edge City*. He might even embrace the resurgence of the personal-discovery-cum-travelogue genre that followed the critical and commercial success of William Least Heat Moon's *Blue Highways*. Jackson was not of an age or mien to indulge in such self-revelatory prose, but he relished firsthand accounts of life along the American road. Even when the authors came to conclusions Jackson would have abhorred, or persisted in recycling tired polemics he had fought to deflate a generation or two earlier, as with Jane Holtz Kay's criticisms of American automobile culture and James Howard Kunstler's diatribes against contemporary "placelessness," Jackson would have applauded their efforts to get out into the American landscape, take its measure, and discern what made it tick—or not tick, as the case may be.[30]

The romanticization of roadside Americana, together with the dearth of classic Jacksonian approaches to be found in contemporary scholarship, raises important questions about the future of odology. The road and the roadside are certainly not lacking for attention, but what are the prospects for the Jacksonian approach to landscape studies in general and odology in particular? Are contemporary road enthusiasts remiss in not continuing along the path that Jackson blazed, or have his observations, goals, and methods become obsolete, or at least less compelling than they were a generation or more ago? Given changing academic climates, what challenges confront landscape analysts attempting to extend Jackson's legacy into the twenty-first century?

On the methodological front, current academic proclivities pose significant obstacles for anyone seeking to emulate Jackson's well-informed yet highly informal approach. Jackson rose to prominence in an era when the academy was more accepting of work that was personalized, synthetic, anecdotal, and belletristic. Younger scholars employing Jackson's rhetorical strategies risk being dismissed as impressionistic, insufficiently "theorized," and politically incorrect. Not only would Jackson's circumspection about sources and research methods create problems for investigators attempting to make their way as academically certified scholars, his willingness to be both a generalist and a generalizer also flies in the face of academic trends. Jackson's stance as the omniscient narrator, his unproblematicized assumptions, his interest in divining broad totalizing patterns, and his invocations of universal human values tend to raise eyebrows—*hackles* is probably a more appropriate word—in contemporary academic circles. In the current critical climate, such claims to universal patterns and broadly shared beliefs are often condemned as ethically and epistemologically untenable, as is the notion that a patrician white male could speak for the beliefs and practices of cultures other than his own.[31]

Many contemporary scholars have gone to the opposite extreme, suggesting that landscapes, and culture in general, should be viewed as a series of individualized performances whose meanings are negotiated by their participants and can be interpreted by outsiders in only the most narrow and qualified terms. Jackson would find these conceits both wrongheaded and dull. He privileged the user's perspective long before it became fashionable and paid close attention to the minutiae of social interactions, but the Jacksonian landscape scholar was more than a journalist or ethnographer. He insisted on placing transitory practices in broader perspective, insisting that the comparative historical element was critical to the field's intellectual vitality. "Without it," he declared, "landscape studies, isolated in the present, are either geography, or what is worse, sociology."[32]

Ironically, many of Jackson's methods and concerns are back in vogue, although they have been upgraded with academically correct theoretical packaging. The phenomenology movement lent stature to Jackson's interest in the experiential nature of space and movement, along with his penchant for drawing large conclusions from subtle and seemingly insignificant social and spatial patterns. His attention to the conflicts between vernacular and official processes presaged the current academic fascination with the contested nature of cultural productions and the ongoing tension between producers and consumers. His emphasis on the user or inhabitant's role in shaping a landscape's forms and meanings has also gained considerable favor in academic circles. Armed with Bourdieu, de Certeau, Lefebvre, and other accredited theorists, progressive scholars now venture into Jacksonian terrain in search of "the patterns of everyday life," "the production of space," and the ways in which ordinary people adapt official landscapes to their own needs and desires.[33] On the stylistic front, postmodern skepticism about traditional scholarly methods, combined with the contemporary culture of self-revelation, has prompted experimentation with some of the mixtures of creative writing, colorful reportage, and conventional academic discourse that enlivened Jackson's eclectic literary output. This embrace of nonelite perspectives and literary self-expression would seem to open the door to a resurgence of Jacksonian landscape studies. Unfortunately, the insights gained by such "theoretically informed" investigations are often mired in mind-numbing jargon and bracketed by methodological blustering that Jackson would have abhorred on rhetorical and epistemological grounds. Jackson was generally conversant with the latest theoretical savants, but he assimilated their ideas and expressed them in compelling, straightforward prose.

Moving from style to content, one is tempted to question the social relevance of the ongoing academic interest in roadside landscapes. During the 1950s and 1960s, when Jackson first addressed the highway landscape, the automobile was radically reshaping American culture. The road, the car, and the landscapes and social patterns they created were exciting, terrifying, depressing, exhilarating, and above all, novel and mystifying. Is that the case any more? Can, or should, the American highway landscape serve as a topic of ongoing public interest and scholarly inquiry into the new millennium? Is there much more to learn about the modern motorway and its architectural accoutrements? Do we really need to parse the finer points of motel design, shopping center location, or parkway development? From a sociological perspective, hasn't the roadside landscape reached the point where it is no longer a striking novelty but a comfortable backdrop for everyday life? Or, in the case of the classic commercial strip, a nostalgic icon on a par with the village green, courthouse square, and small-town main street? Aren't there new landscapes of more pressing concern to those interested in the spatial evolution of American society? What would Jackson devote his energy to today: singing the praises of fifty-year-old transportation networks and rooting out every last fact about archaic architectural fashions, or trying to discover how today's landscapes are taking on new forms and social functions?

The growing fascination with artifacts of the automobile age was a subject of increasing concern to Jackson in his later years. Considering the intensifying zeal with which both scholars and popular writers were celebrating the American roadside, he questioned whether there was "too much enthusiasm, too great a readiness to describe the drive-in, the truck stop, the advertising, and the psychology of the mobile consumer as popular culture, as topics important and attractive in themselves."[34] He

Figure 5.5. Motorcyclist and shopping center, Lubbock, Texas. J. B. Jackson, 1973.

clearly believed that the basic contours of twentieth-century highway history were well mapped, yet he continued to insist that the broader cultural implications of the American road merited further investigation, especially if this research produced new insights into the highway's role as
an evolving social space. He was less enthusiastic about the classic commercial strip, asserting that it had "served its purpose" and had "been
studied and written about to the point of exhaustion."[35]

Despite his ongoing assaults on entrenched academic culture, Jackson
lamented the shortage of well-grounded writing on the American road.
Shortly before he died, he called for further research on historic and contemporary road-related landscapes (fig. 5.5). The evolving social functions
of the highway landscape should be the primary focus, he maintained, not
the morphology of physical features or the pronouncements of professional designers. He insisted that the results of these studies be presented
in short, tightly focused essays, "informative, clearly written, without
condescension or social criticism" and directed toward "the intelligent
layman—not the academic." Jackson outlined several potential areas of
investigation: "Is the automobile now giving greater accessibility? Is there
a new, more folksy kind of tourism? What interests are best served by this

development? Where is it going?"[36] These final exhortations underscore once again that when he looked down the road, J.B. Jackson was not so much interested in the structural characteristics of the highway landscape, but in the roles it played as a setting for social, political, and personal experiences—not as a road in the physical sense, but as a way of expressing our common humanity and attempting to order and understand the world in which we live.

TEACHING AND LEARNING
LANDSCAPE VISION

The chapters in this section all come from experienced teachers. Here these instructors share some of the ways they have taught and learned skills and ideas needed to do cultural landscape analysis.

As a geography professor for more than four decades, Peirce Lewis has championed the tradition of treating landscapes as vital, if often complicated and contradictory, evidence of history and culture. He is known as someone who can confront an audience of students who have never looked seriously at their everyday surroundings and in a single hour forever change the way they see the world. In his chapter, Lewis describes his approach for engaging his classes in the close analysis of two seemingly disparate landscape elements—the ubiquitous war memorial on the lawn of a county courthouse and the generic small-town bungalow.

Like Peirce Lewis, the journalist Grady Clay has been teaching people to see landscapes for more than forty years, but his students have not been in a classroom; they have been the readers of the *Louisville Courier-Journal*, the professional journal *Landscape Architecture*, and the books in which Clay has compiled his lifetime of astute observations of the American city. Clay reaches back to the Renaissance anatomical cross sections of Vesalius, the famous nineteenth-century valley cross sections of Patrick Geddes, and the "stranger's path" of one of J. B. Jackson's most well known essays as inspiration for his own cross-sectional method of learning about the American city. As Clay's chapter reminds us, the interplay of words and sight, and the concepts that we bring to our explorations of a place, lie at the center of landscape analysis.

Lewis and Clay both address an inherent tension in much cultural landscape study: presenting unique local places and at the same time explaining how American farms, towns, and cities resemble one another. In their chapters, Lewis and Clay work from specific examples to more general types. The lack of footnotes and hard facts in J. B. Jackson's essays, by comparison, can leave readers wondering how he arrived at his assertions and speculations. In Clay's chapter we get a glimpse of Jackson's actual method, now visible because a few of his private notebooks and journals have been archived. Like a novelist, and like Grady Clay himself (who in his chapter quotes from his own extensive journals), Jackson shows through his private notebooks and journals how, especially at the beginning of his career, he took very careful written notes of what he saw as he traveled, and those details became the basis for the generic composites that appeared in his writing. Also in his journals, Jackson recorded insights about the meaning of environments that he picked up in conversations. Jackson was a skillful interrogator; he posed simple, friendly questions to local clerks or people on the sidewalk about things he had observed, and he often went away with the kind of field information that cultural anthropologists wait months to find. In a sense, for his entire life Jackson was always an astute outsider, a participant observer of the United States.

As an architecture student, a teaching assistant to Jackson at U.C. Berkeley, and later as a friend, Jeffrey Limerick, now a practicing architect and writer, observed Jackson's deliberate, consummate conversational skills. In his chapter, Limerick relates how Jackson adapted the Socratic method in his teaching and sought to recruit people to landscape studies by giving them the courage to write about the meaning of their own environmental experiences.

In her chapter, design professor Tracy Walker Moir-McClean outlines a teaching challenge from her architecture studio classes: transforming abstract notions such as "sense of place" and "cultural landscape elements" into concrete methods that architecture students can apply directly and consciously to the design process. She reminds us that architectural modernism and abstract, formal emphases have remained pervasive at most American architecture schools, and that these stylistic trends often have little to do with regionalism or local meanings.

THE MONUMENT AND THE BUNGALOW

6

The Intellectual Legacy of J.B. Jackson

In the evolution of modern American geography, few writers or teachers have left a more important and indelible intellectual legacy than John Brinckerhoff Jackson, a man who dominated scholarly thinking about the American landscape for almost half a century. It is fair to say that at the time of his death in 1996, no single individual had done more to enliven the study of ordinary American landscapes; no writer had done more to influence and make respectable the study of seemingly ordinary things.[1] Toward the end of his career, KQED, the public television station in San Francisco, made a documentary film about Jackson, and his interviewer, Robert Calo, caught Jackson airing the spirit of his philosophy:

> My theme has never really varied. I've wanted people to become familiar with the contemporary American landscape and recognize its extraordinary complexity and beauty. Over and over again I've said that the commonplace aspects of the contemporary landscape—the

streets and houses and fields and places of work—could teach us a great deal, not only about American history and American society, but about ourselves, and how we relate to the world. It is a matter of learning how to see.[2]

In October 1998, two years after Jackson's death, a group of some three hundred scholars and designers gathered at the University of New Mexico in Albuquerque to honor Jackson's memory and to assess his intellectual legacy. Although the conferees came from a wide variety of academic and design professions, most came with similar questions in mind. Where do Jackson's ideas lead? What does the study of commonplace landscapes have to offer? What problems does it pose? And what does it require of us, as scholars and as teachers?

LANDSCAPE AS DOCUMENT

Jackson was a prolific writer, and his essays on landscape embrace a wide variety of ideas, arguments, musings, and speculations. Throughout his huge opus, however, one basic proposition persistently recurs. Although it is not original with Jackson, it is fundamental to the intellectual position he espoused: "Wherever we go, whatever the nature of our work, we adorn the face of the earth with a living design which changes and is eventually replaced by that of a future generation. . . . A rich and beautiful book is always open before us. *We have but to learn to read it.*"[3]

In sum, landscape is a historic document that tells a story—actually, multiple stories—about the people who created the landscape and the cultural context in which that landscape was embedded.[4] And, like any document, landscape can be read by those who possess the necessary skills and vocabulary.

Vernacular landscape, furthermore, is a special kind of document. The ordinary landscape is, after all, the only lasting record written by the overwhelming majority of the earth's population who can't write because they are illiterate, or don't write because they are uncomfortable with the use of written language. The landscape created by ordinary people is the main historic record they leave behind—records "written" on the face of the earth.

But what does it mean to "read" landscape? How do we learn to do it? And how do we teach our students the skills of landscape reading?

WHERE THE IDEA OF READING LANDSCAPE CAME FROM

The idea of "reading" landscape is a very old one. In his *History of the Persian Wars,* written about 500 B.C., Herodotus describes the delta of the Nile and speculates about how that curious landscape came to be. But the present-day tradition of landscape reading is an offspring of eighteenth- and nineteenth-century empiricism and the rise of what we might loosely call "natural science." The practitioners of natural science were explorers of the natural universe, who wanted to know what was out there in the world, to catalog omnivorously the things they noticed, to speculate about what things meant and how they related to each other. The best of them were nonspecialists—and aggressively so—who exhibited a catholic curiosity about the world and the things in it. Many of them were collectors and taxonomists, cosmological pack rats who looked at everything and tried to discern order in the seeming chaos of the natural world. Some, like Carolus Linnaeus and Asa Gray, were botanists; others, such as Charles Lyell and Louis Agassiz, were geologists; still others were polymaths, like Charles Darwin and Alexander von Humboldt, who collected information about anything and everything, wherever they found it in the natural world. The best, like Darwin and Linnaeus, tried to fit that information together into ever more comprehensive theories about the way the world was organized and the way it worked.

By the late nineteenth century, curiosity about the natural world had spilled over into the study of human societies, nowhere more forcefully than in the new field of human geography—especially in France, where Jackson was born and spent much of his early life. It was the writings of the French school of human geography *(la géographie humaine)* that J. B. Jackson encountered as a student (and later as a U.S. Army intelligence officer during and after the Normandy invasion of 1944), and that helped ignite his early interest in the vernacular landscape.[5]

In America, that geographic curiosity about human landscapes was brilliantly exhibited in the geography department at the University of California, Berkeley. The leader of the Berkeley School was Carl Sauer, who called himself an "anthropo-geographer" and (like the natural philosophers who preceded him) generally disdained the rigidities of academic boundaries. Even Sauer's later detractors grudgingly conceded that he was brilliant, and nobody could deny his immense influence on students and, indeed, whole fields of humanistic studies.[6] In 1925, shortly after he came to Berkeley, Sauer wrote a highly influential essay titled "The Morphology of Landscape," in which he reiterated the basic message of French human geography: the cultural landscape is the creation of human agency, and it is the business of geographers to decipher how that agency has worked and what it has done to the land.[7] Although that paper has been cited relentlessly, a more mature version of Sauer's views appeared in his 1956 honorary presidential address to the Association of American Geographers, "The Education of a Geographer."[8] In that essay he talks, among other things, about the qualities required of any budding geographer.

"Geography is a science of observation," Sauer says. "The geographic bent [for students] rests on seeing and thinking about what is in the landscape. . . . In some manner, *the field of geography is always a reading of the face of the earth.*"[9] It is no accident that Sauer found Jackson's writings appealing, and that Jackson saw in Sauer a kindred spirit.

Sauer never made the presumptuous claim that landscape reading was the special preserve of professional geographers. In fact, he took some trouble to reject that idea. But for him, landscape reading was something that geographers did, and had to do; it was natural, like breathing, and one couldn't be a geographer (or at least a very good one) unless one did it, and did it well. That was, in Sauer's view, central to the geographic experience.

CAVEATS ABOUT LANDSCAPE READING

Before going on to see where these ideas lead, it is useful to inject some caveats. I do this because the reading of landscape is a pursuit that raises some peculiar and knotty methodological difficulties, and all serious practitioners need to recognize them.

First of all, if we think of common landscapes as documents, it is obvious that they are documents written by many different authors. Rarely were all of those authors trying to "say" the same thing, and that is the reason why the "messages" we read from landscapes often seem contradictory. To say that human landscape is a complex document is a cosmic understatement. In any landscape, a variety of readings is not only possible, but inevitable and even necessary. For those who are seeking final, unambiguous answers about the nature of the human condition, landscape is not the place to look.

Second, the creators of human landscapes do not all receive equal attention from those who try to read it. Some very important landscape makers have been perversely neglected in the traditional literature of landscape reading: women, gay people, poor people, and members of ethnic minorities, to mention but a few. Landscapes that are made by members of the Establishment, by contrast, receive inordinate attention: buildings designed by famous architects or the stately houses of wealthy people. Theoretically, at least, we ought to try to read *all* landscapes, no matter who was responsible for making them. It is especially important to try to do that when we are trying to gain insight into the lives of ordinary, unlettered people. If we truly believe that landscape is a lens that lets us look into the lives and societies of ordinary folk, scholars must necessarily pay special attention to the landscapes those ordinary people created. That does not always come easily. There are plenty of lordly plantation houses strewn across the South, but very few sharecroppers' cabins survive. Thus, our view of landscape is skewed, partly because of what we choose to notice, partly because of what is actually there.

Third, to decipher meaning in ordinary landscapes is inherently more difficult than interpreting other kinds of historic documents. Written documents, for example, like diaries, essays, or newspaper stories, commonly are signed by their authors. They are meant to be read. If scholars are in doubt about what those written documents mean, they can ask the author to explain, or they can read what other commentators have written on the subject. But most ordinary human landscapes carry no signature and certainly cannot be attributed to any single person. Nobody can be tagged for the responsibility of making most commonplace landscapes, and there is seldom any identifiable person we can ask about what those landscapes mean.

Fourth, like all physical artifacts, landscape is a selectively incomplete document. Even in the United States, where human landscapes tend to be fairly new by global standards, the older parts—the ancestors of our present landscapes—have eroded over time, or are gone completely. Although New York City was founded in the early seventeenth century, there are virtually no structures in contemporary New York that predate 1800. Only the street patterns persist, and even some of those have been altered. That is why landscape is sometimes likened to a palimpsest: it is a document, to be sure, but a document that has been partly erased, smudged, and then written over, seemingly by people with illegible handwriting.

Then, too, certain landscapes by nature survive better than others. Parts of the mosaics of Pompeii and the temples of Angkor have survived because they are made of stone. In both places, we have a lucky glimpse at a partial landscape created by a wealthy elite. But the settlements that surely surrounded Angkor and Pompeii have disappeared almost completely, largely because they were made of less substantial materials. The landscape that remains is tantalizingly incomplete, and the landscape of ordinary people is totally gone.

The final caveat is basically epistemological, and it relates not to the landscape as object, but to the eyes and minds of those who set out to read it. Because each of us sees a landscape with different eyes, the same landscape can be seen and interpreted in different ways.[10] Some of these multiple interpretations contradict one another, but that should neither surprise us nor disappoint us. When people set about to interpret the world, contradictions are inevitable. Recently we have heard strident claims that there are "right" ways and "wrong" ways to look at landscape. To take but one example, some "new cultural geographers" have contended that there is a "postmodern" way of interpreting landscape that is inherently superior to old-fashioned ways of looking, which are dismissed as "positivistic" or simply "traditional."[11]

Jackson rejected that idea, and, for what it is worth, so do I. Most of us who knew Jackson admired him for his modesty; not just his personal modesty, but his modest unwillingness to make extravagant methodological claims, his tolerant willingness to entertain diverse views. Landscape is not *the* document; it is *a* document, and as with any document, we should approach it with care, respect, and a healthy dose of skepticism. This view, by the way, is not a counsel of despair—just a modest reminder that all would-be landscape readers need to be cautious and tentative. In reading landscapes, it is often tempting for beginners to be glib—to assert that "this" means "that"—full stop. That is almost never true. Seldom, if ever, does a human landscape convey a single, unambiguous message.

So it is that any attempt to read human landscape confronts practitioners with ambiguity and endless difficulties. But that should not dampen our enthusiasm for the enterprise. Despite all the methodological misgivings and solemn epistemological warnings, the landscape remains out there—waiting for curious humans to grapple with its meaning. Like Mount Everest, it is there. We can choose to ignore it. Or we can try to read it and encourage students to read it, hoping that the lessons we learn will enrich our knowledge of and our respect for the world we inhabit.

And that, of course, is exactly what many scholars are going to do anyway. To those who share the ideas of Jackson, Sauer, and others of similar mind, the landscape is simply too alluring to ignore. We grapple with it because it is there, just as the natural philosophers of the eighteenth and nineteenth centuries set forth as if pursued by demons to explore the far reaches of the world, trying to learn as much as they could about the messy, frustrating, fascinating, wonderfully rich world that humans create and inhabit. Jackson summarized the feelings of many when he wrote in the first issue of *Landscape:* "How can one tire of looking at this variety, or of marveling at the forces within man and nature that brought it about?"[12]

HOW TO READ LANDSCAPE

So, with a song in our hearts, we set forth to read the landscape. But how do we do it? How do we learn to do it? And, as teachers, how do we teach others how to do it?

These are not idle questions. This urge to read landscape that many geographers take for granted is not taken for granted by the public at large, much less our students. No matter how important and interesting we think the enterprise is, it is totally outside the normal experience of most Americans.

I was reminded of that when, quite by coincidence, I received almost identical letters from two former students, who were just getting established as college teachers. I like both of them very much. They are bright, energetic, responsible young scholars, personally engaging, and wonderfully curious. Although neither knew the other was writing, they both asked essentially the same question. I take the liberty of paraphrasing their letters:

> Dear Peirce: Ten or so years ago, I took your undergraduate course about the American vernacular landscape back at Penn State. I liked the course very much, because it introduced me to a way of looking at the world that I had never known before, and which I found very exciting. So here I am, a newly minted Ph.D. in a small university with a flexible curriculum, and I want to organize my own course in the American landscape so that I can share this marvelous insight with my own students. How should I do it? How do I go about teaching students to learn to read landscape? Do you have any tips?

What was I to tell my young colleagues? I held both of them in high esteem, and I wanted to help if I could.

So I did the obvious things: sent them my current course outlines, along with voluminous bibliographic references.[13] I recommended that they read Helen Horowitz's inspired collection of Jackson's writings, with its excellent essay about Jackson.[14] But that didn't answer the real question: how do you teach somebody to read landscape?

To the degree that I had learned some of the techniques, it was because I had the good luck to study with two of the most accomplished landscape readers in North America. One of them was Pierre Dansereau, the distinguished Canadian ecologist, with whom I studied at the University of Michigan before he went off to become associate director of the New York Botanical Garden. Another was the incomparable J. Hoover Mackin, who taught geomorphology at the University of Washington in Seattle—perhaps the best teacher I have ever known. Later on I had the good fortune to go into the field with some accomplished landscape readers in geography: Jim Parsons, John Fraser Hart, Sam Hilliard, Larry Ford, Phil Gersmehl, and Paul Starrs, not to mention some very perceptive closet geographers, such as Joel Garreau and Alan Gowans. For me, it was sheer luck. But unfortunately, teachers cannot import Fraser Hart or Sam Hilliard whenever they want to teach their students how to decipher an agricultural landscape.[15]

So I looked around for pedagogic guidance and found that the pickings were slim.[16] Jackson, for example, generally avoided the question of pedagogy. Like Dansereau and Mackin, he taught by example. As he once remarked to Robert Calo, "I see things that other people don't see, and I simply call their attention to them."[17]

Once more I went back to Sauer's "Education of a Geographer," in search of pedagogic advice that I could pass on. Despite the title of his essay, Sauer wasn't very helpful, at least in answering the questions that had been put to me. According to him, the ability to read landscape somehow comes with the genes. You either have it or you don't:

> There is, I am confident, such a thing as "the morphologic eye," a spontaneous and critical attention to form and pattern . . . *a sense of significant form.* . . . Every good naturalist has it. . . .
> Some of us have this sense of significant form, some develop it (and in them I take it to have been latent), and some never get it. . . . One of the rewards of being in the field with students is in discovering those who are quick and sharp at seeing. And then there are those who never see anything until is it pointed out to them.[18]

Now, I don't doubt that Sauer had a point. Some people are better at visual things than others; I suppose it has something to do with being left-brained or right-brained. But I knew from my own experience that students could be *taught* to read landscape, and it was within the power of teachers to do it.

So I went back and tried to rethink what I had discovered in the process of teaching beginning students to make sense of the commonplace landscapes. Were there any basic guidelines that students had to follow if they were going to learn the art of landscape reading? When I put the question that way, I came to the conclusion that there were two minimum requirements—two things a student had to learn—two precepts, if you will, that a teacher of landscape reading has to pay attention to. I don't submit either one of them as original with me. But I am convinced that they are essential guides when it comes to introducing students to the joys and rewards of reading the vernacular American landscape. And, I might add, both of these precepts sound very simple. They start getting complicated when one undertakes to apply them in the field.

1. Cultivating the Habit of Attention

The first precept is basic and crucial. *Students need to develop and cultivate the habit of using their eyes and asking nonjudgmental questions about familiar, commonplace things.*

Put this in a slightly different way. Students need to get into the habit of trusting the evidence of their eyes—of looking and asking some very elementary descriptive questions. What is that? Why does it look the way it does? How does it work? Why is it there?

Note another thing: the questions are scrupulously nonjudgmental. Teachers should discourage students from making snap judgments about whether they like or don't like something in the landscape. Premature aesthetic or ideological judgments are commonly half-baked, and they almost always get in the way of clear vision, at least in the early stages of serious landscape study. So the first question should always be: "What is that?" not whether I like it or not. This is simply another way of saying the obvious: one can't say anything intelligent about anything unless one can first describe accurately and dispassionately.[19]

To geographers and others who have lived most of their adult lives trying to read landscape, all of this may sound tediously obvious. Why make such a fuss about using one's eyes and asking serious questions about what one sees? The answer is not comforting. Most modern Americans simply don't use their eyes—and they certainly don't use their eyes to look at the commonplace landscape they inhabit from day to day. Australian Aborigines did; it was a matter of survival with them. Most Americans don't—and that includes most American college students.

It's not hard to fix blame for that. The American educational system, both formal and informal, actively discourages the act of looking and thinking about what one sees. Informal education, where most of our students get most of their ideas, says very clearly that looking at landscape isn't something that cool people normally do. In fact, students often get embarrassed when I suggest that they feel the texture of bricks in a building, or wiggle a window shutter to find out if it really works, or get down on their hands and knees to see what a piece of pavement is made of. From their gestures and their body language, not to mention what they say, it's obvious that you're not supposed to go around feeling bricks. People will think you're strange—and the ordinary eighteen-year-old, fresh out of high school, does not like to be thought strange.

Our formal education is just as culpable. Throughout high school, college, and even graduate school, students are inculcated with the idea that reliable information comes only from the written word: from books, journals, or messages on the Web. It's a plain fact that our educational apparatus privileges the written word as a way of getting information, as a way of learning. Look at the typical catalog of college courses, for example. The pages are full of courses in literary analysis and literary criticism. Nearly all history courses are taught from books and lectures—full stop. And, I am sorry to say, far too much geography is taught the same way. Then look for the courses that teach students to gain knowledge from looking at the things that make up the vernacular landscape—and you will look largely in vain. The few courses that do pay attention to visible things tend to focus on famous buildings and high-style paintings—not on what streets and alleys and farms and freeways look like. It's a rare academy that encourages the habit of looking at outbuildings in farmyards, or municipal fire plugs, or the signs in front of fast-food restaurants, or pink flamingos on residential lawns (fig. 6.1).

So our first job, if we want to teach students how to read landscape, is to help them to develop the habit of thoughtful looking and asking questions about what they see in the ordinary landscape they inhabit. Fortunately, that's not hard to do. Bright, curious students pick up on the idea right away, especially in the field, when they are freed from those authoritarian classrooms, with their chairs all bolted to the floor in military formation, and turned loose in the real world to look at real stuff.

Then, too, in a curious way, students are flattered by the idea that a professor thinks it important to look at the world they inhabit. Students are accustomed to professors who think that only Victorian poetry or the laws of thermodynamics are important. Indeed, one main reason that academics are often thought to be stuffy is that they rarely exhibit much interest in the world the students inhabit and the things they deem impor-

Figure 6.1. Vernacular shrine. The conventional academic curriculum provides very little room for the study of commonplace objects in the ordinary American landscape.

tant. Many students are simply delighted when they discover that it's academically OK to go out and look at the parking lots and shopping malls they frequent, or the arrangement of houses and trees and lawns on the residential streets where they live—and then ask serious questions about what they see. To take those students' habitat seriously is, in effect, to take *them* seriously. Many students find this idea astonishing—and exhilarating.

2. Acquiring Vocabulary

The second precept follows logically from the first. *If students are going to look at elements of landscape and describe them, they need to acquire a vocabulary that allows them to describe things systematically and accurately.*

Put it another way. One can't talk about anything, especially something as complicated as human landscape, if one looks at it simply as a kind of goulash of miscellaneous objects, all mixed up in a bubbling random stew. Students can't see order in the world unless they can recognize similarities and differences; a good vocabulary helps them do that.

Figure 6.2.   An alluvial fan, about fifty miles east of Los Angeles. To a geomorphologist, the term *alluvial fan* denotes both morphology and origin.

Geomorphologists, for example, recognize a feature they call an alluvial fan (fig. 6.2). The language is crucial. Two words describe a peculiar kind of land form, with a peculiar and highly recognizable shape that looks from above like an old-fashioned fan, the kind that ladies used to carry to church. But the term also says that we know how that shape *originated*—that we know its history. All alluvial fans are created by running water, by a stream depositing sand and gravel when its volume and velocity drop below a certain point, and the stream is forced to drop the load it had previously been carrying. The term also makes it possible to relate the fan to things around it. Alluvial fans are always younger than both the material beneath them and the bedrock slopes along their flanks. In short, from those two words, *alluvial fan*, geomorphologists know what the feature looks like, how it came to be, what it's made of, and how the feature relates to surrounding elements in the landscape. And because all alluvial fans are created by streams that are overburdened, geomorphologists can go on to ask other, more sophisticated questions: Why is this stream behaving the way it is? What's been going on here, to create this form in this particular place? These are excellent questions, but one cannot ask any of them unless one first knows what an alluvial fan is, and how to apply that term.

The same principle applies in other fields. In plant ecology, certain species of plants are signals of ecological change—but one has to recognize and identify the plants before one can begin to speculate about what sort of change is happening. Agricultural geographers give names to certain kinds of barns and outbuildings because those structures are clues to what kind of farming is being conducted. If a certain kind of barn is consistently being abandoned or altered, while another kind isn't, that is evidence of a particular kind of agricultural change. But one can't talk about barns intelligently unless one can first give them names and know what those names refer to.

THE CASE OF BELLEFONTE

Two examples from Bellefonte, Pennsylvania, illustrate how the accurate use of vocabulary can help students get their teeth into the act of landscape reading. Bellefonte is a small town that I have used from time to time as a laboratory for my own work.[20] It is the county seat of Centre County, close to the geographical center of Pennsylvania, and a dozen or so miles from my university—so it's a convenient place to take students on field trips when I'm first trying to show them some of the ways that human landscapes can be read.

As the students and I walk the streets of Bellefonte, I introduce them to various kinds of technical vocabulary—botanical, technological, demographic—to describe what we are seeing, but the most important vocabulary in this initial stage of landscape reading is that of architectural history. There is good reason for that. The central elements in many human landscapes are buildings—houses, office buildings, barns, factories, warehouses, and so on. They are quintessentially "significant forms," to use Sauer's language. People take buildings very seriously: they are expensive, they last a long time, and their exterior appearance is often interpreted as a reflection of the person who created it or who now inhabits it. Furthermore, architectural styles and forms provide important clues to the age of a building and the economic status of its builder. If one hopes to read the meaning of a town's landscape, for example, it is useful—often necessary—to know what was built when, in order to comprehend the town's chronology and determine when the local building owners decided to make major investments in the town—in short, to use buildings as a visible barometer of past economic and social conditions in the town.

Figure 6.3.   The Centre County War Memorial, Bellefonte, Pennsylvania. This monument was erected in 1904, in the fashionable Beaux Arts style of the day. The county courthouse is in the background.

Before students can begin to talk intelligently about the appearance of buildings, however, they need a certain level of architectural vocabulary—and, unfortunately, most Americans do not possess that vocabulary. So, before taking students to Bellefonte for the first time, I give them a crash course in postcolonial architectural history—specifically of building facades. I ask them to learn what an Italianate house looks like, for example, and how it differs from Gothic and Queen Anne, and I ask them to learn some dates, so that when they see a neighborhood of Italianate houses in Bellefonte, they will know that it is probably older by a decade or two than the Queen Anne neighborhood next door.

What Vocabulary Can Do: The Monument and the Bungalows

In the course of a day's field trip through Bellefonte, my students and I encounter two things that the normal student, in the normal course of daily life, would not be likely to pay much attention to. The first is the War Memorial in front of the county courthouse, at the head of High Street (fig. 6.3). Standing in front of the monument is a dignified bronze

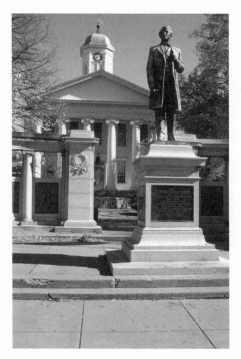

Figure 6.4. Centerpiece of the War Memorial. The statue commemorates Andrew Gregg Curtin, governor of Pennsylvania during the Civil War, and Centre County's most famous citizen. The Curtin statue is a formidable expression of Establishment Bellefonte in its most dignified form.

statue of Andrew Curtin, Bellefonte's most famous citizen, who was governor of Pennsylvania during the Civil War and a potent supporter of Lincoln and the Union cause (fig. 6.4). After the war he was the American ambassador to Russia.

The monument is an elaborate celebration of Centre County's role in helping to fight America's numerous wars. Along with a fair bit of martial statuary, it bears the names of all the county's citizens who served in the military in wartime: during the Revolution, the War of 1812, the Mexican War, the Civil War, the Spanish-American War, the Philippine Insurrection, World War I, World War II, Korea, and Vietnam. There are four long rows of bronze tablets, all closely engraved with the names of veterans (fig. 6.5). It is quite an array.

The second thing—or rather set of things—that students are likely to overlook is a scattering of California bungalows, largely located in a middle-class residential neighborhood several blocks from the courthouse. The monument and the bungalows don't seem to be related to each other, and to most students, they don't seem very interesting, either. Typically, students glance at the monument and dismiss it. "Just another war memorial. What's

Figure 6.5. Bronze plaques on the War Memorial. These tablets bear the names of every citizen of Centre County who served the nation in a time of war. In all, they display about four thousand names.

the big deal?" As for the bungalows, the beginning student sees them as no more interesting than the monument. "Just a bunch of old houses. If you've seen one, you've seen 'em all. Don't all towns have things like that?"

The Monument　Now the war memorial—like any artifact in the land-scape—can be read on several levels. It is a memorial to the citizens of Centre County who served in the military—that much is obvious. But that monument is an extraordinary thing to see in the main square of a supposedly tranquil little town in Quaker Pennsylvania. For most of its history, Bellefonte was just a very small place in an isolated and sparsely populated rural county. Some of the county's early settlers likely came to America to evade military conscription in Europe. Yet there are more than four thousand names on that monument! It bespeaks a bloody history, and it raises forceful questions about the popular roots of American militarism—questions that abstract discussions in the classroom aren't likely to raise.

On another level, the monument, with all those names in bronze, reveals a good deal about the town's ethnic composition at various stages in its history. There are more than two thousand names of Civil War veter-

Figure 6.6.   Detail of War Memorial plaque. The names on the monument's bronze plaques are nearly all of British, Irish, or German origin, evidence of Bellefonte's ethnic makeup at the time of the Civil War.

ans on the monument, and nearly all are of British, Irish, or German derivation (fig. 6.6). There is a conspicuous absence of names from Scandinavia and Eastern or southern Europe, not to mention Asia and Latin America. And there are no Italian names at all, a seeming paradox, since a considerable proportion of Pennsylvania's contemporary population is of Italian ancestry. Perhaps a quarter of the students in an average class at

Figure 6.7. Bonfatto's Restaurant, about a block from the War Memorial. Present-day Bellefonte has a good many citizens of Italian origin, but the monument provides evidence that the migration from Italy did not occur until after the Civil War.

my university are likely to have Italian names. But not in Civil War Bellefonte. What happened between then and now?

There are a good many Italian Americans in Bellefonte today. Standing at the monument, one can look down High Street to Bonfatto's Restaurant (fig. 6.7), and just a little way down Allegheny Street is the onetime Roma Family Restaurant, where a much respected former mayor, Gino Fornicola, liked to drink his morning coffee. And there is no shortage of Italian names on the gravestones in the Catholic cemetery, just a few blocks up the street. Suddenly, a few students begin to realize that one doesn't need special training in history or geography to make some intelligent guesses about the streams of foreign migration that washed through the streets of small Pennsylvania towns in the last third of the nineteenth century. Plenty of students find this sort of thing highly interesting, especially if their name happens to be Capparelli or Berducci, or if their great-grandmother arrived in Pennsylvania from Sicily or Calabria in 1905.

But the architecture of the monument permits yet another reading—and this is where a knowledge of architectural vocabulary exhibits its power. The monument is right out of the textbook: neoclassical beaux arts. The students know—because they had that crash course in architectural

Figure 6.8.   Union Station, Washington, D.C. This was the keystone of Daniel Burnham's 1900 McMillan Plan to rebuild monumental Washington in Beaux Arts style with all the stops pulled out. Union Station was designed as the gateway—both real and iconic—to a magnificent new federal city.

history back in the classroom—that the style, in this particular form, originated in Second Empire France, but they also know that this particular manifestation is peculiarly American. The date on the monument is 1904—and the architecture is plainly derivative of Daniel Burnham's Great White City at the 1893 Columbian Exposition in Chicago. It also bears a strong resemblance to Burnham's McMillan Plan buildings in Washington, D.C.—Union Station (fig. 6.8) and those white marble buildings that line the Mall. In 1904, that Bellefonte monument was, architecturally, very up-to-date. With its elaborate classical detailing and its formidable statue of Bellefonte's leading citizen, it is also very Establishment.

The monument is, in effect, a powerful political statement, nothing less than architectural propaganda. It is unapologetically boastful. It asserts and glorifies America's connection with a purified and high-minded classical tradition. These are America's roots, the monument says, and they're Bellefonte's roots, too. They go back to the glory that was Greece and the grandeur that was Rome. For a little country town in the Appalachians, that is not exactly a modest idea. But Bellefonte was a serious place, and meant itself to be taken seriously by residents and visitors alike.

Figure 6.9.   Postcard of Uncle Sam at the 1893 Columbian Exposition in Chicago. Burnham's Great White City is in the background, along with samples of American naval might. A similar triumphant sentiment is apparent in the architecture of the Bellefonte War Memorial.

At the same time, just like Union Station in Washington, the monument was a proclamation of America's new political, military, and technological power, which had destroyed the last remnants of Spain's once-mighty overseas empire just six years before. That same power would send Theodore Roosevelt's "Great White Fleet" sailing around the world—America's mailed fist in a white glove—only three years later. The statue of Governor Curtin reinforces that Establishment message: Bellefonte's first citizen is central to this patriotic experience. "Look at us! We're Americans! We can do *anything!*" (fig. 6.9).

For the brighter students (Sauer would have liked these kids), this kind of thing comes as a revelation. Theodore Roosevelt and Daniel Burnham aren't just shadowy figures from the pages of an arid textbook. "Roosevelt and Burnham are right here," the monument says, "and they want to talk to you." That is not a familiar experience for most undergraduate students.

Now there is plainly much more that can be said about the monument—about its overt and covert meanings. One can dispute what I have argued so far, and one can surely provide alternative readings of the Bellefonte monument.[21] But this reading, however debatable, would not have been possible without a rudimentary vocabulary of American architectural history.

Figure 6.10.   A quintessential California bungalow, c. 1900.
The bungalow is aggressively equipped with features of the
contemporary Arts and Crafts movement. The natural, uncut
stone, hand-split unpainted shingles, and undisguised beams
and rafters are ostentatious evidence that the house was made
by hand. The form of the house is characteristically bungaloid,
with its low-slung profile, large overhanging eaves and extensive porches.

The Bungalows   By the time we arrive in Bellefonte, the students have
acquired enough vocabulary to recognize a California bungalow when
they see one (fig. 6.10). They know, for example, that such houses derived
from the work of Pasadena architects like the brothers Greene and Greene
during the 1890s and early 1900s, and that their adoption in the East was
one of the first signals that California was no longer an isolated western
territory but was becoming a major center for domestic innovation, reaching even into the isolated and conservative valleys of central Pennsylvania
(fig 6.11). They know that simplified versions of those bungalows were
built in vast numbers in the eastern United States during the 1910s and
1920s, and they know also that the Crash of 1929 essentially killed them
off as a popular domestic style.

Those bungalows, then, are index fossils of residential growth during
the 1920s, and their presence in Bellefonte is fairly typical of most American towns of that period. A few of the Bellefonte bungalows, furthermore, carry the faint earmarks of the Arts and Crafts movement—and
here's where a knowledge of architectural vocabulary allows the students
to see those houses in a new light.

Figure 6.11. A fairly typical Bellefonte bungalow, c. 1920.
Uncounted thousands of bungalows like this one were built in
the eastern United States between World War I and the Great
Depression. The simplified form of bungalow pictured here was
the choice of most eastern builders. Although the typical bungalow form survives, many of the high-style Arts and Crafts
features have been watered down or are missing entirely.

Back in class, while they were still learning their vocabulary, the students learned about the Arts and Crafts movement, first promoted in England by social critics such as John Ruskin and William Morris and then
adopted and publicized in the United States by architects such as Greene
and Greene in Pasadena, and by designer-promoters like Gustav Stickley
in his *Craftsman* magazine, founded in 1900. The best of Bellefonte's
bungalows display a fairly watered down Arts and Crafts style, and an ad-
mirer of Greene and Greene would probably sneer at them. But some of
them, however simplified, incorporate a few Arts and Crafts gestures:
rough-cut undressed stone, hand-split shingles, exposed rafters, imper-
fectly fired brick, and sloppy mortar joints. "Look," the designer is telling
us. "These houses were not made by machines; they were made by hand,
and the mark of the craftsman's hand can be seen everywhere."

In short, these bungalows are not just old houses; they have political
implications, just as the War Memorial does. In the spirit of John Ruskin,
who had inveighed against the railroads and factories that were despoiling
his beloved English countryside, and in the spirit of Lewis Mumford, who
lamented the excesses of American urbanism, these Arts and Crafts designers were protesting the worship of rampant technology, which they

saw as inhuman and inhumane. They were, through their designs, urging a return to an older, simpler, and supposedly more "natural" America.

Now, it is stretching things a bit to say that these particular houses were political statements. The bungalows in Bellefonte are far removed from the elegant and flamboyant Greene and Greene originals in Pasadena. The designs for these likely came from pattern books, and the builders may or may not have even heard of the Arts and Crafts movement. Very likely not.[22]

But the architectural provenance of those houses is clear, and it comes from a social philosophy deeply at odds with the bellicose jingoism of the War Memorial. Just as the monument reassures Bellefontonians that progress is wonderful, the future is bright, and Americans can do anything, the bungalows (or at least their immediate ancestors) convey a very different message. In our mad pursuit of power and progress, these Arts and Crafts bungalows are saying, Americans have really botched things. The machines that were supposed to liberate humanity have in fact dehumanized us, made us slaves. "We must mend our ways," the bungalows are saying. "Let us get back to simpler times, when men and women could take pride in honest work."[23]

WHERE DO WE GO FROM HERE?

What are students to make of all this? They learn the powerful message that, as J. B. Jackson put it, "landscape is history made visible."[24] The students discover that ordinary human landscapes offer them a chance to look into an older world—the parent and grandparent of the world they inhabit. But they could not have done that until they had first absorbed the two precepts I described earlier. The students had to get over the idea that the stuff of commonplace landscapes is boring; they had to open their eyes and their minds at the same time, to see landscape in a new way. And they had to learn a rudimentary vocabulary that allowed them to identify and give names to things in the landscape, so that they could connect those things with larger ideas.

The Bellefonte monument and bungalows, of course, are just samples. The world is full of artifacts that permit a glimpse into past worlds that were just as complex as the one we inhabit today—just as riven with controversy—where people, just as they are today, were simultaneously optimistic and pessimistic about the world they inhabited. The people who created the monument and bungalows were thinking many of the same thoughts that we think today. They were torn by the same kinds of hopes and doubts about a new and unfamiliar world that was suddenly thrust upon them.

Now, I don't mean to be glib. My readings of the monument and the bungalows are certainly not the only possible readings—and they may not even be correct readings—although naturally, I like to think they are. But my argument goes beyond a particular reading of a monument, bungalow, or some other artifact in the landscape. I am arguing that we can teach students to read landscape by getting them into the habit of looking, and by teaching them the vocabulary that allows them to identify and classify recurrent significant forms. If they learn to do that, they will have acquired the raw materials to do something quite wonderful. They can start to learn from landscape, not by listening to lectures from me or some other teacher, but by learning, on their own, to see a world they had never seen before. And that will start to happen when the student says first, "Oh gosh, look at that." And then, a while later, the student says, "Oh! I see!"—and means it in the most literal sense of the word.

When that happens, teachers have done their job and can go home. Mr. Jackson, I believe, would have liked that.

CROSSING THE AMERICAN GRAIN WITH VESALIUS, GEDDES, AND JACKSON

7

The Cross Section as a Learning Tool

George Steiner, in his essay "Word against Object," noted, "The uses of language for alternity . . . for illusion and play, are the greatest of man's tools by far. With this stick he has reached out of the cage of instinct to touch the boundaries of the universe and of time."[1] So it is that Brinck Jackson—with his own self-made stick, *Landscape* magazine—eloquently reached out to touch the boundaries of his personal universe and to make them our own. It was he who, in good company, introduced the world to his Southwest, and vice versa; also in *Landscape,* he created his notion of the "Stranger's Path" as a way of seeing another important part of the American landscape.

I fell under Brinck Jackson's spell in the early 1950s, via early issues of *Landscape,* which led to letters between us and then to his visit to Louisville in 1957, while I was on the news staff of the *Louisville Courier-Journal.* Brinck arrived at my front door in what he called his "little English car," an occasion that I celebrated with an interview in the *Courier-Journal.*[2] Brinck's explorations, his persistent questioning of both the

Kentucky landscape and its inhabitants, entranced me equally as his host and as a journalist.

By that time, I was already testing my own methods for quickly coming to grips with strange cities—an assignment being thrown at many reporters covering the runaway urban and suburban expansion after World War II. My method started with attention to words that could be used for generic urban places. Growing up in Atlanta, I had been taught that Atlanta was "the center of the universe," and Peachtree Street the ultimate main drag. Later, living in Cambridge, Massachusetts, had suggested to me that I feel neighborly toward Boston, which saw itself as "the hub of the universe." Living in Alaska had sharpened my awareness of being "outside," a long way from "stateside."[3] Jackson strengthened this early interest in generic places.

Eventually, the cross-section trip became my own stick, my own special learning tool. By the 1970s, I had finagled a grant to finance an exploration of cross sections; with it, I penetrated—with varying degrees of rigor—some thirty-two cities, many of them new to me. The use of cross sections to understand complicated situations is hardly my own discovery. The cross-section examination is an ancient device for studying almost anything, from insects to geographical regions. The essence of the cross section is that it forces us to confront changes and differences that we might not see in everyday life. Cross sections gain their explanatory strength by revealing adjacencies and contrasts; they set up juxtapositions that spark our awareness and suggest analyses. Cross sections are not necessarily straight lines, or even the first lines that one might cut; they require work and experimentation in the choice of the section line in order to gain their revelatory powers.[4]

THREE CROSS-SECTION PIONEERS: VESALIUS, GEDDES, AND JACKSON

Three observers, in particular, have pointed the way to my own cross-section method. Andreas Vesalius, the Renaissance anatomist, pioneered the method for medicine. In the late Victorian period, Patrick Geddes used the idea of a valley cross section for urban education and for city and regional planning, making the cross section a visual device for understanding the unity and complexity of a large geographical unit. J.B. Jackson had his own humanistic reconnaissance methods, many of them learned during his World War II experience, for exploring and explaining the meanings of cultural landscapes. Except for their unbridled, venturesome curiosity, their penchant for large intellectual and geographical enterprises, and their upper-class beginnings, these three precursors to my own cross-sectional studies could hardly have been more different observers. Nonetheless, their methods share a key attribute with my own: they based their knowledge and explanations in empiricism, in the intellectual organization of what one can observe firsthand.

Andrew Wesel, in Latin called Andreas Vesalius, is said to have invented the sectional teaching of anatomy. He was born in 1514 and became a brilliant medical student at the University of Paris, where he criticized the usual forms of dissection, later becoming a radical teacher of anatomy. He had begun the study of anatomy at age fourteen, and at age twenty-three he became full professor of anatomy at the University of Padua (Padova, in modern Italy). As one physician has put it, "Familiar with the classics, he added French, Italian, Hebrew, and Arabic and made the human body the true Bible of anatomy."[5]

Some accounts make it seem as though Vesalius just walked in, underwent a stiff two-day verbal examination, showed his skill with the scalpel, and was *in:* doctor of medicine, magna cum laude, installed in the chair of surgery and anatomy. However, until his arrival as a professor at the University of Padua, anatomical dissections were done—if at all—clumsily, by barbers, while professors stood about and made comment. Church authorities then held that good Christians should not mess with dead bodies, which belonged only to God. Vesalius broke tradition and the harmonious barbershop monopoly by enlisting students to dig up fresh corpses, illegally, after dark. The corpses were smuggled into school, sometimes piece by piece, for Vesalius to dissect himself, in full view of packed anatomy classes. He gets credit for having invented the graphic method of anatomy, for he followed his own dissections with detailed illustrations, exposing the body's interior to eager students. His detailed engravings of cross sections (fig. 7.1), when published under the title *De humani corporis fabrica* in 1543 in Switzerland, revolutionized the understanding of human anatomy, corrected hundreds of prevailing errors about the human body, and sent a shock throughout the European world. The book was said to be one of the most beautiful medical textbooks of all time.[6]

Vesalius's Italian engraver sent his plates across the Alps on mule back to get them printed at Basel by a Swiss printer. The engraver wrote the printer to encourage him to tell his salesmen (a rough translation here), "Sell the hell out of this one! It'll make our fortunes." And it did, especially for the young Vesalius. But Vesalius came under censure for heresy, and at age twenty-eight, during the Inquisition, he gave up his anatomy

Figure 7.1. Vesalius cross section. Most of the woodcuts in
Andreas Vesalius's monumental
De humani corporis fabrica
(1543) illustrated various stages
of anatomical dissection, but
some, such as this cerebral cross
section, employed diagrammatic
abstraction.

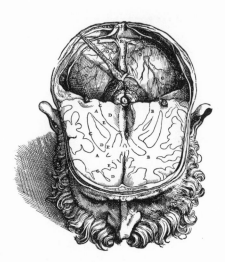

specialization in disgust, destroyed his notes, and took up the general
practice of medicine. His great works, however, live on.

It's a long jump from Vesalius in the sixteenth century, some 960 miles
from Padua, to nineteenth-century Edinburgh and the great oddball Scottish biologist, Patrick Geddes. But Geddes, too, conceived new uses for the
cross-section method. Born in 1854, he grew up in Edinburgh a rambunc-
tious, try-anything kid and seems later to have been transformed into a
natural teacher, attracting students from all over, including his later ad-
mirer and biographer, the American philosopher Lewis Mumford.

In the 1890s, Patrick Geddes created on the hillside above Edinburgh an
"Outlook Tower" atop a multistory mansion that he had transformed into
a home and school. The tower had a panoramic view over Edinburgh, ideal
for teaching and surveying the surroundings. It has been called "the first
sociological laboratory in the world."[7] On the top floor, Geddes installed a
remarkable camera obscura, a teaching device that projected onto a round,
mirror-topped table in a darkened room an enlarged image of the valley
below, around which his students could gather.

But in addition, as an intellectual and visual tool to analyze the urban
region, Geddes invented what he called the "valley section," a variation of
the geographer's traverse—a traditional learning device for recording a
linear experience through new territory. Geddes's valley section panorama covered a wide span: from mountain pastures down to commercial port. It was first exhibited in a grand civic panorama designed for the
now famous Cities Exhibition at Chelsea, London, in 1911 (fig. 7.2). His

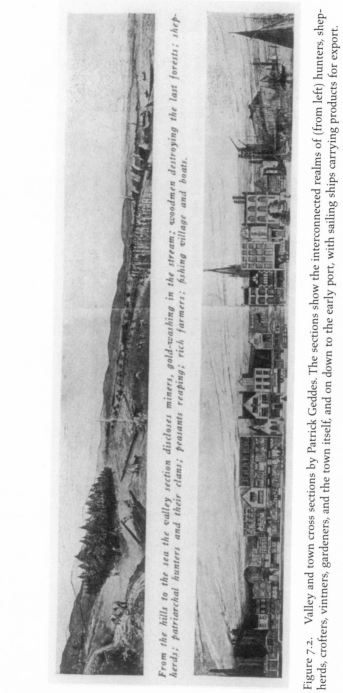

From the hills to the sea the valley section discloses miners, gold-washing in the stream; woodmen destroying the last forests; shepherds; patriarchal hunters and their clans; peasants reaping; rich farmers; fishing village and boats.

Figure 7.2. Valley and town cross sections by Patrick Geddes. The sections show the interconnected realms of (from left) hunters, shepherds, crofters, vintners, gardeners, and the town itself, and on down to the early port, with sailing ships carrying products for export.

gigantic painting showed a typical nineteenth-century valley in cross section, with a fishing village and port down at the right, and the landforms slowly ascending upward to the left. As viewers followed the upward path they crossed city streets, outskirts, hop fields, vineyards, and market gardens with cattle, arable lands, and sheep farms on higher grounds; and then onward and upward, into the turf of upland hunters, foresters, gold miners, and quarry workers, and then finally into the mountaintops.

The valley section was the epitome of perfect town form in the Scotland of that day. In more contemporary lingo, Geddes had invented a pictorial flow diagram: Down from the woods came the game and the pelt; down off the fields came harvests for the miller, baker, and town grocer; and down off the pastures came sheep and cattle—fleece for the crofter and woolen mills, cattle to the slaughterhouse and the shoemaker's shop. Finally, from the little town wharf, the local products got loaded into small ships, and off they sailed to markets, bringing back profits to shoemakers and cheese makers and crofters in a classic economic cycle—a progressional pageant from start to finish, a complete story in one panorama. There is no better way for coming to grips with a complex urban environment than Geddes's valley section when it is adapted to the modern metropolis.

Geddes set all this forth for American readers in a series of articles published in *Survey* magazine in 1925, illustrated by Hendrick Willem van Loon.[8] In one sense, Geddes was saying, "You could stand on the dock and watch the economy of all Scotland unfold before your very eyes." This notion of seeing visual clues to large-scale economies runs through many fine histories.

For instance, I recall a local historian, whose name escaped my notes, at one of those civic-uplift conferences in the Piedmont Crescent region that I covered in the 1960s, proclaiming to his audience, "You could stand on the street corners of Greensboro, North Carolina, and watch the great American cotton textile industry on its slow migration, out of the granitic river valleys of New England, down through the scrawny cotton-mill towns of the Carolinas, onward and outward to Singapore and Taiwan." Patricia Nelson Limerick, that most eloquent historian, has said it another way: "Reconceived as a running story, a fragmented and discontinuous past becomes whole again."[9]

Such is the sort of reconceptualization and generalization that we expect from the writings of John Brinckerhoff Jackson when he suddenly stands back from the evidence of travel and of history and asks the seminal questions: not merely, "What's the history of this particular place?"

but the far more demanding questions of "How do places like this come to exist?" "How do they work?" and "What do they mean to us today?" It was clear, during Jackson's editorship of *Landscape*, that his consuming curiosity about the generic street, town, and countryside was opening them all up to new interpretations.

Among the many writings of J.B. Jackson that helped shape and sharpen my understanding, I single out one essay, "The Stranger's Path." It describes a traveling stranger's arrival by bus, truck, or car to encounter a typical southwestern county seat. Jackson's route was not so much a straight line, as, in his words, "movement along a pretty well defined axis," in the gridlike street pattern of the small city. The traveler's path would proceed from the run-down district around the old railroad depot, past the ranch-supply houses, pawnshops, and whorehouses, onward past the produce market (or its warehouse equivalents) to Court House Square, and possibly thence past lawyers' offices and banks.

Jackson reminded us that "stranger" did not always mean "tourist." Strangers, he said, were often people who came to town "for a day or two . . . not very prosperous, often with no money at all." They were people looking for a job, or on their way to a job, or salespeople calling on local retailers. In the 1950s, most of them were men. Although much of the stranger's path was "loud, tawdry, down-at-the-heel," it exuded the excitement of "the city as a place of exchange," a place also "dedicated to good times." The path, he noted, was "at its gayest and noisiest and most popular from Saturday noon until midnight."[10]

Jackson originally published his article about the path with his own generic diagram of the center of a small southwestern city (fig. 7.3). The stranger's path, Jackson wrote, "rarely if ever touches on the fashionable retail district or the culturally conscious civic center . . . housed in remodeled old mansions." Instead, it usually merges into the financial section of the city: "When the Path has reached the region of banks and hotels—usually grouped around one or two intersections in the average small city—it has lost much of its loud proletarian quality, and about all that is left is a newsstand with out-of-town papers, a travel agency, and an airline office on the ground floor of the dressy hotel." The activity of the path, he said, often rose again outside of town, "along some highway strip."[11]

In 1957, Jackson still resisted the idea that fancy suburban shopping centers might become "the civic centers of the future." The shopping center, Brinck wrote, "no matter now big, how modern, how beautiful, is the *exact* opposite of the Path." The shopping center's public, at least in those days, was almost exclusively composed of local housewives and children,

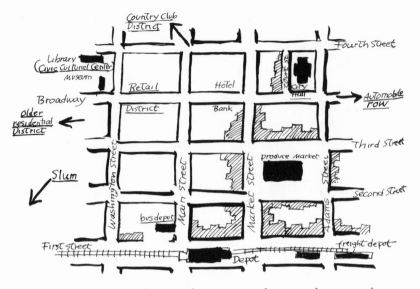

Figure 7.3.   J. B. Jackson's diagram of a generic southwestern downtown, from "The Stranger's Path," 1957. Jackson's visitor arrived by bus, car, or rail and proceeded from the more seedy, run-down warehouse and skid row areas past the produce market and through to the business district of town.

not visiting single men. The shopping center, he continued, "imposes a uniformity of taste and income and interests, and its strenuous efforts to be self-contained mean that it automatically rejects anything from outside." Including, as it did, skid row at one end, and the local Great White Way at the other, Jackson said, the moral of the stranger's path was clear: "the Path caters to every pocketbook, every taste," and welcomed—in fact relied upon—outsiders, the people who were absolutely new to town.[12]

Jackson reminded designers in 1957 (when typical American city planners were actively trying to tear down much of their local stranger's path) that they might see a more positive future for the mixtures and public nature of the path. And in comparing the American stranger's path to two of the best-loved European streets, the Ramblas in Barcelona and the Cannebière in Marseilles, he echoed Geddes's port-town section. Both of these streets, he wrote, consisted of "more than a mile of tree-lined boulevard with more trees and a promenade down the center," and they linked "the harbor (the point of arrival) with the uptown area." Neither had fashionable shops. Their public was "composed of a large cross section of the population of the city, men, women, and children, rich and poor, strangers and

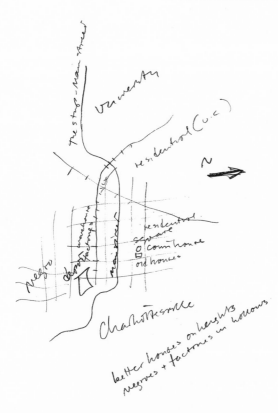

Figure 7.4.   J. B. Jackson's reconnaissance sketch map of Charlottesville, Virginia, 1957. In his detailed travel journals, Jackson often included diagrams of the towns he visited—a shorthand method probably honed as a World War II intelligence officer. He notes locations of "the strip," "Main Street," university, depot, and square, and observes, "better houses on heights/Negroes and factories in hollows."

natives." To walk up such a street, Jackson added, was "to be part of a procession, part of a ceaseless ceremony of being initiated into the city and of rededicating the city itself."[13]

Jackson's notion of the stranger's path retains many other characteristics of a good cross section. He notes and explains the juxtapositions discovered along the route. He brings new areas into view: his route (and the words he uses for it) helps city residents see differences in urban districts and places that local people would not normally visit or know. And like the cross sections of Vesalius and Geddes, Jackson's brand of urban analysis took in the large view and was soundly grounded in empirical, firsthand observations. From his surviving travel journals, now available to scholars, we can see that Jackson's generic diagrams and notions of American public space were built upon careful notations and summaries of whole towns (fig. 7.4). His travel notes show his skills, equal to those of a good journalist or novelist, in picking up cultural clues from what he could see and from his casual interviews with the people in a locale.[14] His unique gift was seeing beyond the local variant to the generic landscape element.

Jackson and I had many things in common beyond our inherent interest in exploring the American landscape and our roots in journalism. At one point I even proposed that Jackson and I could make economic sense by merging the background operations of our magazines: In the 1960s, we were both struggling outside the mainstream of American publishing. With *Landscape*, Jackson was attempting to bring his enlarged vision and a growing circle of like-minded authors to an influential international audience. I was working to take a hidebound quarterly magazine, *Landscape Architecture*, usually published late, with a significant deficit and a small professional audience, to a larger and more diverse readership, and to secure it a larger income. Jackson's printer was in Vermont, mine in Augusta, Maine. Our offices, in New Mexico and Kentucky, respectively, were "out there someplace," in that vast unknown territory between the coasts.

Thus it was, in 1972, after we had both attended one of those professional conferences that was dragging Santa Fe kicking and screaming into the world of mass tourism, that Jackson and I made our way around Santa Fe's plaza, past Native American women selling their goods. Over a long lunch, Jackson and I talked subscription prices and balance sheets, and we cursed printers, and I made my pitch about combining forces. I think he'd heard all this before, for surely I was not the first to spot Jackson's work as significant and his magazine as an important magnet for good ideas and good readers. Well, in due course, he turned my proposal down. But such was his generous nature that out of these negotiations we became lifelong friends—a much better bargain indeed. In the ensuing years, *Landscape* magazine attracted imitators, while *Landscape Architecture* attracted competitors. We were moving in different worlds.

Jackson and I shared a hankering for maps, especially the earlier hachured variety, which we had encountered in World War II. Those who have followed Jackson's career will know that he grew up doing one Grand Tour after another, a proper little boy soaking up European languages along the way, and that in World War II he was an intelligence officer for the U.S. Army's Ninth Infantry Division as it fought its way across Europe. Jackson became a multilingual expert at penetrating enemy lines, bringing back prisoners for interrogation, and ransacking French castles for maps and local studies to help the Allied troops negotiate rough country ahead. Jackson was memorably noted in a wonderful essay by the famous wartime columnist Ernie Pyle.[15]

I too had done a bit of ransacking in France, after encountering a rare dumping ground for maps of the English coast, prepared by the German army for the cross-Channel invasion that never came off. These German maps had been captured by the British, whereupon—because map-quality paper had disappeared during the Nazi occupation—the British had turned the maps over and on the back sides had printed their own maps for the coming Allied invasion of Germany. I stumbled into a room full of these maps, discarded because they were off-register; they were being used as wrapping paper. The Brits kindly gave me a batch, which now reposes in the University of Louisville Library. Such maps as Jackson and I scouted in Europe offered penetrating glimpses into long-gone landscapes. They excited both of us in different times and places.

Jackson's eloquence reached cross-country to touch the faculties at Harvard and the University of California, Berkeley, who opened to him their admiration, their curricula, and their students. It was lucky for me that during the fall and winter of 1973, I was lecturing at MIT, just down the Charles River from Brinck at Harvard, and I managed to bridge the gap between one end of Massachusetts Avenue and the other and to sit in on Brinck's memorable lectures.

THE GRADY CLAY URBAN CROSS-SECTION METHOD

Our intertwining histories, Jackson himself, his stranger's path, and his Harvard lectures were logical inspirations for some of my own journalistic ventures, both in print and in a TV documentary. Another important influence was the work of Kevin Lynch.[16] But I found that Jackson's cross section of a cow town, like the cross section of Geddes's hill and harbor town, had some definite limitations. Sections like these could cope only with isolated portions of the modern American city. Meanwhile, from the 1950s onward, movers and shakers were reshaping the city and the entire city region. The American city was becoming a processor, if not monopolist, of power and information. The city's outskirts, suburbs, and exurbs were becoming dumping grounds for all the excess energy of a rich and wasteful postindustrial society.

To better understand the effects of that expanding urban power, to tap those flows of information, I concluded that one must traverse the complete metropolitan area as a continuous experience: going in one side, continuing through the midsection, and emerging out the other side of the entire urban region. So, beginning in the late 1960s, I set out to work all the way through the commuting range of what economists call the "functioning economic area" of thirty-two modern cities in the United States. These cross sections each start and end at the outer edges of the functioning economic area; from these edges, at least 5 percent of those employed in the urban region commute every day into and around that region. The cities I studied on one western trip included Boulder, Denver, and Durango, Colorado; and Scottsdale and Phoenix, Arizona. Other cities I have "cross-sectioned"—some more thoroughly than others—include Louisville, Frankfort, and Lexington, Kentucky; Worcester and Boston, Massachusetts; Baltimore and Columbia, Maryland; Atlanta and Savannah, Georgia; Cincinnati and Columbus, Ohio; Detroit and Ann Arbor, Michigan; Terre Haute, Indianapolis, and Columbus, Indiana; St. Louis, Missouri; Kansas City, Salina, and Manhattan, Kansas; and Los Angeles and Newport-Irvine, in California.[17]

Along the way, in 1989 I joined the team of geographers prompted by publisher George Thompson and led by Professor Karl Raitz to explore a portion of U.S. Highway 40. Their work is summarized in a two-volume study, *The National Road*, with a concluding coda by Raitz and me.[18]

In order to make the most of a cross-section analysis as a learning device, I developed a set of self-imposed and much tested guidelines, which one might call "The Basic Rules of a Grady Clay Urban Cross Section":[19]

1. The cross-section route must span the entire range of daily commuting, covering the full size of the "commutershed," using specified routes (not always the best-known streets!) as a spine for the trip.

2. The route must continue in one general direction and not double back on itself. Ideally, the direction of movement should cut diagonally across the traditional gridiron pattern of the city streets and end roughly 180 degrees opposite the beginning point.

3. When the route gets boring or repetitive, turn off. To turn is to learn. Often the hidden spaces just off the main routes tell a different story, allow the student of the city to compare what's up front with another reality out back. Turning off from a predictable or familiar route increases the intensity of one's gaze, the receptivity of one's senses. If one turns into threatening territory, pupils dilate, muscles tense, sweat exudes—and learning speeds up.

4. The route must deal with the city center, whether the historic center, the civic center, or the geographic center (that is, where all roads once came together at a historic crossroads). This might be the original point of attachment (such as a port landing, canal basin, an intersection of nineteenth-century turnpikes, or a railroad station), the zero milestone, courthouse square, or another designated central place.

5. The section should touch and explore the historic district of the city, answering the question, "How did this place come to be?"

6. The cross-section route must cope with the zones or neighborhoods from which come the city's major flows of exportable goods and services, and therefore the essential source of local income from distant markets.

7. The section should include at least one dying area; for instance, slums that seem beyond recall, an abandoned warehouse district, a mill or factory district undermined by foreign competition, or a mansion row on the skids.

8. The route should encounter at least one growth area, where booming firms burst through their walls, and workers' parking expands all bounds; where land development is under way; where roadside billboards announce zoning changes and new construction to come.

9. The section route should explore ethnic enclaves, old and new.

10. The section should explore at least one area of the best residential addresses, where fashion and ambition dictate that the new wealthy jostle for space with old families or carve out their own turf; where Volvo and Mercedes agencies cluster, where the footprints of status striving can be seen in certain styles of plantings, residential architecture, and decor.

11. The section should pursue, at least in part, one "main drag," a route that starts next to the original point of attachment and ends up in an automobile strip in suburbia—ideally, the variant I have come to call an "alpha street" (described later in this essay).

12. The cross-section route should bring its travelers into at least visual contact with the major topographic feature of the area, be it the closest navigable waterway or the dominant local peak or escarpment.

13. At some point, the cross section should provide an overlooking view of the city, preferably from a high point. This may require getting out of the car and climbing a hill or taking an elevator to the top of a prominent building. In general, don't get car bound. The truly experimenting student of a city will stop the car fairly often, get out, and explore as necessary on foot.

14. The cross section should be fun. This is the wild card in the deck, the subjectivity among these more objective criteria. Do not ignore alluring diversions, and of course, stop as necessary at places for rest, food, and respite.

15. Finally, remember that a single trip along even the best-planned cross section is never enough. Periodically, come back and run the section again to watch the city (and the appropriate route of the section itself) change over time.

In common with many other educational experiences, such a cross-section trip tends to screen out the hard parts; it smoothes everything down to automobile grades and eliminates dead ends. A route like this can be a shortcut for getting to know your own hometown or any other community, to literally "learn from the street."

In 1976, I published an urban cross section for my hometown of Louisville, Kentucky, in the Sunday magazine of the former *Louisville Times* (fig. 7.5). Although the land along either side of the route has seen many changes since then, the section is still a good way to structure a firsthand running encounter with a changing urban realm. The route moves its followers through two centuries, two states, four counties, and innumerable states of mind. It is distinctly *not* a fine-home tour. The route begins about thirty miles east of downtown Louisville, in the small country town of Shelbyville, Kentucky. The first twenty miles take travelers along U.S. Highway 60 through the kind of white-fenced, widening-vista farmlands that still are evidence of the old, pre–Civil War plantation system; the current owners are wealthy Louisville or Bluegrass country horse-raising or "white-fencing" farmers (fig. 7.6). Other city influences are subdivisions whose billboards in 1976 prominently displayed financing by one of the large downtown banks. A Ford Motor Company plant was the first industrial invader of the 1960s into the then-placid commuter countryside. The plant was a self-conscious effort by the Louisville–Jefferson County Planning Commission to spread out growing industries formerly packed into older, closer-in routes. Along that portion of the route, virtually everything new—houses, apartments,

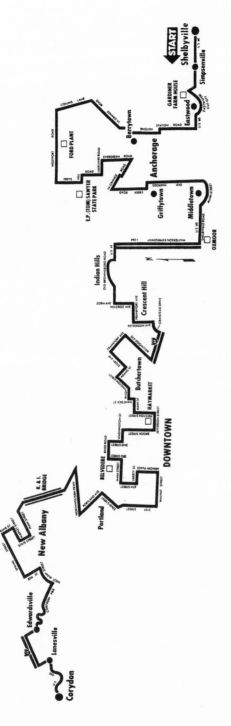

Figure 7.5. The Grady Clay cross-section route for Louisville, Kentucky, 1976. In order to cover the entire "commutershed" of the city, the section runs for fifty miles, from Shelbyville, through downtown, to Corydon, Indiana. The K & I Bridge has since been closed, forcing travelers to detour westward via the I-64 bridge. Drawing by Steve Durbin for Grady Clay, "Cross Section: An In-Depth Tour of Louisville," *Scene* (magazine section of the *Louisville Times*), Saturday, August 28, 1976, pp. 13–15.

Figure 7.6.   Open meadows, with expensive wooden fencing and prize livestock, along U.S. 60, east of Louisville. Evidence of the region's pre–Civil War plantations, areas like these are today most likely to be owned by wealthy Louisville families.

stores—was a by-product of the new jobs plunked down in the open countryside.

Several portions of the Louisville cross section emphasize sharp social divisions. To the west of one north-trending section of the route is Berrytown, a low-density black community with roots in the post–Civil War communities of freed slaves. Directly to the east are larger, mostly white-owned farms and estates. A later section of the route reveals the distinctly New Englandish, white suburb of Anchorage, with such high-status trappings as large residential lots, roads lined with mature trees, and more distinctly Kentuckian private trotting tracks and stables. A mile later the route plunges suddenly through a sharp status and income break and into the mostly black Griffytown.

Finally, approaching the old suburb of St. Matthews, the route passes into the city limits of Louisville itself, through the former suburb of Crescent Hill, in part along Peterson Avenue. With a 13 percent grade, Peterson Avenue is the city's steepest street, paved around 1900 with bricks set on edge, to give horses' hooves good traction. The route continues through the Butchertown neighborhood. In the 1970s, Butchertown was undergoing upgrading and boutiquing and was newly experiencing the retail festivities of street fairs. It had its own "mayor" and semigovernment. Citizens in Butchertown fought for the city's first down-zoning from industrial to residential to stop the expansion of industry and the razing of houses.

Production and trade, past and present, predominate in the adjacent Haymarket District, along the wide block of Market Street that once saw tobacco hogsheads auctioned in mid-street. Closer to the former city center are the giant warehouses of the Belknap Company, once hardware suppliers to the entire South. The warehouses have been converted into offices, but they remind the traveler of Louisville's historic role in long-distance wholesaling and retail supply. The cross-section route moves quickly past Third and Fourth Streets, with occasional examples of the Victorian mansions of the old city's business owners.

Louisville's Main Street, in the 1970s as today, is abustle with "hamburgered" tourists mingling with black-suited bankers down from their nearby office towers. Along the Riverfront Plaza and Belevedere, parks and pedestrian river overlooks remind visitors of the prime importance of the Ohio River Falls as the reason for Louisville's original settlement and the city's nineteenth-century dominance of the entire region. Along Main Street, imposing cast-iron storefronts, some surviving from the 1860s to the 1880s, have been joined by the modern forty-story First National Bank Tower and the decidedly postmodern headquarters tower (designed by Michael Graves) of the for-profit Humana hospital company, which looms over the commercial district (fig. 7.7).[20]

Southwest of the old center waterfront and commercial district, the cross section takes its followers along West Walnut Street, formerly the separate black business district, and then past a general urban devastation zone, through public housing projects from the 1930s and 1960s, and finally past Fifteenth Street, where urban renewal officially and visibly stopped. Then starts the West End, most of whose residents are black.

In the original version, the cross section took motorists across the remarkable old K & I Bridge, the only combined railroad and highway bridge for hundreds of miles on the Ohio River; it had special turnoff points where motorists could stop and enjoy the river views. That bridge has been closed, forcing travelers to detour westward via the I-64 bridge, and once on the Indiana side, to rejoin the original cross section on New Albany's Main Street. Quickly moving out of New Albany toward the west, for three miles the route follows a narrow, steep-sided Appalachian-type valley, with houses uphill from the road to the right, houses down to

Figure 7.7. Commercial buildings of different eras along Main Street in downtown Louisville. The facades of nineteenth-century retail and warehouse structures contrast with the looming Humana Building, and behind it, the First National Bank tower, all near the historic Ohio River landing at the center of the city.

the left, and fields out back. Next, drivers have to brace themselves for higher speeds as they turn onto Interstate 64 and cross a high plateau that has a climatic zone different from Louisville. In winter, occasional deep snows fall here, weather that hardly penetrates the warmer, valley-bound towns around the Falls.

My 1976 cross section ended at Corydon, Indiana, about twenty miles due west of downtown Louisville. The area to the north of Corydon was then booming with new drive-ins, a new shopping plaza, and housing developments. From there, it was only a twenty-five-minute drive along Interstate 64 back to Louisville. A cross section today would probably have to start even farther east than Shelbyville and continue past Corydon, as the 5 percent commutershed of Louisville has grown substantially. Indeed, one of the realities of urban life is change. A cross-section tour of a city, like any map on which it might be drawn, is, in a sense, out of date the minute it is published. My 1976 route simply seized a moment in time and said, "For now, this is my route."

The Louisville cross section satisfies most of my self-imposed criteria, except for one. It does not explore any of Louisville's "alpha streets" for a long distance. What I have called an "alpha street" is a street that starts by the original point of attachment, cuts through the dying mill or factory district, then through the city center, office district, and courthouse square, proceeds uphill along the decaying mansion row (where one can often find men's clubs or funeral parlors taking over the large old houses), and then out to an automobile strip in the suburbs. Not all alpha streets will touch every one of these bases, but they all bear close inspection. I have delighted in looking for the alpha street wherever I travel. It is not listed in the city directory or in guidebooks, but one can usually dig it out of the city's built fabric.[21] In Louisville, the street might be Third Street, which my cross section route only touches upon.[22] Other examples include St. Charles Street in New Orleans, Main Street in Houston, and Meridian Street in Indianapolis.

The idea of taking people through a cross section—in the case of Louisville, from old plantation country, through new horsey suburbs, over sharp social divides, past commercial strips, and through four downtowns and a host of places most people seldom encounter—is to help them learn, by juxtaposition and contrast, all the parts and peoples that make a city work. And by driving a cross section and thinking about it, residents make the city more their own.

REGIONAL AND NATIONAL CROSS SECTIONS

My cross-section technique, at least for a drive that can be done in a single morning or afternoon (or, with breaks for walking and eating, in no more than a day) works best in small and mid-size cities. In very large cities, such as Los Angeles, Chicago, Boston, or New York, a full cross section might take a very long driving day, or perhaps two to three days.

And we should remember that cross sections can encompass whole regions. Returning from a visit in Denver, I tested the regional idea of a cross section by asking myself how I could tell—without stopping to ask or looking at a map—when I was leaving "the West" and reaching "the East." Colorado was part Rockies, part Great Plains; both parts of the state are still distinctly western. As it turned out, the East was on the wet side of the ten-inch-per-year rainfall line, which extends north-south through mid-Kansas. The East was where there was enough moisture to support the flying insects that I began smashing on my windshield as I drove. The

East was where I no longer shared the highway with tumbleweeds. The East was where tough and thorny Osage orange trees, surviving from the days before barbed wire, began to show up along the fencerows. And the East was where they quit selling Coors beer, at least in the days when Coors and its highway billboards could be found only in the West.

So entranced was I with the possibilities of cross sections that I and some others in Louisville obtained financial backers for a half-hour television documentary about human-made geographic change, directed by Clay Nixon and broadcast in 1982 via Channel 15 Public Television in Louisville. Beyond that, I did some reporting and commentary on "The 600-Mile Yard Sale," held every spring along both sides of two-lane U.S. Highway 127, from the outskirts of Cincinnati to Gadsden, Alabama.

In the mid-1950s, the writer George Stewart applied the idea of a cross section to the entire continent in his masterful book, *U.S. 40: Cross Section of the United States of America.*[23] Obviously, for such an extended section, my urban rules needed to be amended. Stewart used U.S. 40 to structure his section, starting from the road's beginning in Atlantic City, New Jersey, and following it, without a detour or side trip, to its end in San Francisco, California. Along the way, he stopped to photograph and research ninety views that epitomized their section of the route. Stewart proved yet again that we can learn a great deal from what we can see from the street, road, and highway.

THE STREET AND HIGHWAY VERSUS THE INTERNET

My notes from Jackson's lectures at Harvard remind me that one day he started the hour with one of his typical great generalizations. "The road," he said, "is a political installation to create a society." Then he confessed, "We [Americans] have a road romanticism . . . [and] no one is more attached to the road than I, and no one sorrier to leave it than I."[24] On that point, however, Jackson and I had come to a fork in the road, for in the 1950s I had analyzed the first Kentucky highway built to the new Interstate standards and was shocked at what I found. I then reported, and later insisted, that we were laying the groundwork for the most expensive settlement pattern the world had yet invented: a pattern of misplaced investment.[25] By 1954, Americans had begun to overinvest in superhighways, to subsidize suburbia with cheap mortgages and low gasoline and capital-gains taxes, all of which cut away at city vitality, further separated rich and poor, and drained life from cities and small towns.

Today, another form of overinvestment is pervading the country. We are being smothered, on our own computer screens, with everything we want to know, all at once. Personal observation, as our ultimate testing ground, is being overshadowed by the excitements of virtual realities, mass-produced secondhand via computers. Although Vesalius and Geddes most likely would have embraced the computer and learned to cruise the Web with, or ahead of, their students, neither they nor Jackson would have abandoned—nor should we consider downgrading—firsthand evidence in exchange for the current explosion of secondhand information about the world.

Meanwhile, that world moves in on us, via cross-border migrations, global competition, worldwide standards of currency, weights, and measures, and terror. We can all learn from J. B. Jackson the rigorous necessity of taking our own hard look at the world's presumptions as they are carried out upon the landscape. Never has it been more necessary to practice the skills of personal observation as the beginning, and ultimate, test of all understanding. Vesalius gave us one great proof of that. Jackson and I have joined Geddes in enjoying a lifetime spent in firsthand observation of changes that both threaten and enliven this world.

It is never enough—no matter how necessary—to find out merely how a given place was shaped, formed, and influenced over time, or how many computer-generated versions of it we can manipulate. The great questions, which cross sections help us to answer for ourselves, are: How do such real places as these work in everyday life? And, Toward what kind of future are they propelling us?

JEFFREY W. LIMERICK

BASIC "BRINCKSMANSHIP"

8

Impressions Left in a Youthful Mind

From the late 1960s through most of the 1970s, J.B. Jackson was at the height of his formal teaching career. During that time, he introduced several thousand students on both sides of the country to cultural landscape studies. Through his engaging lecture style (enlivened by his dry, often self-deprecating sense of humor), his use of the Socratic method in more informal discussions and conversations, and his spirit of intellectual inclusivity in inviting others to join him, Jackson sought to interest his students in the everyday landscape. More often than not, he succeeded.

In 1970 I was one of the two hundred students at Berkeley to take J.B. Jackson's survey lecture course on the American landscape. I loved it. That year, Jackson had taught at Harvard in the fall and Berkeley in the winter quarter, where he gave both a seminar course on the European landscape for the geography department and a lecture course on the American landscape for the College of Environmental Design. I was an architecture student but was also interested in architectural history. It seemed important to know the history of the landscape in order to understand the buildings that sat within it. The themes and patterns that Jackson presented in the course went a long way toward explaining why the world is organized the way it is. I've been trying to understand its patterns and its logic ever since.

As a student, I tried to make the most of talking with my favorite teachers during their office hours, to get a deeper understanding of their lecture topics. Some faculty seemed annoyed at being disturbed. Jackson loved to talk with students and made them feel quite welcome as he spurred their interest in the cultural landscape. With his encouragement, I wrote my paper on the growth and development over time of the area of Sacramento where I had grown up. When I asked if he needed a teaching assistant for the next year, he offered me the job.

Thus in 1971, I found myself helping prepare handouts, keeping track of papers and grades, sorting slides, and refiling Jackson's note cards. The primary benefit of being Jackson's teaching assistant was having a chance to talk with him about his lectures and all manner of other things, and to hear his thoughts at greater length than he had time for in class.

Jackson was about sixty-two years old in 1971, with gray hair in a butch haircut. He was a short man (about five foot six), looked a bit like Buster Keaton, and was absolutely full of energy. He often walked at a clip that many people would consider jogging, and he had an erect, almost military bearing. In those days at Berkeley, one rarely had occasion to mention the military in a positive light, but I did happen to tell Jackson that my electrical engineer father was a captain in the army reserves. Jackson himself had been a captain with military intelligence in France during World War II; I was surprised to learn that this was when his interest in the landscape and patterns of human use and development had first surfaced. He ended his military career as a colonel.[1]

Professor Jackson always dressed in a shirt and tie, dress slacks, and a Brooks Brothers sport coat when he lectured, but he wore this outfit with thick-soled motorcycle boots (fig. 8.1). He rode a large black BMW motorcycle to and from school and had a heavy black leather jacket and a star-spangled red, white, and blue helmet, like the one Peter Fonda wore in *Easy Rider*. He loved to take to the highway every chance he got. When I would ask him what he had done over the weekend, he usually told me he had spent time on the bike, riding out to look at the farms and towns of the Central or San Joaquin Valleys or up to check out lumbering operations on the North Coast. He showed little or no interest in scenery of the Ansel Adams variety, or in the areas most frequented by tourists. "Wilderness" held little attraction for him; he clearly preferred to study

Figure 8.1.   J. B. Jackson with graduate students at University of California, Berkeley, 1980.

how people used and shaped the everyday landscape and made their places within it. If I wanted to get a rise out of him, I could usually get a sour grimace by merely mentioning the overly precious tourist town of Carmel or someplace like it.

Jackson loved to look at vernacular and process-oriented industrial buildings, but he claimed to have little interest in the high art work of architects. It was only several years later that he told me he had actually gone to architecture school briefly with the thought of becoming an architect himself—a thought he had quickly abandoned. He found that he could tease me by making fun of some of the "high art" architecture and architects I admired. And yet I realized how many architects Jackson counted among his extensive and diverse network of friends.

One of them was Charles Moore. I had worked for Charles in his Connecticut office the summer before and had heard a few of his Jackson stories. Charles and two of his partners, Donlyn Lyndon and William Turnbull, had been early contributors to *Landscape* magazine.[2] Don had even prepared a scheme for Jackson's proposed house in La Cienega, near Santa Fe, New Mexico. Charles explained that the Lyndon scheme had cost too much and that Brinck had decided to design a cheaper one himself. When I later asked Jackson about that, he had explained that the Lyndon design was lovely, but it had been far too complicated and too much a self-conscious art object for his taste.[3] He much preferred the high-ceilinged, vernacular-inspired adobe he had designed for himself. He had made a few concessions to art, however, such as the large formal entry court.

Jackson loved his house in La Cienega and, according to Charles, saw himself as a *patrón*, much to the irritation of some of his neighbors, who didn't like being told what to do by this "Yankee." And yet, he didn't seem to miss his New Mexico home when he was living in a guest suite at Harvard's Eliot House or in a similar arrangement at Berkeley. Home, I came to realize, was wherever Jackson found himself.

In class or in his office, Jackson spoke little about himself. If you knew enough to ask them, he would answer specific questions about his childhood in Europe and New England, his time as a student at Wisconsin and Harvard, his tour of duty as a cowboy in New Mexico, or his impressions of his many friends and acquaintances. But he would quickly change the subject to something he considered more interesting—and he had a wide range of interests. He also had some very strong opinions and could be dogmatic or rigid from time to time. Conversations with him were usually freewheeling things that covered an incredible range of topics: roads and fences, the organization and logic of the commercial strip, the national grid, Taylorism, lawns, railroads, changing small towns, the implications of the node-on-a-line organization of freeways for modern life, the evolving form of cemeteries and shopping centers. His manner could range from formal and proper to low key and casual, but he rarely revealed much of a personal nature.

Jackson seemed to have something of an oppositional temperament, as well as a ready sense of humor. If I made a disparaging remark about how ugly I thought parking lots or the commercial strip were, he would often take the opposite side and argue vigorously for the beauty of crisp painted lines on black asphalt or the clarity and adaptability of roadside commercial buildings, until I could either work him into a corner (a rare outcome) or give up myself (a more common outcome). He certainly seemed to enjoy the sport of argument. He also seemed to work constantly, reading specialized magazines from the library that had originally been intended for city managers back in the twenties, motel managers in the forties, or bicyclists at the turn of the twentieth century. He always took fastidious notes on file cards, which he would then place in a large steel file box.[4]

Figure 8.2.   J.B. Jackson as guest lecturer at University of California, Berkeley, 1980.

In 1971, Jackson had thousands of note cards, each covered with information on various aspects of the landscape. The number of cards seemed to be growing all the time, and I suspect that Jackson may have had many more note cards stored elsewhere as well. His note cards were his main resource whenever he was preparing a lecture or writing one of his books or articles, though I gather that they recorded only a fraction of what he had in his head.[5] Part of my job was to help him refile the cards into the various categories and subdivisions he had created—a sometimes rather puzzling personal system of classification. He used to joke that the box contained enough material for half a dozen good books, if only he could find the time to work on them. The book he was researching and writing at the time I was helping him with his class was *American Space*, which was published the next year.[6]

Jackson's lecturing style was relaxed and conversational in tone (fig. 8.2). He referred to his notes but seemed to use them primarily to stimulate his thoughts and to keep himself on the subject. Each class seemed to follow a fairly consistent pattern. I would hand out mimeographed outlines of the lecture or other information sheets, while Jackson placed an outline of key topics in the day's lecture on the board. He would then talk for roughly forty minutes. After that he would illustrate the ideas in the lecture with perhaps ten minutes of slides and restate his conclusions. The slides were hardly artful. A good many of them seemed to have been taken from the seat of Jackson's motorcycle, some while he was apparently still moving. Still, they got the point across. If there was time left, students could ask questions. Discussions often continued at his office after class.

Jackson wrote about how and why he structured his course on the American cultural landscape as he did in his essay "By Way of Conclusion: How to Study the Landscape."[7] That essay was written in 1978, not long after Jackson had retired from teaching, and it explains his strategy in organizing his lectures more clearly than he was able to explain it in 1971. I suspect that he was revising and refining the course as he gained experience both with his subjects and as a teacher.

A brief summary of the course is probably in order. Jackson began it by examining the landscape of the colonial period and the early nineteenth century, along with the forces and processes that shaped it. This not only provided a better understanding of our vernacular history than places like Disneyland or tendentious socioeconomic texts, but, in Jackson's words, "it is an excellent and relatively painless way of learning about the purpose of landscape studies, for it deals with the familiar, more or less simple archetypes. . . . We can only start to understand the contemporary landscape by knowing what we have rejected and what we have retained from the past."[8]

Around the middle of the term, he moved into the study of the modern landscape, which began to emerge in the middle of the nineteenth century and was, in the mid-twentieth century, approaching full flower. Jackson was, in his words, trying "to discover when some of [the modern landscape's] characteristics first made their appearance, rather than [dwelling] on the disappearance of the old."[9] To do this, he focused upon basic elements of the landscape—the land used for farming, the house, the railroad (things the students thought they understood)—and looked at the forces that had transformed them over time into something very different. Jackson would then bring his analysis and examples up to the present. The country road, for example, had begun as an element we had previously paid little attention to—a simple dirt path that enabled people to get from

their home farm to town; in the time shortly after the American Revolution, however, "the building of roads became a matter of national concern,
and from then on it began to play a role in the landscape until (as we
know) it [became] the most powerful force for the destruction or creation
of landscapes that we have."[10]

During seminars and office hours, Jackson's manner was less formal,
more Socratic. Students who came to him expecting clear, concise answers
to their questions often left disappointed or confused. He was much more
likely to use leading questions to explore what *they* thought about the
topic, why they thought it, and where they might find additional information for themselves. Bob Calo captured Jackson in action in a 1988
KQED-TV documentary about Jackson's view of the cultural landscape,
when a high school student who had been assigned to interview people on
the street happened to select Jackson out of the crowd (emphasis in the
original).

Student: What are the biggest problems in the downtown area?

Jackson: Well now, don't you ask *me*. *You* give the answers. It's your
            paper that you're writing. What do *you* think the problem is?

Student: I'm supposed to ask you.

Jackson: Well, you must have some idea. Do you think there are
            problems here? What would they be?[11]

Jackson wanted to stimulate students' interest in the topic and encourage them to speculate and try out a wide range of ideas. As a consequence,
he had little patience for students who clearly lacked enthusiasm or interest in the subject or the class. But conversations with a bright student who
came in with good questions and plenty of intellectual curiosity could be
magical.[12] Jackson would set out to win the student to his cause, using
words like *our* and *we* in phrases like "in *our* field" to help the student
feel a part of the enterprise. He tried very hard not to discourage any student's genuine interest.

This emphasis on a positive approach was carried over into the way
Jackson treated student papers and exams. He preferred comments to be
positive and encouraging in tone. He asked me to suggest rough grades
for exams, which he would often raise to avoid discouraging the students.
He felt that in the long run, grades weren't nearly as important as the
ideas and attitudes toward the subject that the students took with them.
Jackson seemed to enjoy many of the papers he read, explaining, "I enjoyed them not only for their content—they often revealed obscure historical information—but because they seemed to be based on childhood

memories and family traditions." He learned a tremendous amount from the papers about how people "know" towns and cities, about family customs and rituals, farming practices and beliefs. But he also was quite taken with papers that dealt with sensory experiences of the landscape. These were rare. "This kind of landscape perception is something no instructor can teach," he wrote. "We can only be grateful when it comes our way, and encourage students to record such fleeting memories as these and share them. They often make a whole landscape, a whole season, vivid and unforgettable."[13]

I recall one Berkeley student who came in during office hours to discuss his paper on the old Key System transit line in the East Bay. The Key System had developed from a horse-drawn streetcar line in the 1880s to become an extensive network of electric trolleys, all converging on a ferry dock in Oakland to take people across the bay to San Francisco and Sausalito. The dock, with its ferry slips, was shaped like a large old-fashioned door key, giving the system its name. Jackson warmed to the topic immediately. He began asking leading questions to stimulate the student's imagination. "Why do you suppose that most of the car dealerships and repair garages in Berkeley are along San Pablo or Shattuck Avenues?" he asked. "Why are the small neighborhood commercial shopping centers in Berkeley and Oakland located where they are?" "Why is the Claremont Hotel where it is?" "When and where were the first gas stations in Berkeley built?" Both the student and I knew that Jackson considered this topic to be important.

After some time spent tossing ideas about, Jackson went to his filing cabinet and took out a current map of the East Bay to place next to the student's map of the Key System. Spreading the maps out, he began to explain his seemingly unrelated questions. It turned out that he had researched the Key System himself at some point and could see relationships among a variety of things for which the old streetcar lines were the glue. For example, when people used to ride down to the original transit lines in a horse and buggy, they would need to stable the horse during the day. Stables, carriage dealers, and blacksmiths tended to situate themselves along the trolley lines, which ran up San Pablo and Shattuck Avenues. The blacksmiths who sold and repaired carriages became the first automobile dealers in the area, converting their buildings into auto dealerships. Gas was originally sold by the auto dealers or by hardware stores, but soon was sold by independent dealers, who would set up shop near major intersections of the transit lines. Most of the small neighborhood commercial areas grew where streetcar lines crossed and pedestrian traffic was heavier.

Eventually, these areas became enshrined in the Berkeley and Oakland zoning codes as light commercial areas. The Claremont Hotel was built by the owner of the Key System to stimulate business on a new line, while also encouraging people to buy lots and build houses on available land along the route. In fact, most of the development in the Berkeley and Oakland hills up through the early 1930s was accomplished by developers and the streetcar lines working hand in glove. The routes they chose largely shaped the street patterns of the East Bay, which remain to this day.

The student went from being merely interested in his topic to being fascinated with it. I was reminded once again of how a transportation system that had gone out of business during the 1950s was still in evidence in the pattern of city streets and neighborhoods, if you just knew how to interpret what was there to be seen. Things are situated where they are for reasons, Jackson always reminded us, though the reasons may not be readily apparent now; you have to dig out the story as it unfolded over time to understand how and why things have changed. The patterns run deep. The landscape embodies values and functional decisions, made over time, which have a long-lasting influence. This lesson has stayed with me and still shapes the way I look at the world around me.

After graduation and a year spent working in an architect's office in Sacramento, I decided to enter the graduate program in architecture at Yale and to study with Charles Moore. Eventually, I found myself teaching there while also working in the office of a local architect. My wife, Patty (Patricia Nelson Limerick), and I met not long after I arrived in New Haven. She was a graduate student in Yale's American Studies program. Not much later, we went up to Cambridge and I introduced her to Jackson. It was at this time that I was quietly invited to call him "Brinck, " a name he reserved for friends. I went from being addressed as "Limerick" to being called "Jeff." Brinck took to Patty immediately, easily welcoming her into his network of friends and colleagues. It wasn't long after we both started teaching at Yale that we found the opportunity to invite Brinck to give a talk at Trumbull College for our students. Brinck was delighted with the idea. He announced his intention to have one of his graduate students drive him down to New Haven on his favorite back roads through Massachusetts and Connecticut. "It will be good to get him out of Cambridge so he can learn something about New England firsthand," Brinck confided.

American Space had been published a few years before and was still making quite a splash. One of the senior professors heard that Brinck was coming and insisted that we have dinner at his house before the talk. *He* would then introduce Brinck. This was a professor with whom one did not argue. He knew that I had worked for Brinck briefly and confided that he too was a good friend of Jackson, adding conspiratorially that he thought Brinck's latest book was a bit thin. This offered an important lesson on the customs and folkways of intellectuals. Only a few weeks before, Brinck had told me that he thought this professor's latest book was quite inflated.

The day of the talk came. Brinck arrived and dinner was carried off with a great deal of good humor, and of alcohol being consumed by most of the guests and our host. We then made our way to the Trumbull Common Room, which was packed to overflowing with enthusiastic students. Our host made a flowery introductory speech, telling the students how thrilled we should all be to have the opportunity to hear Brinck. He then retired to a large wingback leather chair and fell sound asleep.

Brinck began his engaging and entertaining talk, catching a new group of students in his spell. A faint but steady snore began to come from the armchair. Brinck ignored it. It got louder. Still he ignored it, not giving the slightest hint that he was even aware of it. Only during the question-and-answer period did that mischievous sparkle creep into Brinck's eyes. Finally, a student asked a question that Brinck said would be best put to our host. "Too bad," he said in a deadpan manner, "that he had to leave us earlier." As usual, the audience was completely won over, which I suspect had been Brinck's aim all along.

Patty and I saw Brinck from time to time in the mid- to late seventies. By 1980, when Patty was hired by the Harvard history department to teach the history of the American West and I gave up teaching to work with the well-known architectural firm Cambridge Seven, he had retired and returned full time to La Cienega. John Stilgoe took over his courses at Harvard, and Paul Groth took his courses at Berkeley.

When we moved to Boulder, Colorado, in 1984, we would see Brinck's name in the papers whenever he came through the area to deliver a talk for one group or another. Our meetings at these events were brief and infrequent, though we did write occasionally and remained on good terms. Finally, a few years before his death, I was in Santa Fe and had the opportunity to visit Brinck at his home in La Cienega (fig. 8.3). I called to see if he would like a visitor. "By all means," he said. He gave me some rather convoluted directions and things were set.

I arrived at the appointed time to find Brinck out by the road, clearing some weeds. He was dressed in work clothes and seemed noticeably smaller, thinner, and older than he had just a few years before. He was,

Figure 8.3.   J.B. Jackson House, La Cienega, New Mexico, 1970. Designed and built by Jackson in 1965, it was placed on the National Register of Historic Places in 1999.

however, still sharp and alert. He had an incredible tan from doing part-time landscape and maintenance work. "It's good exercise," he explained, though I suspected that the story was probably more complicated than that. Brinck took me through the house, heading for the kitchen for a cup of tea. In the course of our typically rambling conversation, some topics seemed like well-worn paths. Others seemed new and fresh. He mentioned that he was getting frustrated with the signs of his advancing years. It turned out that he had just recovered from what he described as "a light case of pneumonia" and had been released from the hospital the day before. "It made me awfully weak," he confided. "Why, I was only able to work half my normal shift this morning before I got tired and had to quit. But it's good to get back to work, and I'll be feeling more myself and be back to full time in a day or two." At this point Brinck was in his mid-eighties. His illness could have easily done in someone half his age. He was not one to give up easily.

    J.B. Jackson was never shy about sharing his ideas and opinions about the people and processes that have shaped and are shaping the landscape, or eliciting opinions from students and colleagues. Just as the old Key

System, though long out of business, continues to influence and shape the communities of the East Bay, so Brinck continues to influence and shape his readers' and his students' perceptions of the American landscape. He has given us a lot to think about. It is a pleasure to have known him and to have his observing and questioning attitude permanently installed in our minds.

TRACY WALKER MOIR-MCCLEAN

OBSERVATIONS OF FAITH

9

Landscape Context in Design Education

The commonplace aspects of the contemporary landscape, the streets and houses and fields and places of work, could teach us a great deal not only about American history and American society but also ourselves and how we relate to the world. It is a matter of learning how to see.

J. B. Jackson, *Discovering the Vernacular Landscape*, 1984

Architectural designers often emphasize the formal, visual, and spatial aspects of design at the expense of factors that respond to human culture and comfort. In many schools of architecture, this predilection for purely visual issues is inculcated during first-year design courses, when students are asked to temporarily suspend consideration of historical and cultural issues while they learn the language of space and form. Educators often discourage attention to human issues because beginning students have difficulty addressing both the clarity of basic formal patterns (the usual primary goal of beginning studies) and human needs. As a result, students may receive an unintended message: "Do not look at social or cultural influences. They are not important." The importance of form can be seen in popular introductory texts, such as Roger Clark and Michael Pause's *Precedents in Architecture*, and Frank Ching's *Form, Space, and Order*.[1] In the ensuing classroom years, students become comfortable applying the vocabulary of abstract modern form and composition to discussion and analysis of the built environment. While abstract form pleases the aesthetic eye and mind, however, it does not engage the full spectrum of human sensation, needs, desires, and activities, unless designers integrate that same spectrum into the creative act.

During later years of the curriculum, architecture schools call for the reintegration of cultural and historical issues, but human considerations too often remain marginalized. Heavy course requirements in technical and professional subjects also limit the number of university elective classes that architecture students can take, so they have less exposure to upper-division research and interpretive skills in history, anthropology, geography, natural sciences, or in arts other than architecture. Cultural historians and geographers communicate largely through words, and they analyze artifacts for cultural ideas and social meanings; among traditional academics, visual information—the channel that designers understand best—is clearly secondary and may even be largely ignored. Further compounding this difficulty, many histories and contemporary studies of architecture and cultural landscapes ask different questions than designers do and typically do not address the formal vocabulary and compositional strategies that are of primary interest to design students. The historical sources of most use to designers include detailed physical descriptions of artifacts and spaces, patterns of movement, visual connections, and scale relationships, as well as photographs, maps, or other graphic depictions. For a designer, a good picture or diagram is worth more than a thousand words.

In upper-level architectural design studio classes at the University of Tennessee, I work to integrate the abstract, formal inclinations of designers with the broader cultural contexts of design projects. Simultaneously, I try to bridge the communication gap between designers and cultural landscape scholars. As a first step, I introduce students to historical and cultural geographic approaches for interpreting patterns of human settlement and changes in those cultural landscapes over time. Then students reinterpret these patterns as designers—finding abstract or modern versions of form, space, and composition. In these studios, the ultimate goal is to awaken students' interest in visual and organizational patterns created by cultural activity in the landscapes that surround them and thereby to encourage the cultivation of lifelong habits of seeing and investigating the history of place, landscape, and building types. Examples from "Water, Wood, Spirit: Mountain Baptist Faith and Grace in the City," one of a series of elective studios that focus on Appalachian eastern Tennessee, show this teaching method in action (fig. 9.1).[2] Similar sequences of research, discussion, diagramming, field survey, design rehearsal, and final project

Figure 9.1.   Field survey photograph of Mount Hebron Primitive Baptist church-house, photographed by student survey team Stacy Andrick and Ben Whittenburg for a class assignment to visit and document existing Baptist church-house sites in east Tennessee. The photograph documents the location of the church-house building relative to the rural road and the open side yard. Social activities commonly occur in these open side yards, since church-house interiors are reserved for purely spiritual purposes.

design could be adaptable to design studios for other places, cultures, and building types.

My methods for studying regional context have been strongly influenced by the work of J. B. Jackson and have been refined through traveling, living, and practicing architecture in the western, mid-Atlantic, midwestern, and southeastern regions of the United States. From Jackson I learned to see landscape context as a living accumulation of history and occupation of place—as a composition that is always changing. This sense of active, ongoing construction in the landscape appeals to the sensibilities of design students. Jackson was not a designer himself, so he did not explicitly show how to integrate landscape context as an influence for new design. However, he taught many architects how to decipher order in the seeming tangle of cultural landscape. Those who teach or practice design can learn a great deal about this subject from the writings of Denise Scott Brown, Robert Venturi, Charles Moore, Donlyn Lyndon, Kenneth Frampton, and Douglas Kelbaugh.[3]

ESTABLISHING AN ACTIVE SENSE OF HISTORY

Before a designer can begin to read cultural landscapes with an informed eye, that eye needs to be educated both through historical research and through exploration of specific sites. Architectural educators organize their investigation assignments in different ways, but the shared aim is to develop a comprehensive and systematic approach to predesign research. This research typically examines a set of physical issues ranging from large to small scale: At the large scale are the entire building type, its site, the immediate area surrounding the site, and regional or citywide influences on the site and building. At a medium scale are floor plans, the intended interior uses of space, forms (solid masses and the spaces that surround or exist inside those masses), the entry sequence, interior circulation requirements, the relationship of interiors to exteriors, heating, cooling, ventilation, structural systems, and construction materials. At the smallest scale are details such as hardware and lighting fixtures, or how different building parts are joined together. In the following discussion, the artifacts under consideration may be a landscape considered as a whole, an outdoor space, a building, a piece of furniture, a tool, or other objects altered or created by human activity. For architecture students, the most familiar unit of investigation is the general building type. Studies that compare variations within a single building type are called "typologies," although for writers such as Jackson, the term "landscape element" served equally well.

To learn simple, basic methods of historical research, design students need to engage directly in the collection of cultural history for the building type under consideration. So I send them out, often suggesting that they work in teams, to retrieve information from university and small-town libraries, map rooms, community historians, museums, county historical societies, and government archives. Inclusion of everyday, gossipy, vernacular history is also useful as a supplement to traditional "objective" scholarly sources. In this spirit, I also encourage students to draw on their own knowledge, family histories, photographs, and artifacts and to seize every opportunity for informal conversations with people they encounter in the field.

Some students resist scholarly forms of writing and thus resist ideas presented in a classic academic voice. Their anti-intellectual bias often works against a professor's efforts to bring discipline and rigor to inquiry. Thus, J.B. Jackson's style of integrating everyday history and field observation with critical scholarly knowledge is particularly valuable for demonstrating to students that academic learning is complementary, rather than antagonistic, to direct experience and action.

In the east Tennessee studio, the assigned tasks included identifying an appropriate site and designing a building for worship, as well as fellowship settings (both outdoor and indoor), for a small Baptist congregation. Each of the students designed for an assumed congregation that espoused a different subdenomination within the broad range of Baptist tradition. The appropriate sites for each congregation thus varied. A missionary congregation might prefer a central location in town; a Regular Baptist congregation, a more modest, withdrawn place; the Evangelical Church of God Broadcast, a ridge top for the best radio and television transmission. The background cultural-research topics for the studio included Appalachian Baptist traditions, customs, and beliefs; geographic and anthropological surveys of the area's existing Baptist churches (the activities inside those houses of worship, their locations, and building forms); and natural aspects of the locale that influence or interact with cultural practices, such as seasonal cycle, climate, forest building products, and topography.

Invaluable research collections for student use ranged from government records and reports in the Tennessee Valley Authority archive in Chattanooga, Tennessee, to the Museum of Appalachia in Norris, Tennessee, a collection of everyday artifacts labeled with handwritten notes describing their use. City and county planning commissions, as well as state, local, and federal regulatory offices, also provided copies of plans, building codes, and clarification of gray areas in those documents. The list of useful sources can also include interdisciplinary discussion groups and list-serves, course syllabi and reading lists, and the reports of various social service and educational task forces. Note that not every student had to search every type of source. Design studio education often emphasizes teamwork, especially in the data-gathering stages of design. Thus, different students went to different places for research, and then in studio the students compiled a group set of notes and comments.

To overcome their inexperience with primary sources, I give students suggestions to help them engage with and interpret local history. In the Baptist studio, the readings included descriptions of religious practices in Howard Dorgan's *Giving Glory to God in Appalachia: Worship Practices of Six Baptist Subdenominations* and other sources.[4] Students copy passages that resonate with their evolving sense of the project's central concepts and translate written descriptions of plan organization and other spatial relationships into diagrammatic sketches. Students need to realize, as historians do, that personal interpretation is unavoidable in writing

Figure 9.2.   Graveyard and side view at Heiskell Church, in the 1990s. Note the large side windows and shade trees. From a student survey by Stacy Andrick and Ben Whittenburg.

history and deciphering culture. I encourage them to establish an active dialogue with source material, particularly texts that argue or present a distinct position or theory and also texts and artifacts that have no apparent author. In class handouts, I direct students to treat the text as a dialogue between themselves and the author—to write notes as though they could ask questions, agree, and argue in person with their sources.

Once the students acquire enough background to begin to read landscapes and artifacts with a sense of history, the next task is for them to synthesize their new knowledge so it will be accessible and usable during the rest of the design process. Students learn, for instance, that traditional Baptists consider a church a house for the Lord's spirit, so these Baptists refer to their sanctuaries as "church-houses." Church-houses are found along arterial roads in a wide range of contexts: urban, suburban, and rural. Their size and their general external form are similar to local houses, and they are appropriate for an intimate spiritual relationship between congregation members and God. Interior and exterior finishes of Baptist church-houses are plain, so that nothing distracts worshippers from the essential spiritual dialogue. Large side windows connect interior space to exterior grounds. The grounds may not be large, but they usually include a shade tree or a small grove of trees and at least a small social yard, sometimes with benches and tables for outdoor meals and celebrations, or a fellowship circle of benches for outdoor religious meetings (fig. 9.2).

Central to an understanding of the church-house form is the Baptist conception of spirit. Spirit in east Tennessee Baptist faith is an experience of intimate communion and communication with God and the bounty and beauty that God has provided. God's spirit is seen as a gift; one receives it gladly when and however it comes. Spirit comes at many times and in many ways: at private moments; with family and friends; in a Sunday morning service song that blends the many into one; or in the extraordinary moments of light and presence for which Appalachia is renowned. Thus, a church-house is only one of the many places that spirit can be experienced in the landscape. In east Tennessee, some baptisms are still held, open-air, in local rivers and lakes and attended by a gathering of one or more congregations. So it is important to study church-house structures in relationship to elements of their site context that symbolize nature, particularly those mentioned in the Christian Bible. In studio, students are encouraged to respect and continue these ties between spirit, land, and religious practice by designing for off-site or outdoor baptisms and for open-air services and fellowship spaces.

DISCUSSION AND DIAGRAMMING

Beginning during the background research work and continuing throughout the design process, students diagram cultural and formal relationships as they discover them. Diagrams are particularly important because they are a designer's method for taking notes about visual, spatial, and formal order and organization. Diagrams can include two-dimensional sketches or three-dimensional study models. As drawings, diagrams follow conventions similar to finished architectural drawings—perspectives, or plans, sections, and elevations—but vary in the level of abstraction. A diagram expresses one or two related ideas clearly and simply, while a final presentation drawing simultaneously expresses many ideas. Their simplicity makes diagrams much faster and easier to read than composite drawings. Thus, diagrams are excellent tools for quick communication of formal concepts during individual critiques of student work, in group discussions with the entire studio group, and in the final jury reviews held at the end of the project.

I guide group discussion and individual diagramming with an outline that relates local history to the range of design scales discussed here. This is an agenda for a class meeting rather than an outline for a lecture. My notes anticipate diagram studies, which the students will need both to understand and to explain the correlation between spatial patterns and cultural patterns. I pose my main outline headings to the students in the form of questions and let them determine the rhythm of discussion and fill in content from their readings. Rather than presenting factual or analytical information myself, I try to lead students to the pleasure of discovery and sharing with one another. To draw out hesitant students or bring the discussion back to points that have not been thoroughly examined, I might ask, "What design elements, organizational patterns, or materials do local church-house buildings associate with this cultural habit, functional use, or aesthetic value?"

In the Baptist studio, early diagrams analyzed the interplay between the composition of spaces and the cultural patterns of performance of religious rituals and social activities. To assure an appropriate fit between building forms and cultural patterns, students diagrammed how members of a congregation moved through their churches during such important religious and fellowship rituals as lay preaching, baptism, and foot washing. One assignment challenges the students to diagram how members of a Regular Baptist congregation change their seat location in church as they progress through roles as visitor, unsaved member, and sometimes saved member or church elder. Important outdoor activities for east Tennessee Baptist churches include sunrise services, outdoor lessons, and "dinner on the grounds," a potluck feast following Sunday services. Later, during field surveys, students repeated this diagramming process independently, to consolidate the lesson (fig. 9.3).

By the end of the diagramming discussion sessions, the students' historical background work was organized into a single, shared, draft outline for the building typology of Baptist church-houses, organized by the already established hierarchy of design issues. For example, this outline addressed the physical, visual, and spiritual connections between context and site, the approach to the site, the subareas of the open space surrounding the church, building masses, entry and facade, interior spatial progressions, circulation between events in an activity sequence, rooms and room relationships, body scale elements such as stairs and doors, and tactile details such as door handles and pew benches. This activity outline serves two purposes: first, it provides a checklist to guide observations during subsequent windshield surveys, and second, it serves as a draft for the space and activity program needed later in the design process. The plan, section, and three-dimensional diagrams accompanying this outline are the equivalent of architectural programming diagrams. For architects, "programming" connotes the description, in words and diagrams, of influ-

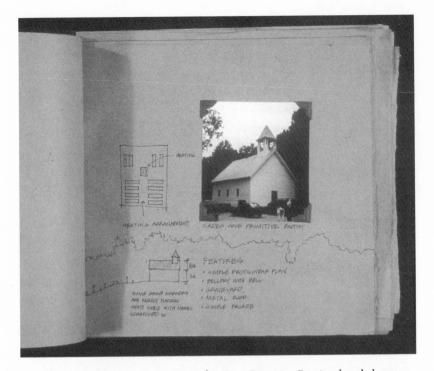

Figure 9.3.   Field survey notes on Cades Cove Primitive Baptist church-house, by student Richard Coleman. His notes document and diagram a seating arrangement described in assigned readings for the course, the location and character of the graveyard, and architectural features that contribute to the building's overall character.

ences that affect the order and organization of a building's spaces. The result of programming is a report, called the program. This report describes the activities, functions, and influences each particular space or group of spaces in the building and site must accommodate. The program can be quite short—a list of well-known room types with the minimum sizes for each—or it can be a long, detailed report (fig. 9.4).

FIELD SURVEYS

Historical background research and diagramming give the students the tools to begin reading the landscape—to have the experience of "Wow, I just read about that. Now I can see how it really occurs on site." As

Analysis Assignment: Building Blocks of Faith and Congregation

Intro: The new Baptist worship site you design may differ in form from tradi-
         tional precedent. However, conceptual divisions that organize tradi-
         tional church-house site relationships will organize relationships on the
         new site—a contemporary continuation of original faith and spirit.

Goals: 1. Identify elements and organization of (traditional) east Tennessee
            Baptist worship sites investigated in class;
         2. Identify spatial "building blocks" and the meaning and use associated
            with each;
         3. Express type and character of relationships between these blocks.

Notes: Diagrams should reflect differences in Baptist prototypes specific to
         practices of your client denomination. Several different meanings of
         uses may be associated with a single spatial block or pathway. (Human
         use and spirit can seldom be reduced to a single desire or motive.) For
         example, a spatial block may be associated with or contain: a worship
         hall, fellowship place, center of warmth, center of spirit, center of grace
         and salvation, home of God, etc. Each student should select divisions
         and "meanings" and relationships that fit with his or her growing un-
         derstanding of the precedent.

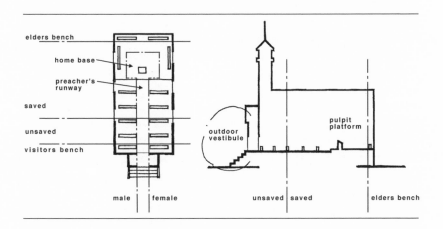

Figure 9.4.   Selections from a diagramming assignment, with the instructor's
sample diagram of typical spatial divisions in Primitive and Regular Baptist
church-houses.

J.B. Jackson has written, when you begin to connect with your everyday surroundings, you "begin to see the landscape with a different eye and to see what you had not seen before."[5] Studio field surveys are similar to but less rigorous than a survey by a cultural geographer or vernacular-architecture historian. Students do not count mile positions on roads or precisely measure and locate elements on sites. Instead, they take photographs and make field notes, sketches, diagrams, and rubbings (of material textures, for instance) and collect renewable artifacts (leaves, small stones, debris) to document their observations. In addition to studying elements and patterns in cultural landscapes during their surveys, architecture students also take careful note of the palette of building materials that vernacular builders have used. For the Baptist studio, wood construction and the characteristics of wood that has naturally weathered were closely observed in the field. During this phase of the design studio, students also read library references about timber materials and wood construction processes and visited lumberyards and woodworking shops to study woodcraft and wood finishes, grain, and other characteristics of wood firsthand.

The first field trip needs to be done as a class, so that the instructor can introduce students, on site, to cultural landscape observation skills. The outline and notes from earlier discussions help to structure the fieldwork so that the architectural issues are explored in a systematic manner. The instructor acts as an unobtrusive guide and audience for students and asks them to share observations, identify patterns, and refine their reading of the landscape. Above all, the instructor and students need to treat the process as an intellectual game in which the objective is to delight and amuse one another with observations and insights. Pleasure sets the habit. Following discussion, the instructor needs to coordinate student diagramming of the pertinent issues.

For a designer attuned only to abstract form and focused only on buildings, the outdoor space surrounding a Baptist church-house may appear to be only a dirt yard. However, with the advantage of background research, the patterns of grass and dirt, arrangement of shade trees, benches along the church-house wall, and open-air shelters can be seen as a functional lobby space, overflow seating for large services, and a place for the outdoor dinner on the grounds. Even an empty yard can be imagined to be full of people. The door is only one of the many connections between the church-house interior and the outside; important visual, aural, and olfactory connections also are transmitted through the large side windows. Inside a church-house, older, more traditional Baptist congregations spatially express distinctions between the saved and unsaved, male and female, and members and visitors by the arrangement and direction of the pews or benches, as well as the location of seats relative to the pulpit, entrance door, and center aisle. The rear wall of a church-house is usually windowless; portraits of deceased church elders are often hung on this wall, facing the congregation, so the preacher is surrounded and supported on all sides by the congregation, both past and present.

After the first field visit, I assign individual field surveys but suggest that students travel in groups to conduct the work. That is more fun, and more effective as well, as students continue to share and compare their observations. For this phase of the studio, I provide the students with several documents: a written description of the survey assignment, which sets both the process and the atmosphere for the individual surveys; a copy of the discussion outline to guide observations; good maps; and prescouted route suggestions for windshield surveys. Although I do suggest initial routes, I also encourage students to look for and explore other roads and sites. With luck, the students experience the excitement that comes when, as Jackson put it, "You turn off the broad highway, leaving the panoramas behind, and follow a dirt road that humps straight ahead out of sight."[6]

Following field surveys, a final discussion and set of diagrams refine the class's understanding of the relationships between cultural and formal patterns and their possible variations. Students teach one another by sharing diagrams, photographs, and artifacts from their field surveys and by reading one another's field books. By this time, students should have a firm grasp of the potential interactions between scholarly research, direct observation, and architectural analysis as a basis for a designer's response to place, in addition to a growing appreciation for the idea that every place—famous or vernacular—has a rich and unique sense of history and culture. Students should be left with the feeling that they have only scratched the surface of culture as a design informant. The habit of investigating historical building types, places, and landscapes can easily, and pleasurably, continue after graduation.

DESIGN REHEARSAL

In architectural design studios, instructors often assign short rehearsal problems so students can practice selecting and manipulating some subset of the issues and elements that the entire design will eventually require.

Figure 9.5.   A student's solution to the container exercise. The three images in Brandon
Pace's container reflect the studio themes of
water, wood, and spirit. The container design
reflects the reclusive and simple character of a
Regular Baptist congregation.

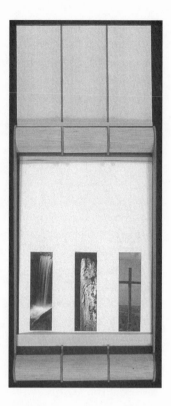

One rehearsal might focus on abstract formal elements such as overarching design ideas, form vocabularies, or spatial conditions; another rehearsal might focus on tangible issues such as materials or structural
systems. To this typical agenda of preliminary exercises, I added in the rehearsal project for the Baptist studio a request that the students explore
the cultural influences on locating, containing, and enclosing a historical
spirit. Each student's task was to construct a container (book, box, designed envelope, or folio) for his or her collected field notes, diagrams,
sketches, photographs, and artifacts (fig. 9.5).

The written guidelines for this phase of the studio reminded students
of the traditional Baptist family Bible, which is not only a container for
the word and the spirit, but also a repository of social history, with flowers pressed at favorite verses, scraps of writing, photographs of loved ones,
and births, marriages, and deaths recorded on the inside cover. Students
were asked to relate the manner in which their container enclosed,
opened, or revealed its contents to the manner in which spirit is revealed

within the Baptist faith, the church-house, and the surrounding church landscape. Students were also asked to develop some abstract visual qualities (open/closed, bound/free, simple/complex) to express the character and spirit of their client congregation.

Since exploration of wood construction was an objective of this studio, the rehearsal assignment encouraged students to use wood products (including paper) and also challenged them to capture the spirit, sensuality, and characteristics of wood as a material in the construction and craft of the container. Group presentation of these containers provided another chance for students to share ideas and to learn from the insights of their colleagues, before each of them began an individual design solution for a Baptist church-house and its site.

INTEGRATING CULTURAL LANDSCAPE CONTEXT INTO DESIGN

When architects complete their preliminary studies and begin an actual building design, they commonly begin with what French-trained architects at the turn of the nineteenth century called a *parti*—an organizing pattern or overall concept for a building. Sketch diagrams and three-dimensional models explore circulation and relationships between areas in the building itself and the surrounding context, the position of the building and other elements on the site, and the general shape and size of the building. Because a parti provides both an intellectual and a formal framework on which the rest of the design is based, the choice of a parti is a critical juncture in the design process, especially in a studio seeking to foster a more nuanced response to cultural landscape context. Ideally, but without being too complicated, the parti synthesizes patterns of historical and cultural context, social uses, and spatial forms identified earlier and brings them into a consistent overarching scheme—and, ultimately, a unified building design.

Parti development exercises, echoing the format of earlier diagramming assignments, allow the students to follow a now familiar routine of visual synthesis (fig. 9.6). Earlier research, observation, and distillation of cultural and formal patterns will lay the groundwork for students to manipulate and transform these patterns in their subsequent designs. Thus, existing cultural patterns of activity may continue, while the student designer is freed to transform the design in response to contemporary sensibilities, materials, and technology.

In the Baptist studio, parti exploration identified "centers of spirit" in community, fellowship, and neighborliness, in nature, and in holiness—

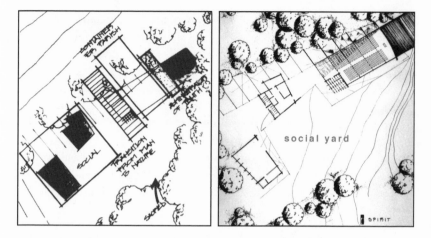

Figure 9.6. This parti diagram by student Stacy Andrick identifies functional areas important to a Regular Baptist congregation (9.6a). From left to right: buildings and an outdoor yard used for social purposes (within the square labeled "social"); an open-air porch and vestibule that provide a transition between social and religious areas (in the hatched box); the congregational space (labeled "container"); a speaker's platform (labeled "administrator of truth"); and a wooden platform for outdoor services (black box). In the final plan developed from this parti (9.6b), note that Andrick's solution eliminates the steep steps found in traditional church-houses, replacing them with an open-air porch easily accessible to congregation members with limited mobility.

that is, proximity to God. Next, the students selected a site suited to the spirit of their congregation. After students had developed an appropriate parti and selected a site and the general outline for their building, their next task was to clarify and extend their scheme.

In general, as design development continues, the size and degree of detail in the drawings increase to make inconsistencies more visible and correctable in the next version of the design. Working over several weeks, with individual critiques at each student's desk and with an occasional "pin up" of rough drafts of designs shown to the whole class, students and instructor systematically develop the key spaces and spatial progressions, and elaborate on and adjust relationships between conceptual intent, parti, functional program, and site context. The instructor's intent, at this time, is to keep students focused on their synthesis of cultural, natural, and formal patterns in the design.

Similar to the danger of setting aside human factors in some early design studios, the danger during design development is fixating on form

Figure 9.7. Sunlight study model for a Regular Baptist church-house. Keith Allen's final design model displays a traditional organization of elements: central preaching platform, a change in floor height to divide the elders' space from the main congregation area, and a windowless rear wall.

making as divorced from considerations of history, culture, and place. To avoid this, I suggest that students test their design alternatives by examining the implications of each alternative at all scales of experience (the overall parti, the middle scale, and at the level of design details) and to imagine their design options as they might be seen from a range of relevant critical perspectives (cultural historian, ecologist, member of the congregation, visitor to the church-house, or professional designer).

In the Baptist studio, when these stages of research, diagramming, fieldwork, and design were successful, students began to routinely link formal and historical patterns to create a locally grounded sense of place in their individual designs. This was evident in solutions that included the appropriate outdoor spaces and in sensitivity to interior details such as wider aisles for lay preaching, traditional seating patterns, including the elders' bench and the visitors' bench, and the appropriate enclosure or openness appropriate to special rituals such as foot washing (fig. 9.7).

Accommodation for Baptist rituals, the local climate, and the local site did not necessarily hinder the student designers' creative manipulations of light, space, and form, or the contribution of the designer's own sense of spirit. However, creativity can cause potential conflicts that also offer potential for learning. One student, for instance, included a clerestory opening in the roof of an open-air worship shelter, producing the potential for a vertical shaft of sunlight that would project down, somewhat mysteriously, into the front of the space. Lighting effects of this sort are fairly common in Roman Catholic churches often studied in history courses; however, this type of light might directly contradict a Baptist sense of plainness. In traditional Baptist church-houses, sunlight enters horizontally, from the side windows. Contrasts such as these provided points of discussion in the final review and subsequent comparison of the students' designs.

Perhaps it is asking too much of a single, upper-level elective studio emphasizing cultural landscape context, such as my east Tennessee studio, to temper the pervasive abstract, formal emphasis in architectural education. However, one studio can introduce questions of where and how architectural designers might search for precedents and methods of incorporating cultural landscape methods into design practice. In recent years, in their search for patterns that suggest form, designers have turned to industrial efficiency, semiotics, French literary theory, and fractal geometry, among other sources of inspiration. However, none of these are as fully engaged as cultural geography or anthropology in the messy, everyday complexity of human life. Studying the cultural landscape offers designers sources of cultural patterns that provide a rich counterpoint to formal abstraction and bring the lives and cultures of those who live in the places we design—including ourselves—into our work.

After graduation, the pressures of architectural practice usually leave too little time to study historical and cultural context for each project in the way that students did in the Baptist studio. Nonetheless, students will informally use these research skills as professional designers and to enrich their own personal experience of the places where they choose to live. They will know how to quickly consult the types of written references and area experts that they used in the studio. Indeed, many of the architects who are well known for their ability to design with a sense of cultural context have taught themselves the kind of thinking and seeing that students learned in the Baptist studio. By following J. B. Jackson's suggestions and example, students can begin, with their own everyday lives, an ongoing curiosity about, and research of, cultural patterns. Exposing students to tools and methods of cultural landscape research in just one studio class can start them on lifelong habits of seeing historical and cultural contexts as an inherent part of their professional careers and their approach to the world.

QUESTIONING THEORETICAL
ASSUMPTIONS

The architectural historian Gwendolyn Wright provides an appropriate beginning to this section when she warns of the dangers in what she calls "modern vernaculars"—the specialized expert languages that so often defensively isolate one discipline or school of thought from another, and that separate scholars in the humanities from design practitioners, journalists, preservationists, and environmentalists. She also warns against the tendency of many groups to "harbor the belief that theirs is the only intelligent (or responsive or creative) way to engage important topics." Wright counsels us to "acquire fluency in multiple modern vernaculars"; to learn to experience the world from multiple perspectives, as J. B. Jackson did; and to write accessibly as a sign of tolerance for those many perspectives, disciplines, professions, discourses, and publics.

George L. Henderson, as a geographer and self-confessed skeptic in the realm of cultural landscape studies, sorts out the flexible and divergent uses of the term *landscape* into four discourses—ongoing scholarly debates predicated on specific sets of theoretical questions and assumptions.

Henderson reminds us that intellectual interpretations of the built world are inherently political and are inevitably linked to one's sense of what "ought to be" in society and space. He is a skeptic, but not a nihilist. His chapter suggests that each discourse has had, and might still have, both positive and negative ramifications for society.

Richard Schein applies the normative dimension of landscape studies, introduced by Henderson, to a series of racialized landscapes—as he describes them, "places particularly implicated in racist practice and the perpetuation of (or challenge to) racist social relations." With examples from Lexington, Kentucky, and the early suburbs of St. Louis, Missouri, Schein shows how landscapes can be built to reify and normalize racial and class segregation.

In his chapter, the historian Mark Fiege addresses the relationship of humans to nature. He figuratively stops in front of a common western No Hunting sign and then helps us see how such signs reflect what he calls "the intersection of two monumental, and sometimes opposing, forces": property rights and nature. Fences, he notes, rarely create a genuine boundary in the natural world. Instead, ecological continuities foster social alliances across those boundaries to generate a space that he calls the "ecological commons."

Even as briefly introduced as theory is in this section—as modern academic vernaculars, as discourses, normative dimensions, or ecological imperatives—the question of some readers may be, "Why bother with theory at all?" The answer resides in the efficacy of theoretical frameworks in guiding cultural interpretation and criticism (especially in selecting salient examples from among the plethora of landscape elements and issues that are present in even the most mundane urban or rural scene); in judging the depth and quality of other people's work; and in mediating the ever present political, social, and economic aspects of landscape.

GWENDOLYN WRIGHT

ON MODERN VERNACULARS AND J. B. JACKSON

10

J. B. Jackson unfailingly played the role of devil's advocate. To raise questions about someone's usual perspective—as a speaker or a listener, as a reader of words or images—helps keep both parties from fixating on any one set of conventions. It therefore seems only appropriate to honor Jackson by continuing his iconoclastic determination to look closely at words, places, and ideas that are too easily dismissed or taken for granted. This attitude of his pertained not only to mainstream intellectual life, but also to alternative cultures and to individuals, including any friend who enjoyed his correspondence.

Some observers have taken Jackson's cantankerous stance far too literally, however, leading them to infer that Jackson was hostile to architects, historians, geographers, and other intellectuals, which is simply untrue. Deeply respectful of learning in all these fields, he was indeed intolerant of self-righteousness in any of them. His criticism extended even to sanctimoniousness in landscape studies, as his correspondents can again testify. Nor is it true, as some have claimed, that Jackson abhorred the "arid terrain" of European theory; he objected only to its abuse by pretentious academics.

In the 1980s, late in his life, as he became increasingly aware of the inequalities as well as the wonders in the vernacular world, Jackson and I had intense conversations about Foucault. As far as I could tell, Jackson had read most of Foucault's work and deeply admired what one could do with it, but he felt no need to cite Foucault as a mark of scholarly legitimation—he even felt an aversion to it. As Daniel Defert has recently argued, Foucault himself would probably have agreed.[1] So too would Michel de Montaigne, who four centuries ago criticized as "jugglery . . . [t]hose complications and convolutions of language with which the scholars drive us into a corner."[2]

Of course, the seeming straightforwardness of Jackson's prose should not be taken too literally, either. It represents the surface of a carefully honed presentation; his writing followed in the tradition of great essayists like Montaigne, whom he so admired, as his lectures did that of skilled American storytellers. Jackson too chose not to announce his sources or his strategies, despite the prodigious effort and multiple appropriations that underlay the finished product.

Something of this quirky spirit animates my title, though my text will take a more academic (and therefore less dexterous) stance, openly seeking to probe the characteristic meanings of certain terms and concepts often associated with Jackson. In particular, most people think of the words *modern* and *vernacular* in fundamental opposition to each other. Progressive Western architects have embraced this bifurcated image at least since Marc-Antoine Laugier's writings on the "primitive hut" in the mid-eighteenth century (fig. 10.1).[3] In an expression that is only now being abandoned, it is often said that the modern seeks an expansive universal dominion through a heroic break with history, while the vernacular, firmly grounded in one distinctive setting, is presumed to remain unchanging, innocent of history.

At least since the late eighteenth century, Western culture has located the vernacular in two literally "marvelous," supposedly unchanging spatial milieus—both conspicuously outside modern cities. A celebration of indigenous traditions in the European or American countryside extolled distinct regional or national folk virtues, including an idyllic harmony between humans and nature. Likewise, a fascination with "the primitive" mapped and justified the West's control over the exotic landscapes and cultures being colonized abroad.

Figure 10.1. The personification of architecture and the primitive hut. This classical illustration of a primitive hut accompanied the 1755 edition of Marc-Antoine Laugier's *Essai sur l'architecture.*

This history indelibly linked the vernacular with other romantic concepts of the era: the "traditional peasantry" (in contrast with the unruly urban working class); the "authentic folk" of European and American nationalism; and the "civilizing mission" of colonialism, claiming at once to preserve the "authentic" pasts and modernize the backward economies of recalcitrant subjects.[4] Therefore, as a generic concept supposedly unconcerned with politics, the vernacular became an amalgam of the specific settings and distinctive groups that constitute these broader, more overtly politicized categories. Inevitably it took on many of the problematic underpinnings of these parallel ideologies.

One such problem concerns artifice. The historian Eric Hobsbawm has brilliantly analyzed "the invention of tradition" since the nineteenth century, inspired in part by the anxiety of loss in the aftermath of the Industrial Revolution.[5] In a similar vein, the anthropologist James Clifford depicts how, from its earliest stages, modernism has "constructed the traditional" as a category in opposition to itself, whether as antidote or impetus for change.[6]

Such artifice depends in part on seeming to exist outside of history. Like the traditional, the vernacular has come to evoke a timeless realm beyond the reach of social tensions or commercial ambitions. Certainly we are all aware of this tendency among various neotraditionalists, but what about the remarkably similar phenomenon in modernism's declaration of a break with history?

For both, the abstraction of an eternal present depends on two imaginary temporalities, distinct but closely intertwined. One is a vision of traditional stability and unity in a past that is about to be lost forever. Some praise this world as stable and harmonious, while others criticize it as tedious and backward; both opinions elide the fact that their past is a pseudohistorical fabrication. This illusion in turn allows, even encourages, fantasies about the present, whether they derive from self-righteous efforts to preserve or re-create that imagined world or from boldly innovative images that proclaim a radical new departure—what Alan Colquhoun has called a "flight into the future."[7] This project bestows a similar legitimacy, sometimes even an urgency, upon the respective causes and aesthetics of both neotraditionalists and the neo-avant-garde.

A related spatial dichotomy also exists. Although the vernacular may seem exotic, perhaps provocatively enticing, in a distant time or place, both groups typically recast it as prosaic, indeed offensive, when it is closer to home.[8] After all, with a few notable exceptions, one is likely to hear praise for the "timeless vernacular" of Dogon villages, the "ingenious creativity" of Brazilian favelas, or the "community harmony" of eighteenth-century American townships, but only snide dismissals of "mindless commercialism" in American shopping centers and suburban houses, or the "violence and anomie" of urban street corners and apartment buildings (figs. 10.2 and 10.3).

The exception again proves the rule. Some present-day academics find congeniality and ingenuity in contemporary American vernacular environments such as single-room-occupancy hotels, trailer parks, or commercial strips. With a few exceptions, most of them are unwilling to find any problems in this domain, preferring to focus their criticism on the invidious invasion of "European theory."[9] This focus denies the careful deliberation, segregation, and controls that underlie such phenomena. By seeming to be both everywhere and inevitable, these more proximate modern vernaculars inhabit another vague, placeless domain outside of history, rather than decentering established historical categories.

The supposed opposition between modern and vernacular keeps us from seeing an intriguing interdependency, which in turn supports

Figure 10.2. Dogon huts in Mali. Photograph from Bernard Rudofsky, *Architecture without Architects* (New York: Museum of Modern Art, 1964), p. 36.

Figure 10.3. Commercial strip. J. B. Jackson took this photograph in Richmond, California, in 1967.

Figure 10.4.   The "successful arrangement of the urban living space" around a medieval Italian piazza. Even ardent modernists valued the collective vernacular of European medieval cities and towns, believing these spaces demonstrate a functionalist aesthetic of asymmetry and community cohesion that validated their own work. From Walter Gropius, *Apollo in the Democracy* (New York: McGraw-Hill, 1958), p. 31.

authoritarian control over intellectual cohorts. So long as the vernacular remains distant in time and place, it actually serves modernists as a justification for their own visions (fig. 10.4). Respect for an "authentic vernacular" purifies the modernist, inwardly and outwardly demonstrating at once a benevolent tolerance of difference and an ambitious desire for improvement. In much the same way, traditionalists need the looming danger of disruption and destruction they associate with the modern vernaculars of contemporary life. The threat of such intrusions legitimates the authority of political, social, or architectural autocracies whose leaders have assumed responsibility for protecting their "authentic vernacular" from any modernist contamination.

A shift to some other words might help clarify these contentions. In the 1990s it became common to hear talk about hybridity and dislocation as quintessential contemporary phenomena. Once again, it does not mat-

Figure 10.5.   Forecourt houses from Frijoles Village Plan (now Aldea de Santa Fe), New Mexico. New urbanists draw from various American vernacular typologies, including early Hispanic plazas and courtyard houses.

ter whether one embraces the purported disorientation of modern life or deplores it. In fact, recent scholarship in history, anthropology, and archaeology consistently emphasizes the high level of change and conflict in all so-called traditional societies. Moreover, especially if we look at cities, the actuality of these supposedly stable, cohesive vernacular cultures has always been based on what the historian Ernst Bloch called "nonsynchronisms," by which he meant the coexistence of tradition and innovation in all people's lives; of different, even opposing cultures living alongside one another; of inequalities and tensions that sustain any social stability, even as they lay the groundwork for change.[10]

This undermines poststructuralist theorists and deconstructivist architects, who boldly announce their own awareness of chaos and contingency, mistakenly claiming them to be distinctive characteristics of late-twentieth-century life. Equally missing the point, neotraditionalists insist they can reclaim the social cohesion, moral order, and wholesome beauty of a chimerical golden age before such fractious disorder arose (fig. 10.5). It is easy to criticize nostalgia, but we must recognize that the avant-garde, through its unrelenting opposition to historical complexity, defines itself in terms of a very similar past. In both cases we are dealing with constructions, almost pure inventions, inflected by self-serving ideological agendas about the present.

But why should the word *vernacular* seem either so alluring or so dangerous, whether it is applied to the past or to the present? An exploration of etymology offers some insights. A vernacular is, of course, the native or indigenous language of a particular district or nation. Originally it meant a local oral dialect concerned with the routines and improvisations of everyday life. Vernaculars stood in contrast to the universality of Latin and the elevated topics discussed by the elite, who used Latin for politics and jurisprudence, for communicating with one another, and, for centuries after the end of the Roman Empire, for scholarly writing and Catholic theology. Past or present, someone speaking in the vernacular might invoke proverbs but rarely abstract theories or learned quotations (other than from the Bible or similar religious texts). Vernaculars deal with matters in the here and now, with daily life, rather than with theoretical abstractions. They are decidedly the languages of the street and the home, used to barter for goods, joke with friends, comfort a child, praise a meal, taunt a foe, entice a lover.

Vernacular words and cadence are by no means dull. What is said often resounds with an imaginative, playful, or surprisingly poetic ring; in antagonistic circumstances it can be provocative, even threatening. Nor are vernaculars inevitably parochial, for they encourage the indigenous pride that leads to trade and cultural creativity as well as warfare. Ordinary speech is a subtle art whose *poēsis* and theory of practice generally operate below the surface. The practice is social; the goal, at once instrumentality and pleasure.

To be sure, there is considerable risk of romanticizing in this characterization of ordinary speech and quotidian life. Tedium, restrictions, indeed many kinds of oppression, are inescapable and often overwhelming. But does that preclude any response other than unmitigated disdain, critique, or celebration? At the very least, while vernaculars encourage creativity as well as tradition, they never deny the multiple constraints that curtail the free play of creativity—in particular those imposed by society, history, and power (fig. 10.6). After all, the Latin word *verna* referred to a slave who was born in the master's house and thus tied to that place in perpetuity, an association based on control, not choice.

Yet no power is absolute, and the vernacular realm celebrates even momentary human efforts to transmute or resist the forces of drudgery and oppression. Legends, jokes, and other subversive stories hold a special place of honor in everyday conversations. Certain kinds of settings can, in turn, remind people of alternative narratives and sustaining fantasies where the wisdom of authorities can be ignored—at least for a brief time.

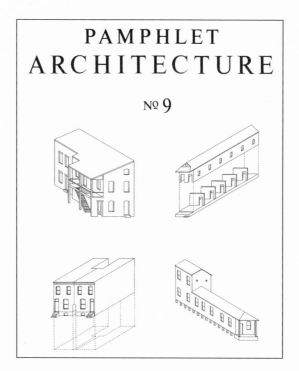

Figure 10.6. Steven Holl's sketches on the cover of his *Urban and Rural House Types in North America* (1982). These sketches show a young modernist's empathy for the simple geometries of ordinary American dwellings from different regions.

Such places include both public and private settings: the grand, glitzy casinos of Las Vegas and the crowded, expensively decorated living rooms that are the pride of many ordinary houses and apartments.

If most intellectuals disdain the provincialism and vulgarity of the vernacular, others have on occasion found much to admire. Think of Dante and Petrarch in Florence, Chaucer in Britain, all in the fourteenth century; or Faulkner in the twentieth-century American South; or contemporary architects such as Alison and Peter Smithson, Robert Venturi and Denise Scott Brown, Frank Gehry, Dan Solomon, or Steven Holl. They all discovered compelling qualities in vernacular languages: a vigorous, earthy physicality; a tolerant acceptance of difference and contingency; and a wry ingenuity, a continual process of tinkering with, improving, or playfully

Figure 10.7.   Castro Commons, infill housing, San Francisco. Here, Daniel Solo-
man and Associates paid homage to the white clapboard backs of nineteenth-
century houses in San Francisco.

personalizing something produced within a system (fig. 10.7). These qualities, signaling a new aesthetics of cultural plurality, often seem absent in
the words and designs of the contemporary elite.

Admittedly this response usually derives from a desire for personal inspiration and collective regeneration in one's own artistic or cultural
world. There is seldom a profound understanding of (or even respect for)
the cultural intricacies that sustain these alternative verbal or visual languages, nor a willingness to criticize the problems that do exist. Differences and complexities all too often melt into a bland collective entity
such as "the American people," "Hispanic culture," "the working class," or
other "authentic" vernacular voices.

Even so, the vernacular inevitably forces politics into the aesthetic
realm, not so much in a declaration of the architect's own political stance,
but rather in terms of tangible evidence of legal rights, social norms, economic conditions: the material conditions of owners, builders, residents—
and of all those who are ignored or left out. Even building materials play
a central role in this process, composing an emotive realm of sensory and
semantic associations on the one hand, and an economic domain of pro-

Figure 10.8.   Italian immigrant family eating dinner in the kitchen of their New York City tenement, 1915 (photographer: Lewis Wickes Hine). Although Hine probably appreciated the close family life and family rituals, he also hoped that middle-class people would feel uncomfortable about the forced overcrowding and lack of adequate sunlight and fresh air.

duction and employment on the other. Most of us would concur that modern vernacular materials are not limited to wood and stone; they include iconoclastic materials such as concrete block, chain-link fencing, and poured concrete, as well as less conspicuous steel frames, cheap plastics, and computer-generated imagery. But is this concession sufficient?

An exploration of material conditions extends as well into the realms of political and moral life. To challenge elite ideals of taste does not eliminate matters of judgment, but rather recasts them to include issues of inclusion, authority, transformation, and cultural diversity. Other sets of questions then come to the fore, such as how to distinguish between differences that reveal alternative forms of human expression and those that signal imposed inequalities, or how to reconcile unbiased description with critical interpretation. Fortunately the effort to address these competing ambitions can itself spur creativity. Consider, for example, the documentary photographer Lewis Hine, who sought to convey both what should be appreciated and what should be changed in his subjects' lives and their environments (fig. 10.8).[11]

Several quite varied contemporary intellectuals—including Michel de Certeau, Henri Lefebvre, Pierre Bourdieu, Alf Ludtke, and Andreas Huyssen, as well as J. B. Jackson—have taken on the ambiguous cultural space that lies between a critique and an appreciation of today's vernacular world.[12] Focusing on situated knowledge in specific places, they seek to understand how—despite the real and invidious pressures of global capitalism—many people nonetheless manage to create something positive, pleasurable, even proud in the context of their daily lives.

For example, in *The Practice of Everyday Life*, Michel de Certeau, the French historian turned philosopher, extols the ways in which human beings continuously transform the routine, repetitive world of the commonplace into something else: a memory or an incentive, a secret hiding place or a public stage, a momentary zone of pleasure or a site of resistance. Whereas the first volume of Certeau's book poetically evokes the creative possibilities of walking city streets, the second draws in even closer to home, quite literally, to look at neighborhood gossip, family rituals, and the potential rewards of domestic tasks such as cooking. For *Les arts de faire* (the original subtitle of Certeau's second volume), his coauthor, Luce Giad, seized upon that splendid Anglicism *making do*, a verb form that captures the ongoing amalgam of creativity and constraint in all aspects of the vernacular domain.

One could say that Certeau, Jackson, and others like them engage in translations between various modern vernaculars. Indeed etymologically, *translation* means "carried from one place to another," transported across the border between one language or nation or cultural group and another. Such a process occurs first and most obviously between words and the human experience of ideas, things, and spaces. It must also negotiate between conscious or unconscious intentions and actual effects, exploring "what an idea does," as the American pragmatist philosophers often put it.[13] The process can never be complete, of course, nor can it always avoid some misunderstanding of the original text, up to the level of a significant distortion of its original meaning. Some scholars have argued that all translation entails displacement, alienation, and appropriation for new purposes.[14]

The process of translation certainly does open up language, challenging words and ideas once taken for granted, reminding us that meanings are never really fixed. The new idiom, while potentially deforming, can also be creative and pleasurable, especially for the speaker but also for listeners, who enjoy an unexpected cadence or an "error" that casts new light on the implicit rules and constraints of their own language. This is not to

Figure 10.9. The photographer Bill Owens with his family and in-laws, from Bill Owens, *Suburbia* (1973).

say that the translator is free to do anything (though some would seem to think so); rather, it is to say simply that possibilities become fluid. One can rediscover a sense of wonder in the playful alliteration of a common phrase, or admit the pretentious abstraction (the "jargon," in Theodor Adorno's 1964 critique) that obscures a word that had seemed so eloquent.[15] Experimentation becomes not merely possible, but inescapable.

What happens between national languages—translating between English and Spanish, for example, or Japanese and Turkish—also occurs with cultural languages such as professional discourses (geography, architecture, landscape history, and so forth) or class and generational dialects. Here one must negotiate not only between words and forms but also between hierarchies, accommodating various modes of speaking and writing, diverse strategies for describing and judging space, different rights to speak and be. At the most fundamental level, there is a process of translation between drawing and building, or between the spoken language of most people and the written prose of intellectuals or architects—languages that are, after all, circumscribed vernaculars that cannot be understood everywhere they are heard (fig. 10.9).[16]

There can be no single authentic lingua franca in such an endeavor, although it is nonetheless tempting to impose one. Even certain educated people didactically reject the language of expertise, insisting that only "the people" have the real truth (rather like Johann Gottfried von Herder's enthusiasm for the "natural poetry" of the *Volk*).[17] Of course, most of their colleagues simply ignore explanations and opinions that are not phrased in terms of the privileged discourse of academia or professionalism. Both approaches are isolationist. At best they treat translation as a routinized chore of simplification—"dumbing down" to please a client or entertain a popular audience—rather than as a creative and demanding opportunity.

Indeed, a certain defensive arrogance easily isolates disciplines or professions not only from the public, but even from one another. Without saying so aloud, many groups often harbor the belief that theirs is the only intelligent (or responsive or creative) way to engage important topics; its power is untranslatable, like the ancient names of gods. They tend to reject another discipline's language as too vague or too rigid, to repudiate someone else's theoretical perspective as unduly romantic, formalist, or biased in some other manner. Practitioners and other "realists" often denounce theorists, and vice versa, at once fearing and refuting the power of the other's language to decimate their own. Such parochialism is not so far from the narrow xenophobia of those American populists who are suspicious of any language but English, convinced that it is (and has always been) a universal mode of communication. I am reminded of a discussion about bilingualism I overheard in Texas a few years ago, in which one exasperated man sputtered, "Well, why can't they learn English? It was good enough for Jesus!"

To acquire a new language requires prodigious effort, although the work will in time become invisible. It also demands individual self-confidence and tolerance. One must be willing to make verbal transgressions, to speak with an accent, even to forget things that once came easily. The process tests the resonance of every language—and of language itself. Not so coincidentally, one's original mode of speech suddenly becomes unconventional too, providing the chance to rethink its implicit rules, its limitations and possibilities.

Of course, both national and disciplinary vernaculars have themselves evolved over time, sometimes from rather homely origins that contravene their present-day academic exactitude. It was in this spirit that Montaigne created the essay as a literary form in the late sixteenth century, treating the *essai* as, literally, a trial, a self-exploration to probe his own responses to different subjects and situations, both near and faraway, responses at once consistent and fluctuating. Then and now the form demands accessible language, abstention from pretense, and an openness to all sorts of unexpected alternative forms of wisdom.

These same intentions informed much of Brinck Jackson's life and work at the edge of the university world; they can animate professional and academic life within the academy as well. Rather than being constrained by disciplinary blinders, we can continually strive to liberate ourselves, as Jackson did, to experience the world in more than one place, from more than one perspective, drawing on more than one mode of description and analysis. Both the means and the goal entail ongoing efforts to acquire fluency in multiple modern vernaculars.

GEORGE L. HENDERSON

WHAT (ELSE) WE TALK ABOUT WHEN WE TALK ABOUT LANDSCAPE

For a Return to the Social Imagination

11

A view, a place, a picture, an angle on the world . . . a *landscape*. How many meanings of that word might there be? Anyone who has been a student of landscape for even a short period of time, or who has read the dictionary entry, for that matter, will surely discover that the meanings are multiple, and perhaps multiplying. But how do these meanings serve the cultural and social critique that is the point of much landscape scholarship, and how does such critique itself generate landscape meanings? That landscape *has* multiple meanings, that it is a concept and refers not just to a portion of the external world, or to actual material places—seen, depicted, walked through, or built—is well worth contemplating, or recalling, as would be the case for readers of J. B. Jackson's many essays. Landscape is worthy of attention as a concept because shifts in meaning may slip by unnoticed, and once they do, the reasons to study and appreciate landscape critically, whatever concept of it is adopted, may also be forgotten. The risk of this sort of recuperative work, however, should not be overlooked, perhaps especially by those who need no reminding about the multiplicity of landscape: What exactly *are* the reasons to foreground landscape, and are they defensible? Because the answer depends on what is meant by *landscape* in the first place, much can be gained by clarifying what it is we talk about when we talk about landscape, and what else we might then have to say. Not least is the recognition that such talk raises important issues—for instance, matters of social justice and norms—that the dominant landscape concepts may be ill-equipped to resolve.

COMING INTO THE COUNTRY

The recent history and treatment of landscape (and some strongly affiliated concepts) in geography is one way to begin looking at landscape discourses. At least, the route through geography is the one I know best. Geography is my home, and certainly it has nurtured the conceptual richness of the landscape idea. But where there is conceptual richness there is also likely to be entrenchment and allegiance to particular variants of the concept. To speak of landscape as a concept, or as discourse (as is the case here), draws scorn from certain quarters and applause from others. There is nothing at all wrong with such divergent responses. On the contrary, to unmask oneself and say something about how one has crossed into Landscape Country, and about what one has seen and done there, seems only sensible. Then follows more honestly a summation and appraisal of how landscape study might presently stand with its theorists, students, and practitioners.[1]

Through geography, I found more than one point of entry. One was through cultural geography in the mid- to late 1970s. The timing was crucial, because these were the peak years of a particular sort of challenge to the postwar manifestos that had claimed positivism as geography's cutting edge. The positivist geography of the 1950s and 1960s had sought to redefine the field exclusively as a search for immutable laws of human behavior, with quantitative methods as the privileged route to their discovery. A few years on, however, an influential group of cultural geographers made cause with their colleagues in the humanities, where the study of meaning, values, creativity, and felt experience remained paramount.[2] This loose-knit group proclaimed a new, humanistic geography. Translated into actual curricula, the humanistic approach was eclectic, to say the least. Our undergraduate readings, for example, involved a quick look back at Berkeley geographer Carl Sauer's rumination that as places develop they acquire a distinctive "personality." This was followed by more reverent paging through J. B. Jackson, more revered because he wrote of modern, everyday landscapes where we students personally had lived, and long hours with geographers of the mind, such as Yi-Fu Tuan and David Lowenthal. From there the curriculum ventured into the rigors of continental thought, especially Gaston Bachelard and Rainer Maria Rilke, who would take rapturous flight into the cosmos one moment and plunge earthward into the microgeographies of human existence the next.[3] Methodologically, the point was that landscape was to be taken in not just through traditional fieldwork, and still less through mere counting, but through any of the literary, visual, and tactile arts that gave voice to the gestalt, the spirit and holism, of landscape and place.

Also in the 1970s, the study and practice of landscape architecture became a haven for the landscape-minded at our university. In studio courses, the examples of Ian McHarg and Roberto Burle Marx loomed large, and we were schooled in the belief that landscape design was a matter of cultural life or death. For this reason, landscape study was a calling of the highest order.[4] But a specifically modernist approach reigned supreme when it came to actual design. No project was relished more than that which allowed us to work on a fresh, clean slate; that way we kept our ideas on landscape and spirit of place pure. Somehow, though, Bachelard always eluded the blueprint. Could felt, lived, and accumulated experience really be *designed*?

By the mid-1980s, at the beginning of a graduate program in geography, I was reaching out to the disciplines of American Studies and social history, through which scholars such as Leo Marx, Henry Nash Smith, and Annette Kolodny had had a decisive impact on the study of American landscape. But a clear difference marked their work. Here was a group of writers for whom landscape was not quite the sacred, even fetishized, terrain that it could sometimes be in humanistic cultural geography and landscape architecture. Rather, the focus was more on actually existing social and political formations: no clean slates. Continuing on the social-formation trajectory, I forked left and headed toward social theory and radical political economy. With wholly new cohorts, I pored over the other Marx and paged slowly through the works of Anthony Giddens, David Harvey, Henri Lefebvre. And here again was landscape, though spoken of more in terms of "space" or "social space"—terms more suggestive of the distinctive theoretical stance toward which I began to move at the beginning of my graduate training. "Land(scape) and life," the old Sauerian couplet that sang of cultural cohesion and adaptation, gave way to the drumbeat of new keywords: social construction, social conflict, and power relations. For we were moving on to the realists now and sought to understand the role of space in the larger debates that raged through the social sciences and cultural studies: structure versus agency, modernism versus postmodernism, Fordism versus post-Fordism.[5]

These are some of the possible encounters with landscape study, then. Readers will have to decide whether the itinerary is wholly idiosyncratic; likely it is not—one can indeed spot a landscape oeuvre. So let us ask: Is it not a little beguiling that all through these intellectual twists and turns, landscape has always been there; and not merely because it is a slice, pure and simple, of the external world to be explained, but rather because landscape is also a highly flexible concept? Other landscape aficionados will undoubtedly have encountered that flexibility in their own ways, subject to their own experiences. But for all those intellectual turns, for all those politically variable perspectives, there has been a concept of landscape considered to be useful to the task at hand. Perhaps this is a testament to the tenacious value of the landscape concept, that it has a broader underlying meaning pulling together the many inflected meanings. More likely, the persistence of landscape results from the very differences in what landscape has been said to refer to—much more, in fact, than to a simple portion of the physical world—and therefore in what there has been to see and understand. Landscape's persistence through many scholarly and political divides is not the only thing worth pointing out, though. As if to structure those differences in what landscape is said to be is the fact that landscape study has been put into service for at least two distinct purposes: to think about the world as it was and is—a *positive*, descriptive meaning for landscape—and to think about the world as it might be—a *normative* and sometimes prescriptive meaning for landscape. These purposes do relate to each other, but in complicated ways.

It is useful to bear in mind this tension between normative and positive modalities, for they signal not just different meanings, but different reasons why landscape study ought or ought not to be worthy of attention. The central questions thus include the following: What sort of landscape discourses have been the dominant ones, and what ontologies do they claim for landscape? What are some of the limits of these differently defined landscapes? And do the ontologies in which the dominant landscape discourses are themselves embedded actually position landscape as a necessary arena of social transformation?

THE FOUR DOMINANT DISCOURSES ON LANDSCAPE

To ask, "What are the dominant ways in which the study of landscape has proceeded, and with what dominant conceptions?" and "What ends do different conceptions of landscape serve?" is to join a popular endeavor: the critique of the "self-evident." Examples come to mind easily. Race and gender, once viewed as objective facts, are seen now as changing social constructions and are studied in genealogical and political terms. This is not to imply that critique of this kind is a recent invention. Thus, when Marx redefined capital as a particular relationship between people, rather than as mere money or accumulated wealth, as it is still considered by most economists, he saw something radically new and gave a familiar word an utterly different meaning that, in turn, necessitated social critique, just as it was founded upon social critique.[6] Landscape, like race, gender, or capital, has a conceptual life, a life of usage, that is ripe for analysis.

Landscape scholarship has been formed around at least four discourses. The first of these encases landscape within a particular kind of social formation, bounded in space and time. This is the Germanic idea of the *landschaft*, the mutual tethering of community and land. A "folk" creation, landschaft is largely rural, historical, and socially stable. A second conception of landscape is landscape as social space. Unlike landschaft, for which mortality is possible—and likely—this second notion of landscape contemplates no such fate. For as social space, landscape is no *particular* social formation, but rather human place and space of any kind, anywhere. A third discourse on landscape is the epistemological landscape, that is, the legible, material record of human practice and belief. This landscape discourse can clearly intersect with the first and second discourses, but with an emphasis on the notion that landscape tells all. The final landscape discourse considered here is landscape *as* discourse. Call this the apocryphal landscape, the landscape as a mode of dissemblance: the "lie of the land," as geographer Don Mitchell puts it. Landscape as discourse is the idea that the landscape is an ideological expression, particularly one that aestheticizes power and subjugation. A lot of ground can be covered with these four, a number chosen to be suggestive, not exhaustive.

Landscape as Landschaft

This discourse makes landscape more or less synonymous with the rural, with community, more or less small in geographical extent, more or less characterized by a balanced fit between people and land, more or less sustained by the use of local resources under the terms given by a more or less shared, vernacular technology. This landscape discourse is interested in time-honored folk forms such as settlement, housing, farm buildings, fences, cemeteries, and so forth. It emphasizes processes of the folk-cultural transmission and diffusion of these material culture elements and stresses cultural continuity and preservation. It admits the environments of small rural towns, insofar as they preserve and express local or regional ways of life, but it is threatened by most forms of modernity (though it has long been symptomatic *of* modernity) and industrialization, by the allegedly inauthentic, and by the unleashing of the urban monster over the land. When operationalized, this notion of landscape, with its obvious normative coloration, describes the world that most Americans have lost. But this very discourse *may* take an interest in things contemporary, especially if they bear the vestiges of the landschaft. Thus, the single-family suburban dwelling surrounded by lawn, so characteristic of American residential suburbs, may be considered a landschaft holdover.

This discourse was for many years a staple theme in texts on landscape in human geography. The idea is strong in Sauer and his student Fred Kniffen. It is lurking in Donald Meinig's well-known essay on symbolic landscapes in *The Interpretation of Ordinary Landscapes*. A similar vision suffuses historical works such as the late René Dubos's exquisite and moving treatise on the spirit of place, *A God Within*, and, likewise Donald Worster's *Rivers of Empire* and Carolyn Merchant's *Ecological Revolutions*. The strong argument for this vision of landscape belongs particularly to John Stilgoe's *Common Landscape of America*.[7]

Landscape as landschaft is so linked to associated ideas of the folk, the community, stewardship and husbandry, nature, the region, and the nation, that a history of its origins is long indeed.[8] Certainly its origins are diffuse, both geographically and ideologically. The salient point is landschaft's modern appeal, partly for its romantic reaction against the perceived alienation and anomie of contemporary life in the industrialized world, and partly as a warning of the ecology movement that industrial society is exceeding the earth's carrying capacity. Both inside and outside the academy, landscape as landschaft—as a way of knowing the world in sensual and communal terms—partakes of the revolt against supposedly value-free, positivist science. At its heart, landscape as landschaft is a normative discourse.

In certain ways, this take on landscape has everything to recommend it. Landscape as most essentially about sustained community life, local knowledge and know-how, and the careful stewardship of nature is a powerful vision. In particular, its implicit argument that a concept of landscape ought to be inextricably linked to a concept of what the good life could be appeals to one's moral sense.

But there are problems. One is simply that if this notion of landscape really refers to a world we have lost, if landscape has effectively ended and turned into not-landscape, as Stilgoe insists, then landscape is, conceptually, not very useful for the present. Indeed, this version of landscape is simply chock-full of narratives of decline. Even if I tend to occasionally enjoy that well-greased, downward slope of complaint, it is just another alien and alienating story to my students, who have limited patience with things that decline. We ought to make landscape of sturdier stuff; indeed, most do.

There is another, more interesting problem with this first version of landscape, and that is, these landscapes were themselves implicated in the processes of their own historical transformation. The categories "landscape" and "not-landscape" are related, not separate. This was too little examined in the landscape-as-landschaft mind-set, since form was readily mistaken as content and process. One passage from Stilgoe's *Common Landscape of America* will serve as an example. Stilgoe writes, "In order to discover the shapes of the past, one must read the shapes of the present as one reads a palimpsest, looking for details perhaps overshadowed by newer building and then ascertaining their evolution and contemporaneous meaning." This reading will ostensibly reveal vestiges of landscape—that is, artifacts on the land produced between 1580 and 1845—when landscape, not cityscape, dominated. Quoting Stilgoe again: "Taken together [these vestiges] are landscape. Mixed with subsequent forms and spaces, they are the contemporary confusion called 'the man-made environment.'"[9]

Stilgoe points to the dichotomous poles of landscape and man-made environment with only the thinnest suggestion that there might be a line of historical, causal connection between them. Such is the desire to see the past as more stable, more ordered, more settled than "now," that it is quite difficult to see how "now" could have happened, how anything could ever have changed. That is, what else but certain elements of the precapitalist world itself can explain the demise of that world? Those processes of commodification, of specialized and separated land uses, of alienation of labor from the land, of pressures to increase production—those processes that would put an end to the world of the landschaft—emerged, in part, from that world. In this very regard (call it the dialectical sensibility) the story is quite effectively told for the New England case by Carolyn Merchant's *Ecological Revolutions*. Also quite effectively, a New Mexico example is given by Don Usner in *Sabino's Map,* concerning the town of Chimayó, New Mexico.[10] Thus, cultural continuity is ultimately, at a fine enough scale of analysis, continuous with its own discontinuance. But it remains difficult to see this if one is working with an overly bounded and reified notion of landschaft.

Moreover, the idea of the landschaft-landscape has been useful in the grander project of obscuring the past, even as we invoke landschaft ostensibly to remember the past. And therein lies another problem. The historical reconstruction of "Colonial Williamsburg," Virginia, provides an example in the form of an old plantation, Carter's Grove. For a long time, museum administrators avoided the fact of slavery in their re-creation of Southern landschaft there. But after a time, they gave way to realism, which is to say legitimate political pressure, and built slaves' quarters, which are now an integral feature of the entrance to Carter's Grove. Celebrated throughout the plantation site are rurality, the development of local resources and know-how, and the rule of cultural adaptation. Landschaft, Southern style and West African style, dwells here, admitting of social hierarchy, for sure, and letting visitors know that slavery meant a mean existence. But also asserted is the fact that slaves were not mere victims; they were cultural exiles reproducing and modifying West African folkways and foodways. How reassuring that is, and how easily the whole re-creation merges with landschaft America as the stable, peaceable kingdom. The trouble with this way of imagining landschaft, though, is that it's so . . . *nice.* These are designer slave quarters, in a designer landschaft. The museum that is Carter's Grove has no room for any budding Frederick Douglass whispering inflammatory words, plotting to dash his owner's brains against a rock. The most the master's going to get is spit in his soup.[11] America reenacts Revolutionary War encampments and Civil War battles, not slave insurrections, and there is an idea of landscape to help hide the contradiction.

Landscape as Social Space

Landscape is also constituted as everyday space and place—as built environment in all its forms, including the "contemporary confusion," as Stilgoe has put it. In this incarnation, landscape is set up in such a way that it could never die, for it is simply human-made place and space as they are from one moment to the next, across any time period we happen to be interested in. In this conception of landscape, it's not that places as we know them don't change, it's just that we also refer to what comes next as a landscape. Dozens of urban residential blocks could get torn down to make way for eight high-speed express lanes, and we would still call those express lanes elements of the landscape. Landscape here extends beyond those fetishized constellations of dwellings, barns, croplands, and woodlots to include apartment buildings, street corners, junkyards, gas stations, train depots, convenience stores, tract housing, shopping centers, and more.

This second landscape discourse is a fundamental theoretical move away from the first; such is the difference between folk landschaft and popular landscape tastes, between a particular kind of everyday life and all the spaces of everyday life everywhere. The shift is radically relativizing. How was it accomplished? What is its appeal? J.B. Jackson's influence has probably been without equal. Though he held out the possibility that landscape was a particular kind of organized space, his populist vision, which surveyed landscapes past and present, implied that landscape was not a historical artifact, not a lost art.[12]

Landscape as everyday social space has its appeal, I think, in the recognition that the normative requirements of landscape as landschaft do not describe the conditions of life for most Americans. Life may not be lived in reference to the maypole anymore, but if it is lived in reference to the daily commute on a highway, that does not make the commute (or the highway) any less meaningful. Therefore, if landscape is everyday social space, and if such space really is full of meaning, then we have much interpretive work to do. Such work began to fill the pages of the geography journals by the 1970s. This second landscape discourse is also in full accord with the conclusions of contemporary cultural theory that culture is everywhere.[13] In the academy, especially in the discipline of cultural geography, one implication of such a theory is clear. Expensive fieldwork in faraway places is not required. A more democratic conception of landscape in some ways also democratizes the practice of geographical scholarship. (The recognition that our own landscapes can be studied qua landscape comes with a bit of irony, however, if one other academic development is considered. Postcolonial theory and the recent emphasis on diaspora studies has recast ostensibly local cultures and landscapes in hemispheric and even global terms.)[14]

Because this second landscape discourse can address rapid and visually dramatic social and economic change, the shocks of the postwar period are open for interpretation. Indeed, these changes cry out for interpretation (and have perhaps helped to elevate the second discourse to its privileged position): huge growth in high-tech and office-park development, in suburban residences, and in new suburban locations for manufacturing, retailing, and wholesaling; profound disinvestment in older urban-core areas and the entrenchment of urban poverty; the rise of edge cities, gentrified urban neighborhoods, and theme entertainment complexes.[15] The second landscape discourse always leaves new interpretive work to do.

Another appeal of landscape as social space is that no *particular* political commitment is required for its study. For this is landscape as "conservation of mass": social space, per se, is neither created nor destroyed; it simply changes form. Its scale may be large or small; it may have nothing to do with community. The concept of social space has no stake in any particular relationship among human beings, nor between humans and nonhuman nature. It is urban, it is rural, it is everything in between. For a whole generation of landscape observers and commentators it's simply that ever present entity, the American scene.

However, even in this most neutral of landscape concepts, there are problems. The reconstituted notion of landscape is often simply too neutral. In no way does it offer a conception of how things ought to be; in many studies, especially those that give themselves over to the delights of pop and mass culture, it seems reasonably content with how things are (or were). The celebrated images come easily to mind: a stretch of Art Deco storefronts, a trailer park, a garden suburb, an aerial view of a highway cloverleaf interchange, a grid plan, a back alley, a junkyard. A manhole cover. If the normative impulses of the first concept of landscape shackle us too much to the past (and a particular vision of the past at that), this second landscape concept cannot find its political bearings and runs amok. For all this notion of landscape can tell us, a stretch of Art Deco storefronts is as worthy of attention as is a sweatshop in Los Angeles's garment district. The history of manhole covers is as compelling as that of trailer parks. Perhaps it is, perhaps it is not. But at its worst, this concept of landscape—as a concept of landscape—cannot tell you why it would or would not be; it offers no reason why a history of every sidewalk crack in America should not be required reading. In order to make the case as to why one feature might warrant more attention than another, why tenement districts really might be more important than sidewalk cracks, this second landscape concept either has to play an ontological second to some other framework of analysis that tells us which categories to privilege, or a different concept of landscape will have to be pressed into service.

This second concept might be traced back to the Kantian notion that things present in a given space have a functional relationship to one another. There is some truth to that, but Kant didn't necessarily imply that what relates them *begins* in that shared place. By extension, if we want to understand how people put their world(s) together, the contiguous elements of landscape are not necessarily the best place to start. This point can be made by reflecting on a particular landscape. Near a university where I once taught, a stretch of road has along it a number of shops, among them a Starbucks, a Coffee Plantation, and a Cafe Latte. There are also some clothing stores: the Gap, the White House, and several others with less brand-name recognition. The Cafe Latte is locally owned and has only the one location. The Coffee Plantation has several Arizona locations but is owned by a national coffee emporium, Gloria Jean. Starbucks, by contrast, is not only national but now international, focusing on Pacific Rim locations in Japan, Korea, Singapore, and the Philippines. In the late 1990s Starbucks bought out a couple of coffee shops in London and thus gained a toehold in the U.K. market. The Gap is also both national and international, but the White House seems to be only a national chain, and even then is concentrated primarily on the East and West Coasts.[16]

The point? This landscape cannot tell you about the ownership structures and circuits of capital that brought it into being. Nor is the exact spatial arrangement of these stores necessary to the circuits of capital that placed them there. This landscape is a nifty heuristic device that tells us about intensely competitive markets and capital's persistent search for profitable harbors, not least amid the capes and bays of once-disinvested neighborhoods. But did I need to begin with this landscape in order to discern the dynamics of capitalist competition? Even that question is not quite right, because the point, I think, is that whether one begins with one landscape or a dozen landscapes, we are dealing with phenomena that, while leaving their traces in individual locales, are themselves constituted at much larger, even dizzying, geographical scales.

A final problem is relevant here, though I will return to it at greater length later. The second concept of landscape often comes with the claim that looking at landscape is a first step toward greater understanding of social and cultural processes. On first hearing, that seems reasonable enough. But it doesn't take much reflection to begin to see that this is not a very convincing argument for studying landscape itself, if intervention in undesirable (because unjust) social and cultural processes is the point. Poverty, sexism, racism, ethnocentrism, homophobia—these are problems that do not begin in landscape, but in human relationships, social relations, and social structures. To be sure, they may produce landscapes or materialize in landscapes, but to begin with landscape analysis can be obfuscating at worst and diverting at best. The relationship between socio-cultural norms and this landscape discourse tends to be indeterminate.

The Epistemological Landscape

Related to the second conception of landscape is a third, which could be called the epistemological landscape: landscape as the material revelation of human practice and thought. In a sense, this landscape discourse is an offshoot of the second one, or of a particular set of arguments that reveal why certain settings are of importance. The epistemological discourse postulates quite explicitly that the landscape tells us important things about who we are as a society and a culture. It ostensibly reveals what might otherwise remain hidden and verifies truths that are difficult to face. In this conception, landscape study becomes useful for showing us aspects of society that have been little noticed because theorists simply did not look carefully enough at the actual physical world.

An example in this vein is geographer Paul Groth's work on the single-room-occupancy hotels that once populated virtually every American downtown, but that since the 1920s have fared poorly.[17] Decades of urban theory and planning took scant notice of the existence of SROs and of their function as affordable shelter. Once ubiquitous in the urban land-scape, they have only recently registered in the minds of landscape schol-ars. In important ways, landscape analysis can reveal a presence that oth-erwise remains largely hidden. In this sense, the landscape never lies, as both Grady Clay and Peirce Lewis have said.[18] Landscape can quite liter-ally be "ground truth."

It's hard to take issue with this elegant, straightforward principle. But if the larger point is to argue that the good landscape, like the good soci-ety, is that which operates as a humane, democratic habitat, then the real point is that we have to decide what sort of social relations we want in the first place. At root, then, what accounts for the vast gaps in wealth be-tween rich and poor residential districts? One could do worse than begin to answer this question with an examination of the social relations of class and race.[19]

It is true that for the epistemological landscape discourse, the landscape is a social space that is one with social relations. One simply can't know society without knowing its spaces, and one can't know social space with-out knowing the social relations that constitute it. The two are mutually constitutive. As an argument for why landscapes and spaces are important foci of research, the implication is clear. *Any* good account of the social world, of social realities, must take account of its spaces and would be fatally flawed if it did anything less. In some sense, the argument for landscape study comes to fruition here. This social-spatial approach has found a major champion in Edward Soja, whose early work in the field is summarized in *Postmodern Geographies*. This argument is also foundational in the work of geographer Allan Pred—his *Place, Practice, and Structure* being an excellent example. Building on the work of such social theorists as Henri Lefebvre and Anthony Giddens, and in Pred's case on a deep involvement with so-called time geography, Soja and Pred are concerned with landscape as an explicitly dialectical construction in which, as Pred puts it, the spatial becomes the social, and the social becomes the spatial.[20] The idea here is the refusal to conceive of social and spatial relationships apart from each other. Spatial forms and processes are the medium and outcome of social structure and agency, while social processes are themselves the medium and outcome of spatial ones. This may sound something like landscape-as-everyday-social-space discourse, but there is a difference. The society-and-space perspective to which Soja, Pred, and many others subscribe means nothing without the conflict model of social theory to back it up. Thus, very particular social relations tend to be invoked, those formed around the major axes of social difference and struggle: class, race, ethnicity, gender, and sexuality.

The dialectic of society and space has revolutionized thinking in human geography since the mid-1980s, but not so much because earlier workers in the landscape field did not know that landscape reflected and shaped society. Rather, the revolution had to do with the conflict model just mentioned. If we are to ask what the conditions of emergence were for the society-space dialectic and what its appeal is, we would need to point out the adoption of Marxist approaches across many of the social sciences in the 1970s, especially in sociology, anthropology, and geography. (Radical approaches in geography and other social sciences have greatly increased since then.)

Marxist perspectives have yielded two things that are pertinent to this discussion. One, of course, is its conflict model of social structure and change, especially its willingness to put social difference and unequal power relations in the foreground. That is, if landscape is everywhere, as our second discourse stipulates, and if everywhere, or nearly so, there is evidence that all is not well, nor has been well, with the body politic, what does geography have to say about that? Marxism gave it much to say, and it is through Marxism that much has been said.[21] Apart from giving geographers a way to theorize and otherwise come to terms with social difference and struggle, the contribution of Marxism relevant here is its willingness to grapple with causation and social structure. Again, if landscape is everywhere, and if everything is in a sense a landscape worth looking at, from John Doe's front yard to New York's Central Park, Marxism suggests that certain things (e.g., those that reveal class struggle and the overlapping relations of class, race, ethnicity, gender, and sexuality) are more worthy of attention than others, because they are more *constitutive* of social structure, social difference and conflict, and, ultimately, social change. This injunction contains an explicit criticism of the voluntarism inherent in some versions of humanistic geography and of humanistic geography's own incomplete critique of positivism. Even as radical approaches in geography fanned out beyond Marxism, the point was to "do" social theory and, at the same time, reformulate it around space to say something about conditions not of our choosing—capital, or class, or race, or gender—and not get lost in the multifarious details of the uses, constructions, and meanings of landscape.[22]

However, even here there are problems. As an argument, the society-space perspective can seem somewhat disingenuous. In this discourse, although the real world is claimed to be structured as a social-spatial dialectic, it is actually the social that has driven the development of the theory. Geographers, including me, almost always use social relations pertaining to class, gender, race, and ethnicity as the ontologically prior categories. Our arguments are first and foremost arguments about society. More to the point, the society-space dialectic is an argument *from* society *to* space. Once the social relations and categories are firmly on the agenda, it is easy, and illuminating, too, to include space and see how *it* is constituted, and constituting. But in actual theoretical procedure, it is the social that leads to and tells us what's interesting about the spatial. And rightly so, or we would fall into those cracks in the sidewalk.

Lest misunderstanding arise, the point is not that the society-space *dialectic* needs to be strengthened. The point is that a return to the social "half," as it were, is in order, with a greater sense of what is at stake. We need to be reminded of David Harvey's original argument with spatial science in his seminal book *Social Justice and the City:* space matters, but an elaboration of social justice matters first.[23] For example, a geographer may conduct a study that examines the ways in which the social relations of production on the shop floor or across some industrial district are expressed in spatial terms, perhaps a panoptic arrangement of workers and managers in the factory; but it does not follow that to secure a higher wage or resist the alienation of labor, the solution is to rearrange workers in space (though there may well be forms of spatial inequality).[24] These are problems that are first and foremost problems among groups of human beings, what we think human beings' obligations to one another ought to be, and what processes might be put in place so that more meaningful and effective debate over those obligations can ensue. It is not, therefore, a conception of space that tells us what is reasonable about a "reasonable" wage. Rather, it is a particular conception, or conceptions, of society—of social relations—that clues us in. Failure to take this distinction seriously has resulted in a most curious lacuna, recently noted by geographer David Smith. Remarking both on Harvey's engagement with moral and political philosophy (which I take to be the central arena for wrangling with normative conceptions of the social) in *Social Justice and the City* and on what has become of that engagement in human geography more broadly, Smith writes:

> Harvey recognized that a more detailed examination of [social justice] principles would be required to build a spatial theory around them. However, the subsequent development of human geography revealed little progress in this direction, despite a massive accumulation of literature on social justice in other fields. So, when Harvey returned to the subject at book length twenty-five years on [in the 1996 book *Justice, Nature, and the Geography of Difference*], his central question of the "just production of just geographical differences" was virtually the same as before.[25]

The meaning is clear enough. We geographers have become very good at spatializing, but have engaged the larger project insufficiently—thus, wanting now to speak directly of a radical normativity, we are at a loss for words.

The Apocryphal Landscape

Yet another way in which scholars have constituted landscape as a subject of study is the discourse of landscape as ideology. We might refer to this discourse as the apocryphal landscape; landscape as a way of seeing, especially a way of seeing that relishes the gaze, that asserts power by privileging perspectival vision, which, far from being a mere way of seeing, informs the actual, material making of places. (One typical story told by landscape scholars notes the trajectory from landscape painting to land planning; that is, from a way of seeing that became materialized in the perspectival and compositional conventions of landscape painting and then materialized further in the actual design and building of places such as gardens and rural estates.) In cultural geography, this "way of seeing" approach to landscape owes a great debt to the English cultural historians John Berger, John Barrell, and Raymond Williams. *Social Formation and Symbolic Landscape,* by Denis Cosgrove, is perhaps the apogee of this mode of landscape analysis. Taking his cue from the cultural Marxism of Berger, Barrell, and Williams, Cosgrove argues that this definition of landscape arose along with capitalist social relations, which fostered a vision of land as property to be owned, managed, and viewed. Land was physically shaped as a thing to be viewed, as property that provided pleasure in the facts of ownership visually displayed, usually to other landowners and at the expense of the less pleasant, gritty facts of labor and production.[26]

In a foreword written for his recently reprinted book, Cosgrove links the conditions of its original publication in part to the humanistic challenge to the scientific method and to the desire "to incorporate into the discipline an open acceptance of subjective modes of study"—modes of study that aimed to decipher a people's consciousness, intent, and meaning. That he sought to do so through Marxism also involved him in some specific debates, especially concerning the historical transition from feudalism to capitalism and the relations between base and superstructure. Cosgrove, no longer a Marxist in more recent work, nonetheless frames a new idiom for landscape study: it ought to *historicize* subjectivity and *politicize* it in some sort of coherent, theoretical framework.[27]

From this perspective, the fourth landscape discourse has an important similarity to the first, landscape as landschaft. Here again, landscape is construed as a specific social formation, a specific cultural practice, which means that—unlike the second and third landscape discourses—it has a beginning and possible ending. It is a historical narrative. Yet, the similarity stops there. For Cosgrove, capitalist social relations gave birth to the need for a reconceptualization of landscape, while for Stilgoe, capitalism brought landscape to an end. For the former, landscape is a type of lie we live with; for the latter, it is a truth we have lost. The appeal of the landscape discourse invoked by Cosgrove is that it could potentially be applied to the present, in as much as capitalism lives on.

At the same time, Cosgrove reminds us that there is more to capitalism than its social, economic, and cultural spaces: land itself. One should not miss that Cosgrove's take on landscape arose at virtually the same time as the social-spatial discourse, and that both concepts tap the Marxist root.

But during the years following publication of Cosgrove's book in the 1980s, landscape and social space tended to fold into each other in radical geography, and the usage of "social space" tended to dominate. Something was thereby lost: "the matter of nature," as geographer Margaret Fitz-Simmons put it in a stinging critique of contemporary radical geography published in *Antipode*.[28] Radical human geographers, taken with the analysis of society and space, were not paying nearly enough attention to the physical world and the manner in which the production of social space was also a matter of the production of "social nature": the human transformation of first nature into second nature. In this regard, the latent legacy of Cosgrove's book is that it could have preserved landscape—historicized subjectivities and land/nature inclusive—as a subject of study distinct from but related to the study of space, more than it actually did. In retrospect, Cosgrove's book is more tantalizing than ever. It teases with the idea that, as opposed to the second landscape discourse, landscape is not just anything we want it to be, but rather is profitably seen as (1) a *historicized, politicized* formation specific to Western capitalism and (2) the ongoing creation of "social nature."

While Cosgrove has a very specific argument to make about landscape and capitalism, his thesis also belongs to a larger family of arguments, which takes as its subject all the ways in which actual material places and their design can be traced to specific ideologies of any sort. Seen this way, Cosgrove's book, Yi-Fu Tuan's canonical *Topophilia* (published in 1974), and James Duncan's *City as Text* (from 1990) are nearly siblings, despite their respective Marxist, structuralist, and poststructuralist approaches. The analysis of landscape as the material expression of some individual or group notion of the ideal has since been applied to a wide range of planned places, from urban street grids, suburban cul-de-sacs, and parkways to palace grounds and backyard garden designs. In sum, these studies of landscape as ideology explore the meta-argument that ideas can have material consequences that naturalize and many times conceal those very ideas.[29]

Landscape analysts who have examined these material consequences in order to discover what ideas hide in the material built environment and whom they protect—analysts who are interested in how landscape works as spectacle—have done some of the best service to landscape studies.[30] This is because, among other things, they pose landscape *as* an idea (usually a hegemonic idea held by a power elite) and, for the most part, challenge such ideas on egalitarian grounds. Yet such work will always have to proceed with caution, for two reasons. One is that the ideological power of designed places is not necessarily synonymous with what happens in those places. Hegemony is not destiny. Michel de Certeau warns precisely against this assumption in *The Practice of Everyday Life*. He urges spatial analysts to sensitize themselves to the everyday defiance of and ongoing negotiation with planned, gridded space, a notion for which Cosgrove and Duncan (not to mention J.B. Jackson) have considerable sympathy, and which Don Mitchell has especially confronted in *The Lie of the Land*.[31] Warnings such as Certeau's, along with a general crisis among geographers over how they should represent social and cultural practice—let alone why and for whom such work should be done—have inspired a small methodological revolution: geographers are turning their attention to fine-grained, ethnographic approaches developed in anthropology and sociology in order to ferret out the hidden details of resisted, negotiated landscape.[32]

But the warning needs to be reiterated, with a second reason to be cautious. Everyday forms of agency and resistance threaten to become trivialized. Agency and resistance, once pushed to the margins, now appear to be everywhere. Perhaps with the theorization of the pedestrian has come the pedestrianization of theory. The initial motives were sound enough: through the use of social theory, geographers learned that the point of their discipline was to study (and change) society, and therefore, landscape ought to be seen critically as a vector of social injustice. Landscape, seen this way, thus became its own reason for study. But through the social theory lens, geographers now see instances of oppression, domination, and exploitation everywhere; they see resistance and politics on all sides. A new set of questions now arises for the new millennium, as Harvey and others have indicated.[33] What are the forms of resistance and agency that really count, as we contemplate a plausible, socially just society? Which forms are to be supported and nurtured? Which forms have yet to be initiated? Of course, everything is political, but perhaps some things are more political, more urgent than others? In what ways, if at all, can landscape study, and the conception of landscape, help with answers to these questions? Are J.B. Jackson's celebrations of the great improvised, vernacular spaces of America enough?

ON THE BRINK: FORGET THE PLUMAGE, PITY THE DYING BIRD

Different landscape concepts rest on different ontologies, on varying notions of what the world is like and what's worth pointing out about it—

that much we can depend on. And very worthwhile for new conceptions and studies of landscape will be a discourse that defines landscape as a necessary and integral component of reconstructed, more just social relations. What is also needed is a concept of landscape that helps point the way to those interventions that can bring about much greater social justice. And what landscape study needs even more is a concept of landscape that will assist the development of the very idea of social justice. To achieve this, geographers and other landscape analysts will need to engage in a more sustained conversation with the disciplines of moral and political philosophy concerning the enumeration of basic human rights and the modes of their defense. To date, our labors on landscape have brought us only so far. We have invoked the landschaft only to romanticize or misremember the past. Alternatively, under the sign of everyday landscape, we have expertly charted vernacular environments of all kinds, only to lose ourselves in the terra incognita of relativism. We have turned to the epistemological landscape as a way of reading our own palms for some hidden truth we need to know about ourselves as a society, while, as David Smith concludes, forsaking the social imaginary per se. We have proposed an apocryphal landscape that, in giving material expression to ideas, cannot but reflect ideology and dissemblance. And no sooner do we appreciate that ideology is not utterly hegemonic, than we see forms of resistance everywhere without a meaningful political compass. It could be that the landscape concept is as good as it's going to get, even when the scale is enlarged enough to incorporate what Doreen Massey calls the "global sense of place."[34]

But are the insights about social existence that these landscape concepts afford the keys to social change? Can they tell us what kinds of social change are needed? Landscape scholars should not simply assume that landscape study has a place in what is to be done.[35] Our efforts to intervene in landscape must be tested against a whole set of other issues: the concern for security, safety, and joy in one's work; the struggle for wages that guarantee a share in the good life; the question of who gets to decide what work is, what work gets done, and what goods get made; the fight against excessive personal and corporate accumulation of wealth and power; the idolatry of the market.[36] The list could go on, but the study of landscape, that thing which so often evokes the plane on which normal, everyday life is lived—precisely *because* of the premium it places on the everyday—must stand up to the facts of a world in crisis, to the fact that the condition of everyday life is, for many people, the interruption or destruction of everyday life. Is this a question of putting landscape analysis aside? Not really. Rather, we might take up the project of devising a normative discourse on landscape that defines landscape as a social arrangement, and a society-nature arrangement, to be brought into being. What I am proposing is difficult to think through, to say the least, and I do no more than try to name a set of problems here. Moreover, the literatures of moral and political philosophy are themselves daunting, dense, and full of disagreement (one expects no less!), while the material world changes daily. For woven through the places where we live, holding them together individually and collectively, are lines of connectivity, now global in scope. These impose the nearly impossible burden of having to sort out our allegiances—why should a people's allegiances remain local, or regional, or national? "How far should we care?" as David Smith puts it.[37] Where would the landscape yet to be defined and achieved begin, and where would it end?

It is possible to expect too much from the concept of landscape, but none other than J.B. Jackson suggested raising the bar. (As has that senior teacher to many students of landscape, Henry Glassie, whose recent book offers some pointed reminders about political commitment—and the explicitly leftist tradition—in material culture study.)[38] The questions concerning morals, ethics, and political commitment—the tension between landscape as "positive" and "normative" study—are trumpeted in an early Jackson essay, "To Pity the Plumage and Forget the Dying Bird."[39] What was the point of local beautification efforts, Jackson wondered, if local economies were in the throes of abject poverty? If landscape was to be about not only surfaces, but also alertness to social structure, and to fairness and justice, Jackson reminded us it would also have to be about questioning how far the study of landscape can take us and how landscape could be redefined in terms of concern with social and economic justice. And it would have to be about whether it even made sense to start with landscape. Alas, Jackson did not answer the question, even though he concluded that any definition of a beautiful landscape would have to include the full participation of all and the economic means to do so. In that essay a concept of landscape began to form that included at its heart a notion of human capability. We could do worse than return to that sort of thinking. Certainly, there are now more guideposts than ever in the fast-growing literatures of social justice, including the work of Iris Marion Young, whose controversial thoughts on those built environments and spatial arrangements that might foster the formation and protection of group rights have been of much interest to geographers. Her work, and the work of numerous others, has helped promulgate an incipient social justice "turn" in human geography.[40] Rereading Jackson's essay reminds me that we have been too fond, on the one hand, of thinking that landscape is "good to think" because it lets us see things in their contexts; on the other hand, we have been less fond of putting landscape and landscape study into context. Either way, much is at stake, and only a return to the social imaginary will tell us why.

RICHARD H. SCHEIN

NORMATIVE DIMENSIONS OF LANDSCAPE

12

American cultural landscapes have many interpreters. Academics and scholars from a half dozen fields—architects, landscape architects, and other design practitioners; historic preservationists; planners; and even commercial developers—all share a fascination with the tangible, visible scene that transcends disciplinary boundaries. In moments of optimism, this professional fascination is shared with the group that so many writers fervently hope exists, that is, the "lay audience" of men and women who actually notice their everyday surroundings and ask questions about its order, form, history, and meaning. While professional and lay fascination may be shared, educational backgrounds vary widely. Thus it is unreasonable to expect that all people stand on common ground when it comes to defining terms, recognizing or claiming philosophical stances, or even agreeing on exactly how to delineate the cultural landscape itself. Consequently, there are disagreements and debates about such issues. The disagreements and debates can be academic, when they are played out on the pages of scholarly journals, or more informal, as in the implicit assumptions underlying a particular "take" on the landscape. Other discordances arise from the simple fact that some landscape enthusiasts of different backgrounds barely know that the others exist.

These disagreements and debates are central to landscape study. They are the essential mechanisms through which our ability to understand and appreciate the cultural landscape and its role in American life is honed and improved. While dwelling exclusively upon the more conceptual or theoretical aspects of landscape study can seem a rather esoteric or arcane—even tedious—exercise, nevertheless it is an important responsibility. The task generally is made easier, and clearer, through empirical explication, by "grounding" the discussion in real places where the cultural landscape is implicated in the everyday lives of real people. This essay will do that. What follows is, first, a discussion revolving around the theoretical question of landscape's normativity, which will be, second, grounded in several examples of racialized landscapes, places where American ideas about race take tangible, visible form, and where those forms and ideas not only speak about some collective American past, but also serve as cultural signposts toward our collective future.

THE CONCEPTUAL ISSUE

While commenting on a theoretically dense essay on the cultural landscape, Donald Meinig wrote to me that "one basic matter that never comes through in these ever so serious presentations . . . is . . . any sense of aesthetic appreciation, of sheer pleasure and personal satisfaction, from the lifelong activity of landscape looking, and contemplation, and the sort of thing I found so attractive in Hoskins and Jackson."[1] This sentiment no doubt resonates with many landscape scholars and enthusiasts. The sheer pleasure and personal satisfaction gained from the view, from the assemblage of the landscape, is what first drew most of us to landscape study. We may then have been excited by understanding how landscapes work, by studying their histories, their meanings, and their place in American life. Yet the distinction implied between aesthetic appreciation and serious theoretical considerations of landscape also is troubling. An aesthetic appreciation is not simply reducible to the vagaries of individual understanding, for individuals themselves are inextricably part of a social and cultural order; their "beholding eye" is not autonomous, but is bound up with experience and training in a larger world. Nor is the "aesthetic" an objective, natural, essentialized category of understanding in a modern world. A contemporary landscape aesthetic is reliant upon vision and, often, shared notions of spatial order, which in turn constitute an episte-mology; and that epistemology, like other seemingly "commonsense" ap-proaches to social life, is a product of its place and time.[2] Recognizing that the aesthetics of landscape transcend individual interpretation, are un-avoidably embedded in various social contexts, and are not universally understood or agreed upon is a distinctly antimodernist perspective. It is redolent of J. B. Jackson's own approach to the cultural landscape and leads to an awareness of the normative dimensions of any landscape and of any landscape interpretation.

At its simplest, the idea of the "normative" has to do with prescribing norms, of suggesting what *ought* to be. The meanings of the word can be traced to a combination of the investigations of logic, aesthetics, and ethics, as if these things should be considered inseparable and always in concert. J.B. Jackson, especially in his pseudonymous moments, appears to have held to that inseparability, at least regarding the cultural landscape. He wrote, "to be a part of a landscape, to derive our identity from it is an essential precondition of our being-in-the-world, in the most solemn meaning of that phrase." He continues, "no landscape, vernacular or oth-erwise, can be comprehended unless we perceive it as an organization of space; unless we ask ourselves who owns or uses those spaces, how they were created and how they change."[3]

Helen Lefkowitz Horowitz has reminded us that in *Landscape* maga-zine's opening essay, Jackson bound the aesthetic with other concerns. Seeing the landscape from the air, Jackson wrote, "stirs us not only be-cause of its beauty and vastness but because of its meaning." By the mag-azine's second year, Jackson was calling for a human geography that in-cluded a focus on "Man the inhabitant's effort to re-create heaven on earth," a normative turn if ever there were one.[4] It does not require a great leap of faith to see in Jackson's writings—or perhaps more often in the writings of his pseudonymous Ajax, A.W. C., A.W. Conway, and H.G. West—a morality that could easily move from cultural criticism to nor-mative prescription—and thus link the two. As Jackson put it in 1963, "We are *not* spectators; the human landscape is *not* a work of art." Jackson noted that we can (or ought to) find new criteria for evaluating the worth of a human landscape not by focusing on its "esthetic qualities or its ca-pacity for making money," but rather by "abandoning the spectator stance and seeking to identify ourselves and our desires with the landscape, by asking ourselves how any man would fare who had to live in it. What chances does it offer for freedom of choice of action? What chances for meaningful relationships with other men and with the landscape itself? What chances for individual fulfillment and for social change?"[5] These concerns presage by thirty years a set of debates, or more accurately a theoretical (r)evolution (minus an attention to gender specificity) within geographical literatures on landscape, at least, that attempt to centrally position the cultural landscape within ongoing processes of social and cultural reproduction.

One of the most cited quotations regarding the American cultural landscape comes from Peirce Lewis: "The human landscape is our unwitting autobiography, reflecting our tastes, our values, our aspiration, and even our fears, in tangible, visible form."[6] Very few landscape scholars would disagree with this observation. Indeed, we often read any number of landscapes to make claims about the past and about contemporary social change. Yet this approach to the cultural landscape suggests that landscape primarily is the *result* of human activity, material evidence that can be read to make any number of cultural observations. In many ways, this formulation is the hallmark of an empiricist scientific tradition in cultural geography that, in a sense, leaves the landscape itself out of social and cultural processes (it is inert and exists as the detritus or spoor of cultural activity). That tradition, and its underlying assumptions, have since been the subject of twenty years of theoretical reformulations, which have been wide ranging. They have included questioning the underlying assumptions or key concepts in landscape interpretation (for instance, asking just who, or what, is the "culture" in a cultural landscape, or pushing further the textual metaphor of reading);[7] highlighting the ontological and epistemological origins and ramifications of the landscape concept (for example, linking landscape to epistemologies of vision and spatial order);[8] and contextualizing our understanding of ordinary landscapes through interpretive lenses such as gender, class, race, power, and political economy.[9] Along the way, postempiricist links have been forged between landscape interpretation and the social theory of Michel Foucault, Michel de Certeau, and Pierre Bourdieu.[10]

In short, postempiricist approaches to cultural landscapes have begun taking seriously the assumption behind J.B. Jackson's concern for the landscape as capable of providing for social change. The cultural landscape is not merely the result of human activity. It is both a material thing and a conceptual framing of the world—a visual and spatial epistemology. As such, the cultural landscape is an important, even constitutive, part of social and cultural processes (no longer simply inert, or just detritus or spoor, but something central to the reproduction of human activity).

Through its symbolic qualities, the cultural landscape serves to naturalize or concretize—to normalize—social relations. Additionally, the landscape's normalizing, normative capabilities simultaneously make the landscape central to the ongoing production and reproduction of place and identity. The cultural landscapes of the United States reflect and are symbolic of individual activity and cultural ideals, as they simultaneously are central to the constitution and reinforcement of those very ideals.[11] In short, the landscape is not innocent. Its role in mediating social and cultural reproduction works through its ability to stand for something: norms, values, fears, and so on. Through our ability to read landscapes, those very norms, values, and fears are perpetuated, reproduced, or challenged. This power of landscape makes it inescapably normative.

RACIALIZED LANDSCAPES

To illustrate these normative dimensions of landscape, I will rely here on several examples of racialized landscapes—American cultural landscapes that are particularly implicated in racist practice and the perpetuation of (or challenge to) racist social relations. These examples are all drawn from work in progress, which is focused on St. Louis, Missouri, and Lexington, Kentucky. They all deal with "race" in the sense of black-white relations, primarily because my ideas about racialized landscapes have been honed in Lexington, a city that is historically embedded in white-black relations above other racial and ethnic categories. Furthermore, most of these examples are about the white construction (and here, deconstruction) of particular landscapes. Such is the state of the work in progress. None of this is to deny the utility of the concepts presented here for a broad, nonessentialized understanding of race to include any racialized group in an American context. Nor is it to deny the importance of a normalized whiteness in the American cultural landscape, or the conceptual "othering" that takes place in white "pure" spaces vis-à-vis black "dirty" spaces. Nor is this to suggest that African Americans are completely powerless and unable to either effect their own landscapes or to resist those foisted upon them by a dominant white, racist hegemony.[12]

The sociologists Michael Omi and Howard Winant have described the concept of *racial formation* as "the socio-historical process by which racial categories are created, inhabited, transformed, and destroyed." Additionally, racial formation "is a process of historically situated *projects* in which human bodies and social structures are represented and organized." The concept of race becomes a matter of "both social structure and cultural representation," and the ideological linkages between those moments of racial formation take place through racial projects.[13] Clearly, a racialized landscape is a racial project, one that is not only sociohistorical, but also sociospatial. As such, a racialized landscape serves to naturalize, make normal, or provide the means to challenge racial formations and racist practices.[14]

It is not hard to imagine a cultural landscape reflecting dominant norms and values regarding race in the United States. For example, we need only trace the twentieth-century historical geographies of racial zoning, racial covenants, and redlining by banks, realtors, and mortgage lending agencies to realize the extent of an American apartheid undergirded by racist ideology.[15] And it does not require a great leap of the imagination to see how, once inscribed upon the earth's surface, such spatial orderings and their concomitant cultural landscapes perpetuate racist ideologies and practices. The archives of the Missouri Historical Society preserve a map showing African Americans as a percentage of total population in St. Louis, by census district, taken from the 1930 census (fig. 12.1). The map shows three distinct concentrations of African Americans in the city's east-central and north-central areas. Those areas displaying a dense concentration of African Americans (ranging from 37 to 73 percent of the tract's total population) are confined by a boundary line on the map, labeled the "Negro District (Real Estate Exchange)."

Here is a case of redlining based on racial prejudice, in which particular areas of the city were cordoned off as financial danger zones on the basis of their African American population (fig. 12.2). This racism not only reflected common financial practices in 1930, but also contributed to future disinvestment and the downward spiral of livability for a racialized inner-city landscape.[16] In time, the appearance of such inner-city cultural landscapes became seen as "naturally decayed," something unavoidably associated with African American "ghettos." The mere sight—and site—of such ghettos, as racialized landscapes, became associated with allegedly inexorable city life cycles, with the "normal" machinations of urban sociospatial processes.[17]

Another example drawn from St. Louis begins with a streetcar suburb opened three miles beyond the city limits in 1893. Kinloch Park (fig. 12.3) was meant for white suburban expansion, but an apocryphal tale suggests that through the agency of a white Kinloch resident who saw the need for servants immediately proximate to the new subdivision, several African Americans were able to settle in the tract's southeast corner; this last

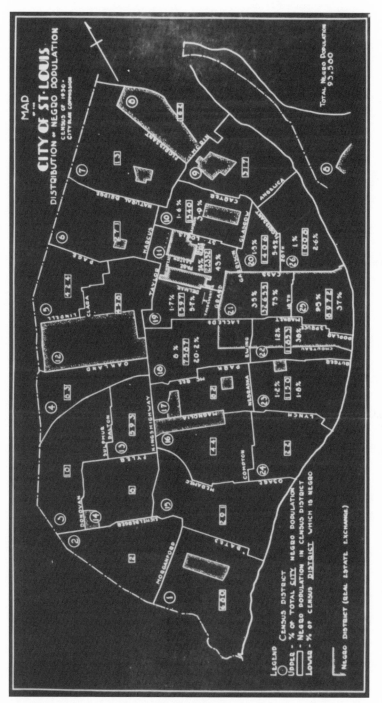

Figure 12.1. Map of the City of St. Louis, 1930. This map illustrates the process of redlining by highlighting what the city's real estate exchange termed the "Negro district." North is to the right; at the bottom of the map is the Mississippi River.

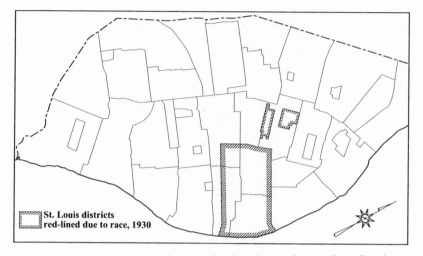

St. Louis districts
red-lined due to race, 1930

Figure 12.2. St. Louis, 1930. This map clearly indicates the racially redlined districts.

point, at least, is verified by another early map of the area (fig. 12.4). The subsequent demand for house lots by African Americans prompted the Olive Street Terrace Realty Company to purchase farmland immediately adjacent to Kinloch (around and including the Henry Lix farm, shown in fig. 12.3) and to lay out South Kinloch Park exclusively for African Americans, who moved there over the next twenty-plus years.

Although South Kinloch Park was intended for African Americans, the realty company insisted upon first selling the lots there to white investors, who immediately resold them to African Americans at a standard 100 percent profit rate. Apparently, the realty company was unable to use "Negro" purchase notes as secure collateral on bank loans, thus prompting this scheme, whereby the white realty company and its investors made handsome gains.

The establishment of an all-black suburb created a cultural landscape reflecting racist practices at the time. Furthermore, the suburb's timing was propitious, for it coincided with broader, even national, racial issues. In the eastern and midwestern United States, this period is known for the burgeoning northward migration of African Americans. Regionally, the East St. Louis race riots in 1917 intersected with that migration. In a general context of white animosity toward competition from newly arrived black (and foreign) labor, African Americans were the victims of white prejudice that stemmed from a union strike in 1917. The months of May, June, and July, especially, saw daily harassment and beatings of African

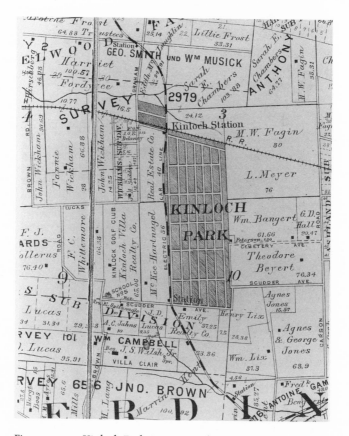

Figure 12.3. Kinloch Park, Missouri. The original street grid of this 1893 "streetcar suburb" can still be seen in the contemporary St. Louis landscape. The neighborhood is now due east of St. Louis Lambert International Airport and the Interstate 170 corridor. North is to the top of the map.

American workers in East St. Louis, and many black residents fled for St. Louis proper, across the river.[18] The proposal of a racial zoning ordinance for St. Louis in 1916 and the pending U.S. Supreme Court case of *Buchanan v. Warley*, which would overturn the legality of racial zoning (1917), were acknowledged by the developers of South Kinloch Park as incentives for real estate sales.[19]

South Kinloch Park must have seemed paradoxical to its residents at the time, serving as both a safe haven of sorts for the many African Americans who had moved there by 1920, and as an example of forced segregation in the context of broader Jim Crow–era discrimination. In ad-

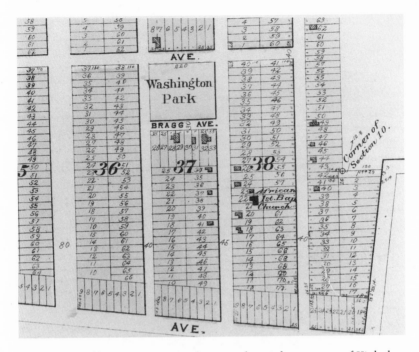

Figure 12.4. African American residences in the southeast corner of Kinloch Park, mostly along Jefferson, Washington, and Jackson Avenues. Note the presence of the African First Baptist Church.

dition to reflecting contemporary racist practices (and, perhaps, middle- and working-class African American preferences for a relatively secure residential environment), South Kinloch Park also came to stand for normal practice and thus became, as a racialized landscape, a normative one as well. Here, as in many places throughout the United States, was a seemingly benign solution, in the form of residential segregation, to the "problem" of mixing the races.

This solution, which perhaps seemed so normal in the 1920s, had reached its extremes by the 1990s. South Kinloch Park today is known simply as Kinloch, and it is visible from the air by passengers landing at Lambert International Airport as a seemingly abandoned and overgrown green space in the midst of the suburban sprawl of St. Louis County. If you rent a car at the airport and try to drive into Kinloch, the task will be daunting, for the area is virtually cordoned off by what is locally known as the "Kinloch wall"; only a few through streets connect its internal street grid to the greater St. Louis street network. In the 1920s, after

South Kinloch Park was clearly established as an African American suburb, the surrounding white suburb of Berkeley and the black South Kinloch Park "divorced"; the town of Kinloch was incorporated in 1948, becoming one of a handful of all black towns in the United States.[20] The core of the newly incorporated Kinloch was the original South Kinloch Park subdivision, but it also included those lots in the original (ostensibly all white) Kinloch Park that had first been sold to black servants. Although Kinloch appears to have seen a brief period of prosperity, today it is only a remnant of its former self.

All-black towns did not become the norm across the American landscape, but Kinloch, as a seemingly natural course of (sub)urban development, served as a racialized, normative landscape, capturing both the negative aspects of the ideology of forced segregation and the potentially positive social ideas of black self-governance and economic security in the face of overwhelmingly racist odds. The case of nearby Berkeley reminds us that African American landscapes are not the only ones that are racialized and normative. The acceptance of the original Kinloch Park's "all white" status is the other side of the sociospatial coin, which speaks to the tacit understanding that, for the most part, suburbs in the United States are white. Donald Meinig has written that the suburban landscape in the United States is a particularly salient symbol of nationhood, of who we are as a people, especially at the turn of the twentieth century.[21] Yet not surprisingly, most images of the suburbs are images of whiteness.[22]

Two other salient examples come from Lexington, Kentucky, a prosperous city of approximately a quarter million residents that reigns over the urban hierarchy of central and eastern Kentucky.[23] Lexington was founded in the late eighteenth century as part of the westward-moving American urban frontier. The city enjoyed a brief period as the primary entrepot of the urban West, but its inability to industrialize enough to compete with nearby Louisville and Cincinnati forced the city to draw upon its cultural heritage as an outgrowth of plantation Virginia, and it became known as the Athens of the West. For most of the nineteenth century, the city remained the Fayette County seat, an elite-dominated market center for the fertile livestock, hemp, and tobacco lands in the surrounding Bluegrass region. By the time of the Civil War, the county's population was evenly divided between blacks and whites; by 1870, the city itself reflected that same demographic profile, as numerous African Americans fled the central Kentucky countryside in the war's aftermath.

The city remained a regional economic and social center in the waning years of the nineteenth century, but it also began to be known along na-

tional, and eventually international, circuits of capital as northern industrialists bought in to the region's horse farms; it was then that the region's signature landscape of "gentleman horse farms" was created as a
place of conspicuous consumption.[24] These developments did little to
change the existing social structure of the agricultural and mercantile
inner Bluegrass, however, which had long been divided along general lines
of white-black and rich-poor—except, perhaps, to introduce national so-
cialites to central Kentucky. Those members of the national elite inter-
acted with central Kentuckians through their sympathies with the local
elite, or by employing labor on the farms and racetracks. Only after World
War II did Lexington really begin to join the twentieth century, primarily
by attracting clean industry such as IBM and General Electric and
through the dramatic expansion of the University of Kentucky thanks to
the G.I. Bill. Today, Lexington is perhaps a postindustrial city, with less
than 3 percent unemployment. It relies on the university and the service
economy for the bulk of its economic activity. The city is, for the most
part, a rich place, a migration destination, with no rust-belt industrial decline or decay and no out-migration.

In many ways, however, Lexington is struggling to join the twenty-
first century, especially in terms of its race relations or, more accurately, in
terms of the structural imperatives of racism that are embedded in so
many of the city's social, economic, and political institutions. The city still
embodies in many ways its nineteenth-century legacy, including its cultural landscape and its social relations. Perhaps the most obvious reminder
of this legacy is the courthouse square, centrally located and displaying
the usual plaques and statuary of such civic spaces, which are especially
prevalent in the South, where the county is the most important unit of
local government. Although the square contains memorials to veterans
and crime victims of the twentieth century and at least one historic plaque
about the county's first schoolhouse, it is dominated by statues celebrating the Confederacy. For example, on the front lawn of the courthouse
stands an enormous statue of General John Hunt Morgan astride his
horse (fig. 12.5). Morgan was a Lexingtonian, a historical rogue of sorts,
and he is venerated as the "Raider of the Confederacy" for his exploits in
Kentucky and Tennessee, which successfully diverted Union troops from
the primary battle lines.

The northwest side of the courthouse is known as "Cheapside," and it,
too, displays reminders that although Kentucky was officially neutral during the Civil War, the plantation-dominated Bluegrass was somewhat
more certain of its sympathies. If you ask local folks about the origin of

Figure 12.5. The John Hunt Morgan statue on the courthouse lawn, Lexington, Kentucky.

the name Cheapside, and you are not met with blank stares, you are likely to get one of two answers: either the site was named after the London market of the same name (and central Kentucky, like Virginia, is an Anglophilic place); or the name refers to the fact that, because "better quality" slaves were sold in nearby trader's shops, only the "poorest quality" slaves were sold at auction, and the so-called cheap side of the courthouse was indeed the site of an infamous slave market where surplus labor was sold down the Ohio River to the westward-migrating cotton belt.

Contemporary Cheapside contains no reminder of that infamy. The market's exact site is dominated by a statue of John Breckinridge, variously vice president of the United States and a U.S. senator before he officially joined the Confederate cause and rose to become the Confederate secretary of war. Yet this is undoubtedly a racialized landscape, one that captures in its historical form the Confederate sympathies of central Kentucky, albeit sympathies that resurfaced only toward the end of the nineteenth century, when the statuary was erected.[25] Throughout the post-Reconstruction South, the beginnings of Jim Crow were marked with similar local testimonies to the Lost Cause, and the result was a normative landscape standing for what ought to have been and, by implication, for what ought to be. In a more contemporary sense, Cheapside is still a normative landscape of slavery and racism, simply through the seeming invisibility of those ideas on the site—at least to the uninitiated, usually white visitor; many African American Lexingtonians are all too aware of the site's legacy, for they carry an alternative mental map of the city that continues to mark such sites through oral tradition. Most white Americans believe that the past is irrelevant, particularly regarding slaveholding in the South. And many whites also believe that the civil rights gains of the 1950s and 1960s have eliminated all vestiges of the racism so evident in slavery's social formation, despite mounting evidence of a civil rights backslide in recent years.

Cheapside continues to be a racialized landscape in that it masks the full story of the square's (and the region's) past, favoring the glories of the Confederacy over the shame of its best-known socioeconomic institution. And it is normative in its tacit perpetuation of the assumption that what "ought to be" forgotten is the place of Lexington in that world of the past, even though so many of the city's contemporary social issues can be directly traced to the institution of slavery, and to the influx of former slaves to the city after 1865. Issues as seemingly diverse as residential segregation patterns, the occupational structure at the University of Kentucky, support for public transportation, and downtown redevelopment schemes still bear the traces of nineteenth-century racial patterns and processes.

The normative role of cultural landscapes is also exhibited in Lexington's recently constructed Thoroughbred Park, about six blocks southeast of the courthouse (fig. 12.6). Lexington's twenty-first-century prosperity is not readily evident in its central-city landscape. The city decentralized with a vengeance in the mid-twentieth century, and its galactic-city urban morphology makes it like hundreds of other American cities and towns whose strip shopping centers and suburban malls are doing fine while the central business district languishes from economic abandonment. Like so many U.S. cities, Lexington sought a remedy through entrepreneurial action in the 1980s and formed several public-private partnerships in order to reshape its downtown, in terms of both activity and image.[26] One of those partnerships created Thoroughbred Park, although in an unusual variation on the national theme, the partnership was more private than public. Thoroughbred Park was essentially a gift to the city from the Triangle Foundation, a local nonprofit group of horsemen and businessmen. The Triangle Foundation first acquired the land in five separate parcels that now make up the 3.1-acre park. It then raised eight million dollars—

Figure 12.6. Thoroughbred Park, Lexington, Kentucky. Bronze horses race to the finish pole in this recently built park east of the city's courthouse square.

including donations of half a million dollars or more from local enterprises such as Toyota Motor Manufacturing, Ashland Oil, a famous horse farm, and the Humana Corporation—and hired a sculptor and a nationally known landscape architect. By 1992 the Triangle Foundation was able to donate the completed park to the city. It is a remarkable space on first glance, and that glance is best achieved from an automobile approaching from the south. Superbly crafted lifelike bronze horses race to a finish line, backed by a series of fountains, all in front of a rolling hillside reminiscent of the Bluegrass countryside, including a reference to the region's famous stone fences and more bronze horses grazing in the near distance.

Lexington's mayor praised the park and the Triangle Foundation as catalysts for downtown rejuvenation. The local newspaper heralded the site's transformation from one of urban decay to one of pastoral beauty. The president of the venerated local thoroughbred racetrack called the whole package an example of common enterprise for the public good. A past president of the foundation claimed that there could be no more appropriate a park than this one, symbolizing Lexington's international equine reputation. The landscape architects proclaimed that the countryside imagery of the park captured the essence of the region. Newspaper headlines boldly praised the park for capturing the city's identity and noted that it was universally admired.[27]

Yet all is not as it might seem; we need to look this gift horse in the mouth. Thoroughbred Park is a racialized landscape, best interpreted through an attention to its site and its imagery. The park is strategically located at one terminus of the central city's one-way street system; it is visible by automobile only from two roads that approach the central city from the primary suburban ring and two major interstate highway exits. It is the southern gateway to the central city. The site is also a node in a century-old historical geography, a place that joins and separates several functional areas of the city. The site of Thoroughbred Park was once the spot that joined the city's retail zone along Main Street; its wholesale and industrial district, focused on a railroad corridor that crossed Main Street at that point; and two residential districts. The first was a white, middle-class zone extending southwest from the central business district along a streetcar line, the second an African American residential district that had grown from a small urban appendage created to house newly freed blacks at the end of the Civil War.

By the 1890s, the future park site had housed a lumberyard and a hemp factory, among other commercial uses. To cross from the African American residential district into the burgeoning middle-class white suburb required a pedestrian to cross no fewer than a dozen railroad tracks and sidings and to negotiate any number of quasi-industrial hazards. By the 1980s, when Thoroughbred Park was first conceived, the site had changed in the particulars of occupation, but not in its function. The hemp factory and lumberyards were long gone, the railroad had been rerouted around the city, and auto-related businesses marked the southern edge of the central business district, but the scene appeared run-down, and it still demarcated a sharp socioeconomic gradient between the southwest part of the city (96 percent white, with average housing values over $100,000 and average rents greater than $600 a month) and the northeast part (86 percent African American, $25,000 average housing values, and less than $150 average monthly rent), known locally as the "East End" and coded as the ghetto. The new Thoroughbred Park hillside displaying the grazing horses was literally built for the park to effectively hide the East End from view for anyone approaching the central city (fig. 12.7). The hill visually masks the ghetto and funnels travelers onto Main Street. Thoroughbred Park, occupying a critical node in the city's long-standing social geography, has been captured by the dominant (white) power interests and made to reify and normalize traditional social boundaries of urban racial and class segregation. For anyone driving into the city, the East End is now out of sight and out of mind. More complexly, the park's siting suggests not

Figure 12.7. Thoroughbred Park, Lexington, Kentucky. A newly built hill representing the rolling central Kentucky countryside hides Lexington's East End from the view of passing motorists.

only benign neglect of the inner city, but also an active attempt to hem in and discipline, by partition and enclosure, a less-than-desirable space in the eyes of the powers that be.[28]

Beyond capturing space, the re-creation of this node as Thoroughbred Park also proclaims a victory for one vision of the past and the future of Lexington, a claim borne in no small part by the park's imagery, which is carefully constructed to represent the region's racing and breeding legacies. The images serve as historical iconography in both their form and their antecedents. The sculptor who created the park's statuary, Gwen Reardon, was meticulous in her attention to detail. In her own words, she was "real obsessive about knowing my subject." She traveled to the Smithsonian in order to measure the bones of the racehorse Lexington, now immortalized in the park. She obtained clothes and measurements from famous jockeys, including Willie Shoemaker and Pat Day, in order to accurately cast the figures racing the thoroughbreds to the finish pole.[29] Numerous plaques, mostly dedicated to famous and wealthy men, line one of the park's walkways, a tribute to the money and vision behind the thoroughbred industry and a hall of fame for the industry's past.

The racing imagery so elegantly displayed in Thoroughbred Park does make sense within one framework of interpretation. Horses are important to the Lexington and Bluegrass economies, and they do appear to hold a special place in the hearts of many central Kentuckians, of all ethnicities. The horse motif is widespread in the region, and Lexington is a world center of the thoroughbred industry, which can legitimately trace its roots at least to the early nineteenth century. The match between the park and the countryside is well done, and is thus seen as normal. The park is deemed authentic, and is thus legitimate. It stands for a regional identity. Indeed, the park and the Bluegrass landscape it represents are part of a long tradition of elite symbol making. Wealthy northern industrialists such as Joseph Widener, James Cox Brady, and William Wright earlier in the twentieth century hired landscape architects to create the region's signature landscape. That landscape includes the twin spires of Churchill Downs (which were, until recently, pictured on the Kentucky license plate), white or brown four-board fences and rock fences lining rolling country roads, horses grazing in the middle distance, and barns with prominent cupolas. The imagery of both the central Kentucky countryside and Thoroughbred Park thus is carefully groomed and linked by association in the popular imagination with other Kentucky traditions: mint juleps, Stephen Foster's ballad and state song ("My Old Kentucky Home"), derby hats, and perhaps even the once-ubiquitous black lawn jockeys.[30]

However, the park and the Bluegrass imagery tell only a part of the story, even of the thoroughbred industry. Stories of the stable hands and grooms, for example, are missing. There is no mention of any jockeys by name, especially not the African American jockeys who dominated an earlier era of thoroughbred racing. Where is the plaque to Isaac Murphy, for example? Murphy was an African American jockey (born in 1861) who won the Kentucky Derby three times and who still holds a record for winning 44 percent of all the races he rode. In a bit of spatial irony, many of the people missing from the park's visual story once lived just behind it, in the East End, for the region's premier racetrack prior to the 1930s was less than a half mile east of the site, at the edge of the neighborhood now hidden from view.

In Lexington in the year 2001, there appeared to be little challenge to the elite-dominated imagery that characterizes Thoroughbred Park. Such is the practice of society and politics in central Kentucky. The park reflects and perpetuates not only a particular view of the horse industry, but also a general statement about the operation of local politics. And if no one challenges the imagery of the Bluegrass landscape in particular, there is no hint of challenge to the choice of the thoroughbred as an icon, despite the importance of other industries and institutions that might claim a similar centrality to the region's identity, such as the University of Kentucky or Toyota Motor Manufacturing Corporation, or even tobacco. At the park dedication, the local newspaper noted that Thoroughbred Park is a tribute to the horse and a place that signifies heritage, family values, and the natural beauty of the Kentucky countryside.[31] Each of these claims is, of course, problematic. Still, the park is normative in its attempt to promote those ideals. As a racialized landscape, the park is a three-dimensional visual and spatial display that naturalizes long-standing social and racial practice in this part of the country, both in the form of the park and in the processes that gave it form. The park reifies Lexington's racial and spatial boundaries, boundaries that are both Cartesian and social. That it probably does not do so intentionally makes the park's normative dimensions even more insidious.

CAPTURING THE NORMATIVE

Each of the racialized landscapes described here can be seen as a kind of autobiography, in that each captures social or cultural norms, values, and fears. Each of these examples also captures in concrete form, and normalizes, some prescribed social, racial, class, economic, or political order that not only stands for the past and present, but also inescapably embodies power relations that make claims on the future. While the normative dimensions of these landscapes may be inescapable, that in no way suggests that each of these landscapes should be seen as standing for unchangeable ideas and ideals. The normative dimensions of any landscape operate at a structural level: unconsciously promoted and unrecognized as anything other than "common sense." Yet in locating these normative aspects, we open possibilities for denaturalizing the appearance and operation of that scene. The possibilities for individual agency, the power to challenge such structures, thus are heartening.

First, no landscape is ever read or used in exactly the manner intended by its creator. There is always the possibility of resistance in and through the landscape. In Thoroughbred Park, for example, there is nothing to stop a local grassroots movement focused on this now-public park from raising money in order to erect a statue or plaque to Isaac Murphy. The simple act of contributing to the visible form of the park would help subvert the elite-politics-as-usual tenor of the site, and a memorial to Murphy would stand in the future as a reminder of both the objection to one version of the park's original narrative and the important contribution of historical figures like Murphy to central Kentucky's economy and regional identity. Second, the act of calling into question the social and cultural values embedded in any cultural landscape is a great first step, even a leap, toward an approach to landscape interpretation that recognizes the protean nature of meaning and symbolism in the cultural landscape and, by implication, in the society and culture of which it is so central a part. Finally, the argument presented here is in no way meant to deny the possibilities inherent in what Stephen Daniels calls the duplicity of landscape.[32] It ought to be possible to acknowledge the normative dimensions of the cultural landscape and simultaneously take some personal pleasure from the tangible, visible scene. The real danger lies in the claim to an apolitical aesthetic serving to mask or hide or normalize potentially racist social and cultural ideals and practice, as in the cases presented here.

MARK FIEGE

PRIVATE PROPERTY AND THE ECOLOGICAL COMMONS IN THE AMERICAN WEST

13

Travel through the rural American West and, sooner or later, you will come across a seemingly innocuous sign. Usually metal or cardboard, a little rusty or weathered, it is often fixed to a wood post in a fence strung with barbed wire. It faces outward, toward the public right-of-way, perhaps a road, trail, forest, prairie, or stream. To its rear is a private landscape, private property, filled with pasture or crops but also grass, brush, trees, and other plants. It states in bold letters: NO HUNTING, or NO HUNTING WITHOUT PERMISSION, or PRIVATE PROPERTY—NO HUNTING, or some variation of that basic message (fig. 13.1). To the student of landscape, if not to the hunter pursuing game, it seems straightforward and uncomplicated, perhaps even a little quaint: another small, fading relic of the rural western past. You glance at the sign, but your impulse is to move on; your trained and sensitive eye perhaps already has picked out more prominent and worthwhile features of the cultural landscape. What's that over there? A log cabin? A rail fence? A hay derrick, perhaps?

Figure 13.1.　No-hunting sign, irrigated landscape, Colorado. Such markers indicate the importance of property boundaries in the cultural landscape but also suggest the ways in which nature, in this case wildlife, crosses boundaries.

But wait—if you really want to learn something new about western American landscape, you will not head off so quickly; no, you will linger for a moment and ponder the sign more intently. That small piece of the real West is not so insignificant as you might first think. Indeed, it carries a meaning, and contains a history, far deeper than the surface message that it projects. So ignore the cabin, the rail fence, and the hay derrick for a moment. Contemplate the sign, unpack and examine its deeper meaning, and take a fresh look at western American landscape and western geographic space. That sign, which at first might seem so small and inconsequential, stands at the intersection of two monumental, and sometimes opposing, forces.

One of those forces, as the sign suggests, is private property. Property rights have always been at the heart of America's attitude toward land and other natural resources. In the rural West, citizens have elevated those rights almost to the level of a religion. That sign on the fence, and others like it (PRIVATE PROPERTY, or NO TRESPASSING), are not simply warnings; they are virtual testaments of faith in an ideology built on the prem-

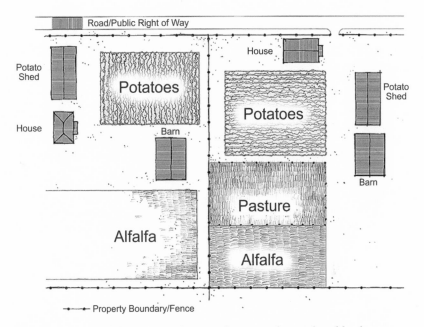

Figure 13.2. Divided nature. In the typical privatized agricultural landscape, property owners divide the land and, within each parcel, harness nature for capitalist production and to serve individual self-interest.

ise that humans can, and should, divide nature into precisely measured quantities (in this case, acres of land) that a person can own absolutely (fig. 13.2). As Senator Kay Bailey Hutchison of Texas has said, summing up much of this sentiment, "Private property, under our Constitution, is sacrosanct." And in the West this zeal has grown only stronger in recent years, as demonstrated by the property-rights movement and its belief that environmentalists, federal bureaucrats, and urban liberals are waging a "war on the West" to strip the region's people of their lands.[1]

But as powerful as it is, the property-rights ideal cannot completely withstand the pressure of an even more powerful force about which the sign on the fence only hints: nature. Private property is fixed and static; it places boundaries around parts of nature and assigns exclusive rights to the use of those parts. Yet as the sign suggests, a private property boundary and the fence that objectifies it cannot bound nature completely. Just as surely as a deer will leap over the barbed wire, so other animals, plants, microorganisms, soil, water, fire, air, sound, and other components of the biophysical will cross that boundary. And just as surely as these things will do so, humans will want to follow. The fleeing deer will tempt the hunter, and the hunter may even think, contrary to the sign and contrary to the law, that it is right to follow. In fact, when virtually any part of nature transcends the fence, so a human, in one way or another, will be tempted to cross, too. This, then, is the deeper story embedded in the NO HUNTING sign: a landscape of rigid property boundaries, a greater world of fluid ecological relationships, and the social conflicts and compromises that emerge from their interaction.

The property-rights movement, of course, denies much of this story by seeking to collapse the tension between property and ecology into a simplistic morality play in which authoritarian bureaucrats and scheming environmentalists trample on the rights of the virtuous citizenry. But it is important to understand that this current issue is but a part of an old and complex conflict between property and ecology in the American West. The fighting over modern policies such as the Endangered Species Act (passed in 1973), the power that such policies give public officials to regulate private land, and the smoldering anger of many westerners are not small problems easily dismissed. But they are only the latest chapter in a much longer and more varied history that goes back virtually to the beginning of European-American settlement in the West. Scratch the broader surface of the western American landscape, as we have scratched the surface of the NO HUNTING sign, and this history begins to come into focus.

Before we delve into the western landscape any further, however, some explanations and definitions are in order. My analysis of private property and ecology relates to a growing, vibrant body of scholarship that deals with public space in American history. This scholarship itself is related to a current national debate regarding the meaning of civic life in America.[2] Social historians, architectural historians, geographers, and other scholars have done much to illuminate the social and political conditions that have gone into the production and regulation of public spaces such as sidewalks, streets, parks, courthouse squares, shopping malls, and other sites. However, it is my contention that the inclusion of ecology—of relationships among organisms and their environments—can open another point of view in this debate. Ecological relationships generate public space as much as do social and political circumstances. Whenever and wherever these relationships (for example, an organism to its habitat) transcend property lines, and whenever and wherever human interests follow those mobile forces of nature, they in effect create a public arena in the midst of a privatized landscape. I call this form of ecological public space the *ecological commons*.[3]

This concept draws on the work of several eminent landscape scholars. The geographer Hildegard Binder Johnson pointed out some of the ways that the rectangular survey has been ill suited to ecological conditions such as varied topography. J. B. Jackson articulated the notion of the vernacular landscape: the informal, spontaneous use of space unsanctioned by official laws and rules. More recently, the geographer Edward Soja has defined what he calls "Thirdspace," a concept that attempts to encapsulate the fluid, interacting social, historical, and spatial influences on human experience. Following Johnson, the ecological commons encompasses the ways that nature transcends property boundaries that are based on the rectangular survey. Drawing on Jackson, the ecological commons describes vernacular land uses that take place in the broader ecological landscape that coexists with private-property regimes. And like Soja's Thirdspace, the ecological commons reflects the complex, simultaneous, interrelated forces that generate western American space. Like Soja, I try to resist reducing the story to simple oppositions—private versus public space, private property versus ecology—or to the simple resolution of those oppositions. Like Thirdspace, the ecological commons is a flexible, contingent space that exists in opposition to private property but also in complex relationship to it.[4]

In using the concept of the commons, I am borrowing a term that scholars have used somewhat differently from the way I use it here. In conventional parlance, a "commons" or a "common property resource" refers to spaces or resources to which a group of people exercises collective rights. Access to the space or resource is limited to that group, and strict rules govern its use. An Indian band's hunting ground, a national forest, or a river are typical examples of common spaces or resources.[5] My adaptation of the commons is not intended to counter or overturn these more conventional uses of the concept. Rather, my purpose is simply to stretch the definition to fit the ecological conditions that I find operating in the midst of private-property regimes. And indeed, my use of the term and its conventional applications are not necessarily far apart. After all, a deer herd, even one that moves across private space, can be a conventional commons resource; so can the water that flows across the private space; so, too, can any number of other moving, interrelated parts of nature. It is my argument, though, that as they move, these parts of nature (deer, for example) transform the private space itself, and the earth itself, into a sort of commons. To what extent, after all, can an organism be distinguished from its habitat, or water from the ground through which it flows? Moreover, even parts of nature that humans do not want, and which they seek to destroy (weeds, diseases, animal pests), easily cross boundaries and so compel humans to view otherwise privatized landscapes in collective and public terms.[6]

The relationship between private property, ecology, and the ecological commons, however, is best understood not through abstract explanations but through examples grounded in actual historical experience. These examples could be gathered from across the western American landscape. I will choose only a few, involving water, plants, and animals, and I will examine them as they operate across the West, but mostly in a place I know best—the irrigated landscape of the Snake River Valley in southern Idaho.[7]

Water is, perhaps, the one part of nature that most resists privatization and for which a NO TRESPASSING sign makes the least sense. The hydrologic cycle, the grand movement of water through the land and the atmosphere, in effect creates an aqueous commons that we might call, in a variation of the basic concept, the hydrological commons. As rain or snow, water falls to earth. Plants absorb and then transpire it, sending it back into the atmosphere. Some of the water trickles into aquifers. Some of it, too, passes through the moist, fleshy bodies of animals, which drink deeply and then sweat and urinate. Eventually, most of the water gathers in streams that flow to the ocean, where evaporation and cloud formation begin the cycle again. Under such conditions, water moves irrespective of the abstract lines that separate private plots of ground. A few westerners, at least, have realized this. "A lesson learned early," states the official history of Idaho's soil conservation districts, " . . . was the myth of boundary lines. . . . How one farmer manages his or her land affects the amount and kind of water and the amount of sediment that neighbors downstream must deal with. Sediment, floods, pollution, and other water problems don't stop at artificial boundary lines."[8]

But the logic of western American attitudes toward nature, including water, more often has operated in the opposite direction, toward privatization and the establishment of boundaries. And so water management in the arid West has always reflected a tension between the ideal of absolute ownership and the reality of the hydrological commons (fig. 13.3) Western irrigation farmers have tended to be fiercely possessive of this precious resource. "You can take my wife, but if you take my water I'll kill you," is a popular phrase in irrigated regions of the West, uttered only partly in jest. And irrigators will often speak of a river or stream from which they divert water to their fields as belonging to them.[9]

But to what extent can someone actually own water, possess it absolutely? Not easily, and certainly not completely. The aqueous commons of the hydrologic cycle has governed water use in the West as much as the private-property ideal has governed it. In Idaho as elsewhere, one can

Figure 13.3. Irrigation canal, Idaho Falls vicinity, early 1900s. Fluid, evanescent, seldom stationary, water resisted the drive to privatize the western American landscape. Irrigation conduits, their banks, and the water itself served as corridors for the movement of flora and fauna among farms.

legally own rights to a specific amount of water in a stream but cannot own the stream itself—after all, how can a person possess something that is perpetually moving? Only when water diverted from a stream passes onto private land, and only when the landowner uses it, does it become physical property. Even then, water's inherent instability makes its possession problematic. Water in a ditch legally may be physical property, but that water is still only a subsidiary stream in the broader commons that is the hydrologic cycle. An irrigation farmer, for example, will not use all the water that flows from a stream onto his or her land. Depending on environmental factors (mostly soil type, crop type, and the physical condition of canals and ditches), a substantial amount of water will seep into the ground, out of control and out of possession. And when that seeping water passes underneath the boundaries that separate one farm from another, the hydrological commons appears with sudden vigor. In such circumstances, private property is less important than the hydrological unity of the land (fig. 13.4).

This was a lesson that Idaho irrigation farmers learned during the 1910s and 1920s. In some areas, water from canals and farms on high ground seeped downward and waterlogged the soil of low-lying farms, making it difficult for the people there to raise crops. The water that farm-

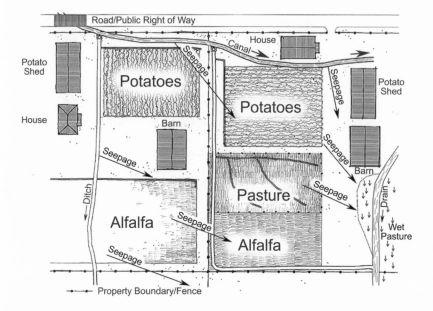

Figure 13.4. The aqueous ecological commons. Following the hydrologic cycle, surface and subsurface water crosses property boundaries and thereby links discrete, private land parcels in a hydrologically unified public landscape.

ers had so jealously guarded became, ironically, a serious nuisance. To remove the excess water, irrigation districts and companies excavated drains, deep ditches below the level of fields and canals. Most irrigators recognized that seepage and drainage were community problems and that farmers on high land, not just those occupying low ground, should pay for the drains. A few people occupying high ground, however, disagreed, and took their objections to court. Why should they be held responsible for the condition of someone else's property? But the courts found against them, and by 1925, drainage fees levied on farmers who occupied high land constituted an established principle in Idaho irrigation. Seepage had transformed a landscape of private farms into a hydrological commons, a condition that the law at least tacitly recognized.

The example of the hydrological commons shows that people cannot easily detach property from nature; or, put another way, they cannot easily detach a part of nature (such as water) and confine it within property boundaries. Nature does not work that way. And this becomes even clearer when one considers the webs of life that stretch across and unite vast areas of private land. Here again, one finds a tension between the drive to create ecologically and socially autonomous spaces and a natural world that often overwhelms such artificial divisions.

Property ownership based on the rectangular survey is in part a system of confining plants and animals in rigid spaces, boxes almost, where those living things can be made to serve individual self-interest. Within these fenced fields, pastures, and ranges, people seek to arrest and control, if not outright stop, biological processes. Here they regulate the life course—growth, maturation, and decay—and exclude and even destroy unwanted organisms. Mostly they are successful in this endeavor, as the West's abundant fields and flourishing herds demonstrate. But to what extent can landowners completely confine nature in boxes, even their crops and livestock? How autonomous—how sacrosanct—are their private spaces, really?

Much as water courses over the land, so does an astonishing array of living things. We have the example of the deer leaping the barbed-wire fence (and the hunter tempted to follow). But that is only the barest hint of the flying, crawling, floating, migrating, swirling diversity of life that passes through private land. Idaho's irrigated landscape in the early twentieth century provides an interesting case study of the life forms that have swept over private spaces and transformed them into an ecological commons. Weed after weed (Russian thistle, dodder, bindweed, and more) spread across freshly plowed soil, their seeds carried by the wind, in the fur and guts of livestock, in batches of crop seed, in railroad cars, and in the very substance that made agriculture possible in this arid place: water. Along with weeds came swarms of insects: the beet leafhopper, which carried the curly-top virus that killed sugar beets, one of the state's most lucrative crops; the alfalfa weevil, which infested the state's most important forage crop; the Mormon cricket, a voracious creature that quite literally marched, en masse, across fields, devouring plants; or the bees that flew between farms, pollinating flowering crops. Birds—geese, magpies, sparrows, and many others—moved across the land, feeding and nesting as they went. Last but not least were the mammals—gophers, ground squirrels, marmots, muskrats, beavers, badgers, jackrabbits, and coyotes—that consumed crops, burrowed into canal banks, or pursued other mammals. Like many environments in the West, the irrigated landscape was a privatized landscape, but property boundaries did virtually nothing to stop mobile organisms (fig. 13.5).

How western Americans have responded to these organisms proves the existence of the ecological commons just as surely as do the organisms themselves. When weeds, insects, diseases, birds, and mammals cross

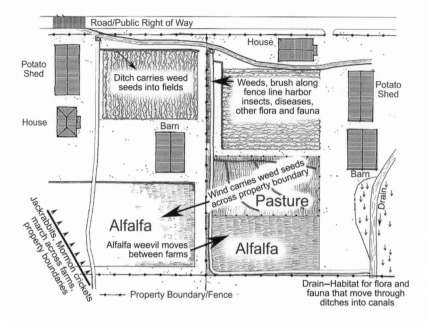

Figure 13.5. The biotic ecological commons. Uncontrolled organisms cross property boundaries, in effect creating a single biologically and socially unified public landscape.

property boundaries, they encourage people to see the landscape not just as the sum of its many private parts, but as an ecological and social whole. Irrigation farmers in Idaho in the late nineteenth and early twentieth centuries, for example, understood that they could best resist weeds, viruses, or jackrabbits by working together, not individually. What one person did (or failed to do) on his or her private land mattered to adjacent landowners, and coordinated resistance was the most effective response. Westerners still understand this. People in one Montana locality recently asserted that indeed they can save their area from "noxious weeds," but only if "we pull together as a community in one concerted effort."[10]

The ways in which westerners have pulled together have tended to diminish the importance of property boundaries, and with them the fences and the signs that divide neighbor from neighbor, property from nature, insider from outsider. Western Americans have engaged in all manner of activities consistent with the ecological commons. During the early twentieth century, for example, Idaho and many other western states enacted legislation that empowered county officials to enter the private property of neglectful landowners to destroy weeds, insects, or rodents. By authorizing the public transgression of private space, these statutes tacitly acknowledged that property rights in the ecological commons must be qualified. Western states, too, passed measures that quarantined diseased plants and animals and that permitted public agents to enter private land to destroy diseased livestock. Such measures generated some opposition from landowners, who believed that the statutes violated their property rights. But such opposition did not detract from the truth of the matter: that when government officials crossed property boundaries in pursuit of weeds or other mobile organisms, the ground on which they walked was less private space than it was an ecological commons.[11]

These official actions, furthermore, were related to folk practices that took place within the ecological commons. Idaho irrigators, for example, drawing on habits of mutual assistance characteristic of rural Americans, erected community fences to collectively protect their individual farms from ground squirrels, crickets, and other animals. And when jackrabbit populations periodically irrupted and thousands of the animals moved onto irrigated fields to consume alfalfa and other crops, neighboring farmers resurrected an ancient form of communal hunting: the drive. Hundreds of men and boys encircled the "jacks," drove them into a wire enclosure, and clubbed them to death (fig. 13.6). Folklorists, historians, geographers, and other students of landscape have devoted little if any attention to these vernacular forms of cooperative land management. We know little of the precise physical characteristics of community fences, for example. Some were made of woven sagebrush, others of lumber and woven wire. But these vernacular structures and practices are important. Whenever a community fence went up, or whenever the locals held a rabbit drive, the outlines of a landscape less private than public, less fragmented than ecological, less formal than vernacular, came into view.

These are but a few examples of the ecological commons as it has operated in the American West. There is more complexity to this phenomenon, of course, than a few stories of seeping water, weeds, or rabbit drives can convey. But such stories should make us think twice the next time we are ready to overlook those NO HUNTING or NO TRESPASSING signs. To ignore those small pieces of culture is to accept a constricted view of western, and American, landscape. To ignore them is to assume that certain cultural categories (private property, private and public space) are solid, when in fact they are really quite unstable. To ignore them is to overlook a small opening that leads to a wider view of the ways in which humans struggle with the land and with one another to structure and give meaning to their world.

Figure 13.6.   Rabbit drive, southern Idaho, early 1900s. Mobile organisms, in this case jackrabbits, migrated irrespective of property boundaries. At such moments, farmers often behaved less as individualists and more as communitarians as they banded together to confront the biota that threatened their collective landscape.

Property boundaries and the fences and signs that demarcate them occupy a Thirdspace, as Soja would call it, in which ecology and culture intersect. Examining this intersection reveals that the social construction of space involves more than simply the imposition of human systems on the land. Space is not merely a cultural form painted on the canvas of nature; private property is not just a rigid geometric system laid down on a pliant and vulnerable earth. Space, private property included, is indeed social, but it is always formed out of an ongoing, complex interaction with earth, water, atmosphere, and living things. Boundaries and ecological processes constantly reshape and reconstitute one another; private property requires perpetual defense and modification in the face of a broader world that is perpetually moving. Private property may be ideologically sacrosanct, but ecologically, socially, and legally it is not. Nor is public space simply a product of social and political conditions, as scholars have usually depicted it. As the ecological commons shows, public space—civic space—is also profoundly ecological.

If we take this wider view of our landscapes, we can see numerous examples of the ecological commons beyond relatively discrete localities like

Idaho's Snake River Valley, and beyond the American West and even the United States. Traces of the ecological commons are virtually everywhere, and they transcend not only property lines but also numerous other kinds of borders. When wildfires sweep across boundaries, as they did in Colorado, Montana, and other western states during the summer of 2000, they unite individual people and public agencies in mutual efforts to address a common landscape problem. When farmers on the Great Plains sink wells into the Ogallala aquifer and begin to pump it down, they link their individual fates, and the fates of their respective communities, to the condition of a shared, public body of underground water. When salmon migrate from the Gulf of Alaska up the Columbia and Snake Rivers to spawn in Idaho, they swim through a thicket of some seventeen jurisdictions, bringing together disparate polities, agencies, and cultures to confront the issue of whether the fish can survive extinction or not.[12]

Cultural boundaries and national borders, too, mean less in the face of the ecological commons. When AIDS, influenza, or the common cold pass from one person to the next, these viruses penetrate the innermost recesses of the body, instantly submerging that most prized space, that most prized possession—the individual, autonomous self—in a larger disease pool that grows more global with each passing year. When the Colorado River trickles to a thin, salty stream at its delta, the use of the river in the United States can no longer be clearly separated from conditions on the Mexican side. And when the wind carries dioxin burned in U.S. incinerators and furnaces into the Canadian Arctic and, finally, into the bodies of Inuit people, it offers yet another telling reminder of the many ecological and social links that transcend the boundaries that we imagine on the earth's surface. (Confronted with evidence of this tragedy, an official with the North American Commission for Environmental Cooperation declared that "we must revise our concept of neighbors.")[13]

Such a catalog of examples, however, should not pass for deeper analysis. The ecological commons and its problems and potentials need more study. This phenomenon needs to be examined through not only American but also a broader North American history, across time and across space. When that has been done, perhaps we will have a better understanding of ourselves and our landscapes, and perhaps we will be able to transcend our narrow, rigid views and find our place in an ecologically complex and contingent world.

INTERPRETING TWENTIETH-CENTURY
URBAN LANDSCAPES

The authors of the last section of this book, each from a different academic discipline, apply current cultural landscape practice to four very different parts of the American city and suburb. In doing so, they provide ample proof of the ongoing adaptive characteristics of landscape studies.

Architectural historian Jessica Sewell reminds us of the importance not only of seeing what *is* in the physical landscape, but also the power of experience and imagination as lenses for confronting social conflict and instigating political change. Using examples from San Francisco in the early twentieth century, Sewell compares the mixed-gender experiences of supposedly "rational, male" office buildings and office work with supposedly "impulsive, female" department store interiors and shopping. Sewell shows how the actual mixture of genders in the buildings themselves and on downtown sidewalks and streets provided venues for women to convert male voters to the women's suffragist cause in the California election of 1911.

Louise Mozingo, as a landscape architect and historian of that profession, applies a cultural landscape approach to the discussion of expensive high-style settings. She shows how corporate executives and their landscape architects consciously recast features of the nineteenth-century urban parks movement into suburban research campuses, estate-style headquarters, and office parks to serve the new social structures of corporate management. She also provides an excellent example of the general truth that what we *can't* see, what is *not* in view, may be more important than what is within sight.

In the next chapter, city planner James Rojas takes us on a personal tour of the East Los Angeles street and neighborhood where he grew up. He brings to life a working-class district of the American city that non-Latino readers might never understand without a local guide. His image of "home," as he says, was not "the house where I slept at night," but "the excitement and fascination of the street." Rojas moves us along his East Los Angeles street from Antojitos Denise (a taco stand) to the sidewalk where Carmen, the "corn woman," sets up her barbecue grill, and moves on to private front yards, all packed with outdoor social activity. On the way, he identifies generic landscape elements for what he calls the "Latinoization" of districts in other American cities.

In the final chapter, historian David Sloane examines the decentering of traditional health care from large institutional hospital settings and genteel medical offices to outpatient clinics and even surgical centers now open for business in roadside commercial strips. Seeing a surgery center next to a pizza parlor and a copier shop, he suggests, will be common in the near future. These new locations indicate the blurring of former distinctions: between traditionally educated physicians and alternative medical practitioners such as chiropractors and acupuncturists, between doctors and patients, and between commerce and professional practice.

In these studies of change—suffragettes realizing their spatial powers, corporate executives adopting park and estate trappings, Latinos modifying old bungalow neighborhoods, and health care providers relocating and redefining their services—we can see that *landscape*, as a term, continues to enjoy the potential of new applications and new meanings.

JESSICA SEWELL

GENDER, IMAGINATION, AND EXPERIENCE IN THE EARLY-TWENTIETH-CENTURY AMERICAN DOWNTOWN

14

In "The Word Itself," J.B. Jackson defined cultural landscape as "a composition of man-made or man-modified spaces to serve as infrastructure or background for our collective existence . . . which underscores . . . our identity and presence."[1] Cultural landscapes consist not only of physical spaces, but also of the way people think about and experience those physical spaces. Paul Groth, building on an unpublished manuscript by J.B. Jackson, has defined landscape as "the interaction of people and place: a social group and its spaces, particularly the spaces to which the group belongs and from which its members derive some part of their shared identity and meaning."[2]

People's interaction with spaces includes creating a built environment, experiencing it, and imagining it. Experiencing a space consists of using it on an everyday or occasional basis and includes how an individual feels in that space, in response to both its physical and social environments. Imagining a space consists of thinking about a space, for example as safe or dangerous, as an ethnically marked space, or as a space identified with a particular activity or social group. Experiences and imaginations are particular to an individual, but shared experiences and shared ideas about the nature of a space come together to create collective cultural experiences and imaginations. These shared experiences and understandings of a landscape are the cultural aspect of cultural landscapes. However, how the experienced, the imagined, and the physical landscapes interact is not a subject that has been explored in depth by cultural landscape scholars.[3] This paper is an attempt to begin to fill that gap.

IMAGINING AND EXPERIENCING GENDERED LANDSCAPES

When we try to understand gendered landscapes, starting with the imagined and the experienced landscapes is essential. Unlike many ethnic and subcultural landscapes, gendered landscapes are only rarely marked as gendered through physical design, and when they are, it is primarily through interior design, decoration, and other relatively temporary means, rather than through the design of buildings or streets themselves. However, by starting from how spaces are *experienced* as gendered and *imagined* to be gendered, we can understand how aspects of the physical landscape that do not appear at first to be related to gender actually reflect and shape gender in the American city.

In common speech, a gendered landscape often means a space used particularly by men or by women, such as a pool hall or a fabric shop. These spaces are experienced as gendered because the people in them are nearly all of one gender. The same space can be experienced as differently gendered when used by different groups. The gendering of a late-twentieth-century football stadium is quite different when hosting the Lilith Fair, an all-female rock festival, than when it is used by the Promise-Keepers, a male Christian revivalist group. This gendering of a space through the gender of the people within it is one aspect of experience in gendered landscape.

However, landscapes that are used by both men and women are not neutrally gendered, even if men and women are there at the same time. Men's and women's experiences of the same place can be quite different. For example, women in public places are aware of the possibility of being harassed and, especially at night, are constantly aware of the potential danger of rape; they tend to keep as much as possible to well-lit and populated areas. Men, although they may be concerned about mugging, experience these same places without this sexual wariness, this necessity to always be on guard because of their gender. Women also often find themselves belittled and taken advantage of by the staff in places considered to be male terrain, such as car-repair shops. The ways men and women feel within a space, and are treated in it, constitute another crucial aspect of the experienced gendered landscape.

Different gendered experiences are created in part through a landscape's place in the cultural imagination—for example, through a shared assumption that a certain space is more appropriate (or safe) for people of one gender than for those of the other. Many streets at night are not imagined to be socially appropriate spaces for women, so that women on these streets at night have a legitimate fear of being mistaken for a prostitute either by passersby or by the police. Other spaces, such as knitting stores or lingerie shops, are not generally considered appropriate for men. Thus, the way spaces are imagined to be gendered shapes people's experience within them, often making a man in a female space or a woman in a male space feel uncomfortable and vulnerable. Imagined gendered landscapes shape not only men's and women's experiences, but also the social imagination of gender and of society as a whole. As the following case study will show, how people imagine public space to be gendered influences who is imagined as a member of the body public and thus who has the authority to speak publicly and to participate in public decision making.

Looking at imagined and experienced landscapes does not mean ignoring the physical landscape. Instead, imagined and experienced landscapes are essential lenses for understanding the physical landscape. Beginning with imagined and the experienced landscapes, then, allows us to see how they respond to and are shaped by the design of the physical landscape. For example, as many feminist critics have detailed, the creation of suburbs was based on the assumption that the space of the home was most appropriate for women, and the space of the city and of waged workplaces was primarily masculine. Thus, the creation of the physical landscape of suburbs and a largely nonresidential downtown was based on a gendered imagining of home and work landscapes. The suburbs, in turn, shaped men's and women's experiences of home and of the city, making it increasingly difficult for women to combine household work and wage work because of the physical separation of these landscapes.[4] By examining how a landscape is experienced on a daily basis by men and women, and how that same landscape is imagined, we can better recognize the physical features that contribute to its gendering.

Early-twentieth-century San Francisco provides a good case study for examining the interrelations of imagined, experienced, and physical gen-

Figure 14.1. The Mills Building, 220 Montgomery Street, San Francisco. This large office block, designed by Burnham and Root, was built in 1891.

dered landscapes. How downtown San Francisco was imagined to be gendered, how these imaginings were enacted in the physical landscape, and how that physical landscape was experienced had important impacts on the changing roles and perceptions of women. In particular, how downtown San Francisco was used for gendered political purposes in the California woman suffrage campaign of 1911 shows the importance of the imagined, experienced, and physical downtown landscapes to political action.

THE IMAGINED LANDSCAPE OF DOWNTOWN SAN FRANCISCO

Like all turn-of-the-century downtowns, the physical and imagined downtown of San Francisco reflected the waning, but still powerful, gendered ideology of separate spheres. In this middle-class ideology, men and women were understood as fundamentally different creatures, with separate spheres of interest and skills, focusing on the home and domesticity for women and the larger world and work for men. Women were believed

Figure 14.2   The White House department store, 255 Sutter Street, San Francisco, in 1909. This high-class department store, designed by Albert Pissis, was built in 1908 to replace an earlier store destroyed by the 1906 earthquake and fire.

to be endangered by strange men, and thus when the cares of the household took them outside the home, for example to shop and run errands, spaces were created to segregate them from potentially dangerous men. A wide range of late-nineteenth-century public spaces, including libraries, banks, post offices, restaurants, and hotels, provided special ladies' windows or ladies' lounges to keep men and women separate.

In keeping with this segregation of male and female public spaces, two important segments of the early-twentieth-century American downtown, the office landscape and the shopping landscape, were imagined as separate and gendered. Both of these centralized, specialized uses of space were primarily nineteenth-century inventions, and each was epitomized by a new architectural form. The paradigmatic building of the metropolitan business landscape was the office block or skyscraper, with many floors of offices (fig. 14.1). The paradigmatic building of the shopping landscape was the department store, a large establishment selling a wide range of goods, especially clothing, dry goods, and furnishings (fig. 14.2).

These buildings, and the landscapes they epitomized, were imagined as distinctly gendered: offices as a realm of masculine efficiency, power, and modernity; the shopping district as a realm of feminine consumption, irrationality, and display. Though women worked in offices and men in stores, these landscapes were still imagined as single-gendered, with the gender served in each space predominating—the businessman in the office and the female shopper in the stores. Descriptions of shopping and office landscapes in San Francisco guidebooks emphasized these gender assignments, both through who was described as inhabiting a space and by the language used to describe the landscapes themselves, emphasizing display, leisure, and whim for the feminized shopping landscape and production, hurry, and purposefulness for the masculine office landscape. The female "strolling shopper" was repeatedly contrasted with the "hurrying businessman."[5]

In the literature of the period, San Francisco's office landscape was usually described in primarily architectural and quantitative terms, with enumerations of such facts as the number of offices and floors in each building and dollars made in annual trade. A typical description read: "This district presents the most modern and artistic development of the 'skyscraper' style which ranks probably as America's foremost contribution to architecture; and nowhere else do office buildings present such a uniformly neat and clean appearance."[6] The guide went on to list prominent buildings, including the height in feet for each, but said nothing of the people and activity within these impressive structures. Another San Francisco guide contrasted Kearny Street, the center of the shopping district in 1903, with the business quarter, briefly described as "even more exclusively the haunt of men than Kearny Street is of women."[7]

The imagined masculinity of business was reflected in the physical landscape. Offices were not in fact an entirely male space, as from the 1880s on an increasing number of women did clerical work in downtown offices. However, designs that emphasized male power and female marginality, though they could not reproduce the "Eve-less paradise" of earlier offices, made it clear that women were tangential to the masculine spaces of commerce.[8] Even in office spaces full of female workers, the primacy of masculinity was made clear by male oversight, often physically expressed by raised workspaces for men, as well as by the rigid gridlike organization of the workspace, which allowed no room for personalization (fig. 14.3).

Angel Kwolek-Folland, in *Engendering Business*, describes some of the ways in which masculinity was marked in early-twentieth-century offices through design, decoration, and organization of space. For example, exec-

Figure 14.3 Office at Metropolitan Life, 1896. Late-nineteenth- and early-twentieth-century offices such as this one were highly controlled and tightly organized spaces. Notice the male supervisor, who is standing, and the male clerks along the right wall, whose desks were raised above the level of the long tables used by the female employees.

utive office spaces, libraries, and board rooms used a design language borrowed from masculine domestic spaces such as dens, including fireplaces, dark wood, leather, and animal skins (fig. 14.4). With these designs, male executives showed that they were at home in the office environment while simultaneously marking the office as a male space.[9]

The organization of space within office buildings was also used to emphasize men's higher status and legitimacy. Analyzing the Victor Talking Machine company building of 1917, Kwolek-Folland argues that the placement of men's bathrooms prominently and conveniently on every floor, near the public stairway, and of women's bathrooms "at the end of a crooked corridor, behind the vault and the service stairway," such that women "had to make their way down the entire length of the building" emphasized the status difference between men and women workers.[10]

Figure 14.4. Executive library at Metropolitan Life, c. 1900. This male executive space was modeled after masculine domestic interiors and masculine spaces such as residential hotels and private men's clubs. The heavy furniture, leather, dark woods, and books all mark it as a male space.

Many larger offices also segregated male and female workers spatially and temporally. Men and women not only worked in separate rooms, at separate tasks, but also ate in different lunchrooms and even had different workdays and lunch hours, so that they would not share elevators when moving to and from their offices.[11]

In parallel to this imagined "Eve-less paradise" of the office landscape, the downtown shopping landscape was conceptualized by department store owners as a largely segregated female landscape, in which mostly middle-class women did the work of consumption—shopping for the family and themselves. Edward Filene even called his store an "Adamless Eden."[12] Published descriptions of department store space emphasized its femininity, making the male owners, managers, buyers, and clerks invisible. This 1910 description of a department store, taken from a business magazine, epitomizes such gendered descriptions:

Buying and selling, serving and being served—women. On every floor, in every aisle, at every counter, women. . . . Behind most of the counters on all the floors . . . women. At every cashier's desk, at the wrappers' desks, running back and forth with parcels and change, short-skirted women. Filling the aisles, passing and repassing, a constantly arriving and departing throng of shoppers, women. Simply a moving, seeking, hurrying, mass of femininity, in the midst of which an occasional man shopper, man clerk, and man supervisor, looks lost and out of place.[13]

Department stores were imagined by their owners as complete female worlds, self-contained cities providing a wide range of goods and services. In the case of San Francisco's Emporium in 1910, the list of services included the following: "a parlor with papers, periodicals and writing materials; a children's nursery; an emergency hospital, with trained nurse in attendance; a Post Office Station; a Western Union telegraph office; a theater-ticket office; a manicuring and a hair-dressing parlor and a barber shop; public telephones; a lunch room; an information bureau; [and] always some free exhibition in the art rooms."[14] This range of goods and services all provided under one roof theoretically made it possible for women shoppers to do all their downtown errands without ever setting foot outside the store. The wide variety of shops along the outside sidewalks and most of the nonretail services of the downtown, such as the post office, hairdressers, and restaurants, were duplicated within department stores. Department stores even had their own security force, in part to protect the women shoppers, as well as to protect the owners from theft.

Department stores were also designed as spaces of excess and spectacle, which was considered appropriate for women, whose assumed emotional irrationality and love for beauty, advertisers and retailers believed, made them susceptible to being wooed by commodities.[15] The department store was designed to stimulate women's desires through visual display as well as music, light displays, food, and other aspects of festival. A 1901 study of women's shoplifting argued that the dream world of the department store overstimulated women until "temptation is so strong, surging desire so powerful, so impervious, so irresistible that the act is accomplished before reason has time to plead its cause."[16]

In contrast to the rational, quantitative descriptions of the business district, descriptions of San Francisco's shopping landscape emphasized people, atmosphere, and emotion, as the following quotation from a 1903 guidebook put out by the California Promotion Committee illustrates:

"Hosts of fair ladies trip its stony pavements, looking with absorbed attention at window displays of silks and laces, coats and curtains, or casting glances at the latest walking exponent of fads and fashions. Some are lured by the fragrant aroma or tempting window exhibition into the sanctuary of ices and candies; others succumb to the florist, and thus money circulates by the caprice of feminine fancy."[17] Here, shopping was conceptualized as a process of impressionable women being lured in and eventually succumbing to luxury goods, a tale of seduction with chocolate candy, rather than a man, as the lover.

To seduce women with goods, the design of department stores focused largely on interior spectacle, created both through display of goods and through architectural setting. Department stores presented a plethora of goods, seductively displayed in luxurious settings, overwhelming shoppers with colors, quality, and quantity (fig. 14.5). Unlike the spare and orderly rows of desks of the office landscape, the department store made use of excess, exoticism, and choreographed disorder.

The interior space was often organized around a breathtaking central atrium, frequently capped with a stained-glass roof that transformed the daylight into something more spectacular. This atrium functioned as a stand-in for the out-of-doors, providing the daylight that was denied the store by enclosed display windows. The space in the atrium could even be read as mimicking the street outside, because the several stories of selling floors surrounding it created the same cavernous effect as did tall buildings lining a downtown street. Both the range of goods and services provided within the department store and the design of its interior thus suggested that it could function as a safe, controlled, beautiful, feminine replacement for the downtown shopping district as a whole.

THE EXPERIENCED LANDSCAPE OF DOWNTOWN SAN FRANCISCO

In the social imagination, office and shopping landscapes were distinctly gendered spaces, with primarily male offices separate from female shops. The design of offices and department stores reflected and reinforced this idea of separation, using spare masculine design language for offices and feminized spectacle for department store interiors. However, men's and women's experiences of these landscapes did not fit the imagined ideals. Examining photographs of San Francisco's downtown and mapping the location of businesses in the city directory, I have found that these landscapes, rather than being physically separate, actually shared spaces in the

Figure 14.5. "Interior Electrical Display." Rotating lightbulb-covered cones suspended from the ceiling, strings of lights, printed muslin, and eight to ten thousand Japanese paper napkins were used to create this effect in a department store interior. In the early twentieth century, trade magazines published photos of model displays such as this one, encouraging the creation of elaborate window and interior displays and explaining how to replicate them.

same buildings. Because downtown shops and offices had many of the same requirements, such as easy accessibility by public transportation, a dense concentration of people and businesses, and proximity to banks, the same area of the city was ideal for both. Because ground-floor locations, which were essential to stores, were not particularly important for offices, landlords found it financially efficient to rent their ground-floor spaces to shops.[18]

This real estate situation led to a standard building type within the downtown shopping district that combined shops on the ground floor with several stories of offices above. This building type predominated along the stretch of Market Street most shared by the shopping and office land-scapes (fig. 14.6). Even the Emporium department store housed offices in its facade, in addition to its mercantile space. To counteract this overlap

Figure 14.6.   Market Street looking west from the Phelan
Building, 1909. From left are the Pacific Building, the Commercial Building, and the Emporium. The Emporium had an imposing entrance for its department store at the middle of its facade,
while the more modest office entries were placed at either end.

between gendered landscapes, the shopping space and office space were
well segregated within these buildings, which generally had separate entrances for shops and offices and no communication between the two sections within the building. In the view of Market Street shown in fig. 14.6,
the separate entrances for shops and offices can be seen most obviously in
the Emporium, which provided an entrance to the department store
through a two-story central archway and entrances to offices through the
smaller doorways at either corner of the building. This physical segregation, like the careful separation of men and women in offices, reflected the
imagined separation of men and women and their activities downtown.

However, men's and women's experience of the San Francisco down-town contradicted this imagined separation between the sexes. In order to get to these carefully gender-sorted buildings, both men and women took streetcars or walked the streets leading downtown. Within the down-town, they shared the streets and sidewalks onto which the streetcars, stores, and office buildings opened, thus creating a mixed-gender land-scape (fig. 14.7). Early-twentieth-century guidebooks described Market Street, the core of downtown, as a cosmopolitan mixture, "the thorough-fare alike of the strolling shopper and the hurrying businessman."[19] Mar-ket Street was described as the space of mixture not only of men and women, but also of classes and races, as in this 1912 description from *Care-Free San Francisco:*

> Actor, soubrette and ingenue, both professional and amateur, soldier
> and sailor, clerk and boulevardier, workingman and workingwoman,
> a dozen tongues, a dozen grades of color, a dozen national cos-
> tumes—miner from the desert, cowboy from the range, chekako or
> sourdough from Alaska; upper, lower and half world; full of the joy
> of being, of forming one of the lively throng, exchange greetings
> more or less conventional, gaze in the brilliant store windows,
> buy—or hope to—and go to dinner, clubward, homeward, to restau-
> rant and boarding-place.[20]

Unlike the mixed-gender realm inside the office building, which was carefully controlled (both through doormen, elevator operators, and man-agers policing behavior and through spatial and temporal separations be-tween the sexes and the classes), the social landscape of the downtown sidewalk was relatively unpoliced. Furthermore, because the sidewalk was both part of the imagined female-gendered landscape of shopping and of the imagined male-gendered landscape of offices, the gendering of the sidewalk realm was ambiguous; it was a space that belonged both to men and to women. Its nature changed throughout the day, with workers (imagined to be male), shoppers (female), or pleasure-seekers (couples) dominant at different hours, as expressed in *Care-Free San Francisco:* "Before noon Market Street is a bustle of business men. At noon the bright-eyed blooming youth of the office forces debouch for luncheon and a 'how d'ye do.' Then come the down-town cars to discharge shopping matrons, and forth come the butterflies of leisure and of pleasure. Towards the half light the bees buzz out again and turn drones for the hour before dinner (the five-o'clock promenade)."[21]

Figure 14.7. View north on Powell Street and east on Market Street, c. 1910. Notice the mixture of men, women, and children.

SUFFRAGE AND DOWNTOWN SAN FRANCISCO

In the woman suffrage campaign of 1911, suffragists made use of the ambiguous gendering of the sidewalk realm. Because the downtown sidewalk was a space frequented by men, as well as a space within which women had some legitimacy to speak, it became an important site of many suffrage actions focused on the necessary task of getting men to vote for women's voting rights. For example, in one of the first major campaigns, suffragists convinced store owners throughout the downtown to decorate their windows in yellow, the suffrage color, as one suffragist put it, "the florist's by having flowers of the suffrage color, the milliner's and the dry goods by hats and goods of our color, the stationer's by filling the window with suffrage books and periodicals."[22] "To point the reason for the color, copies of the prize poster, in dull olives and tan, lightened with yellow and flame, gave the campaign cry 'Votes for Women'" (fig. 14.8).[23]

More than half of the suffrage street speeches in San Francisco during the 1911 campaign also took place at major intersections along Market Street. The street speech campaign climaxed the night before the election, in a rally involving five thousand people, at least four automobiles, multiple speakers, and the famous diva Lillian Nordica. The rally began on Stockton Street, at the east side of Union Square Park, the center of the downtown shopping district, where the audience heard Mme. Nordica give a pro-suffrage speech and sing "America" and "The Star-Spangled Banner." She was followed by a speech by Dr. Charles F. Aked, a prominent pro-suffrage debater, which Mme. Nordica publicly approved of "by nodding her head and crying 'Hear, hear' when the speaker clinched the points of his argument." Then Mme. Nordica went back to her hotel, and automobiles filled with suffrage speakers took up posts at the four corners of the square and carried on four separate open-air meetings.[24]

On one well-advertised day, suffragists, described by Selina Solomons in *How We Won the Vote in California* as "prettily costumed young saleswomen, with golden bannerettes, offering their wares," sold pro-suffrage postcards.[25] They set up their sales posts, according to one local newspaper, "at every street corner where traffic is busiest, at the entrance to all the big office buildings and the most patronized stores."[26] Suffragists also set up shop in a storefront just a few doors down from the Emporium, decorating their window with yellow placards and posters, yellow chrysanthemums, and "Votes for Women" banners; they pulled sympathizers in with the "constant distribution of leaflets on the sidewalk in front of the store, day and evening, until 9 P.M."[27] With this storefront

Figure 14.8. "Votes for Women," poster by B. M. Boyé, 1911. This was the winner of a highly publicized poster competition sponsored by a coalition of San Francisco woman suffrage organizations. It was the main image used in the campaign and was reproduced on postcards and stamps as well. In the original image, the woman's clothing is a light yellow, and the halo behind her head and the trim of her gown are a darker yellow.

headquarters, suffragists made themselves visible and easily accessible to a wide range of the populace, including, as the suffragists reported, "workingmen and workingwomen of all degrees," who came in "at noon and on the way home to dinner in the evening."[28] The storefront headquarters functioned as a suffrage store as well as a political office.

Downtown sidewalks and the transportation leading to the shopping district were, of course, a major focus of advertising posters of all types. Suffrage posters appeared not only in store windows, but also in all the streetcars leading to Market Street, and pro-suffrage slogans, written in letters a foot high, were posted on piles in the harbor, where they could best be seen from ferries approaching the terminal at the foot of Market Street. Suffragists were proud that at Market Street near Fourth Street, "the largest business center of the city," they had erected the most prominent piece of suffrage advertising, a "large, permanent, electric sign" reading "Votes for Women."[29]

The mixed-gender nature of the public space of the sidewalk not only provided women with a legitimate venue for political speech—aimed both at other women and at men—but, equally important, it also accustomed both men and women to a joint occupation of public space. Sharing public space with members of the other gender helped make shared participation in public life more imaginable. That the sidewalks of Market Street were in the symbolic heart of the city made this common territory that much more significant. As women shared this central public space with men, the idea of sharing power and responsibility in the public sphere became more imaginable. Men's and women's experience of the downtown landscape helped to change their imagination not only of that landscape, but also of appropriate gender roles. The idea that shared use of public space should lead to shared participation in the public sphere is notable in a speech that Fannie McLean, a schoolteacher and suffrage activist, made to members of women's clubs during the campaign:

> The woman of today takes a larger and more gracious place in the world. We are now co-thinkers and co-workers with man, in the same world, living in the same houses, using the same public conveyances, attending the same colleges, buying our food and clothing at the same shops; and why not be co-voters as to the management of this common environment and as to the basic principles of the democracy which produces this environment?[30]

In this speech, McLean argued that women should have an equal control over the spaces they shared with men, rather than remaining powerless because voteless. She was able to make this claim only because women not only shared that space, but also had a cultural claim to that space. Downtown sidewalks, streetcars, and shops were not male spaces that women also used, but rather areas that were gendered as mixed, as part of the realms of both men and women.

EXPERIENCE VERSUS THE IDEOLOGICAL IMAGINATION

The downtown landscape, as experienced, undercut the ideological separation of genders and contradicted the imagined gendered landscapes of shopping and offices. The hybrid office-shop buildings that lined Market Street and many other streets in San Francisco's downtown were an important element of the new downtown landscape of the early twentieth century. Their full significance is visible when we address their relationship to imagined and experienced gendered landscapes. In their architectural design, these buildings reflected the imagined separation of men and women, offices and shops. However, by combining female-gendered shops and male-gendered offices within a single structure, they created an experience on the sidewalk that contradicted this goal of gender separation. Asking about experience as well as imagination, we see the ways in which the imagined landscape can be contradicted and broken down by everyday use, even when the buildings, at first glance, appear to have supported gender segregation. Examining both imagined and experienced landscapes gives us an important tool for understanding the built environment and its role in social change and the construction of gender.

LOUISE A. MOZINGO

CAMPUS, ESTATE, AND PARK | 15

Lawn Culture Comes to the Corporation

Beginning in the 1940s, American corporate management built three new business landscapes at the urban periphery: the corporate campus, the corporate estate, and the office park. In edge-city conurbations they may appear chaotic, but they function as distinct niches of the corporate workplace, contrived with discernible intent. Though they are different in specifics, common motives have fashioned these suburban environments. The purported magic of gazing at greenness lies at these landscapes' conceptual core—magic credited with generating productivity, competitiveness, and public approbation (fig. 15.1).

The emergence of suburban corporate landscapes was framed by the conceptual precedents of the public park and the residential suburb, both material results of what J.B. Jackson termed "lawn culture." By the late nineteenth century, the pastoral public park prevailed as an environmental ideal of the American landscape. Gently undulating grass, serpentine lakes, sinuous pathways, and leafy woodland groves provided urban dwellers a much sought after respite from the dense industrial city, pre-

Figure 15.1. Aerial view of Deere and Company Administrative Center, the quintessential corporate estate. The imposing corporate headquarters, inaugurated in 1964, sits in the center of 720 sylvan acres well outside the industrial downtown of Moline, Illinois.

sumably with salutary physical and moral effects as well. The application of this pastoral ideal to residential districts by real estate speculators formed exclusive suburbs typified by open lot houses, coordinated infrastructure, limited building heights, and expansive, unfenced front yards presenting a continuous street-side landscape. Both the public park and the residential suburb conjoined gentility and greenery.[1]

The prevalence of automobile transportation that began the 1920s expanded the scale and scope of the suburbs, a process that accelerated after World War II. The ever sprawling suburbs encompassed other development types besides single-family housing: parkways, highways, strip shopping centers, drive-in movie theaters, and retail malls. The last suburban development types to crystallize (and the last to receive scholarly attention) are the interrelated corporate campus, corporate estate, and office park.

Corporate management initially built and occupied the *corporate campus*, a suburban workplace for industrial scientists. Modeled on the American university landscape, the corporate campus consisted of several office and laboratory facilities focused around an inner green or quadrangle. Inspired by the corporate campus, top management retreated from the city center to the *corporate estate*, distinguished by a conspicuously grand site, usually of at least two hundred acres, centered on an impressive office structure. Real estate entrepreneurs translated the most elementary attributes of the corporate campus and estate to develop the *office park*, which housed regional managers of national corporations, corporate support staffs, small local corporations, and service businesses.

Together these suburban landscape types served the ranks of white-collar employees of a new twentieth-century economic institution—the managerial capitalist corporation. Since the 1890s, corporate expansion had both required and been facilitated by a rational and professional management hierarchy, consisting of three specialized tiers: lower management, which oversaw production, sales, and purchasing; middle management, which coordinated the activities of lower management and implemented corporate strategies through finance, marketing, and research departments; and top management, which directed the activities of middle managers, allocated overall corporate resources, and plotted competitive strategies.[2]

Managerial capitalism was a necessary precursor to the relocation of corporate managers to suburban offices. One of the principal advantages of this rationalized hierarchy was the decentralization of business decisions, which provided the means to control and guide geographically distant parts of vast corporations. Economic expansion after World War II furthered the adoption and refinement of this management strategy. The differentiated corporate offices were a parallel manifestation of the specialization and decentralization that marked the suburbs as a whole. But in moving to the suburbs, these corporations did more: "greenery," as Jackson stated, is "a way of communicating with others." The new corporate management landscapes connoted both the "relaxation and sociability" of the public park and the "goodwill and approval" of the suburban front yard, and thus elided the actualities of profit-making American business.[3]

MOTIVATIONS

The advent of suburban workplaces for corporate management resulted from either of two business strategies. In one, management separated from industrial production. When Robert Hewitt took over as president of the farm machinery giant Deere and Company in 1955, his initial and most decisive action was to remove his top management from the corporation's sprawling industrial swath along the Mississippi River in Moline, Illinois.[4] He transferred it beyond the city limits to a stunning headquarters nestled within 720 verdant acres. As *Fortune* reported in 1952, corporations were cleaving management from industrial sites "in the hope that this will reduce friction . . . between unionized workers and unorganized office personnel."[5] In the second strategy, corporations relocated away from urban downtowns. In the immediate postwar years, space tightened significantly in central business districts: office staffs doubled between 1942 and 1952, and each individual worker took up more space. In addition, efficient office organization now required flexible, expandable offices with movable partitions rather than fixed walls.[6] The dense, constricted downtown became untenable for rapidly expanding conglomerates such as General Foods, which had been a Manhattan resident since the 1920s.[7] After first seeking adequate space in Manhattan, General Foods exited to a custom-designed headquarters in Westchester County, twenty miles north, in 1954. It was the first of many *Fortune 500* companies to do so.

A peculiar postwar circumstance, civil defense, also spurred the corporate decision to relocate to the urban periphery. After 1949, as civil defense activities rapidly increased, corporate interest in suburban locations also sharply increased. As of 1952, out of twenty-two New York City companies that had consulted with an expert on land acquisitions in suburban Westchester County, each had "privately revealed that, among other things, it wanted to avoid target areas."[8] Among General Foods employees, the scuttlebutt was that the corporation had designed the complex to be used as a hospital in case of nuclear war.[9]

In addition to their presumed safety from atomic warfare, suburban sites allowed corporate managers an extraordinary degree of control over public access to their facilities. Buildings were distanced from public roads, fences discreetly secured sites, long driveways gave ample warning of approaching visitors, and guard houses vetted guests under the guise of giving friendly directions. For the many corporations undertaking military research and development, only ample suburban sites could offer these defensive layouts. By the 1960s, corporations had left behind Cold War concerns and instead were focusing on suburban sites as insulated from disconcerting "urban unrest."[10] Protective measures could be tied up in an appealing bucolic package, altogether less threatening and obtrusive than the urban fortresses that eventually housed some downtown corporations.

These new management landscapes fit hand in glove with the economic goals of the politicians, developers, and bankers in suburban jurisdictions. As *Business Week* reported of 1950s Westchester County, suburban office buildings solved the "threatening problem" that faced predominantly residential suburbs: "Residential areas don't pay their own way unless average [housing] valuations run high." For this, *Business Week* noted, "Office buildings look like a heaven-sent answer. They carry a big share of the tax load, but don't clutter up the countryside."[11]

The landscape provisions attached to these corporate workplaces made them palatable to well-to-do communities known for their idealized, and envied, suburban landscapes. Though power brokers welcomed corporate development, homeowners feared unsightly and noxious industry. Indeed, factories preceded corporate administration in the urban periphery by several decades. The need to distinguish between the environments of genteel white-collar management and gritty blue-collar industry necessitated corporate investment in a green surround. When Dr. F. B. Jewett, president of AT&T Bell Telephone Laboratories, had to convince local New Jersey politicians that his research campus (completed in 1942) would fit into the "high" suburban character of the nearby town of Summit, he repeatedly returned to the site design by the Olmsted Brothers, the esteemed firm of landscape architects founded by Frederick Law Olmsted and carried on by his sons.[12] Universally, suburban authorities imposed height restrictions, limited uses to offices and research laboratories, and dictated the presence of enveloping landscape setbacks. What demarcated executive offices from production plants was not the appearance of the buildings, since from a disinterested perspective offices might look much like factories, but the presence of a generously designed and tended landscape.

Corporate management understood that a landscape surround could appease suburban residents but also, more generally, broadcast a positive public image. While closely controlling public access, corporations orchestrated engaging public prospects from the new parkways and highways that usually flanked their facilities. The site designer of the forerunning General Electric Electronics Park, a 1948 corporate campus outside Syracuse, New York, along the New York State Thruway, promoted the "possibilities and advantages of 'site advertising'" in *Landscape Architecture* and described the importance of "the location, orientation, and treatment with respect to the abutting highway. Here will be our approach; here will be our advertising."[13] Highly visible sites displayed impressive buildings and greenery to a ready audience of passing motorists and, in the process, an estimable depiction of the corporation itself.

Relatedly, large suburban properties yielded the idealized modernist design effect advocated by the architects employed by corporations in the 1950s. Groves of trees, glistening lakes, and rolling lawns buoyed gleam-

Figure 15.2.   Aerial view of the 1956 Connecticut General Life Insurance headquarters designed by Skidmore, Owings and Merrill. On the expansive property
outside of Hartford, Connecticut, the designers and their corporate patron
achieved the modernist design ideal of a gleaming glass and steel building set
amid a bucolic landscape.

ing buildings of glass standing free from the dictates of the street. The
transparent curtain wall of modernist buildings demanded a suitable exterior panorama, for the entire wall was now window. Ultimately, the only
acceptable view was either a dynamic city skyline or verdant pastures, one
the purview of the downtown skyscraper, the other of the new corporate
suburban landscape. As typified by the popular press's reaction to the
1956 Connecticut General Life Insurance headquarters in Bloomfield,
Connecticut—an "important departure from the monolithic piles which
corporations once favored," a "building with a future," and "one of the
finest office structures in the country"—the summary effect of the lus-
trous architecture and lush landscape seized public attention (fig. 15.2).[14]

Corporate management justified the expensive suburban moves and
elaborate landscape provisions as cost effective. Suburban pioneers consis-

tently reported low rates of employee turnover. Management determined that suburban locations increased effective working hours because the convenience of integrated parking spaces captured the employee for the entire working day. The new workplaces discouraged out-the-door distractions and facilitated overtime by minimizing concern about mass transportation schedules and traffic congestion (at least initially).[15]

From the beginning, corporate management expected employees of "a better type" to be attracted by the suburban character and location of the new campuses, estates, and office parks.[16] In 1967, *Fortune* minced no words: "New York is becoming an increasingly Negro and Puerto Rican city. Some companies are reluctant to hire a large proportion of Negro and Puerto Rican help."[17] As characterized by a New York City Economic Development administrator to the *New York Times* in 1971, the "executive decision maker" lived in a homogeneous "ethnic and class community," while his urban employees came "from communities very different in class and ethnicity." The administrator bluntly continued, "It's an older generation in charge trying to reestablish a setting that seems to be more comfortable, more the old way."[18]

Corporate leaders also calculated that bucolic settings could grant their business a competitive edge. At the 1964 opening ceremonies, Robert Hewitt declared that the new Deere and Company Administrative Center would provide "additional inspiration to all of us to be bold, ingenious and creative, to use our imagination in new ways to keep John Deere out in front as a leader."[19] Five years after occupation of the Administrative Center, a staff survey determined that employees overwhelmingly favored the resplendent site and landscape of the Administrative Center over all other elements of the headquarters. Attracting new high-quality personnel became easier, and want ads that included pictures of the center garnered notably higher response rates than those that did not.[20]

The corporate managers who developed the corporate campus, the corporate estate, and the office park were recasting the social engineering of the nineteenth-century public park and the residential suburb to serve corporate capitalism. The landscape designers of the General Electric Electronics Park described the purpose of the carefully composed trees, lawns, and lakes as the creation of a landscape "that bespeaks orderliness, spaciousness, and well-being."[21] Corporations used the aesthetic, mental, and social effects attributed to the public park and the residential suburb to achieve operational efficiency, local acceptance, employee satisfaction, selective discrimination, and favorable self-representation.

THE CORPORATE CAMPUS

Corporations, and the designers they employed, devised the corporate campus because scientists conducting industrial research became crucial to corporate success. By 1940, companies angling to entice and keep scientists in a fiercely competitive labor market realized that the old industrial plants where scientists typically worked conveyed ever less prestige; Americans in general regarded the landscapes of production with growing distaste.[22] Nor did the factory environment continue to match the role that corporations envisioned for the corporate scientist. As the General Motors director of technical employment explained in an address to the American Association for the Advancement of Science in 1946, the scientist "is not recruited as a factory laborer" but rather "for development into a management position."[23] For their part, scientists were wary of corporate strictures, and management needed to provide them with a setting that reflected and reinforced their comparatively independent operations. In 1955, *Business Week* concluded that the notable success of General Electric and Bell Labs in attracting and retaining scientists could first be accounted for because, "Work goes on in a campus-like atmosphere that the brainy youngsters seem to go for."[24]

The defining element of the corporate campus is a central open space that provides a visual focal point for the separate buildings that house administrative, office, and laboratory uses. Like a university campus, this pattern of landscape and structures accommodates complicated underground utility conduits, and in the years after the campus's initial construction minimizes disruption when, inevitably, incremental alterations and additions to buildings and infrastructure take place. The major driveways in the corporate campus begin at the gate or entry, course around the site's periphery, and connect several parking lots, usually one for each building; the encircling driveway pattern also provides essential truck access to each building, for the delivery of laboratory materials (fig. 15.3).

The AT&T Bell Telephone Laboratories, first proposed in 1930 and completed in 1942 on a 213-acre site in Murray Hill, New Jersey, was the model for all corporate campuses to follow, as *Fortune* later attested.[25] Scientists worked in flexible modular laboratories provided with excellent experimental utilities. The three-story height limit, ample landscape setbacks, buried utilities, and specifically white-collar uses (all subsequently codified in unprecedented zoning restrictions) allowed the incursion of a corporate employment center into an exclusive residential suburb (fig. 15.4). Most important, Bell's "campus" initiated and integrated an in-

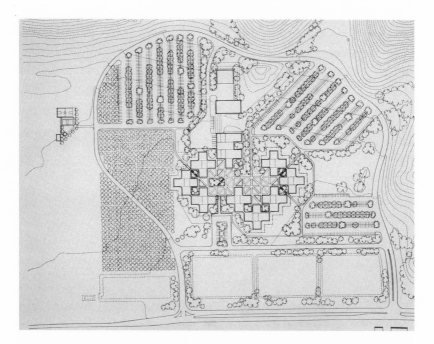

Figure 15.3.   Site plan of the IBM West Coast Programming Center in Santa
Teresa, California. Completed in 1977, the plan iterates the concentric scheme of
the corporate campus first developed in the 1940s: buildings clustered around a
central open space serving as the campus focal point, parking lots ranged around
the buildings, and an access drive encircling the entire site.

dustrial research culture that mimicked the university's encompassing
landscape, prestige, and reputation for independent intellectual inquiry.
Bell Labs is still famous as the site where scientists, supposedly free of
corporate constraints, invented both the transistor and the "bit" in 1948,
revolutionizing electronics and computing.

The 1948 Johns-Manville Research Center, in Manville, New Jersey,
and the contemporary General Electric Electronics Park further promoted
the corporate campus.[26] However, the 1956 General Motors Technical
Center spectacularly refined the precepts of the corporate campus. On a
grand one-by-two-mile property north of Detroit, the architect Eero
Saarinen and the landscape architect Thomas Church designed a modernist manifesto comprised of long, low, glazed buildings, crisp planes of
grass, sharply delineated bosques of trees, and, at the center, a vast rectan-
gle of water (fig. 15.5). The cutting-edge campus design emphasized and

Figure 15.4.   View of the first corporate campus, the AT&T Bell Telephone Laboratories in Murray Hill, New Jersey, completed in 1942. The landscape architects
the Olmsted Brothers designed the campus site and Voorhees, Walker, Foley and
Smith the building architecture.

glorified the modernity of the corporate research enterprise. As a com-
mentator observed, "Here is know-how; here is the vision of industry;
here is tomorrow today—Wednesday on Tuesday."[27] Twelve years in the
making and widely covered in the media, the GM Technical Center elicited
a tide of superlative press. It cost at least $130 million (perhaps more), an
immense expense even with all its enduring public relations value. To
date, no other corporate campus has bested the GM Technical Center.

Future corporate campuses reiterated the initial postwar models and
imitated General Motors with more modest but nonetheless emphatically
modernist designs. By 1960, corporations had also built campuses on the
West Coast. IBM completed the first phase of its principal California operations base in 1958, a 190-acre complex in San Jose that helped to initiate
the now mythic Silicon Valley. The 1960 Ramo-Wooldridge Laboratories
in Southern California were lauded by the designers and critics Christopher Tunnard and Boris Pushkarev in *Man-Made America* as an exemplar
of "industrial urban design."[28]

Figure 15.5. Aerial photo of the one-by-two-mile site of the General Motors Technical Center. Though distractingly spectacular, the fundamental scheme is the same as the more modest versions of the corporate campus. Instead of a grassy expanse, the research facilities face the rectangular lake, an immense watery quadrangle studded with jetting fountains, willow islands, and a sculptural water tower. The glinting dome visible near the lower right of the lake is where styling engineers show off new models of GM cars.

Since the 1950s, the corporate campus has continued to be a remarkably consistent landscape type, while accommodating circumstances of site, region, and business priorities. The 1977 IBM West Coast Programming Center, in Santa Teresa (near San Jose), displays a taut, crisp, high-style geometry within its campus, in contrast to a backdrop of grassland hillsides (fig. 15.6).[29] The 1992 Boeing Longacres Park, outside Seattle, incorporates more recent environmental concerns. An orchard, its rows of

Figure 15.6. View from the interior open space to the hillsides surrounding the IBM West Programming Center, Santa Teresa, California, a corporate campus designed by the landscape architects SWA Group.

trees angled toward a distant view of Mount Rainier, reflects the region's history of apple cultivation. Building on remnant wetlands protected by federal law, a large constructed wetland, surrounded by native woodland, forms the centerpiece of the corporate campus.[30]

THE CORPORATE ESTATE

Corporate campus schemes used landscape design to reconceive the white-collar workplace, retain targeted employee groups, and signal eminent corporate standing. Indubitably successful in these goals, the setting sold the corporation. This lesson was absorbed and amplified in the idea of the corporate estate. For two seminal estate projects—the General Foods headquarters (the very first corporate estate) and the Deere and Company Administrative Center—corporations hired the designers of previous precedent-setting corporate campuses: for General Foods, the architect of Bell Labs; for Deere and Company, the architect of the GM Technical Center.

Built as the seat of the highest corporate echelons, the corporate estate provides the suburban alternative to the striking urban skyscraper. Ample pastoral sites, views unblemished by rude site utilities, and stylish architecture suitably reflect the elite status of top postwar executives. At the same time, corporate estates' extensive and generous landscape engenders

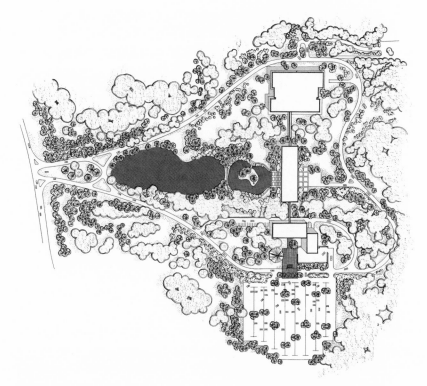

Figure 15.7. The site plan of the Deere and Company Administrative Center, designed by the building architect Eero Saarinen and the landscape architects Sasaki Associates. As is characteristic of the corporate estate, the placement and landscaping of the parking lots hides their presence on the site, particularly from the principal public facade, approach driveway, and office windows.

popular approval, even civic pride, in much the same way that skyscrapers distinguish a city skyline.

Though predated by the 1954 General Foods Headquarters and the 1956 Connecticut General Life Insurance Corporation, the 1964 Deere and Company Administrative Center in Moline, Illinois, has commanded the most renown.[31] It appears simple on the site plan, yet its circumnavigating driveway structures an elegantly dramatic series of views that visitors and employees experience as they enter the site (fig. 15.7). The looping driveway lassoes the building complex, moving from the ravine bottom at the road intersection, then rising along embankments to reveal stunning views across the ponds to the rusty brown Cor-ten steel facades, then banking upward into the woodland groves, eventually arriving at the

principal parking lot, disclosed at the last possible moment, and then drop-
ping back down again to the rear of the building, to provide service access.
In this way, the driveway is an active element in the experience of the
landscape, orchestrating views to maximum effect (fig. 15.8).

The award-winning Administrative Center garnered high praise from
Deere's executives and employees, the local community, cultural critics,
and other corporate leaders; it was a resounding success both inside and
outside the company and remains a cornerstone of the corporation's public relations (fig. 15.9). Images of the center are ubiquitous in Deere publications; the company encourages farmers and the general public to visit
the site and invites particularly good customers to lunch in the executive
dining room, which affords views out over the shimmering ponds. All
subsequent corporate estates have recapitulated Deere's essential elements: low-rise, contemporary architecture set amid many sylvan acres,
with grand entry drives, concealed parking and infrastructure, and verdant vistas.

Two high-profile corporate headquarters added refinements to the corporate estate idea: the 1970 PepsiCo World Headquarters, in Harrison, New
York, and the 1972 Weyerhaeuser Corporate Headquarters, in Tacoma,
Washington. PepsiCo president Donald Kendall extended prestigious display to seigniorial patronage, surrounding his executive office building
with a public sculpture garden of major twentieth-century works. George
Weyerhaeuser particularly insisted on high visibility for his sumptuous
building and landscape. He convinced the state highway authorities to
modify their standard railing design to make the headquarters readily visible from both an adjoining interstate and a passing state highway.[32]

In marked contrast, perceived threats of antiestablishment activism and
skeptical receptions in more affluent suburban communities during the
early 1970s caused other corporations to obscure their presence in the
suburban landscape. Wooded terrain completely enveloped the 1971
American Can headquarters in Greenwich, Connecticut, to create a kind
of a corporate hideaway. Additional corporations wary of public attention
followed suit, including Union Carbide, which built its Corporation World
Headquarters in Danbury, Connecticut, buffered deep within 645 acres of
forest in 1982.

By the late 1980s and into the 1990s, corporations had begun to confront highly motivated and organized local resistance. The latest permu-
tation of the corporate estate might thus be designated as Palladio meets
the Prairie School: it combines historicist architecture with a regionalist

Figure 15.8.   View from the drive at the Deere and Company Administrative Center, an example of the spectacular views of the corporate headquarters throughout the site.

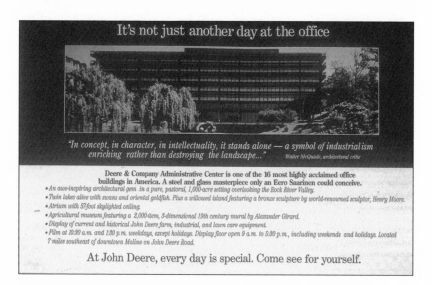

Figure 15.9.   Ad for the Deere and Company Administrative Center in *Destination Quad Cities,* the 1997 visitors' guide to the Moline area.

landscape. The Codex World Headquarters, in Canton, Massachusetts, and the Becton Dickson Headquarters, in Franklin Lakes, New Jersey, attempted to appease local outcries with swank design solutions inspired by European villas and country houses.[33] While certainly partly the result of architectural vogue, these constructions placed a cloak of genteel aristocratic leisure over the busy capitalism taking place within.

THE OFFICE PARK

The developers of office parks built upon two precedents. One was the industrial park—a planned industrial district of warehousing and manufacturing uses first seen in the 1920s. Though quite bare-boned, industrial park development guidelines coordinated infrastructure systems, standardized ample traffic conduits, and set limits on building heights and footprints.[34] The other precedent was the planned residential community, later regularized as the planned unit development, where restrictive covenants controlled every aspect of development for predictable environmental results and assured real estate values. Planned unit developments adhered even more strictly to the suburban aesthetic than industrial parks. They usually included larger open spaces and extensive landscaping and restricted supporting uses other than single-family housing. In both of the first two office parks—the 1952 Office Park in Mountain Brook, Alabama, outside of Birmingham, and the 1955 Hobbs Brook Office Park in Waltham, Massachusetts, along Route 128—developers relied on the landscape to define an ambience desirable to both suburban communities and white-collar tenants.

In office parks, green borders surround structures and parking lots; narrow green strips, often bermed, break up large expanses of asphalt; and landscaped medians and verges outline interior roads. An ample, sometimes showy landscape expanse that usually includes a sign naming the office park fronts the principal road or highway that connects to the distant downtown (fig. 15.10). Cory Jackson, the developer of the Mountain Brook Office Park, identified this visual effect as "looking over the treetops instead of the car tops."[35]

For the local entrepreneurs who built them, landscaping was fundamental to the "definite asset" of office parks: "The attractiveness of a controlled environment."[36] Quite unlike corporate campuses and estates, office parks can take a couple of decades to attain full occupancy. There-

Figure 15.10. The site plan of the Cornell Oaks Corporate Center, an office park in a suburb of Portland, Oregon, designed by the Mitchell Nelson Group. As typifies the office park, each office building is surrounded by a pool of parking delineated by landscape medians and verges. More generous landscape areas front the highway, connecting arterial and interior "parkway."

fore, as buildings are added, the landscape space provides coherence and organization within the development and consistency between it and surrounding residential areas.

Though they gathered far less notice than corporate campuses or estates, office parks were, and continue to be, the most common type of suburban corporate landscape, found in the peripheries of most cities. Early office parks appeared in regional business centers like Birmingham, as well as in major markets such as the Boston metropolitan area.[37] By 1960, developers had begun to build office parks in the suburbs of Omaha, St. Paul, and Kansas City (Missouri), as well as additional ones in both Birmingham and Waltham. By 1965, office parks had opened in suburban

Atlanta, Oklahoma City, Mobile, Tucson, Englewood (Colorado), Asheville (North Carolina), San Mateo (California), Kansas City, Chattanooga, Wellesley (Massachusetts), El Paso, Houston, and Dallas.[38]

In 1965, *Industrial Development and Manufacturers Record* reported that office parks housed "middle executives and their staffs" and "a sales force or regional administrative operation." They constituted the personnel of the expansion and decentralization of postwar corporations. Besides corporate tenants, the office park catered to insurance, accounting, architectural, and engineering firms—professional services expanding to meet growing corporate demand.[39]

By 1970, the term *business park* encompassed the emerging variations of the office park, such as the university research park.[40] During the next decade, office parks expanded in size and often included supporting uses such as hotels, restaurants, and service, retail, and day care centers. Developers increasingly realized the marketing value of the landscape design, which in combination with emblematic graphics (the "signage system"), created a sought-after "address" for the business tenants. With relatively cheap land costs, office park designs could be even more ambitious. At Corporate Woods, outside of Kansas City, the main thoroughfare through the project became a "scenic parkway," and the site's amenities included three miles of trails, a golf course, and tennis courts. Office park developers, convening under professional organizations, agreed that landscape design was "second only to parking in importance." This was "a function of why people moved to the suburbs in the first place," they explained; "to enjoy a pastoral environment."[41]

During the heated speculation of the 1980s, office park plans were marked by an outlandish audacity: huge properties, square-footage targets in the millions, and "photo op" landscape design. The most ambitious was Solana, on the suburban edge of Dallas–Ft. Worth, straddling two towns (Westlake and Southlake) and developed by joint partnership between Maguire Thomas Partners and IBM, the lead tenant. The nine-hundred-acre site contained 7 million square feet of office space (3 million occupied by IBM), a two-hundred-room hotel, an athletic club, and several restaurants and retail and service businesses (fig. 15.11).[42] A large team designed the complex, under the leadership of the landscape architects Peter Walker and Martha Schwartz, who devised the site concept and master plan. Dubbed "Vaux on the prairie" by one critic (a reference to the seventeenth-century splendor of Vaux-le-Vicomte, outside Paris), Solana received worldwide publicity, with coverage in the design press of Japan, Germany, Great Britain, and Italy.[43]

Figure 15.11   View of Solana, an office park in the Dallas suburb of Westlake-Southlake. This widely publicized office park was by the Offices of Peter Walker and Martha Schwartz.

THE DISSEMBLING PASTORAL CORPORATION

The most apparent significance of the corporate campus, corporate estate, and office park is their common role in the relocation of white-collar work. They were the means by which the leaders of postwar capitalism fled the urban core: a vivid abandonment of the city center by the powerful, self-interested parties that keep cities going. This is most heartbreakingly obvious in smaller cities dominated by single corporations, such as Moline, Illinois. There, Deere and Company's exit left a decimated downtown that dwindled for decades. The business leaders who built corporate campuses, corporate estates, and office parks powerfully shaped postwar American urbanism and locked into place the last keystone in the automobile landscape, with all its attendant difficulties. Complacent at the insulated suburban periphery are the people who, like Bill Gates, ensconced in the Microsoft Corporate Campus, run the world.

Beyond their role in reshaping the American city, the import of these landscapes lies in their cheerful reconception of the troubling corporate endeavor. What Richard Walker so aptly terms the American "well-honed taste for the Arcadian look" enabled corporations to mask the ugly results of managerial capitalism.[44] This most useful corporate disguise was clearly enunciated by Gabriel Hauge, a New York business bank president, in a speech at the inauguration of the Deere and Company Administrative Center. He first conceded to the assembly of top industrial financiers and executives: "The creation of wealth is not necessarily a lovely process. People can get hurt, skills can be rendered obsolete, investment can lose value, natural resources have to be put to the uses of man, and in the process beautiful landscapes have to be scratched, trees have to be cut down." He countered that gloomy estimation with the assurance that the Administrative Center would attest to a progressive, public-minded institution: "[We] are witnessing an impressive manifestation of the business community thinking greatly of its functions. I speak now not only of all the efforts that businessmen contribute in their communities unrelated to their own activities, but also of pursuing and seeking excellence in the way this enterprise has achieved it in this great new nerve center for Deere and Company."[45]

At an extreme, the campus, estate, and office park became vehicles for out and out corporate duplicity. The reconstructed wetlands and restored woodlands of Boeing Longacres Park spin a tale of environmental responsibility, of abiding by, even extending beyond, environmental regulations for the public good, of literally having environmental concerns at the core of corporate life. Yet in the same year that construction began at Longacres, *Fortune* singled out Boeing as one of ten egregious corporate "environmental laggards," noting the company's beyond the norm increases in toxic, chemical, and solid waste production.[46]

In the 1951 essay "Ghosts at the Door," J.B. Jackson wrote of the American lawn: "in an indefinable way the lawn is . . . the background for conventionally correct behavior. . . . In America the lawn is more than essential, it is the heart and very soul of the front yard . . . that landscape element that every American values most."[47] With a seductive, dissembling élan, the corporate campus, the corporate estate, and the office park gave corporate capitalism a front yard, with, as Jackson said, "its vague but nonetheless real social connotations."

THE ENACTED ENVIRONMENT | 16

Examining the Streets and Yards of East Los Angeles

My image of home is the street where I grew up, rather than the house where I slept at night. Life inside the house was bleak and indifferent compared to the excitement and fascination of the street.

In 1963, when my family moved to Hendricks Street in East Los Angeles, it was a street in a typical working-class neighborhood, just off Whittier Boulevard, about seven miles east of downtown Los Angeles. The small houses, painted white, with their tidy front yards, created a sense of visual harmony in the neighborhood. Most of the residents were older white couples, with a few Mexican American families mixed in. Initially, I thought my new neighborhood was unfriendly, because many of the elderly couples did not have children and stayed inside their homes. I had moved from an older Latino neighborhood in Boyle Heights, where many members of my extended family were neighbors, and the family had spent much of its free time in the front yard or on the porch.

Within a few years of our moving to Hendricks Street, a large number of other Mexican families moved in. The increase in children greatly

Figure 16.1. The street plan, lots, and small houses of a working-class suburb.
Initially built in the 1920s and 1930s, the streets and houses still set some of the
basic outlines of the enacted exterior environment of Latino East Los Angeles.

changed the quiet and orderly residential streetscape. We would play on
the streets and trample over the lawns. Not surprisingly, as soon as the
number of children increased, fences went up around the front lawns to
keep us out and to police the toddlers and dogs inside the fences (fig 16.1).
Although we had backyards, we rarely played in them, because of their
seclusion and unkempt condition. They usually ended up as the territory
of the unfriendly family dog. Rarely did I even go inside the homes of my
friends; most of the bedrooms were small and dominated by beds everywhere.

As a child, I considered the adult world to exist entirely in our house,
and the world outside, the world my friends and I inhabited, in the front
yards and the local streets. The streets and front yards were accessible at
all times to us; they were the public spaces where we would gather daily
to become part of the larger community. While life on the street may have
looked chaotic to outsiders, to us it was orderly because we understood it.
We found fun, adventure, and comfort outside of our homes.

When people returned from work, especially on the long, warm summer evenings, the street became very active, drawing people out of their

homes. It became a well-orchestrated show, in which everyone had a time and place. People walking, talking, watering their grass, or fixing cars made the evening front yards of Hendricks Street the place to be and to be seen. Age and gender groups controlled different locations: girls tended to play on the front porches and lawns, where they took care of toddlers; boys played touch football and other group contact games on the street. During the late afternoon, my mother would talk for hours to the neighbor over the fence on one side of our front yard. Then, after dinner, she might talk until nightfall to the woman on the opposite side.

Today in Los Angeles County, Latino Americans outnumber Anglo Americans. Of the county's 9.5 million residents, 41 percent are Latino. As greater numbers of Latino immigrants and native-born Mexican American citizens have settled in the suburbs of East Los Angeles, they have brought different use patterns to the existing built environment. The newcomers' former communities—*ciudades, pueblos,* and *ranchos* in Mexico and Central America—were structured differently, both physically and socially, than the American suburb. By examining the patterns by which Latinos have transformed early suburban East Los Angeles, we can better understand the "Latinoization" of urban space throughout Los Angeles and in other U.S. cities as well.

ARCHITECTS AND THE ENACTED ENVIRONMENT

The idea of examining and analyzing the place where I grew up developed during my formal architectural and planning studies at MIT. My architecture professors emphasized the importance of form, while the urban planners examined social issues and policy. Neither group addressed the use of space by real people. Professors would lecture about the built environment and emphasize the order and harmony of "place" as an abstract idea. Although their slides were aesthetically pleasing, they failed to address the behavior patterns of people from different cultures, genders, and income levels.

As I began to look for academic resources to help me understand my cultural background and its distinct use of outdoor space—and how to put it into terms that could be used in my professions of planning and architecture—I did not find much research on Mexican American environments. *The Social Order of the Slum,* by Gerald Suttles, did provide insights into interpersonal, household, and economic relations. Philippe Boudon's *Lived-In Architecture* and Amos Rapoport's *House Form and*

Culture each provided a framework for examining transformations of physical space by cultural and economic forces rather than professional design. Oscar Newman's *Defensible Space* examined the psychological effects of public spaces and their meaning, while William Whyte's *The Social Life of Small Urban Spaces* suggested a method for studying people in public spaces.[1]

These studies charted a method for understanding the relationship between people and the city. However, no one except J. B. Jackson had focused on Latino areas. Jackson's holistic and humanistic approach to understanding cultural landscapes in general and the U.S.-Mexican border region in particular gave me a broad perspective for understanding the Mexican barrios of East Los Angeles. With Jackson as an early guide, rather than examining the barrio only as a part of Los Angeles, I could examine it as part of the greater American Southwest.[2]

In spite of earnest statements to the contrary, architects are largely trained to design buildings, with a strong focus on interior spaces. They often view exterior space primarily as a foreground for highlighting their facades. When architects do take note of human activity, they often see it as a direct consequence of their built forms. For instance, designers study and copy the idealized physical form of the Italian piazza because of its human activity. By reproducing the enclosed spaces of the Italian piazza— or more recently (with the move to the New Urbanism), the village squares of colonial America or the City Beautiful movement—architects believe they can actually create human activity. But architecture alone does not create a sense of place. The way people *use* the space between buildings—the *enacted* exterior environment—is a necessary component of a vital cultural landscape.

Exterior space provides a background for people to manipulate places as they please, much like a movie set. To understand the enacted environment, one must examine people as users and creators of a place through their behavior patterns—patterns affected by culture, space, and time.[3] For example, the housing stock of East Los Angeles was built primarily between the 1920s and 1940s. Neighborhoods of two- and three-bedroom bungalows were produced with front porches, all set back a uniform distance from the street. However, today's tremendous difference in the appearance of the community of East Los Angeles from that of other Los Angeles suburbs (originally built in the same decades) results from the subsequent use of space around the houses. By working and relaxing in these outdoor spaces, neighborhood residents create a spontaneous, dynamic, and animated urban landscape unlike any other in the Los Angeles area. The streets, front yards, driveways, and other spaces around homes bring residents together in East Los Angeles, while in many other neighborhoods and cities these same spaces remain unoccupied, thereby isolating residents.

ELEMENTS OF EAST L.A.'S ENACTED ENVIRONMENT

Listed and briefly described here are key elements of the East Los Angeles enacted environment. Although they are presented in a linear, hierarchical order, from the private front yard to the most public streets and sidewalks, in reality, one often experiences these elements all at once.

People

Very few official signs or landmarks indicate where East Los Angeles begins. However, you can tell when you have arrived because of the large number of people in the front yards and on the streets, engaging in all types of activities. What may look like random groups of people are actually sets of well-ordered interactions in which everybody has a role. Children play, teenagers hang out, and the elderly watch. These roles enhance the street activity and provide security for families, neighbors, and friends. People on the streets in East Los Angeles exercise implicit social control. In each neighborhood area of the district, everyone knows everyone else. If you do not belong, they will challenge you with words or a stare.

Front Yards

The element of the East Los Angeles landscape that most demonstrates the Mexican use of space, while also expressing personal and family identity, is the enclosed front yard. Here, the residents put their faces on the street; the yard is an area they can publicly personalize without interfering with their neighbors. Enclosed front yards function as a work space, party area, or just a place to spend time. Latino front yards vary from elaborate gardens reminiscent of Mexican courtyard houses, to bare, unkempt yards (fig. 16.2).

J. B. Jackson suggests that the front yards in middle-class Anglo American suburbs have become "a space dedicated to showing that we are good

Figure 16.2. An extension of the home. For Latinos, the front yard is not a passive, symbolic patch of grass separating the house from the street, but an actively used, semipublic space.

citizens, and responsible members of the community."[4] Support of community identity, he notes, is measured by how well households uphold neighborhood standards through the upkeep of their front lawns. In the typical American front yard, a balance is struck between the collective and the individual identity. Since most suburban Americans socialize in their backyards, Jackson describes the front yard as a very impersonal space: "No one sits there, no personal objects are left lying." This kind of front yard acts as a psychological barrier separating the private space of the home from the public space of the street.

Although the houses in East Los Angeles were built by non-Latinos, their yards have evolved into a new vernacular form as residents have made changes to suit their needs. Front yards reflect Mexican cultural values as applied to American suburban form: a hybrid of two architectural vocabularies, a new language that uses building elements from both Mexico and the United States. In a sense, the Latino front yard functions like a step-down transformer: all the sights and sounds from the street are scaled down to family size and brought under personal control. Unlike Anglo middle-class suburbanites, who, in effect, pull away from the street, people

Figure 16.3.   A front porch, transformed into a highly social outdoor room.

in East Los Angeles graciously extend their home life toward the street and bring the street's party, work space, and conversation into the front yard.

In the Latino front yard, every change, no matter how small, has meaning and purpose. Bringing the sofa out to the front porch, stuccoing over the clapboard siding, painting the house in vivid colors, or placing a statue of the Virgin Mary in the front yard all reflect the struggles, triumphs, and everyday habits and values of working-class Latinos. The front yards in East L.A. are not anonymous spaces upholding a single community identity, but rather exuberant vignettes of the individual owners' lives. Upon entering one of these enclosed spaces, the residents' private world suddenly unfolds. What appears cluttered from outside the fence becomes as organized as the objects in a room; indeed, the enclosed front yard is almost a like another room in the house.

Because of all the activity in the front yard, the front porch becomes the focal point of the house. Since the rise of the automobile, air conditioning, and television, the use and importance of the front porch has declined in most American homes.[5] However, in East Los Angeles, the front porch has gained a new importance as residents enlarge and expand it for heavy use. Residents sit on the porch to escape summer heat or just to be outside with family, friends, and neighbors (fig. 16.3).

Figure 16.4.   Conversing at the gate. Fences not only play traditional roles of marking private property but also provide a place to socialize.

Fences

Waist-high fences are ubiquitous throughout the residential landscape of East Los Angeles. They outline most front yards and define the streetscape of Latino barrios. Most are visually permeable chain link or elaborate wrought iron. In non-Latino neighborhoods, people also build fences for security and privacy, and some do in East Los Angeles as well. In Latino neighborhoods, as elsewhere, fences define boundaries between public and private space; they create easily defensible spaces and assert ownership. However, in East Los Angeles, fences serve additional purposes. They are places to hang wet laundry, to talk to neighbors, and to sell items. As J. B. Jackson has observed, boundaries not only mark separate ownership, they also can bring people together.[6] In East L.A., fences create a place where people can congregate; they serve as social catalysts (fig. 16.4).

In Latino neighborhoods, fences also solve what might be called "the problem of the front door." When visitors cross an East Los Angeles front yard and reach the front door of the house, they have reached a pivotal part of the home. The front door marks the boundary between an open, public realm and a closed, inaccessible one. Thus, when a visitor and a resident meet at a front door, there is great pressure to define the social relationship: will the visitor be invited in or not? The fence around a front yard telescopes this social threshold from the front door to the front gate.

Taken together, the social uses of the front yards and fences of East Los Angeles transform the residential street into an unconventional plaza with both public and semiprivate zones. On the street, residents and pedestrians participate in a public social dialogue, but in the yards, residents can stay within the semiprivate comfort and security of their outdoor room.

Props

Even outside the fenced yards, no space in East Los Angeles—private or public—is left unused or unmarked. Movable, relatively temporary props help to mark space and to create the enacted public environment of the Latino neighborhood. A table and chair brought to a sidewalk define territory and make people comfortable in open urban space. For men working on a parked car in the street or in the front yard, the car becomes the center of a day's activity. A sidewalk sales table can generate some revenue and become a focal point for neighborhood gossip.

Commercial sidewalks are also transformed with props. Many shopkeepers in East Los Angeles have replaced the glass front wall of their shops with metal doors or shutters, which open to the street during business hours. Shop wares and racks of goods serve to create a flow of activity between store interiors and outdoor spaces.

Sound and paint are additional types of props. From car stereos to mariachis, music in East Los Angeles temporarily controls and defines space. Visually, walls painted vividly, be it with graffiti or murals, are also key places for Latino cultural expression. This tradition, like so much else in the neighborhood, has come to the United States with immigrants from Mexico. There, murals and graphics are important communication tools that date back to European medieval times and the later centuries, when the Spanish arrived in Latin America and had to communicate with the indigenous people there. Pictures, along with words, are still used to give

Figure 16.5. Props for communication and flair. The pictures and words on this *taquería* describe what is sold and also make it a visually exuberant addition to the public space of the street.

directions in Mexico City. For example, a pig's or cow's head indicates a butcher shop, while a cornucopia indicates a vegetable and fruit stand.

In East Los Angeles, very few spaces and walls are left untouched. The flamboyant words and graphics covering many buildings from top to bottom liven up a space; they add a kinetic visual sense to the urban environment (fig. 16.5). Murals used for business advertisement can also be political or religious. Murals painted on the side walls of corner stores not only prevent or disguise graffiti, but also create a visual transition from commercial to residential uses.

In East Los Angeles, the use of props of all kinds creates a unifying human scale of activity. This is true in both residential and commercial areas. Props scale down the commercial landscape to pedestrian size, which contradicts the automobile scale of the major Los Angeles avenues and the city's wide, straight residential streets. Driving through the streets of Latino barrios, all one sees is clutter. When walking, however, one experiences a richly textured visual and tactile (that is, "hands on") landscape that enhances the enacted environment.

Recently, architects and urban designers have employed street furniture, banners, benches, and cart vendors in their designs for festival market places. In these professionally designed public spaces, the props reflect the control of a single owner. Such calculated auxiliary objects function as generic symbols of a pedestrian-friendly environment and as an opportunity for generating more income, rather than as indicators of a specific cultural group. In contrast, the use of props in East Los Angeles is anything but calculated; many props do add to marginal incomes, but more important, they reflect cultural traditions and individual initiative rather than a corporate sales strategy.

Street Vendors

In Mexican cities, informal outdoor selling is very popular, and Latinos have transferred this practice to the United States. In East Los Angeles, the streets provide a backdrop for individual economic survival. Because much of the American urban landscape is not designed for outdoor selling, East Los Angeles vendors have had to be innovative in adapting urban space for their sales. For example, vendors selling on the exits and entrances of freeways transform a space not designed for pedestrians. Vendors also occupy intersections and temporarily convert vacant lots, front yards, sidewalks, and curbs into markets (fig. 16.6).

East Los Angeles vendors vary in their mobility and amount of investment. The most highly mobile, and those with the least overhead, are day laborers who station themselves near hardware stores throughout Los Angeles to compete for menial jobs. If passing motorists show interest in hiring someone and slow down, they are swarmed by work-hungry men. The supply of jobs is always smaller than the number of men available.

Also mobile, but weighed down with their musical instruments, are the many mariachi bands that gather at the intersection of First Street and Boyle Avenue, fairly close to downtown L.A., now referred to as Mariachi Plaza, where they wait patiently for people to drive up and hire them for parties. On the streets of East Los Angeles, other mariachis walk from bars to restaurants, serenading patrons. Additional walking salespeople work the streets of East Los Angeles selling fake flowers, cassette tapes, or other lightweight items.

Some vendors selling similar products find a good semipermanent location for their business and create makeshift tents by attaching sheets of plastic or fabric to buildings, poles, and fences (fig. 16.7). In the past few

Figure 16.6.   Street vendors in East Los Angeles. These flower vendors have temporarily transformed a boulevard median into commercial space.

years there has been an increase in the number of small barbecue stands known as *taquerías,* located mainly on commercial streets in East Los Angeles. On the weekends, many people also sell odds and ends from their front yards. Fences again play an important role, as they can hold up items and delineate the selling space. The yard sales add still more activity to the already lively residential streets.

Still other vendors circulate through the neighborhood's residential streets (and, to a lesser extent, its commercial streets) with carts, cars, or trucks, primarily selling food. Many walk the same beat day in and day out. Pushcart vendors sometimes look out of place on the wide suburban streets of Los Angeles, because most streets were originally designed for cars, not pedestrians. Vendors who conduct business from their car or truck often park along streets or in vacant lots (fig. 16.8). Some of them move several times a day. Large panel trucks or vans outfitted as quick-meal stands, part of the scene in many American cities, are known in East Los Angeles as "roach coaches." They provide lunches at construction sites and dinners in other parts of the neighborhood. Some can be found open again late at night, tapping the market of pedestrians who are out on the street after the bars close.

Figure 16.7. Makeshift shop. This street vendor has found a semipermanent location and has set up a stall with street furniture, a table, and a tarp attached to the fence.

Figure 16.8. Roadside vendor. A parked truck along the road becomes a temporary produce store.

Street vendors have been a part of the enacted environment in Latino East Los Angeles since the 1920s. However, with the rising Latino population in the 1990s, there has been a dramatic increase in street vending. In some communities around East Los Angeles, this type of commerce is now prohibited. Furthermore, many residents complain about the trash the street vendors generate, and permanent businesses complain about unfair competition.[7]

THE CORNER OF OLYMPIC AND ROWAN

Among the most vibrant areas of East Los Angeles are the places where residential and commercial zones meet. The corner of Olympic Boulevard and Rowan Avenue is like many other street corners in this regard. Olympic Boulevard is one of the heavily used four-lane streets that link the various cities of Los Angeles County. The boulevard starts near the beach in Santa Monica and stretches eastward for twenty-five miles, traversing downtown Los Angeles and extending into East Los Angeles.[8] Rowan Avenue is a purely local and largely residential street. Just a half block to the north of this intersection, regional traffic roars by overhead on I-5, the Santa Ana Freeway. A block to the south begins the area of large warehouses and factories along the railroad tracks in the cities of Vernon and Commerce, where many East Los Angeles residents work.

Elsewhere, in typical streetcar-era suburban neighborhoods, the corners of commercial and residential streets are rarely populated; people park their cars and walk to the stores, but they spend little time on the street itself. In East Los Angeles, however, many people congregate on the front and side streets of Olympic and Rowan. Drivers double-park to talk to their friends, or park right on the sidewalk; other drivers slow down to see who is around. The traffic creates a dynamic flow of movement and activity at the corner. As one visitor remarked to me, the residents of East Los Angeles "know how to use a corner."[9]

At Rowan and Olympic, two enterprises set the diurnal rhythm and generate much of the activity. A small but permanent building houses Antojitos Denise, a taco stand on the corner (fig. 16.9). Because of the lack of storage room in the building, food supplies are brought in twice a day by a large truck that parks on Rowan Avenue. Most of the kitchen cleanup work is done on this side of the taco stand, and employees take their lunches and breaks in front of the house behind it. The taco stand has a mural of a traditional Mexican family making and eating tacos on its

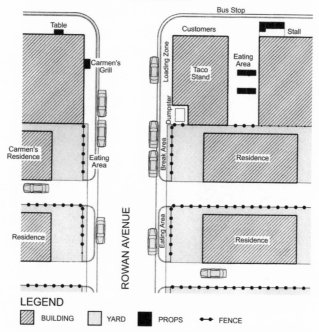

Figure 16.9. Olympic and Rowan. This map of the intersection of Olympic Boulevard and Rowan Avenue shows activity that would be typical from five to seven in the evening, Monday through Friday, when people are returning from work.

Rowan Avenue side. Seating for customers is provided on the other side of the stand, but most customers prefer to eat standing up, facing the street or leaning on the cars parked along Rowan. These overlapping commercial and residential land uses—the workers on break, the customers leaning on the cars—connect the visual excitement of Olympic Boulevard to the neighborhood street.

Across Rowan Avenue from the taco stand is Carmen, *"la mujer del elote"* (the corn woman). Every weekend she sets up her grill, a small table, and some kitchen chairs, and sells roasted corn for a dollar an ear (fig. 16.10). She talks to all the pedestrians, and many stop for at least ten minutes to gossip with her. She lives in a small house only a few feet from the corner, where she can often be seen cleaning the corn in her large front yard.

On the weekends, because most people are off work and the auto traffic on Olympic declines, the rhythm of life changes on nearby streets as

Figure 16.10. *La mujer del elote.* Carmen, the "corn woman" at the corner of Olympic and Rowan, is almost always seen in conversation with passersby.

well. On Saturday mornings, one sees people doing chores in their front yards: one woman dusts off a rug over the fence, another brings out her dinette set to be scrubbed down. Some men wash their cars, others fix their cars or install stereos. Still others sell items from their front yards. In comparison with Monday through Thursday evenings, weekend evenings bring more excitement to these streets. Young teenage girls dress up and buzz around the sidewalks in front of their homes. Teenage boys cruise by in their mini-trucks while the *cholos* (gang members) cruise by in their low-riders. Mariachis walk down the streets ready to serenade residents willing to pay for a song or two. Some bands get lucky and find a birthday, *quinceañera* (the local equivalent of a debutante party), or some other gathering where participants are willing to pay for several songs or a whole evening of music.

Sunday mornings in the vicinity of corners like Olympic and Rowan begin with a strange silence. Early light finds old men collecting the leftover aluminum beer cans and bottles on the streets to recycle them.

Slowly the neighborhood wakes up, as parents set out for church with their small children. Teenagers rise later, dress more fashionably, and attend later mass. Some people return from services, and others return from the corner stores carrying a Sunday paper and a pot of *menudo* (Mexican tripe soup). By afternoon, the block has fully risen and front yard society emerges as people sit on furniture on the front porch or lawn. They greet visiting family members and friends, for whom parking by now has become a problem. Nevertheless, the pace is much slower on Sunday than during the rest of the week. From Monday to Thursday, only the evenings will seem lively, and on the next Friday night, the weekend increase in activity will predictably start again.

EAST LOS ANGELES AS A MODEL CITY

The proponents of New Urbanism currently are searching for ways to recreate social interaction in the public spaces of American suburbs. This new approach to urban design constructs festival marketplaces, creates new plazas and village squares, moves houses closer to the street, and again provides them with porches—all characteristics similar to the vernacular development of outdoor space in my East Los Angeles barrio.[10] Whether or not these initiatives will actually create more social interaction remains to be seen. New Urbanists find inspiration in the historic urban forms of Europe and early-twentieth-century middle-class America, but they rarely look to the street life that exists today in Latino, African American, Asian, and other minority communities throughout the United States. Detailed studies of rich social environments such as East Los Angeles, however, could offer inspiration for filling some of the social voids of suburban America.

J. B. Jackson often reminded his readers that landscapes, even ephemeral ones, provide important contexts for understanding multicultural places such as Los Angeles.[11] Mexican Americans and more recent Mexican immigrants have transformed the once staid bungalow suburbs of East Los Angeles into their own brand of New Urbanism. Clusters of people socializing on street corners and over front yard fences; the furniture and props that make these front yards into personal statements; vivid colors, murals, and business signs; street vendors carrying their wares, pushing carts, or setting up temporary tables and tarps—all contribute to the lively, unique landscape of the barrio, where local residents (not professional designers) have focused their inventive imaginations on the transformation of the spaces in front of and between their homes and stores. The resulting enacted outdoor environment is a fluid place, one composed of front yards and commercial streets, of private and public places unified by human behavior and ideas. These hardworking people, many of them newcomers to this country, have created something many other Americans desire: a vibrant street life, shared public spaces, and the sense of belonging to a community.

DAVID C. SLOANE

MEDICINE IN THE (MINI) MALL | 17

An American Health Care Landscape

In one of his last papers, J. B. Jackson described the rise of the "auto-vernacular" landscape, which he had been chronicling for decades. "The car has taken over," he wrote, "taking the family to the day care center, the Laundromat, the supermarket, the drive-in restaurant, the emergency room at the hospital." The new car-centered landscape represented a shift in daily urban life, since the auto-vernacular was "composed of structures and spaces designed to accommodate the auto as distinguished from spaces designed to accommodate people." Jackson struggled with understanding the scope, meaning, and consequences of this landscape about which he felt so ambivalent.[1] He applauded it as a distinctly American and modern landscape, but he never seemed entirely comfortable with all its ramifications.

Many Americans share his ambivalence. They love the convenience of mini-malls, but dislike their architecture, the loss of older neighborhood-center styles, and the perceived diminished sense of community they represent. However, mini-malls and the auto-vernacular continue to shape

Figure 17.1.   Photograph of the intersection of Wilshire Boulevard and Western Avenue, Los Angeles, 1939. Whittington Collection. The automobile culture of Los Angeles was already thriving by the late 1930s. This intersection was home to the 1931 art deco Wiltern Theatre (right) and the Owl Drug Company (left), with its prominent clock and Coca-Cola sign.

the cityscape; barriers between formerly separate sectors of the landscape are collapsing. For instance, white-collar professionals hold themselves aloof from the older auto-vernacular, as if they were less influenced by the car culture. When Jackson defined the auto-vernacular, he included among his examples such businesses as a gas station, a parking garage, a racetrack, and "the strip" (fig. 17.1). Lawyers, doctors, bankers, academics, and other professionals stood symbolically apart from that landscape.

Some professionals set up their offices outside the urban commercial landscape altogether. Many physicians still worked out of their homes as late as the 1930s; either their patients came to their homes, or physicians traveled to the patient's home for consultation. In small-town America, the central square was neatly segmented into commercial and professional levels. Along Main Street, commercial businesses such as restaurants and banks, drug and grocery stores were downstairs, while the lawyers, doctors, and accountants were upstairs. Downstairs, windows were plastered with SALE and other signs of commerce. Small brass plaques by the doors or discreet window signs with the professional firm's name notified passersby of the appropriate stairs to climb for the desired service.[2] In the post–World War II era, however, these models largely disappeared.[3] Physicians could no longer carry around the diagnostic tools and treatments of scientific medicine in their proverbial black bags. More sophisticated tests and interventions required a clinic or hospital setting. Hospitals, physician groups, and speculative developers, spurred on by the specialization of medicine, constructed medical office buildings on major urban and suburban thoroughfares surrounding the city. In these generic buildings, medicine moved onto the street but did not become part of it.

For instance, Los Angeles's Wilshire Metropolitan Medical Building, which opened in 1964 on perhaps the nation's most famous mid-twentieth-century boulevard, was sited, according to a contemporary advertisement, "just west of the Harbor Freeway and easy to get to from any point in the Southland" (fig. 17.2).[4] It was convenient to "ALL major Los Angeles hospitals," with suites "tailored to meet the individual doctor's specialized needs." The sleek, concrete-and-glass fifteen-story building gave no indication that it was dedicated to the medical arts. Its dark glass doorway offered only an opaque window to passing cars. Along the lengthy corridors of offices within the building, small signs informed passersby of the available medical services. Discreet practices were thus sheltered from the commercial world outside.

Such towers still hold many medical practices, but as people change the way they navigate the city and traverse the health care system, developers are also changing the spatial relationship between patients and providers. In Los Angeles's mini-malls and small shopping centers and along its commercial streets, medicine is becoming more visible in the "auto-vernacular landscape." Practitioners are leaving their medical office buildings for more commercially advantageous locations, creating a new landscape that reflects new health care practices and competition, as well as the maturation of the American drive-in culture.

THE CHANGING LANDSCAPE, MEDICAL AND OTHERWISE

Recently, a more competitive medical market and the rapid expansion of outpatient (or ambulatory) medicine have begun restructuring health care provision in the United States. One change has been that hospitals are being designed to appear more welcoming and accessible.[5] Another change is that health care providers have been forced to search for sites outside of

Figure 17.2.   Wilshire Metropolitan Medical Building, Wilshire Boulevard, Los Angeles, c. 1960s. The
medical office building towers above the street, suggesting the aloof distance of health care professionals
from the world outside.

hospitals that are easy for patients to find and are cheaper to staff. Not
surprisingly, such sites are increasingly found in Jackson's auto-vernacular landscape. Some clinics are freestanding, others situated within a mini-
mall or even a shopping center. In whatever location, these facilities raise
questions about the status and role of medicine in society, and the role of
medicine in reshaping the urban landscape.

Jackson's conception of the auto-vernacular is helpful here. While
changes in medical practice and financing provide a rationale for the relocation of medical offices, the automobile has influenced the siting of the
new facilities. Jackson wrote in 1985, "what makes most American cities
interesting . . . is that . . . they are not pedestrian cities; they are not to be

explored on foot." He noted that the automobile extends the city, opening its horizons even as it sprawls over the land, stretching "for miles and miles."[6] No place better represents the rise of the automotive city, nor more effectively reflects the changing medical landscape, than Los Angeles.[7] As chronicled by a number of recent books, Los Angeles has been a prototype of the sprawling city in the evolving urban landscape.[8] Given the city's importance in this regard, this chapter examines the changing place of medicine and health care in the urban landscape of Los Angeles and in Southern California in general.

Other writers have evoked the freeway or highway as a torrential force sweeping through the urban landscape, but Jackson was entranced with the commercial street. As he observed, the "contemporary street . . . is more like an environmental force, a river or torrent, that has to be controlled with a definite policy in view."[9] With the rising deluge along the commercial street, both consumers and retailers were caught in a new current. Modern-day "mobile consumers" would "think nothing of traveling to a supermarket that has better parking than one located two miles nearer."[10] The flexibility and convenience of the car had altered space and place as well as social choices.

Jackson argued that, in addition, retailers "must learn to attract . . . business in a way they never had to do when customers were confined to a certain familiar area."[11] The battle for retail recognition in the increasingly fast-traveling urban world shaped many commercial trends during the twentieth century. Fighting for space, attention, and customers, retailers strung themselves out over miles of streets, looking to be more accessible, more attractive, more easily noticed, more profitable. Parking became a major issue as early as the 1920s and has only increased in gravity since that time.[12] The use of the car created convenience but diminished recognizability. Imagine someone trying to pick out an address or a sign while walking at three miles per hour, as opposed driving at thirty, forty, or fifty miles per hour. The higher speeds require visual signals to be bold and eye catching.

MINI-MALL MEDICINE

The now ubiquitous mini-mall is symbolic of this new bolder, more aggressive commercial landscape. As Richard Longstreth persuasively argues, the development of the small neighborhood shopping center, whether it's called a taxpayer block, a shopping center, or a mini-mall, spans the twentieth century.[13] Retailers have perfected its design through the decades, changing parking configurations, altering tenant mixes, and adapting to changing architectural fashions. Throughout, the neighborhood center has served its small surrounding market with stores that provide convenience goods. Today, instead of a small grocery store and shoe emporium, you are more likely to find a video store and a restaurant, but the mini-mall's commercial purpose has changed very little.

When we think of these centers, we rarely imagine them housing a health care facility. But increasingly, chiropractors, dentists, acupuncturists, herbal medicine shops, health food stores, and, more recently, primary care clinics and ambulatory surgery centers have moved into the mini-mall. They have moved in because the medical system is undergoing fundamental shifts that have made access, visibility, and expense increasingly important.

First, "managed care" has systematized competition in the health care system. The health care market had long been constrained by controls on admission into the profession, on the extension of admitting privileges to hospitals, and on commercial advertising. Medicine was viewed—and its practitioners viewed themselves—as above the market, just as they placed themselves outside or above the commercial establishments of the auto-vernacular. However, employers' demands for discounted rates of care, and discussions about federal health care subsidies, have made the financial structures of health care more visible to consumers. The rise of health maintenance organizations (HMOs) since the 1970s has fostered competition and encouraged centralization in health care systems, evident in the hospital chains that have become so common. Consumers employed by a relatively large employer or paying for heath insurance themselves have a choice once a year between contending health care plans and providers. Systems compete for patients by promising low-cost, high-quality health care.

The second critical change is the rise and remarkable expansion of ambulatory services. At the beginning of the twentieth century, most outpatient services were for the poor. Through the century, however, new treatments for a wide range of illnesses made long hospital stays unnecessary. In the last twenty-five years especially, medical practice started an ambulatory care revolution. Many hospitals can fill no more than 40 percent of their inpatient beds, even as their ambulatory clinics are jammed.[14] And that represents only ambulatory services in hospitals, not the huge number of ambulatory visits to clinics and individual practices. The monumental hospital was the symbol of twentieth-century medicine (fig. 17.3), but the ambulatory clinic will replace it early in the new century.

Figure 17.3.   Photograph of the exterior of the Los Angeles County Hospital, Los Angeles, 1932. *Los Angeles Examiner,* Hearst Collection. The monumental hospital literally towers above celebrants on opening day, a physical symbol of medicine's authority.

A third shift has been the new legitimacy of alternative or complementary health care practitioners, such as chiropractors and acupuncturists. While each therapy has a particular past that helps shape its place in the present health care landscape, their practitioners have as a group struggled for acceptance among "regular" physicians. Even as regular providers belittle their theories and reject their efficacy, Americans flock to them. A recent Harvard survey estimates that Americans made roughly 628 million visits to alternative therapy practitioners in 1997. Those patients spent roughly $27 billion, almost as much as they did on visits to regular physicians.[15]

The shifts in competitiveness, the ambulatory nature of care, and alternative treatments have all reinforced the spread of mini-mall medicine.

The competitive market for health care consumers encourages the reloca-tion of primary care and some specialty care to facilities more convenient to patients. These facilities are possible because of the high volume of am-bulatory patients. And the new clinics are simply joining alternative care providers who have long been established in more commercial locations. The places where consumers spend their daily lives are along the boule-vards and in the neighborhood shopping centers. Unlike the professional office buildings of the last generation, which were aloof from or situated outside the commercial realm, the new sites for health care are in the commercial complexes next to the pizza parlors and copier shops.

PIONEERS

The pioneer practitioners who moved into the mini-mall and along the commercial street were particularly sensitive to health care consumers' available choices and were the first to overcome resistance to advertising. Alternative care providers have had fewer constraints placed on them, be-cause their services often are not covered by health insurance, nor are they bound by the same regulations as conventional care. Left outside the professional system, the alternative practitioners opened offices in com-mercial buildings, often in ethnically diverse neighborhoods. Then den-tists and eye care practitioners (opticians and optometrists) started relo-cating from professional buildings to more accessible and competitive locations. Changes in the regulatory environment and the rise of compet-itive franchises, especially in the eye care industry, encouraged such inno-vation. Eventually, herbal stores and optical outlets would become typical not only in the smaller mini-malls and shopping centers, but also in the regional shopping malls.[16] These pioneers provided models for the later arrivals.

Alternative care providers have long practiced in Southern California. Chinese herbalists were advertising citywide by the 1920s. Today, chiro-practors, acupuncturists, herbal healers, and other alternative medical prac-titioners are common in mini-malls and on commercial streets. Partly this shift was driven by the diffusion of ethnic minorities out of downtown. Los Angeles is a diverse city, with an equal percentage of Latinos and whites and large concentrations of Southeast and East Asians and African Americans. The Hanmi Plaza, on Eighth Street, houses not only Lim's Acupuncture, but also Medicina General, suggesting the ethnic diversity of the users. However, alternative medicine transcends any single therapy's ethnic origins. Acupuncture practices can be found throughout the region, as can herbal shops. The most visible alternative therapies are chiropractics and herbal medicines. Near Koreatown, for instance, a chiropractic clinic is adjacent to a Mexican restaurant in a concrete, flat-roofed mini-mall with a vaguely Southwestern style. Across the city, in much wealthier, newer Marina Del Rey, a chiropractor and optometrist have facilities on the first floor of a two-story setback center with a faux brick facade.[17]

Dentists and eye care practitioners have already joined the alternative care providers in the mini-mall, looking for the same accessibility and visibility. Dentists have long been community based, but eye care services were usually found in professional office buildings, with the optometrists among the physicians, and the opticians down on the ground floor. Since optical care franchises became legal, they have entered the mini-mall, shopping center, even the shopping mall. Optical shops, such as Pearle Vision and other one-hour shops, have become so prevalent in our malls that we now take their presence for granted. However, as Regina Herzlinger reminds us, in the 1970s, many patients could not shop for eyeglasses because many states prohibited them from obtaining their prescriptions, outlawed advertising, and restricted optometrists from working directly for an optician, all in the name of protecting patients from commercial influences.[18]

RELOCATING PRIMARY CARE

Medical clinics and surgical centers are the newest residents of the mini-mall. The closure of public clinics, the restriction of emergency rooms to insured customers, and the opportunity for private providers to receive governmental payments has propelled the opening of many independent medical centers, particularly in poorer neighborhoods. Freestanding clinics, or, as they are sometimes called, "doc-in-the-boxes," are often inexpensive places to receive minimal medical services. Their quality varies widely. Some are believed to employ unprepared clinicians and charge clients for inappropriate procedures; others provide essential, good-quality care for underserved neighborhoods.

Such small clinics have become pervasive in poorer Los Angeles neighborhoods. Driving down one of the major commercial streets, such as Vermont, Pico, or Western, a dozen medical clinics can be seen within a few

Figure 17.4.   Van Ness Plaza sign, Pico Boulevard, Los
Angeles. At this mini-mall, medical, retail, and fast-food
tenants share equal billing.

blocks. The Van Ness Plaza shopping center is in a low-income Latino
neighborhood near the very busy transportation corridor of Vermont
Avenue. Here, the Drew University health clinic is just doors down from
the nonprofit St. Basil's health clinic, and the Clínica Médica Familiar is
next to the Botánica, all in a heavily Korean neighborhood (fig. 17.4). Private, public; conventional, alternative: All are tucked in neatly next to
Domino's Pizza and the copy shop. All are cheap, nondescript, commercial
one-story wood-frame stucco buildings, ornamented with a single blue
stripe, arrayed in an L-shaped configuration, with a parking lot in front
(fig. 17.5).

Figure 17.5.   Van Ness Plaza, Pico Boulevard, Los Angeles. The nondescript mini-mall is now home to medical offices as well as a botánica, copier shop, and pizza parlor.

While most mini-mall clinics are in poor neighborhoods in rather run-down commercial centers, some are opening in newer centers in wealthier areas. Representative of this trend is the mini-mall at the corner of Highland and Wilshire, just east of the resurgent LaBrea commercial corridor, in the center of a diverse neighborhood, with the wealthy Hancock Park area to the east and Museum Row to the west. This two-story mini-mall has a new, more expensive architecture in a Mediterranean style with a pseudo-postmodern cupola. The center provides local residents with an interesting mix of stores convenient to the nearby businesses on Wilshire and LaBrea. The classic mini-mall categories are all covered: fast food at Fatburgers and Subway; photocopy services at Kinko's; the beauty salon and the cleaners; and semiprofessional services such as an insurance agent. The medical services are in amid them all. Not only are dental services advertised on the mini-mall's sign, but also a small medical clinic, a massage therapist, a chiropractor, and an acupuncturist.

These mini-mall clinics are competing with the expanded networks of stand-alone satellite centers being opened by hospitals and physician groups. The most prominent example of this trend in Los Angeles is the UCLA system of primary care centers, which are opening up in strategic

Figure 17.6.   UCLA Medical Group Clinic sign on
National Avenue, Los Angeles. The UCLA sign com-
petes in the cluttered visual space of commerce with a
McDonald's and a bank in this roadside landscape.

locations throughout the Westside. These centers are almost all one- or
two-story buildings either constructed for or adapted to medical services.
They are situated on prominent commercial streets, such as Wilshire in
Beverly Hills and National in West Los Angeles, and the buildings are
clearly visible, thanks to their big UCLA signs in bright blue and gold, the
university's colors (fig. 17.6). In some locations, only primary care services are offered. In others, primary care services are integrated with spe-
cialties such as pediatrics or women's health.

Most people visiting mini-mall or stand-alone clinics are seeking primary or emergency care, but a growing number are undergoing surgical
procedures. Among the newest innovations in medical practice is the rapid
rise of independent surgical clinics—from around two hundred nationally
in 1970 to more than twenty-five hundred in 1998. Most such centers are
freestanding buildings reminiscent of older professional buildings, offer-

Figure 17.7.   Granville Plaza, Los Angeles. The mini-mall sign (at the center) jumbles surgical center and fast-food restaurant, alternative therapist and regular physician in the new health care landscape. Stop for nachos, then finish with ambulatory surgery; the visit would be emblematic of the changing health care landscape.

ing a spectrum of ambulatory surgical procedures. However, as ambulatory techniques standardize and barriers between commerce and medicine diminish, surgical clinics appear poised to join primary care clinics in mini-malls and shopping centers.[19]

Granville Plaza, designed and built by Richard Donahue in 1988, epitomizes the changing medical landscape.[20] The Plaza is a two-story concrete mini-mall located mid-block along Wilshire Boulevard on the city's prosperous Westside. Its two wings are joined by a center bridge that also serves as the entrance to the mini-mall's underground parking lot. Tenants include several restaurants, Kinko's, and several small businesses. On the eastern upper floor, a chiropractor and a surgical clinic have offices. The surgical clinic is just above the copy shop (fig. 17.7).

On one level, mini-malls like Granville Plaza reconstruct the old Main Street configuration, with the professionals above the retailers. However, the clinics are no longer separated from the commercial image of the street. The plaza's main sign (at the center of fig. 17.7) merges the medical and nonmedical into a single commercial environment: Kinko's, Surgical

Center, Subway, India's Tandoori, Amir's Travel, Chiropractic & Nutritional, and so on. Signs like this one signal a physical and cultural relocation of medicine. Uses that were carefully separated for at least two generations are now mixed in an unruly combination.

A NEW HEALTH CARE LANDSCAPE?

Mini-mall medicine is in its formative stages nationwide. The fundamental changes in the health care system suggest that the medical landscape in Los Angeles (and other Sun Belt cities) will become a national phenomenon. In doing so, these new landscapes raise or reinforce issues about the role of medicine in American society. At this early stage of development, conclusions are impossible to draw, but observations about trends certainly are possible.

First, mini-mall medicine reduces physical and symbolic distinctions between conventional and alternative medicine. Through much of the twentieth century, conventional practitioners marginalized alternative care givers by excluding them from professional associations, conferences, and journals. This institutional exclusion was manifested in their physical separation: alternative practitioners were kept out of medical office buildings and hospitals, the central sites of health care. Mini-mall medicine diminishes these barriers. Chiropractors and acupuncturists are now found in the same commercial centers as pediatric internists and orthopedic surgeons. Commercial signs equate them rather than distinguish between them. Whether similar locations will reinforce the legitimacy of alternative health care is still unclear, but certainly more than at any time in the twentieth century, Americans are less willing to accept conventional proscriptions against such treatments.

Second, mini-mall medicine shifts some of the relationships between patients and providers. Practitioners long ago moved from a cozy, domestic setting to a hierarchical, structured setting in medical office buildings and hospitals. The physical environment of those facilities made clear the powerlessness of patients. Simply finding a doctor's office could be an ordeal in one of the older hospitals, with their maze of facilities. The long corridors of the urban office buildings spoke of the serious business undertaken within the quiet and decorous offices.

In sharp contrast, mini-mall facilities shimmer with signs of informality and welcome. Since this environment is structured to compete for clients, it destroys barriers, opens arms, even yells for attention. Within the offices, attempts may be made to tone down the commercial setting with professional furnishings, but once the barriers are down, it is difficult to reconstruct them. Whether the atmosphere evokes a more equitable relationship between patient (customer-client) and doctor (provider-clinician) is still unclear. Access and diminished physical evidence of power may represent only a commercialization of medicine that weakens medical professionalism and fails to strengthen the collaborative nature of the health care interaction.

Third, mini-mall medicine heightens already existing concerns about the commercialization of medicine. Removing medicine from a location where professional distance and objectivity is valorized to one where the marketplace and competition is recognized may damage the professional standards that have guided the profession. Ambulatory medicine is already less regulated than inpatient, hospital medicine. Patients may, as has already occurred in some instances, believe they are receiving quality care when they actually are not.[21] Such concerns are particularly relevant in the commercially managed, for-profit, primary care clinics sprouting up to serve the working poor, who are unable to purchase private health insurance and are not covered by the limited governmental health insurance programs. In the fluid mini-mall marketplace, such facilities may appear one day and disappear the next, leaving patients with no continuity of care and no accessible record of their illnesses.[22]

Some commentators recognize the dangers of mini-mall medicine for all practitioners. Medicine is among the most honored of American professions. Its practitioners and its clients still view it as a sacred trust, regulated by strict standards and overseen by august professional bodies. The proliferation of mini-mall medicine will be viewed by many as one more example of the deterioration of medicine as a profession and of health care as a public service.

Finally, mini-mall medicine represents a more sophisticated health care streetscape, suggesting the maturity of the drive-in culture, the continuing sophistication of the automotive city, and the next stage in the auto-vernacular landscape. Some commentators will view it simply as another evil attribute of urban sprawl; however, mini-mall medicine is one aspect of a complex evolution in the urban scene that reflects the complicated social and economic relationships that shape the city. For if in "Optimo City," the doctors practiced upstairs on the square, in the mini-mall, the distance between medicine and commerce has shrunk—one more example of how Americans continue to reshape the vernacular city that Jackson so movingly described and so dearly loved.

NOTES

1. GROTH AND WILSON, "THE POLYPHONY OF CULTURAL LANDSCAPE STUDY"

1. For salient recent examples, see the geographer William Wyckoff's *Creating Colorado: The Making of a Western American Landscape, 1860–1940* (New Haven: Yale University Press, 1999); landscape as a guiding textbook theme in William Norton, *Cultural Geography: Themes, Concepts, Analyses* (New York: Oxford University Press, 2000); the landscape architect Anne Whiston Spirn's *The Language of Landscape* (New Haven: Yale University Press, 1998); the landscape archaeologist Richard Muir's *The New Reading the Landscape: Fieldwork in Landscape History* (Exeter, England: University of Exeter Press, 2000); and the architectural historian Dell Upton's "Architectural History or Landscape History?" *Journal of Architectural Education* 44, no. 4 (August 1991): 195–99.

2. For example, see the English literature scholar William Alexander McClung, *Landscapes of Desire: Anglo Mythologies of Los Angeles* (Berkeley: University of California Press, 2000); the anthropologist Barbara Bender, ed., *Landscape: Politics and Perspectives* (Providence: Berg, 1993); the sociolo-

gist Sharon Zukin, *Landscapes of Power: From Detroit to Disney World* (Berkeley: University of California Press, 1991). Since 1988 the Ohio State University Press has sponsored the Urban Life and Urban Landscape Series, edited by the historian Zane L. Miller. In the popular press, see Herbert Muschamp, "Eloquent Champion of the Vernacular Landscape," *New York Times*, April 21, 1996; for NPR, refer to Edward Said's lecture "Unresolved Geographies and Embattled Landscapes" from the weekly series *Alternative Radio*, broadcast December 17, 1999.

3. J.B. Jackson, "The Word Itself," in *Discovering the Vernacular Landscape* (New Haven: Yale University Press, 1984), pp. 1–8; see especially pp. 5–8. *The Compact Oxford English Dictionary*, 1st ed., s.v. "landscape."

4. Eric Hirsch and Michael O'Hanlon, eds., *The Anthropology of Landscape: Perspectives on Place and Space* (New York: Oxford University Press, 1995), pp. 2, 6–8; John A. Jackle, et al., *The Motel in America* (Baltimore: Johns Hopkins University Press, 1996), p. 14.

5. Hirsch and O'Hanlon, *Anthropology of Landscape*, p. 12; Arthur O. Lovejoy, *The Great Chain of Being* (Cambridge: Harvard University Press, 1936), pp. 15–16; Upton, "Architectural History or Landscape History," p. 196. See also John Dixon Hunt and Peter Willis, eds., *The Genius of the Place: The English Landscape Garden, 1620–1820* (Cambridge: MIT Press, 1988), and Denis Cosgrove, "The Idea of Landscape," in *Social Formation and Symbolic Landscapes* (Totowa, N.J.: Barnes and Noble Books, 1984), pp. 13–38.

6. Helen Lefkowitz Horowitz, "J.B. Jackson and the Discovery of the American Landscape," in Jackson, *Landscape in Sight: Looking at America*, ed. Helen Lefkowitz Horowitz (New Haven: Yale University Press, 1997), pp. ix–xxxi, esp. p. xxi; Donald Meinig, "Reading the Landscape: An Appreciation of W.G. Hoskins and J.B. Jackson," in *The Interpretation of Ordinary Landscapes: Geographical Essays*, ed. Donald Meinig (New York: Oxford University Press, 1979), pp. 195–244, esp. p. 210; Hirsch and O'Hanlon, *Anthropology of Landscape*, p. 9. See also Lewis Mumford, *Technics and Civilization* (New York: Harcourt, Brace and Co., 1934); George Perkins Marsh, *Man and Nature; or, Physical Geography as Modified by Human Action* (New York: C. Scribner, 1864). On Marsh, see David Lowenthal, *George Perkins Marsh: Prophet of Conservation* (Seattle: University of Washington Press, 2000).

7. For Germany, see Michael P. Conzen, "The Historical Impulse in Geographical Writing about the United States," in *A Scholar's Guide to Geographical Writing on the American and Canadian Past*, ed. Michael P. Conzen, Thomas A. Rumney, and Graeme Wynn (Chicago: University of Chicago Press, 1993), pp. 3–90, and Preston E. James, *All Possible Worlds: A History of Geographical Ideas* (Indianapolis: Bobbs-Merrill, 1972), pp. 213–54.

8. On British geography, see James, *All Possible Worlds*, pp. 255–79. For examples of the ideas of other influential historical geographers, see H. Clifford Darby, *A New Historical Geography of England* (London: Cambridge University Press, 1973), and Maurice Warwick Beresford, *History on the Ground: Six Studies in Maps and Landscapes* (London: Lutterworth Press,

1957; rev. ed., Stroud, England: Sutton Publishing, 1998). On Geddes, a classic and often-quoted series of articles, "Talks from the Outlook Tower," appeared in the Progressive Era city-planning journal *The Survey*. The series begins with a foreword by Lewis Mumford, "Who *Is* Patrick Geddes?" *The Survey* 53, no. 9 (February 1, 1925): 522–24. On Hoskins, see W. G. Hoskins, *The Making of the English Landscape* (London: Penguin, 1985), and Meinig, "Reading the Landscape," pp. 196–210. See also M. R. G. Conzen, *Alnwick, Northumberland: A Study in Town-Plan Analysis*, Institute of British Geographers Publication no. 27 (London: George Philip, 1960); the Conzen tradition continues in Jeremy Whitehand and Peter Larkham, eds., *Urban Landscapes: International Perspectives* (London: Routledge, 1992). A new semiannual journal of landscape archaeology, *Landscapes*, edited by Richard Muir, began publication by Windgather Press, in the U.K., in April 2000.

9. Michael Conzen, "The Historical Impulse," 56–66. Andrew Clark, the dominant figure in the development of historical geography at Wisconsin, was a Sauer student who set new standards for archival research.

10. Carl O. Sauer, "The Morphology of Landscape," University of California Publications in Geography 2, no. 2 (Berkeley, 1925), p. 46; the manifesto is reprinted in John Leighly, ed., *Land and Life: A Selection from the Writings of Carl Ortwin Sauer* (Berkeley: University of California Press, 1963), pp. 315–50. There is a huge body of literature on Sauer and his traditions of cultural geography; two useful examples are Nicolas Entrikin, "Carl O. Sauer, Philosopher in Spite of Himself," *Geographical Review* 74, no. 4 (October 1984): 387–408, and Kenneth E. Foote et al., eds., *Re-Reading Cultural Geography* (Austin: University of Texas Press, 1994). See also Marie Price and Martin Lewis, "The Reinvention of Cultural Geography," *Annals of the Association of American Geographers* 83, no. 1 (1993): 1–17, and a lively exchange of views led by Denis Cosgrove, "Commentary on 'The Reinvention of Cultural Geography,' by Price and Lewis," *Annals of the Association of American Geographers* 83, no. 3 (1993): 515–17.

11. See Fred Kniffen, "Louisiana House Types," *Annals of the Association of American Geographers* 26, no. 4 (1936): 179–93; and Kniffen, "Folk Housing: Key to Diffusion," *Annals of the Association of American Geographers* 55 (1965): 549–77. See also the works by Wilbur Zelinsky cited in note 50.

12. We have relied heavily on the authoritative biographical work on Jackson done by Helen Lefkowitz Horowitz. See Horowitz, "J. B. Jackson and the Discovery of the American Landscape" and "Toward a New History of the Landscape and Built Environment," *Reviews in American History* 13, no. 4 (December 1985): 487–93. In addition to several chapters in the present volume, other assessments of Jackson's career include Meinig, "Reading the Landscape"; Kenneth I. Helphand, Robert Z. Melnick, and Rene C. Kane, eds., "John Brinckerhoff Jackson, 1909–1996," *Landscape Journal* 16, no. 1 (spring 1997): 1–45 (a collection of several remembrances of Jackson); Paul Groth, "J. B. Jackson and Geography," *Geographical Review* 88, no. 4 (1998): iii–vi; and John Pen La Farge, *Turn Left at the Sleeping Dog: Scripting the Santa Fe*

Legend, 1920–1955 (Albuquerque: University of New Mexico Press, 2001), 217–21 (a biographical interview with Jackson).

13. The School of American Archeology was a companion institution to the Museum of New Mexico, then the center for southwestern archaeology and a mainstay of the Santa Fe art colony. See Chris Wilson, *The Myth of Santa Fe: Creating a Modern Regional Tradition* (Albuquerque: University of New Mexico Press, 1997).

14. Horowitz, "Discovery of the American Landscape," xx–xxiv; Chris Wilson, "A Life on the Stranger's Path," *Designer/Builder* 3, no. 7 (November 1996): 25–28; Robert B. Riley and Brenda J. Brown, eds., "Most Influential Books" [a collection of lists by prominent designers and writers], *Landscape Journal* 10, no. 2 (fall 1991): 173–86, with Jackson's list on p. 174. The Experimental College at Wisconsin was later renamed the Integrated Studies Program.

15. Jackson's early published works include "Prussianism or Hitlerism," *American Review* 3 (April–October 1934): 454–71, and "A Führer Comes to Liechtenstein," *Harper's Magazine*, February 1935, pp. 298–310. His novel was published in New York by W. W. Norton. For reviews, see Ralph Thompson, *New York Times*, July 21, 1938, and Elmer Davis, "People Follow a Parade," *Saturday Review of Literature*, July 23, 1938, 5.

16. The quarterly *Revue de géographie humaine et d'ethnologie* was published from 1948 to 1949 by the geographer Pierre Deffontaines and the anthropologist André Leroi-Gourhan.

17. J. B. Jackson, "The Need of Being Versed in Country Things," *Landscape* 1, no. 1 (spring 1951): 1–5.

18. Jackson cites Maurice le Lannou in "The Vocation of Human Geography," *Landscape* 1, no. 1 (spring 1951): 41; see also the impact of Pierre Deffontaines's *Geographie et religions* in "Human, All Too Human, Geography," *Landscape* 2, no. 2 (autumn 1952): 2–7.

19. *Landscape* readers were attracted by the diversity and quality of its articles, whose authors represented some of the most original writers from an impressive breadth of fields. The authors included the historical ecologist Edgar Anderson; sociologist Herbert Ganz; anthropologist Edward T. Hall; art and architecture historians Siegfried Giedion, Christopher Tunnard, Colin Rowe, and Reyner Banham; geographers Carl O. Sauer, David Lowenthal, Donald Meinig, Yi-Fu Tuan, and Peirce Lewis; novelist Frank Waters; social philosophers Lewis Mumford and Peter van Dresser; journalist Grady Clay; planner Kevin Lynch; landscape architects Garrett Ecbo and Lawrence Halprin; and architects Charles Moore, Denise Scott Brown, and Christopher Alexander.

20. See Russell Jacoby, *The Last Intellectuals: American Culture in the Age of Academe* (New York: Farrar, Straus and Giroux, 1989).

21. Helen Lefkowitz Horowitz has done the most to unravel Jackson's pseudonyms. See chapter 3 of this book and "Discovery of the American Landscape," xxiv.

22. Meinig, "Reading the Landscape," 235.

23. Jackson's collections of essays include *American Space: The Centennial Years, 1865–1876* (New York: Norton, 1972), and *Landscapes: Selected Writings of J.B. Jackson,* ed. Ervin H. Zube (Amherst: University of Massachusetts Press, 1970), published before Jackson's retirement from teaching. Later collections include *The Necessity for Ruins and Other Topics* (Amherst: University of Massachusetts Press, 1980); *The Southern Landscape Tradition in Texas* (Fort Worth: Amon Carter Museum, 1980); *Discovering the Vernacular Landscape* (New Haven: Yale University Press, 1984); *The Essential Landscape: The New Mexico Photographic Survey* (Albuquerque: University of New Mexico Press, 1985); and *A Sense of Place, a Sense of Time* (New Haven: Yale University Press, 1994).

Jackson's teaching years led to two full-scale documentary video programs about him, as well: *Figure in a Landscape: A Conversation with J.B. Jackson,* prod. and dir. Clair Marino and Janet Mendelsohn, Conservation Foundation and the Film Study Center, Harvard University, 1987, videocassette (dist. by Direct Cinema Limited, P.O. Box 69799, Los Angeles, CA 90069); and *J.B. Jackson and the Love of Everyday Places,* prod. and dir. Robert Calo, KQED-TV, 1988, videocassette (dist. by Encyclopaedia Britannica Educational Corp., Chicago).

24. According to Jackson's one-page curriculum vitae, he began his survey lecture course in the Department of Landscape Architecture at Berkeley in 1967 and in 1969 at Harvard, also in landscape architecture. Jackson describes these courses in "Learning about Landscapes" and "By Way of Conclusion: How to Study the Landscape," in *The Necessity for Ruins,* pp. 1–18 and 113–26, respectively. Faculty auditors at Berkeley included Lawrence Halprin, Donlyn Lyndon, Spiro Kostof, Norma Evenson, and Marc Treib. The first half of Jackson's survey course has been recorded, footnoted, and extended in John Stilgoe, *Common Landscape of America, 1580 to 1845* (New Haven: Yale University Press, 1982).

25. Helaine Caplan Prentice, "John Brinckerhoff Jackson," *Landscape Architecture* 71 (November 1981): 740–45.

26. Wilson, "A Life," 27.

27. *Landscape in Sight* was largely complete before Jackson's death; its final publication came the year following. It contains the most complete bibliography of Jackson's writings, compiled by Horowitz. (Jackson did not keep any list of his many articles and book reviews.) In late 1999, two European translations of Jackson's work were in press: a collection of Jackson essays translated into French by the journal *Le Visiteur* and an Italian translation of *The Necessity for Ruins.*

28. See, for instance, A.W. Fawcett (probably a pseudonym for J.B. Jackson), "Help for the Village," *Landscape* 6, no. 3 (autumn 1957): 6–10; J.B. Jackson, "The Urban Cosmeticians; or, the City Beautiful Rides Again," *Landscape* 15, no. 3 (spring 1966): 3–4; David Lowenthal, "Not Every Prospect Pleases: What Is Our Criterion for Scenic Beauty?" *Landscape* 12, no. 2 (winter 1962–63); and Peter van Dresser, "Rootstock for a New Regionalism," *Landscape* 10, no. 1 (autumn 1960): 11–14.

29. Donlyn Lyndon, Charles W. Moore, Sim Van der Ryn, and Patrick J. Quinn, "Toward Making Places," *Landscape* 12, no. 1 (autumn 1962): 31–41; Robert Venturi, Denise Scott Brown, and Steven Izenour, *Learning from Las Vegas* (Cambridge: MIT Press, 1972; rev. ed., Cambridge: MIT Press, 1977). See also Robert Venturi, *Complexity and Contradiction in Architecture* (New York: Museum of Modern Art, 1977); Vincent Scully, *American Architecture and Urbanism*, 2d ed. (New York: Henry Holt, 1988), pp. 229–45; and Denise Scott Brown, *Urban Concepts: An Architectural Design Profile* (London: Academy Editions; New York: St. Martin's Press, 1990), esp. pp. 9–20.

Articles in *Landscape* with a similar theme include Denise Scott Brown, "Mapping the City: Symbols and Systems," *Landscape* 17, no. 3 (spring 1968): 22–25; J.B. Jackson, "Other-Directed Houses," *Landscape* 6, no. 2 (winter 1956–57): 29–35; and Reyner Banham, "The Missing Motel," *Landscape* 15, no. 2 (winter 1965–66): 4–6. See also the collected comments of designers about Jackson in Helphand et al., "John Brinckerhoff Jackson, 1909–1996."

30. Richard E. Nichols, "Defining American Landscape," *Preservation*, March–April 1997, 111–12.

31. Robert Z. Melnick, Daniel Spann, and Emma Jean Saxe, *Cultural Landscapes: Rural Historic Districts in the National Park System* (Washington, D.C.: Park Historic Architecture Division, Cultural Resources Management, U.S. Department of the Interior, 1984); Linda Flint McClelland, Genevieve Keller, and Robert Z. Melnick, *Guidelines for Evaluating and Documenting Rural Historic Landscape*, National Register Bulletin no. 30 (Washington, D.C.: National Park Service, 1990). Cityscape is a project of the Fund for the City of New York; its newsletter is *Cityscape News*.

32. Kevin Lynch, *The Image of the City* (Cambridge: MIT Press, 1960); Lynch, *What Time Is This Place* (Cambridge: MIT Press, 1972); and David Lowenthal, *The Past Is a Foreign Country* (New York: Cambridge University Press, 1985), perceptively explore the paradoxes of trying to preserve human landscapes that are the result of ever changing forces.

33. J.B. Jackson, "'Sterile' Restorations Cannot Replace a Sense of the Stream of Time," letter to the editor, *Landscape Architecture* 66 (May 1976): 194, reprinted in Jackson, *Landscape in Sight*, pp. 366–68.

34. See the *Journal of Architectural Education* 30, no. 1 (1976), a thematic issue titled "Teaching the Landscape" and guest edited by Jackson; and J.B. Jackson, "By Way of Conclusion" and preface, in *Discovering the Vernacular Landscape*.

35. Churchill is quoted in Edward T. Hall, *Beyond Culture* (New York: Doubleday, 1976), p. 106.

36. Early appearances of phenomenological points of view in *Landscape* include Yi-Fu Tuan, "Architecture and Human Nature: Can There Be an Existential Architecture?" *Landscape* 13, no. 1 (autumn 1963): 16–19; David Stea, "Space, Territory, and Human Movement," *Landscape* 15, no. 1 (autumn 1965): 13–16; and Georges Matoré, "Existential Space," *Landscape* 15, no. 3 (spring 1966): 5–6, translated and abridged by Jackson from *L'Espace humain* (Paris: La Colombe, 1962).

Classic studies include Yi-Fu Tuan, *Topophilia: A Study of Environmental Perception, Attitudes, and Values* (Englewood Cliffs, N.J.: Prentice-Hall, 1974); Charles Moore, Gerald Allen, and Donlyn Lyndon, *The Place of Houses* (New York: Holt, Rinehart and Winston, 1974); Edward Relph, *Place and Placelessness* (London: Pion, 1976); David Seamon, *A Geography of the Lifeworld: Movement, Rest, and Encounter* (London: Croom Helm, 1979); and Anne Buttimer and David Seamon, eds., *The Human Experience of Space and Place* (London: Croom Helm, 1980).

Examples of the continuing interest in and reinterpretation of place include Irwin Altman and Setha M. Low, eds., *Place Attachment* (New York: Plenum, 1992), and *Places* magazine, edited by Donlyn Lyndon.

A rich vein of recent geographical research connects politics, perception, and place. See especially John A. Agnew and James S. Duncan, eds., *The Power of Place: Bringing Together Geographical and Sociological Imaginations* (Winchester, Mass.: Unwin-Hyman, 1989), and James S. Duncan and David Ley, eds., *Place/Culture/Representation* (New York: Routledge, 1993). An early bridge between the phenomenological focus on the individual and the more social notions of structuration is Peter L. Berger and Thomas Luckman, *The Social Construction of Reality: A Treatise in the Sociology of Knowledge* (New York: Doubleday, 1966).

37. See Albert Eide Paar, "Environmental Design and Perception," *Landscape* 14, no. 2 (winter 1964–65): 15–17; Edward T. Hall, "The Language of Space," *Landscape* 10, no. 1 (autumn 1960): 41–45; Hall, "The Madding Crowd," *Landscape* 12, no. 1 (autumn 1962): 26–28; Hall, *The Hidden Dimension* (Garden City, N.Y.: Doubleday, 1966); and Robert Sommer, letter to the editor, "LSD," *Landscape* 15, no. 2 (winter 1965–66): 3. See also Sommer, *Personal Space: The Behavioral Basis of Design* (Englewood Cliffs, N.J.: Prentice-Hall, 1969), and Phillippe Boudon, *Lived-In Architecture: Le Corbusier's Pessace Revisited* (Cambridge: MIT Press, 1979).

38. Henry Glassie, *Folk Housing in Middle Virginia: A Structural Analysis of Historic Artifacts* (Knoxville: University of Tennessee Press, 1975). See also James Deetz, *In Small Things Forgotten: The Archeology of Everyday Life* (Garden City, N.Y.: Doubleday, Anchor Press, 1977); Dell Upton, "Vernacular Domestic Architecture in Eighteenth-Century Virginia," *Winterthur Portfolio* 17, no. 2–3 (summer–fall 1982): 220–44.

39. Richard Walker, "Unseen and Disbelieved: A Political Economist among Cultural Geographers," in *Understanding Ordinary Landscapes*, ed. Paul Groth and Todd W. Bressi (New Haven: Yale University Press, 1997), pp. 162–74 (quotation on p. 165).

40. David Harvey, *Justice, Nature, and the Geography of Difference* (Oxford: Blackwell, 1996), p. 204 (emphasis added). See also Henri Lefebvre, *The Production of Space*, trans. Donald Nicholson-Smith (London: Blackwell, 1991; orig. pub. Paris: Editions Anthropos, 1974).

41. See James S. Duncan, "The Superorganic in American Cultural Geography," *Annals of the Association of American Geographers* 70, no. 2 (1980): 181–98.

42. See also Marshall Sahlins, *Culture and Practical Reason* (Chicago: University of Chicago Press, 1970); Clifford James, *The Predicament of Culture* (Cambridge: Harvard University Press, 1988); Frederick Jamison, *Postmodernism; or, the Cultural Logic of Late Capitalism* (Durham, N.C.: Duke University Press, 1991); Cornel West, *Beyond Ethnocentrism and Multiculturalism* (Monroe, Maine: Common Courage Press, 1993).

Within geography, see particularly James S. Duncan, *The City as Text: The Politics of Landscape Interpretation in the Kandyan Kingdom* (New York: Cambridge University Press, 1990); Trevor J. Barnes and James S. Duncan, eds., *Writing Worlds: Discourse, Text, and Metaphor in the Representation of Landscape* (New York: Routledge, 1992); and Richard H. Schein, "The Place of Landscape: A Conceptual Framework for Interpreting an American Scene," *Annals of the Association of American Geographers* 87, no. 4 (1997): 660–80.

43. Anthony D. King, *The Bungalow: The Production of a Global Culture* (London: Routledge and Kegan Paul, 1984). See also King, "The Politics of Vision," in *Understanding Ordinary Landscapes*, ed. Groth and Bressi, pp. 134–44, and John Agnew and Stuart Corbridge, *Mastering Space: Hegemony, Territory, and International Political Economy* (New York: Routledge, 1995).

44. Don Mitchell, *The Lie of the Land: Migrant Workers and the California Landscape* (Minneapolis: University of Minnesota Press, 1996), p. 30. Although Mitchell invokes Sauer and provides a definition of landscape that includes both built space and social process, he bases the bulk of his book on a small set of iconic photographs and the landscape perceptions they embody, in the manner of writers who primarily use images of landscape as their points of departure.

45. Dolores Hayden, *The Power of Place: Urban Landscapes as Public History* (Cambridge: MIT Press, 1995); Setha Low, *On the Plaza: The Politics of Public Space and Culture* (Austin: University of Texas Press, 2001). See also Charles S. Aiken, *The Cotton Plantation South since the Civil War* (Baltimore: Johns Hopkins University Press, 1998); Catherine Nash, "Remapping the Body/Land: New Cartographies of Identity, Gender, and Landscape in Ireland," in *Writing Women and Space*, ed. Alison Blunt and Gillian Rose (New York: The Guilford Press, 1994), pp. 227–50; Gail Dubrow, "Asian American Imprints on the Western Landscape," in *Preserving Cultural Landscapes in America*, ed. Arnold R. Alanen and Robert Z. Melnick (Baltimore: Johns Hopkins University Press, 2000); Kenneth E. Foote, *Shadowed Ground: America's Landscapes of Violence and Tragedy* (Austin: University of Texas Press, 1997); and Leonie Sandercock, ed., *Making the Invisible Visible: A Multicultural Planning History* (Berkeley: University of California Press, 1998). Other applications of these ideas include Paul Groth, "Rooming Houses and the Margins of Respectability," in his *Living Downtown: The History of Residential Hotels in the United States* (Berkeley: University of California Press, 1994), pp. 90–130; and Chris Wilson, "When a Room Is the Hall," in *Images of an American Land: Vernacular Architecture in the Western United States*, ed. Thomas Carter (Albuquerque: University of New Mexico Press, 1997), pp. 113–28.

46. See Anthony Giddens, *The Constitution of Society: Introduction of the Theory of Structuration* (Berkeley: University of California Press, 1984); Pierre Bourdieu, *The Logic of Practice*, trans. Richard Nice (Stanford: Stanford University Press, 1990; orig. pub. Paris: Editions de Minuit, 1980). A very readable introduction to Bourdieu is Garry Stevens, *The Favored Circle: The Social Foundations of Architectural Distinction* (Cambridge: MIT Press, 1998), pp. 36–67. In geography, related work includes Allan Pred, *Making Histories and Constructing Human Geographies: The Local Transformations of Practice, Power Relations, and Consciousness* (Boulder, Colo.: Westview Press, 1990); Allan Pred, *Lost Words and Lost Worlds: Modernity and the Language of Everyday Life in Nineteenth-Century Stockholm* (New York: Cambridge University Press, 1990); and Allan Pred and Michael John Watts, *Reworking Modernity: Capitalisms and Symbolic Discontent* (New Brunswick, N.J.: Rutgers University Press, 1992). A related approach linking individual action and group identity is Peter J. Hugill, *Upstate Arcadia: Landscape, Aesthetics, and the Triumph of Social Differentiation in America* (Lanham, Md.: Rowman and Littlefield Publishers, 1995).

47. See Raymond Williams, *Culture* (Cambridge, England: Fontana Paperbacks, 1981), and *Keywords* (London: Fontana Paperbacks, 1983); John Berger, *Ways of Seeing* (New York: Viking Press, 1973); Denis Cosgrove, "Landscape and Social Formation: Theoretical Considerations," in *Social Formation and Symbolic Landscapes*, pp. 39–68; Denis Cosgrove and Stephen Daniels, eds., *The Iconography of Landscape* (New York: Cambridge University Press, 1988). See also Peter Jackson, *Maps of Meaning: An Introduction to Cultural Geography* (London: Unwin Hyman, 1989), and Stephen Daniels, *Fields of Vision: Landscape Imagery and National Identity in England and the United States* (Princeton: Princeton University Press, 1993). For an American Studies perspective on landscape from Britain, with a notable chapter on landscape painting, see Stephen F. Mills, *The American Landscape* (Edinburgh: Keele University Press, 1997).

48. Edgar Anderson, "The City Is a Garden," *Landscape* 7, no. 2 (winter 1957–58): 3–5 (quotation on p. 3). Anderson's series of influential *Landscape* articles are collected in Edgar Anderson, *Landscape Papers* (Berkeley: Turtle Island Foundation, 1976). See also Mae Thielgaard Watts, *Reading the Landscape: An Adventure in Ecology* (New York: Macmillan, 1957), and J. B. Jackson, "Once More: Man and Nature," *Landscape* 13, no. 1 (autumn 1963): 1–3, in which Jackson comments on how much he has learned from Anderson.

49. See Carolyn Merchant, *The Death of Nature: Women, Ecology, and the Scientific Revolution* (San Francisco: Harper and Row, 1980); Donald Worster, *Nature's Economy: A History of Ecological Ideas*, 2d ed. (New York: Cambridge University Press, 1994); Richard White, *The Organic Machine* (New York: Hill and Wang, 1995); William Cronon, *Nature's Metropolis: Chicago and the Great West* (New York: W. W. Norton, 1991); and Cronon, *Uncommon Ground: Rethinking the Human Place in Nature* (New York:

W. W. Norton, 1996). See also the artful application of physical geography to urban landscape study in Peirce Lewis, *New Orleans: The Making of an Urban Landscape* (Cambridge, Mass.: Ballinger Press, 1976; rev. ed. Harrisonburg, Va.: The Center for American Places, 2003).

50. Key works include Michael P. Conzen, ed., *The Making of the American Landscape* (Boston: Unwin-Hyman, 1990), and "Analytical Approaches to the Urban Landscape," in *Dimensions in Human Geography,* Geography Research Paper no. 186, ed. Karl W. Butzer (Chicago: University of Chicago Press, 1978), pp. 128–65; Donald W. Meinig, "Environmental Appreciation: Localities as Humane Art," *The Western Humanities Review* 25, no. 1 (1971): 1–11; Meinig, *The Interpretation of Ordinary Landscapes;* Meinig, *Imperial Texas: An Interpretive Essay in Cultural Geography* (Austin: University of Texas Press, 1969); Peirce Lewis, "Axioms for Reading the Landscape: Some Guides to the American Scene," in *The Interpretation of Ordinary Landscapes,* ed. Meinig, pp. 11–32; Lewis, "Learning from Looking: Geographic and Other Writing about the American Cultural Landscape," *American Quarterly* 35, no. 3 (1983): 242–61; Karl B. Raitz, ed., *The National Road* (Baltimore: Johns Hopkins University Press, 1996); Karl B. Raitz and John Fraser Hart, *Cultural Geography on Topographic Maps* (New York: Wiley, 1975); Wilbur Zelinsky, *The Cultural Geography of the United States* (Englewood Cliffs, N.J.: Prentice-Hall, 1973; rev. ed., Englewood Cliffs, N.J.: Prentice-Hall, 1992); and Zelinsky, *Exploring the Beloved Country: Geographic Forays into American Society and Culture* (Iowa City: University of Iowa Press, 1994), which collects several of Zelinsky's articles.

Other iconic geographical works include David Lowenthal, "The American Scene," *Geographical Review* 58, no. 1 (1968): 61–88, and John Fraser Hart, *The Look of the Land* (Englewood Cliffs, N.J.: Prentice-Hall, 1973). For lists of university departments that have traditionally offered courses in cultural landscape interpretation in the Jackson tradition, see Paul Groth, "Frameworks for Cultural Landscape Study," in *Understanding Ordinary Landscapes,* ed. Groth and Bressi, p. 213 n. 23, p. 214 n. 30.

51. See Thomas J. Schlereth, *Cultural History and Material Culture: Everyday Life, Landscapes, Museums* (Ann Arbor, Mich.: UMI Research Press, 1990), and *Reading the Road: U.S. 40 and the American Landscape* (Knoxville: University of Tennessee Press, 1997); John R. Stilgoe, *Metropolitan Corridor: Railroads and the American Scene* (New Haven: Yale University Press, 1983); and *Outside Lies Magic: Regaining History and Awareness in Everyday Places* (New York: Walker and Company, 1998).

At a March 2001 conference in Edinburgh entitled "Landscape and Politics," almost half of the seventy-three papers reflected primarily literary interests in landscape, although the conference itself was sponsored by the Department of Architecture at the University of Edinburgh and the Department of Geography at the Open University, Milton Keynes.

52. Grady Clay, *Close-Up: How to Read the American City* (New York: Praeger Publishers, 1973; reprint, Chicago: University of Chicago Press, 1980);

Clay, *Right Before Your Eyes: Penetrating the Urban Environment* (Chicago: American Planning Association, 1987); and Clay, *Real Places: An Unconventional Guide to America's Generic Landscape* (Chicago: University of Chicago Press, 1994). Beginning with some of J.B. Jackson's own collections, Judy Metro, while at Yale University Press, fostered a strong list. George Thompson, first as an editor at Johns Hopkins University Press and then also at his Center for American Places (www.americanplaces.org), has sought out authors and prompted work on subjects ranging from a single Great Plains farmstead to the entire Los Angeles urban region. See also George F. Thompson, ed., *Landscape in America* (Austin: University of Texas Press, 1995).

53. Zube was the first editor to compile a collection of J.B. Jackson's essays; see Ervin H. Zube, ed., *Landscapes: Selected Writings of J.B. Jackson* (Amherst: University of Massachusetts Press, 1970), and Ervin H. Zube and Margaret J. Zube, *Changing Rural Landscapes* (Amherst: University of Massachusetts Press, 1977). The website of the Institute for Cultural Landscape Studies is www.icls.harvard.edu.

54. Richard Walker, "Unseen and Disbelieved," 162, 173.

55. See Stephen Daniels, "Marxism, Culture, and the Duplicity of Landscape," in *New Models in Geography*, vol. 2, ed. Richard Peet and Nigel Thrift (Winchester, Mass.: Unwin-Hyman, 1989), pp. 196–220; Dell Upton, "Seen, Unseen, and Scene," in *Understanding Ordinary Landscapes*, ed. Groth and Bressi, pp. 174–80; and on the related notion of visual delight that accompanies or masks social ill, see Pierce Lewis, "The Architecture of Agribusiness: Reflections on Ambiguity in the Landscape," *Pioneer America* 10, no. 1 (1978): 4–6.

56. Michael Conzen, comments at a special session devoted to J.B. Jackson at the annual meeting of the Association of American Geographers, Fort Worth, Texas, April 1977.

2. NELSON LIMERICK, "J.B. JACKSON AND THE PLAY OF THE MIND"

1. J.B. Jackson, "Learning about Landscapes," in *The Necessity for Ruins and Other Topics* (Amherst: University of Massachusetts Press, 1980), p. 2

2. J.B. Jackson, "The Domestication of the Garage," in *The Necessity for Ruins*, p. 107.

3. J.B. Jackson, "The Sacred Grove in America," in *The Necessity for Ruins*, p. 80.

4. J.B. Jackson, "From Monument to Place," in *Landscape in Sight: Looking at America*, ed. Helen Lefkowitz Horowitz (New Haven: Yale University Press, 1997), p. 174.

5. J.B. Jackson, "Places for Fun and Games," in *Landscape in Sight*, p. 1.

6. J.B. Jackson, "The Accessible Landscape," in *Landscape in Sight*, p. 69.

7. J.B. Jackson, "The Movable Dwelling and How It Came to America," in *Landscape in Sight*, p. 222.

8. Jackson, "Learning about Landscapes," p. 16.

9. J.B. Jackson, "Gardens to Decipher and Gardens to Admire," in *The Necessity for Ruins*, p. 51.

10. J.B. Jackson, "Ghosts at the Door," in *Landscape in Sight*, p. 109.

11. J.B. Jackson, "Chihuahua as We Might Have Been," in *Landscape in Sight*, p. 53.

12. J.B. Jackson, "By Way of Conclusion: How to Study the Landscape," in *The Necessity for Ruins*, pp. 125–26.

13. Jackson, "The Accessible Landscape," p. 76.

14. J.B. Jackson, "The Past and Future Park," in *A Sense of Place, a Sense of Time* (New Haven: Yale University Press, 1994), p. 110.

15. Jackson, "Learning about Landscapes," p. 1.

16. J.B. Jackson, "To Pity the Plumage and Forget the Dying Bird," in *Landscapes: Selected Writings of J.B. Jackson*, ed. Ervin H. Zube (Amherst: University of Massachusetts Press, 1970), p. 145.

3. HOROWITZ, "J.B. JACKSON AS A CRITIC OF MODERN ARCHITECTURE"

1. Although Jackson wrote and spoke frequently about the baroque, he tended to be rather unspecific. My guess is that he was referring to the European style that reigned between the Renaissance and the classical period, roughly 1550–1700. Encountering the Modern movement early in the twentieth century, he identified it with work of the primary European architects of the International Style, such as Le Corbusier, Ludwig Mies van der Rohe, and Walter Gropius.

2. A useful source on Jackson's life is D. W. Meinig, "Reading the Landscape: An Appreciation of W. G. Hoskins and J.B. Jackson," in *The Interpretation of Ordinary Landscapes: Geographical Essays*, ed. D. W. Meinig (New York: Oxford University Press, 1979), pp. 210–32.

3. I interviewed J.B. Jackson on tape on successive days in January and again in late May and early June 1994. Quotations without cited sources come from the verbatim transcript of these interviews.

4. "Our Architects Discover Rousseau," *Harvard Advocate* 117, no. 8 (May 1931): 46–57 (quotation on p. 53).

5. Ibid., pp. 47–48.

6. Ibid., pp. 53–54.

7. *Saints in Summertime* (New York: W. W. Norton, 1938); "A Führer Comes to Liechtenstein," *Harper's Magazine*, February 1935, pp. 298–310; "Prussianism or Hitlerism," *American Review* 3 (April–October 1934): 454–71.

8. H.G. West [J.B. Jackson], review of *Baroque and Rococo in Latin America*, by Pál Kelemen, *Landscape* 2, no. 1 (spring 1952): 31.

9. H.G. West [J.B. Jackson], review of *Early American Architecture*, by Hugh Morrison, and *A Decade of New Architecture*, ed. Sigfried Giedion, *Landscape* 2, no. 2 (autumn 1952): 37–39 (quotation on p. 38).

10. Ibid., p. 39.

11. Ibid.

12. H.G. West [J.B. Jackson], review of *Built in U.S.A.*, ed. Henry-Russell Hitchcock and Arthur Drexler, *Landscape* 3, no. 1 (summer 1953): 29–30; reprinted in J.B. Jackson, *Landscape in Sight: Looking at America*, ed. Helen Lefkowitz Horowitz (New Haven: Yale University Press, 1997), pp. 278–79.

13. This is made explicit in H.G. West [J.B. Jackson], review of *The Golden City*, by Henry Hope Reed, Jr., *Landscape* 8, no. 3 (spring 1959): 37–38.

14. H.G. West [J.B. Jackson], "A Change in Plans: Is the Modern House a Victorian Invention?" *Landscape* 1, no. 3 (spring 1952): 18–26.

15. J.B. Jackson, "The Westward-Moving House," *Landscape* 2, no. 3 (spring 1953): 8–21; Jackson, *Landscape in Sight*, pp. 81–105 (quotation on p. 100).

16. Ajax [J.B. Jackson], "Living Outdoors with Mrs. Panther," *Landscape* 4, no. 2 (winter 1954–55): 24–25; Jackson, *Landscape in Sight*, p. 284.

17. See, for example, Sigfried Giedion, *Space, Time, and Architecture: The Growth of a New Tradition* (Cambridge: Harvard University Press, 1941).

18. J.B. Jackson, "Hail and Farewell," *Landscape* 3, no. 2 (winter 1953–54): 6; Jackson, *Landscape in Sight*, p. 287.

19. The publication date of "Other-Directed Houses"—1956—should be noted in light of similar themes conveyed later in Robert Venturi, Denise Scott Brown, and Steven Izenour, *Learning from Las Vegas* (Cambridge: MIT Press, 1972; rev. ed., Cambridge: MIT Press, 1977). In "An Architect Learns from Las Vegas," Jackson reviewed this book in the *Harvard Independent*, November 30, 1972.

20. J.B. Jackson, "Other-Directed Houses," *Landscape* 6, no. 2 (winter 1956–57): 29–35; Jackson, *Landscape in Sight*, p. 190.

21. Jackson, "Other-Directed Houses," 29–35; Jackson, *Landscape in Sight*, pp. 185–97.

22. P.A. Anson [J.B. Jackson], review of *The Heart of the City: Towards the Humanisation of Urban Life*, ed. J. Tyrwhitt, J.L. Sert, and E.N. Rogers, and *An Approach to Urban Planning; New World Writing*, ed. G. Breese and D.E. Whiteman, *Landscape* 3, no. 1 (summer 1953): 30–31.

In *Landscape*, "P.A. Anson" is obviously a typographical error for the constant contributor P.G. Anson. Because the pseudonym P.G. Anson does not appear until volume 2, no. 3 (spring 1953), it is internal evidence that makes me certain that Jackson was using this name of an eighteenth-century writer as a pseudonym. In this particular review there are two give-aways: a reference to a piece by another contributor elsewhere in the issue, something that would be known by an editor but not normally by a re-viewer; and a correction about the founding date of Harvard, clear in the mind of the editor, who had worked for Harvard's tercentenary in 1936.

23. J.B. Jackson, review of *Landscape for Living*, by Garrett Eckbo, *Landscape* 2, no. 3 (spring 1953): 34–35.

24. J.B. Jackson, "Southeast to Turkey," *Landscape* 7, no. 3 (spring 1958): 17–22; Jackson, *Landscape in Sight*, pp. 289–90.

4. SCOTT BROWN, "LEARNING FROM BRINCK"

1. Robert Venturi, Denise Scott Brown, and Steven Izenour, *Learning from Las Vegas* (Cambridge: MIT Press, 1972; rev. ed., Cambridge: MIT Press, 1977).

2. Philip L. Wagner, *The Human Use of the Earth* (Glencoe, Ill.: The Free Press, 1960).

3. Throughout this essay, quotations from conversations and letters are based on my recollections and are not necessarily verbatim.

4. Denise Scott Brown, "Learning from Brutalism," in *The Independent Group: Postwar Britain and the Aesthetics of Plenty* (Cambridge, Mass., and London: MIT Press, 1990).

5. Not surprisingly, Gans was one of the social scientists published in Jackson's journal. See Herbert J. Gans, "Suburbs and Planners," *Landscape* 11, no. 1 (autumn, 1961): pp. 23–24.

6. Denise Scott Brown, "A Worm's Eye View of Recent Architectural History," *Architectural Record* (February 1984): 69–81, and "Between Three Stools: A Personal View of Urban Design Practice and Pedagogy," in *Education for Urban Design* (Purchase, N.Y.: Institute for Urban Design, 1982), pp. 132–72. Denise Scott Brown, "Urban Concepts," *Architectural Design* profile no. 60, *Architectural Design* 60, no. 1–2 (January–February 1990); dist. London: Academy Editions, 1990; dist. New York: St. Martin's Press, 1990.

7. Helen Lefkowitz Horowitz, "J. B. Jackson and the Discovery of the American Landscape," in J. B. Jackson, *Landscape in Sight: Looking at America* (New Haven: Yale University Press, 1997): p. xxv. Bob's view was mannerist, rather than what later was called Postmodernist. He felt that mid-twentieth-century societal complexities had upended prevailing architectural philosophies and that they called for the breaking of architectural rules, which had become too simple or too simply ideological for the urban and social conditions of the time. Robert Venturi, *Complexity and Contradiction in Architecture* (New York: Museum of Modern Art and Graham Foundation, 1966).

8. J. B. Jackson, "Other-Directed Houses," *Landscape* 6, no. 2 (winter 1956–57): 29–35; reprinted in Jackson, *Landscape in Sight*, pp. 184–97. In the same book, Helen Lefkowitz Horowitz writes, in discussing "Other-Directed Houses": "Jackson's witty delineation of the characteristics of strip architecture predated *Learning from Las Vegas* . . . by sixteen years" (p. xxv; she makes a similar observation in chapter 3, note 19 of this book). The heart of what would become *Learning from Las Vegas* (1972) first appeared in Robert Venturi and Denise Scott Brown, "A Significance for A&P Parking Lots, or Learning from Las Vegas," *Architectural Forum* 128, no. 2 (March 1968): 37–43 ff. Although Horowitz's chronology needs amending, in light of this 1968 publication, her essay augmented my understanding and jogged my memory as I worked on my assessments and remembrances of Brinck.

9. J. B. Jackson, "An Architect Learns from Las Vegas," *Harvard Independent*, November 30, 1972. That best bibliography appears in Jackson, *Landscape in Sight*.

10. Denise Scott Brown, "The Power of Inner Diversity," *Proceedings of the AIA Diversity Conference Building Bridges: Diversity Connections* (Washington, D.C.: AIA, 1995), pp. 4–6; reprinted in *AIArchitect* (May 1996): 22.

11. As in the film *Lawrence of Arabia,* or as Lawrence himself wrote in *Seven Pillars of Wisdom* (London: Jonathan Cape, 1935).

12. Denise Scott Brown and Robert Venturi, "Hotel Mielparque Resort Complex: Nikko Kirifuri, Japan, 1992–1997," in *Venturi, Scott Brown and Associates: Buildings and Projects, 1986–1998,* ed. Stanislaus von Moos (New York: The Monacelli Press, 1999): pp. 270–79.

5. DAVIS, "THE AMERICAN HIGHWAY LANDSCAPE"

1. Gilmore Clarke, "Modern Motor Ways," *Architectural Record* (December 1933): 430; Clarke, "The Mount Vernon Memorial Highway," *Landscape Architecture* 22 (April 1932): 179; Jay Downer, "How Westchester Treats Its Roadsides," in *American Civic Annual, 1930* (Washington, D.C.: American Civic Association, 1930), 165–66.

2. Mumford complained about the automobile's impact in many of his books and in articles, such as "Townless Highways for the Motorist," *Harper's Monthly,* August 1931, pp. 347–56; "The Roaring Traffic's Boom," a three-part series in the *New Yorker,* March 19, April 2, and April 16, 1955, and "The Highway and the City," *Architectural Record* 123 (April 1958): 179–86. Blake railed about the American landscape in *God's Own Junkyard: The Planned Deterioration of the American Landscape* (New York: Holt, Rinehart and Winston, 1964). Keats satirized suburbs in *The Crack in the Picture Window* (Boston: Houghton Mifflin, 1956) and condemned automobile culture in *The Insolent Chariots* (Philadelphia: J.B. Lippincott, 1958).

3. Jackson noted: "As late as 1965 I was booed and hissed at conferences when I mentioned the topic and dared to show slides" (letter, Jackson to the author, March 3, 1993).

4. Jackson was not the first to call attention to the social complexity and visual appeal of the modern roadside landscape. One of the earliest sympathetic appraisals of the new American roadside was James Agee's article "The Great American Roadside," *Fortune,* April 1934, 53–63, 172–77. Agee portrayed the new roadside landscape as a hotbed of creativity and small-time entrepreneurism, as well as a vibrant, if somewhat tawdry, social environment. Walker Evans and the Farm Security Administration and photographers for Standard Oil of New Jersey were also entranced by the automobile's impact on the American landscape. Like Jackson, they recognized the highway's rapidly growing role as a recreational and economic space and were drawn to the visual pyrotechnics and kinesthetic exuberance of roadside commercial architecture.

Jackson's views were even more directly foreshadowed by two articles in publications he was known to favor. An article by Volnay Hurd in the May 5,

1945, *Christian Science Monitor*, "Nazi Zeal for War Efficiency Slighted Beauty in Autobahns," presaged Jackson's criticisms of the interstate highway system. Hurd combined Jackson's keen powers of observation and description. "The American Landscape," an anonymous essay in *Harper's Magazine*, January 1950, pp. 100–101, was even more Jacksonian in style and content. Authored, apparently, by contributing editor John Kouwenhoven, and cast as the first in an ongoing series on the contemporary American landscape, the essay celebrated the serendipitous vitality of unregulated roadsides and condemned modern parkways and freeways as banal, authoritarian, and elitist. The striking similarities to Jackson's views suggest either that he was influenced by Kouwenhoven or that he may have consulted the senior landscape interpreter while contemplating the founding of his own magazine. Jackson began publishing *Landscape* a year after the "American Landscape" series's brief three-installment appearance in *Harper's*.

5. Bernard De Voto, "The Easy Chair: Outdoor Metropolis," *Harper's Magazine*, October 1955, pp. 12–21.

6. J. B. Jackson, "Other-Directed Houses," *Landscape* 6 (winter 1956–57): 29–35; reprinted in Jackson, *Landscape in Sight: Looking at America*, ed. Helen Lefkowitz Horowitz (New Haven: Yale University Press, 1997), pp. 185–97.

7. Jackson, "Other-Directed Houses," *Landscape in Sight*, pp. 187, 189.

8. Ibid., p. 190. The concept of other-directedness was developed by David Riesman, Nathan Glazer, and Reuel Denny in their best-selling exploration of the contemporary culture of conformity, *The Lonely Crowd: A Study of the Changing American Character* (New Haven: Yale University Press, 1950). The authors proposed that Americans had previously been "inner-directed," observing an internalized ethos of duty and social propriety derived from a long legacy of classical, Judeo-Christian, and Enlightenment values. Modern Americans had supposedly lost confidence in this internal compass and were primarily "other-directed," catering to the reactions of their immediate audiences and basing their behavior and values on cues provided by the increasingly dominant cultures of consumption and entertainment.

9. Jackson, "Other-Directed Houses," pp. 187, 191.

10. Ibid., pp. 190–94 (quotations on pp. 192, 190).

11. J. B. Jackson, "The Abstract World of the Hot-Rodder," *Landscape* 7 (winter 1957–58): 22–27; reprinted in *Landscape in Sight*, pp. 199–209 (quotations on p. 205).

12. J. B. Jackson, "Auto Territoriality," *Landscape* 17 (spring 1968): 1–2. "The Social Landscape" and "The Public Landscape" were originally presented as lectures at the University of Massachusetts in autumn 1966. They were published in Jackson, *Landscapes: Selected Writings of J.B. Jackson*, ed. Ervin Zube (Amherst: University of Massachusetts, 1970), pp. 147–60. Hall's pathbreaking work on proxemics and nonverbal communication included *The Silent Language* (Garden City, N.Y.: Doubleday, 1959) and *The Hidden Dimension* (Garden City, N.Y.: Doubleday, 1966).

13. In "Two Street Scenes," *Landscape* 3 (spring 1954): 4–5 (reprinted in *Landscapes,* pp. 107–12), Jackson contrasted Santa Fe's vibrant street life with the fate of a city where traffic planners had streamlined the flow of traffic but killed the street as a forum for public life.

14. "Limited Access," *Landscape* 14 (autumn 1964): 18–23; "To Pity the Plumage and Forget the Dying Bird," *Landscape* 17 (autumn 1967): 1–4 (reprinted in *Landscape in Sight,* pp. 355–65). In "The Highways," *Landscape* 3 (summer 1953): 3, Jackson insisted, "We will have decent appearing highways only when we have planned and zoned highways."

15. J.B. Jackson, "Dictatorship of Highway Engineers," letter to the *Christian Science Monitor,* May 8, 1957; reprinted in *Landscape Architecture* 47 (July 1957): 504–5.

16. Grady Clay, "Main Street 1969," *Landscape* 7 (autumn 1957): 1–4; Boris Pushkarev, "The Esthetics of Freeway Design," *Landscape* 10 (winter 1960–61): 7–15; Reyner Banham, "The Missing Motel," *Landscape* 15 (winter 1965–66): 4–6.

17. J.B. Jackson, review of *Return to Taos,* by Eric Sloane, *Landscape* 10 (winter 1960–61): 15; Jackson, review of *U.S. 40: Cross Section of the United States of America,* by George Stewart, *Landscape* 3 (summer 1953): 28–29.

18. Robert Venturi, Denise Scott Brown, and Steven Izenour, *Learning from Las Vegas* (Cambridge: MIT Press, 1972; rev. ed., Cambridge: MIT Press, 1977).

19. Jackson expounded on these issues in "By Way of Conclusion: How to Study the Landscape," in *The Necessity for Ruins and Other Topics* (Amherst: University of Massachusetts Press, 1980), pp. 113–26; "A Pair of Ideal Landscapes," in *Discovering the Vernacular Landscape* (New Haven: Yale University Press, 1984), pp. 9–57; and "Roads Belong in the Landscape," in *A Sense of Place, a Sense of Time* (New Haven: Yale University Press, 1994), pp. 187–205 (quotation on p. 191).

20. Jackson, "A Pair of Ideal Landscapes," p. 27.

21. J.B. Jackson, "Country Towns for a New Part of the Country," in *Discovering the Vernacular Landscape,* pp. 79–80; Jackson, "Working at Home," "Looking into Automobiles," and "Truck City," in *A Sense of Place,* pp. 135–45, 165–69, 171–85, respectively; Jackson, "Of Houses and Highways," *Aperture* 120 (late summer 1990): 64–71. Jackson remarked on the transformation of the road into a place itself in "The Road Belongs in the Landscape," *A Sense of Place,* p. 190.

22. While Jackson welcomed the growing interest in road-related research and other forms of landscape studies, he lamented that the fruits of these labors were directed primarily at a narrow audience that he disparaged as the "bibliographical, Ph.D., conference-oriented class" (letter, Jackson to the author, October 8, 1992).

23. Jackson characterized the much romanticized cabin courts and mom-and-pop roadside establishments of the 1920s and 1930s as "the decaying refuse" of the early automobile age and derided the bulk of postwar highway

architecture as "a second jungle crop of ill-planned, ill-designed, uneconomic enterprises" ("Other-Directed Houses," *Landscape in Sight*, pp. 186, 189).

24. Two classic scholarly overviews of American roadside history are Warren Belasco, *Americans on the Road: From Autocamp to Motel, 1910–1945* (Cambridge: MIT Press, 1979), and Chester Liebs, *Main Street to Miracle Mile: American Roadside Architecture* (Boston: Little, Brown, 1985). General examinations of American highway development include Bruce Seely, *Building the American Highway System: Engineers and Policy Makers* (Philadelphia: Temple University Press, 1987), and Mark Rose, *Interstate: Express Highway Politics, 1939–1989* (Knoxville: University of Tennessee Press, 1990). Academic studies of specific genres of roadside architecture include John Jakle and Keith Sculle, *The Gas Station in America* (Baltimore: Johns Hopkins University Press, 1994); John Jakle, Keith Sculle, and Jefferson Rogers, *The Motel in America* (Baltimore: Johns Hopkins University Press, 1996); Richard Longstreth, *City Center to Regional Mall: Architecture, the Automobile, and Retailing in Los Angeles, 1920–1950* (Cambridge: MIT Press, 1997), and *The Drive-In, the Supermarket, and the Transformation of Commercial Space in Los Angeles, 1914–1941* (Cambridge: MIT Press, 1999).

25. Letter, Jackson to the author, November 11, 1993.

26. Jackson's classic diatribe against the academy appeared in the introduction to *Discovering the Vernacular Landscape*, in which he complained that the academic embrace of landscape studies had changed the focus of the field from the landscape itself to archives, library stacks, and the analysis of literary and artistic interpretations. "If the academic community thinks this is an important contribution," he declared, "this is where I depart from the academic community" (p. xi).

27. Letter, Jackson to the author, "Sunday," ca. 1994.

28. Letter, Jackson to the author, September 28, 1994.

29. The critically praised volume *Meditations on a Theme Park: The New American City and the End of Public Space*, ed. Michael Sorkin (New York: Hill and Wang, 1992), launched Jackson on a tirade about the slavish devotion of American scholars to European theorists. "I found the book a confirmation of what American universities have been accused of," he lamented, "a fascination with French intellectual fashions [and] a total ignorance of middle America." Jackson was dismayed that a book purporting to explain the American landscape was based primarily on French critical theory, bolstered by occasional contemporary newspaper accounts, with little fieldwork and scant reference to the substantial body of work on the topic produced by American geographers and social historians (letter, Jackson to the author, November 11, 1993).

30. Joel Garreau, *Edge City: Life on the New Frontier* (New York: Doubleday, 1991); William Least Heat Moon, *Blue Highways: A Journey into America* (Boston: Little, Brown, 1983); Jane Holtz Kay, *Asphalt Nation: How the Automobile Took Over America and How We Can Take It Back* (New York:

Crown Publishers, 1997; Berkeley: University of California Press, 1998); James Howard Kunstler, *The Geography of Nowhere: The Rise and Decline of America's Man-Made Landscape* (New York: Simon and Schuster, 1993).

31. While Jackson asserted that landscapes reflected "a common, unchanging human nature," he meant this in the broadest psychological terms; he asserted that every community developed its own culture and associated landscape (*Discovering the Vernacular Landscape*, pp. 28, 42–43).

32. Even an excess of historical context was better than too little or none at all. "History makes a landscape part of our culture and part of our own past," Jackson continued, "and even when it threatens to become antiquarian or reactionary, it makes the experience of a landscape very much more revealing" (letter, Jackson to the author, February 11, 1995).

33. Influential academic treatises offering "theoretical grounding" for some of Jackson's ad hoc approaches include Pierre Bourdieu, *Distinction: A Social Critique of the Judgement of Taste* (Cambridge: Harvard University Press, 1984); Michel de Certeau, *The Practice of Everyday Life* (Berkeley: University of California Press, 1984); and Henri Lefebvre, *The Production of Space* (Oxford: Blackwell, 1991).

34. Jackson, "By Way of Conclusion," p. 317. "What the advent of the automobile, now a hundred years in the past, has done and continues to do to our old systems of roads and streets is a familiar story," Jackson observed in "The Accessible Landscape," in *A Sense of Place*, p. 7.

35. Letter, Jackson to the author, March 3, 1993.

36. Letter, Jackson to the author, May 19, 1996. Expounding on this theme in an earlier missive, Jackson pronounced: "Whenever young writers or students send me a specimen of their work and ask me what can be done with it in the way of publication, my response—inevitably ignored—is to rewrite it significantly, shorten it and eliminate all obscure references. Then it should be sent to any one of a dozen journals of opinion: the *New Republic, The Nation, The Atlantic, Harper's,* the magazine section of the Sunday newspaper, even the *Wall Street Journal.* . . . This is the educated, more or less open-minded public you should aspire to address—NOT fellow students or faculty members" (letter, Jackson to the author, April 23, 1996).

6. LEWIS, "THE MONUMENT AND THE BUNGALOW"

1. As Helaine Kaplan Prentice put it in a much quoted remark: "He freed us of the guilt of enjoying what we saw." H.K. Prentice, "John Brinckerhoff Jackson," *Landscape Architecture* (1981): 740–46 (quotation on p. 741).

2. *J.B. Jackson and the Love of Everyday Places*, prod. and dir. Robert Calo, KQED-TV, 1988, videocassette (dist. by Encyclopaedia Britannica Educational Corp., Chicago).

3. J.B. Jackson, "The Need to Be Versed in Country Things," *Landscape* 1, no. 1 (1951): 4–5. Emphasis in the original.

4. For an elaboration of this argument, see Peirce Lewis, "Axioms for Reading the Landscape," in *The Interpretation of Ordinary Landscapes: Geographical Essays*, ed. D.W. Meinig (New York: Oxford University Press, 1979): pp. 11–32.

5. Jackson was a complex and sometimes enigmatic man, and the evolution of his ideas has been documented in biographical essays by Donald Meinig ("Reading the Landscape: An Appreciation of W. G. Hoskins and J.B. Jackson," in *The Interpretation of Ordinary Landscapes*, pp. 195–244) and by Helen Lefkowitz Horowitz ("J.B. Jackson and the Discovery of the American Landscape," in Jackson, *Landscape in Sight: Looking at America* [New Haven: Yale University Press 1997]: pp. ix–xxxi). Horowitz's book also contains a fine sampling of Jackson's writings, as well as a comprehensive bibliography of his work. In addition, two excellent documentary films contain extensive interviews with Jackson and with a variety of his friends, admirers, and critics. See *J. B. Jackson and the Love of Everyday Places* and *Figure in a Landscape: A Conversation with J.B. Jackson*, prod. and dir. Clair Marino and Janet Mendelsohn, Conservation Foundation and the Film Study Center, Harvard University, 1987, videocassette (dist. by Direct Cinema Limited, P.O. Box 69799, Los Angeles, CA 90069).

6. Marie Price and Martin Lewis, "The Reinvention of Cultural Geography," *Annals of the Association of American Geographers* 83 (1993): 1–17.

7. Carl O. Sauer, "The Morphology of Landscape," University of California Publications in Geography 2, no. 2 (Berkeley: 1925): 19–53; reprinted in *Land and Life: A Selection from the Writings of Carl Ortwin Sauer*, ed. John Leighly (Berkeley: University of California Press, 1963).

8. Carl O. Sauer, "The Education of a Geographer," *Annals of the Association of American Geographers* 46, no. 3 (1956): 287–99; reprinted in *Land and Life*, ed. Leighly, pp. 389–404. Subsequent citations of this article refer to *Land and Life*.

9. Sauer, "Education of a Geographer," pp. 392–93. Emphasis added.

10. D.W. Meinig, "The Beholding Eye: Ten Views of the Same Scene," in *The Interpretation of Ordinary Landscapes*, pp. 33–50.

11. The criticisms come from a variety of sources in a variety of forms, many of them under the rubric of "postmodernism" or "the new cultural geography." For a sample of that literature, see Donald Mitchell, *The Lie of the Land: Migrant Workers and the California Landscape* (Minneapolis: University of Minnesota Press, 1997), esp. chap. 1.

12. Jackson, "The Need to Be Versed," 5.

13. A goodly selection of the literature of landscape reading up to the early 1980s is cited in Peirce Lewis, "Learning from Looking: Geographic and Other Writing about the American Cultural Landscape," *American Quarterly* 35, no. 3 (1983): 242–61; reprinted in *Material Culture: A Research Guide*, ed. Thomas J. Schlereth (Lawrence: University Press of Kansas, 1985), pp. 35–56.

14. Horowitz, *Landscape in Sight*.

15. They can, however, urge their students to read Hart's excellent book about agricultural landscapes: J.F. Hart, *The Rural Landscape* (Baltimore: Johns Hopkins University Press, 1998).

16. There are two rare exceptions. George Stewart's classic *U.S. 40: Cross Section of the United States of America* (Boston: Riverside Press / Houghton Mifflin, 1953; reprint, Westport, Conn.: Greenwood Press, 1987), is a wonderful combination of prose and photographs depicting and interpreting the ordinary landscapes along transcontinental U.S. Highway 40. It is a remarkable portrait of the United States just before the arrival of the interstate highway system, but an even more remarkable venture into the art of reading ordinary landscapes. Even though Stewart is describing landscapes that have largely disappeared (or are fast disappearing), the book can be read with pleasure and profit by anyone who is seriously interested in the United States.

The second classic is Grady Clay's brilliant *Close-Up: How to Read the American City* (New York: Praeger, 1973; reprinted, Chicago: University of Chicago Press, 1980). Clay is Stewart's equal in his introduction to the art of landscape reading. The book masquerades as a primer, and it ostensibly deals with cities, but it is essential reading for anyone interested in reading the contemporary American landscape, urban or rural.

17. Horowitz, *Landscape in Sight*, p. xxiv, quoting from the film *J. B. Jackson and the Love of Everyday Places.*

18. Sauer, "Education of a Geographer," 290. Emphasis added.

19. I am not suggesting that would-be landscape readers abdicate their ethical or aesthetic standards. I am only suggesting that in the early stages of learning to read landscape, one needs to cultivate the ability to describe a landscape accurately before one passes judgment on its moral or aesthetic properties.

20. See, for example, Peirce Lewis, "Small Town in Pennsylvania," *Annals of the Association of American Geographers* 62, no. 2 (1972): 323–51; reprinted in *Regions of the United States*, ed. John Fraser Hart (New York: Harper and Row, 1927), pp. 323–51.

21. For another way of reading monumental architecture, see David Harvey's masterful essay on the church of Sacre Coeur in Paris, and its political meaning, as seen from a Marxist perspective: Harvey, "Monument and Myth," *Annals of the Association of American Geographers* 69, no. 3 (1979): 362–81.

22. For example, the bricks on those Bellefonte bungalows were made to *look* handmade, but in fact they are not; they were just mass-produced to look as if they were. The foundation stones are commonly discovered to be concrete blocks, poured in casts to make them look like rough-cut stone. The idea of mass-produced or even machine-made Arts and Crafts materials, of course, is a violent contradiction in terms, a cruel irony that turns the basic message of the Arts and Crafts movement on its head. Stickley would have been horrified by the pseudo-handmade bricks and fake-stone foundation blocks.

23. That is not the last time Americans would hear that message. Charlie Chaplin makes the same pitch in the 1936 movie *Modern Times*, and the hippies of the 1960s were on the same wavelength. *Plus ça change, plus c'est la même chose.*

24. Horowitz, *Landscape in Sight*, p. x.

7. CLAY, "THE CROSS SECTION AS A LEARNING TOOL"

My thanks to Chris Wilson for connecting me with the notes and diagrams from Jackson's travel journals, and to Paul Groth for his help in translating my initial symposium talk and earlier discussions of my cross-section method into this new version.

1. George Steiner, "Word against Object," in *After Babel* (London and New York: Oxford University Press, 1975), p. 224.

2. Grady Clay, "Human Geography Finds Kentucky Lovely, but Is Appalled at Disregard for Landscape," *Louisville Courier-Journal*, August 25, 1957.

3. Common terms for generic urban places and city processes structure three of my books: *Close-Up: How to Read the American City* (New York: Praeger Publishers, 1973; reprint, Chicago: University of Chicago Press, 1980); *Right before Your Eyes: Penetrating the Urban Environment* (Chicago: American Planning Association, 1987); and *Real Places: An Unconventional Guide to America's Generic Landscape* (Chicago: University of Chicago Press, 1994).

4. See the preface to Clay, *Real Places*, pp. x–xiii, and Clay, "Fix 2: Cross Sections," in *Close-Up*, pp. 32–34.

5. Stewart Roberts, *Life and Writings of Stewart R. Roberts, MD* (Spartanberg, S.C.: Reprint Co., 1993). On Vesalius, see also Stephen A. Yesko, "History of Human Dissection," *Medical Record*, April 3, 1940, 238–41; John Farquhar Fulton, *Vesalius Four Centuries Later: Medicine in the Eighteenth Century* (Lawrence: University of Kansas Press, 1950); and Charles Donald O'Malley, *Andreas Vesalius of Brussels, 1514–1564* (Berkeley: University of California Press, 1964).

6. Easily accessible editions of Vesalius's drawings, annotated and translated into English, include Andreas Vesalius, *The Illustrations from the Works of Andreas Vesalius of Brussels* (Cleveland: World Publishing Co., 1950), and Vesalius, *The Anatomical Drawings of Andreas Vesalius* (New York: Bonanza Books, 1982).

7. Philip Boardman, *Patrick Geddes: Maker of the Future* (Chapel Hill: University of North Carolina Press, 1944), p. 172. See also BEE (the *Bulletin of Environmental Education*), no. 33 (January 1974); Helen Elizabeth Meller, *Patrick Geddes: Social Evolutionist and City Planner* (London: Routledge, 1990); and Philip Boardman, *The Worlds of Patrick Geddes: Biologist, Town Planner, Re-Educator, Peace-Warrior* (London: Routledge and Kegan Paul, 1978).

8. Patrick Geddes, "The Valley Plan of Civilization," *Survey* 54, no. 5 (June 1, 1925): 288–90, 322–25, and "The Valley in the Town," *Survey* 54, no. 7 (July 1, 1925): 396–400, 415–16. These were the third and fourth installments of a series of articles for *Survey* that Geddes titled "Talks from the Outlook Tower."

9. Patricia Nelson Limerick, *The Legacy of Conquest: The Unbroken Past of the American West* (New York: Norton, 1987), p. 27.

10. John Brinckerhoff Jackson, "The Stranger's Path," *Landscape* 7, no. 1 (autumn 1957): 11–15 (quotations on pp. 12–13). This article has been reprinted most recently in Jackson, *Landscape in Sight: Looking at America*, ed. Helen Lefkowitz Horowitz (New Haven: Yale University Press, 1997), pp. 19–29.

11. Jackson, "The Stranger's Path," pp. 13, 14.

12. Ibid., pp. 12, 15.

13. Ibid., p. 15.

14. J.B. Jackson, untitled travel notebook, January 1–February 25 [?], 1957. Box 2, folder 3, Jackson Collection, MSS 633 BC, Center for Southwest Research, University of New Mexico. In the same trip throughout the South, in January and February 1957, Jackson also drew sketch maps of Savannah, Georgia, and Culpepper, Virginia.

15. Ernie Pyle, *Brave Men* (New York: Henry Holt and Co., 1945), p. 280–81.

16. Kevin Lynch, *The Image of the City* (Cambridge: MIT Press, 1960). Lynch's seminal book became even more impressive for me when I discovered, while occupying Kevin's office at MIT when he was on leave, that his working papers for that book occupied only three or four modest cartons left stacked on the floor. See also Kevin Lynch and Malcom Rivkin, "A Walk around the Block," *Landscape* 8, no. 3 (spring 1959): 24–34; this often-quoted article was, unfortunately, too long for us to publish in *Landscape Architecture*, and Jackson's *Landscape* came to the rescue.

17. My first New Mexico cross section was done through Albuquerque in 1989, more hastily than the earlier ones. See Grady Clay, "Megalopolis in Passing: The Function of Ephemeral Places," *Mass* 7 (fall 1989): 2–6 (*Mass* is a publication of the School of Architecture and Planning at the University of New Mexico). See also Grady Clay, "A Shot across Boston's Bow," *Landscape Architecture* (September 1999): 224–25.

18. Karl B. Raitz, ed., *The National Road* (Baltimore: Johns Hopkins University Press, 1996), and Raitz, ed., *A Guide to the National Road* (Baltimore: Johns Hopkins University Press, 1996).

19. The rules as given here, in revised form, are based on Grady Clay, "The Grady Clay Urban Cross-Section," in *Right before Your Eyes*, pp. 165–67, and on notes by Professor Christopher (Kit) Salter of a talk I gave at the University of Missouri Department of Geography, Columbia, Missouri, April 17, 1997. On the "point of attachment" (Rule 4), see James E. Vance, Jr., Raymond Murphy, and Bart J. Epstein, "The Internal Structure of the CBD," *Economic Geography* 31 (January 1955): 21–46.

20. For a brisk 1970s view of old and new commercial development in Louisville, and its dilemmas, see William Morgan, *Louisville: Architecture and the Urban Environment* (Dublin, N.H.: William L. Bauhan, 1979).

21. The definition of "alpha street" is from Clay, *Right before Your Eyes*, p. 166; see also Clay, "The Row," in *Real Places*, pp. 32–38.

22. A handsomely illustrated view of mansion life on Louisville's Third and Fourth Streets is Samuel W. Thomas and William Morgan, *Old Louisville:*

The Victorian Era (Louisville: Data Courier, Inc., for the *Courier-Journal* and the *Louisville Times*, 1975).

23. George R. Stewart, *U.S. 40: Cross Section of the United States of America* (Boston: Riverside Press/Houghton Mifflin, 1953; reprint, Westport, Conn.: Greenwood Press, 1987).

24. Journal, Grady Clay, vol. 44 (November 1974): 23.

25. Grady Clay, "Monotony at $1,000,000 per Mile?" and "Gouge, Chop, and Rut," two "Townscape" columns in *Arts in Louisville* magazine, November 1956 and April 1958, respectively, and Grady Clay, "Still Gouging Away," *Landscape Architecture* (October 1968). See also a fine, more recent book on the same theme: Jane Holtz Kay, *Asphalt Nation: How the Automobile Took Over America and How We Can Take It Back* (New York: Crown Publishers, 1997; Berkeley: University of California Press, 1998).

8. LIMERICK, "BASIC 'BRINCKSMANSHIP'"

1. Helen Lefkowitz Horowitz, "J. B. Jackson and the Discovery of the American Landscape," in Jackson, *Landscape in Sight: Looking at America*, ed. Helen Lefkowitz Horowitz (New Haven: Yale University Press, 1997), pp. xvi–xix; John Stilgoe, "'Colonel Jackson,' United States Army," *Landscape Journal* 16, no. 1 (spring 1997): 1–2.

2. Donlyn Lyndon et al., "Toward Making Places," *Landscape* 12, no. 1 (autumn 1962): 31–41.

3. The plan of the Lyndon scheme is shown in the chapter "Assembling the Rooms" (fig. 10), in *The Place of Houses*, by Charles Moore, Gerald Allen, and Donlyn Lyndon (New York: Holt, Rinehart and Winston, 1974). The house Jackson designed for himself is described in Marc Trieb, "J. B. Jackson's Home Ground," *Landscape Architecture* (April–May 1988): 52–57. Donlyn Lyndon's reminiscence about designing a house for Jackson is one of several that appears in *Landscape Journal* 16, no. 1 (spring 1997); see p. 5.

4. The file box and many of Jackson's notes were later given to John Stilgoe, who assumed the teaching of Jackson's courses at Harvard after Jackson retired. Paul Groth, who assumed the teaching of Jackson's Berkeley courses, was also given copies of the notes for his use.

5. Jackson told me that the information on his note cards, while often relatively complete, would remind him of many other things he could use to elaborate upon a subject while talking or writing.

6. J. B. Jackson, *American Space: The Centennial Years* (New York: W. W. Norton, 1972).

7. J. B. Jackson, "By Way of Conclusion: How to Study Landscape," in *The Necessity for Ruins and Other Topics* (Amherst: University of Massachusetts Press, 1980), pp. 113–26; reprinted in Jackson, *Landscape in Sight*, pp. 307–18.

8. Jackson, "By Way of Conclusion," 119.

9. Ibid., 120.

10. Ibid., 122.

11. *J. B. Jackson and the Love of Everyday Places,* prod. and dir. Bob Calo, KQED-TV, San Francisco, 1988, videocassette (dist. by Encyclopaedia Britannica Educational Corp., Chicago).

12. My thanks to Paul Groth, who was Jackson's teaching assistant at Berkeley in the late 1970s, for comparing some of his memories of working with Brinck with my own. Also helpful for refreshing my memory were the reminiscences by other Jackson T.A.s, friends, and students in Kenneth I. Helphand, Robert Z. Melnick, and Rene C. Kane, eds., "John Brinckerhoff Jackson, 1909–1996," *Landscape Journal* 16, no. 1 (spring 1997): 1–45.

13. Jackson, "By Way of Conclusion," 119.

9. MOIR-MCCLEAN, "LANDSCAPE CONTEXT IN DESIGN EDUCATION"

I would like to acknowledge the contributions of the educators, students, and professionals who added questions and comments to the excellent discussion session at the 1998 conference "J. B. Jackson and American Landscape" at the University of New Mexico, and Dr. Benita J. Howell at the University of Tennessee, whose assigned readings for her Appalachian Studies course helped guide my research for the studio course discussed here. I also would like to thank Chris Wilson and Paul Groth for their insightful editorial comments.

1. Roger H. Clark and Michael Pause, *Precedents in Architecture,* 2d ed. (New York: Van Nostrand Reinhold, 1996); Francis D. Ching, *Architecture: Form, Space, and Order,* 2d ed. (New York: Van Nostrand Reinhold, 1996).

2. This studio was offered during the fall semester of 1996. Students in the class included Robert Adamo, Amber Allen, Keith Allen, Stacy Andrick, Chad Boetger, Juleigh Bruce, Richard Coleman, Kristen Grove, Brandon Pace, Frank Taylor, Ben Whittenburg, and Somboon Xayarath.

3. See, for instance, Robert Venturi, Denise Scott Brown, and Steven Izenour, *Learning from Las Vegas: The Forgotten Symbolism of Architectural Form,* rev. ed. (Cambridge: MIT Press, 1977); *Places* magazine, edited by Donlyn London; Kenneth Frampton, "Critical Regionalism, Modern Architecture, and Cultural Identity," in *Modern Architecture: A Critical History,* 3d ed. (New York: Thames and Hudson, 1992), pp. 314–27; Douglas Kelbaugh, *Common Place: Toward Neighborhood and Regional Design* (Seattle: University of Washington Press, 1997).

4. Key sources used in the studio included Howard Dorgan, *Giving Glory to God in Appalachia: Worship Practices of Six Baptist Subdenominations* (Knoxville: University of Tennessee Press, 1987); Catherine L. Albanese, *America, Religions, and Religion* (Belmont, Calif.: Wadsworth Publishing Company, 1981); Joseph Burnley Moody, *The Twelve Ws of Baptism: Lectures Delivered to the Theological Class at Hall-Moody Institute, Martin, Tennessee* (Nashville: Marshall and Bruce Co., 1906); Deborah Vensau McCauley,

"Grace and the Heart of Appalachian Mountain Religion," and Melanie Sorvine, "Traditionalism, Anti-Missionism, and the Primitive Baptist Religion: A Preliminary Analysis," in *Appalachia: Social Context, Past and Present*, 3d ed., ed. Bruce Ergood and Bruce E. Kuhre (Dubuque, Iowa: Kendall/ Hunt Publishing Company, 1991), pp. 355–62 and 362–69, respectively; and Arthur Carl Peipkorn, "The Primitive Baptists of North America," *Concordia Theological Monthly* 42 (May 1971): 297–314.

5. J.B. Jackson, "To Pity the Plumage and Forget the Dying Bird," *Landscape* 17, no. 1 (autumn 1967): 1–4 (quotation on p. 1); reprinted in Jackson, *Landscape in Sight: Looking at America*, ed. Helen Lefkowitz Horowitz (New Haven: Yale University Press, 1997), pp. 355–65.

6. Jackson, "To Pity the Plumage," p. 1.

10. WRIGHT, "ON MODERN VERNACULARS AND J.B. JACKSON"

1. Daniel Defert, "Foucault, Space, and the Architects," *Documenta X— The Book* (Kassell, Germany: Edition Cantz/Abrams, 1997), pp. 274–83.

2. Michel de Montaigne, "On the Art of Conversation," in *The Complete Essays of Montaigne*, trans. J.M. Cohen (1560; reprint, London: Penguin, 1958), p. 294.

3. Marc-Antoine Laugier, *An Essay on Architecture*, trans. Wolfgang and Anni Herrmann (1755; reprint, Los Angeles: Hennessey and Ingalls, 1977).

4. See Eric Hobsbawm and Terence Ranger, eds., *The Invention of Tradition* (Cambridge and New York: Cambridge University Press, 1983), and Regina Bendix, *In Search of Authenticity: The Formation of Folklore Studies* (Madison: University of Wisconsin Press, 1997).

5. See Eric Hobsbawm, "Introduction: Inventing Traditions" and "Mass-Producing Traditions: Europe, 1870–1914," in Hobsbawm and Ranger, *Invention of Tradition*.

6. James Clifford, *Routes: Travel and Translation in the Late Twentieth Century* (Cambridge: Harvard University Press, 1997).

7. Alan Colquhoun, "Three Kinds of Historicism," in *Modernity and the Classical Tradition: Architectural Essays, 1980–1987* (Cambridge: MIT Press, 1989), pp. 3–20.

8. Gwendolyn Wright, "Modern Vernaculars," *Architecture and Urbanism* (Tokyo) 332 (May 1998): 4–9.

9. Paul Groth, *Living Downtown: The History of Residential Hotels in the United States* (Berkeley: University of California Press, 1994); Paul Groth and Todd W. Bressi, eds., *Understanding Ordinary Landscapes* (New Haven: Yale University Press, 1997); Steven Harris and Deborah Berke, eds., *Architecture of the Everyday* (New York: Princeton Architectural Press, 1997); and Neil Harris, *Cultural Excursions: Marketing Appetites and Cultural Tastes in Modern America* (Chicago: University of Chicago Press, 1990).

10. Ernst Bloch, *The Utopian Function of Art and Literature: Selected Essays*, trans. Jack Zipes and Frank Mecklenburg (Cambridge: MIT Press, 1988). The original German references were from *Erbschaft dieser Zeit*, 1935.

11. *America and Lewis Hine, Photographs 1904–1940*. Exhibition catalog by Walter Rosenblum and Naomi Rosenblum, with an essay by Alan Trachtenberg (Millerton, N.Y.: Aperture, 1977).

12. Personal communication with Luce Giad, May 1, 1997. See Michel de Certeau, *The Practice of Everyday Life*, vol. 1, trans. Steven Rendall (orig. pub., 1974; trans., Berkeley: University of California Press, 1984); Michel de Certeau with Luce Giad and Pierre Mayol, *The Practice of Everyday Life*, vol. 2, *Living and Cooking*, trans. Timothy J. Tomasik (Minneapolis: University of Minnesota Press, 1998); Henri Lefebvre, *The Production of Space*, trans. Donald Nicholson (orig. pub., 1974; trans., Boston: Basil Blackwell, 1991), and *Writings on Cities*, ed. and trans. Elenore Kofman and Elizabeth Lebas (Boston: Basil Blackwell, 1994); Pierre Bourdieu, *The Field of Cultural Production: Essays on Art and Literature* (New York: Columbia University Press, 1993); Alf Ludtke, ed., *The History of Everyday Life: Reconstructing Historical Experiences and Ways of Life*, ed. with an introduction by Randal Johnson, trans. William Templer (orig. pub., 1989; trans., Princeton: Princeton University Press, 1995); and Andreas Huyssen, *After the Great Divide: Modernism, Mass Culture, Postmodernism* (Bloomington: Indiana University Press, 1986).

13. For an excellent overview of pragmatist philosophy, see Joan Ockman and John Rajchman, eds., *The Pragmatist Imagination: Thinking about Things in the Making* (New York: Princeton Architectural Press, 2000).

14. J. Hillis Miller, "Border Crossings, Translating Theory: Ruth," in *Topographies* (Stanford: Stanford University Press, 1995), reprinted in *The Translatability of Culture*, ed. Sanford Budick and Wolfgang Iser (Stanford: Stanford University Press, 1996), pp. 207–23.

15. Theodor W. Adorno, *The Jargon of Authenticity*, trans. Kurt Tarnowski and Frederic Will (orig. pub., 1964; trans., Evanston, Ill.: Northwestern University Press, 1973).

16. Robin Evans, *Translations from Drawing to Building and Other Essays* (Cambridge: MIT Press, 1997).

17. See Johan Gottfried von Herder, *Reflections on the Philosophy of the History of Mankind*, ed. Frank E. Manuel (1784; Chicago: University of Chicago Press, 1968). For recent commentary, see, in particular, Geoff Eley and Ronald Grigor Suny, *Becoming National: A Reader* (New York: Oxford University Press, 1996); David Lowenthal, *The Past Is a Foreign Country* (Cambridge and New York: Cambridge University Press, 1985); and Homi K. Bhabha, ed., *Nations and Narration* (London and New York: Routledge, 1990).

11. HENDERSON, "WHEN WE TALK ABOUT LANDSCAPE"

I owe a great debt of thanks to Paul Groth, Chris Wilson, and Charlene Woodcock for their many questions, comments, and suggestions. I have also returned repeatedly to the challenging audience responses provoked by an earlier version of this paper, presented at the conference "J. B. Jackson and American Landscape."

This essay is dedicated to Edmunds Bunksé, my first landscape teacher, and to Simon, my young son, who is about to begin his education in the ways of this world.

1. Throughout this essay I will refer to "landscape" rather than to the "cultural landscape." The volume editors have asked me to explain this. I think the promise of the landscape concept is that adjectives such as *cultural, social, political,* and *economic* ought to be already folded into what we mean by *landscape,* or at least into the best of such meanings. I advocate a conception of landscape that includes the very reasons to pay attention to it. Put another way, could we, in the very first instance, define landscape in such a way that we understand why the cultural, social, political, or economic might matter? At the end of the essay I turn to an early essay by J.B. Jackson for assistance: "To Pity the Plumage and Forget the Dying Bird," *Landscape* 17, no. 1 (autumn 1967): 1–4, reprinted in J.B. Jackson, *Landscape in Sight: Looking at America,* ed. Helen Lefkowitz Horowitz (New Haven: Yale University Press, 1997), pp. 355–65. In that essay, Jackson aimed to say, quite rightly I think, that any concept of landscape is bankrupt when it is not also a participatory concept. In other words, landscape, in our very invocation of it, ought to signify a particular, normative state of social relations.

2. See Richard Peet, *Modern Geographic Thought* (Oxford: Blackwell, 1998), and David Livingstone, *The Geographical Tradition* (Oxford: Blackwell, 1993).

3. Carl O. Sauer, *Land and Life,* ed. John Leighly (Berkeley: University of California Press, 1963); J.B. Jackson, *Landscapes: Selected Writings of J.B. Jackson,* ed. Ervin H. Zube (Amherst: University of Massachusetts Press, 1970); Yi-Fu Tuan, *Topophilia: A Study of Environmental Perception, Attitudes, and Values* (Englewood Cliffs, N.J.: Prentice-Hall, 1974); David Lowenthal and Martyn Bowden, eds., *Geographies of the Mind* (New York: Oxford University Press, 1975); Gaston Bachelard, *Poetics of Space,* trans. Maria Jolas (New York: Orion Press, 1964); Rainer Maria Rilke, *Where Silence Reigns: Selected Prose,* trans. G. Craig Houston (New York: New Directions, 1978).

4. See Ian McHarg, *Design with Nature* (Garden City, N.Y.: Natural History Press, 1969), and P.M. Bardi, *The Tropical Gardens of Burle Marx* (New York: Reinhold, 1964).

5. Leo Marx, *The Machine in the Garden* (New York: Oxford University Press, 1964); Henry Nash Smith, *Virgin Land* (Cambridge: Harvard University Press, 1950); Annette Kolodny, *The Lay of the Land* (Chapel Hill: University of North Carolina Press, 1975); Karl Marx, *Capital,* 3 vols. (New York: International Publishers, 1967); Anthony Giddens, *Central Problems in Social Theory* (Berkeley: University of California Press, 1979); David Harvey, *Consciousness and the Urban Experience* (Baltimore: Johns Hopkins University Press, 1985) and *The Condition of Postmodernity* (Oxford: Blackwell, 1989); Henri Lefebvre, *The Production of Space,* trans. Donald Nicholson-Smith (London: Blackwell, 1991).

6. On social constructions of race and gender, see Elazar Barkan, *The Retreat of Scientific Racism: Changing Concepts of Race in Britain and the United States between the World Wars* (New York: Cambridge University

Press, 1992), and Linda McDowell, *Gender, Identity, and Place* (Minneapolis: University of Minnesota Press, 1999). A useful guide to Marx's notion of capital is David Harvey, *The Limits to Capital* (Oxford: Blackwell, 1982).

7. Sauer, *Land and Life*; Fred Kniffen, "Cultural Diffusion and Landscapes: Selections by Fred Kniffen," ed. H. Jesse Walker, *Geosciences and Man* 17 (Baton Rouge: Department of Geography and Anthropology, Louisiana State University, 1990); Donald Meinig, "Symbolic Landscapes: Models of American Community," in *The Interpretation of Ordinary Landscapes: Geographical Essays,* ed. D. W. Meinig (New York: Oxford University Press, 1979); René Dubos, *A God Within* (New York: Scribner, 1972); Donald Worster, *Rivers of Empire: Water, Aridity, and the Growth of the American West* (New York: Pantheon Books, 1985); Carolyn Merchant, *Ecological Revolutions: Nature, Gender, and Science in New England* (Chapel Hill: University of North Carolina Press, 1989); John Stilgoe, *Common Landscape of America, 1580 to 1845* (New Haven: Yale University Press, 1982).

8. But see the short summary in Kenneth Olwig's "Landscape: Mapping the Traces of a Ghostly Concept," in *Concepts in Human Geography,* ed. Carville Earle, et al. (Lanham, Md.: Rowman and Littlefield, 1996).

9. Stilgoe, *Common Landscape,* p. 29.

10. Merchant, *Ecological Revolutions;* Donald Usner, *Sabino's Map* (Santa Fe: Museum of New Mexico Press, 1995).

11. These observations on Carter's Grove are based upon several visits by the author in 1993. See Frederick Douglass, *My Bondage and My Freedom,* ed. William L. Andrews (Urbana: University of Illinois Press, 1987), p. 197.

12. See Jackson's essay "In Search of the Proto-Landscape" in George Thompson, ed., *Landscape in America* (Austin: University of Texas Press, 1995). See also "By Way of Conclusion: How to Study the Landscape," in J. B. Jackson, *The Necessity for Ruins and Other Topics* (Amherst: University of Massachusetts Press, 1980), in which the tension between "landscape" and "space" as somewhat-distinct, somewhat-identical is in evidence.

13. See, for example, Chandra Mukerji and Michael Schudson, eds., *Rethinking Popular Culture: Contemporary Perspectives in Cultural Studies* (Berkeley: University of California Press, 1991).

14. See, for example, Edward Said, *Culture and Imperialism* (New York: Knopf, 1993), and, especially, Grey Gundaker's brilliant work in *Signs of Diaspora, Diaspora of Signs* (New York: Oxford University Press, 1998).

15. A good review is Paul Knox, ed., *The Restless Urban Landscape* (Englewood Cliffs, N.J.: Prentice-Hall, 1992). A very readable book-length case study is John M. Findlay, *Magic Lands: Western Cityscapes and American Culture after 1940* (Berkeley: University of California Press, 1992).

16. Location data obtained through a September 21, 1998, telephone interview with the managers of these stores on University Avenue, Tucson, Arizona.

17. Paul Groth, *Living Downtown: The History of Residential Hotels in the United States* (Berkeley: University of California Press, 1994).

18. Grady Clay, *Close-Up: How to Read the American City* (Chicago: University of Chicago Press, 1980); Peirce Lewis, "Axioms for Reading the Landscape: Some Guides to the American Scene," in *The Interpretation of Ordinary Landscapes*, ed. Meinig, pp. 11–32.

19. See, for example, Thomas Sugrue's *The Origins of the Urban Crisis* (Princeton: Princeton University Press, 1996).

20. Edward Soja, *Postmodern Geographies: The Reassertion of Space in Critical Social Theory* (New York: Verso, 1989); Allan Pred, *Place, Practice, and Structure: Social and Spatial Transformation in Southern Sweden, 1750–1850* (Totowa, N.J.: Barnes and Noble, 1986); Lefebvre, *The Production of Space;* and Giddens, *Central Problems in Social Theory.*

21. See any work of David Harvey, from *Social Justice and the City* (Baltimore: Johns Hopkins University Press, 1973) to *Spaces of Hope* (Berkeley: University of California Press, 2000); see also Neil Smith, *Uneven Development* (Oxford: Blackwell, 1991); Michael Storper and Richard Walker, *The Capitalist Imperative* (Oxford: Blackwell, 1989); Richard Peet, *Modern Geographical Thought;* or the journal *Antipode: A Journal of Radical Geography.*

22. For a more complete discussion, see Peet, *Modern Geographical Thought;* see also Richard Walker, "Unseen and Disbelieved: A Political Economist among Cultural Geographers," in *Understanding Ordinary Landscapes*, ed. Paul Groth and Todd Bressi (New Haven: Yale University Press, 1997), pp. 162–73.

23. Harvey, *Social Justice and the City;* See also *Urban Geography* 15, no. 7 (1994), a special issue devoted to Harvey's *Social Justice*, edited by Glenda Laws. Andy Merrifield and Erik Swyngedouw, eds., in *The Urbanization of Injustice* (New York: NYU Press, 1997), similarly revisit Harvey's book. For a review of major theories of social justice and what they imply for geography, see David M. Smith, *Geography and Social Justice* (Oxford: Blackwell, 1994).

It is striking that two geographers whose work on the spatiality of social life is widely cited and admired are typically keen to return to social relations (here class relations) as the key site of exploitation. See David Harvey, *Justice, Nature, and the Geography of Difference* (Oxford: Blackwell, 1996), and Neil Smith, *The New Urban Frontier* (London: Routledge, 1996). That geographers and other analysts of landscape *ought* to be concerned with social justice and attendant matters of exploitation and oppression is not an argument that can be "proved." What can be said is that nearly the whole of human geography now points in the direction of a critique of power relations and resulting social constructions of all sorts. The critical human geography that began in the 1970s with Marxist approaches now has high status in human geography at large. A perusal of the last fifteen years of the *Annals of the Association of American Geographers*, as well as other prominent human geography journals (for instance, *Transactions of the Institute of British Geographers, Environment and Planning D: Society and Space*) bears this out. The question, therefore, has become "What is social justice and how might it be brought about?" Not "Is concern with social justice a legitimate area of inquiry?" Of course, that a social-justice tide has risen is not sufficient reason to swim with it. Indeed, if I may mix metaphors, individuals are perfectly free to ignore the tide, let others do the work, and then reap the benefits.

24. On spatial inequalities, see Neil Smith, *Uneven Development: Nature, Capital, and the Production of Space* (Oxford: Blackwell, 1991).

25. David M. Smith, *Moral Geographies: Ethics in a World of Difference* (Edinburgh, Scotland: Edinburgh University Press, 2000), p. 137; Harvey, *Geography of Difference*.

26. John Berger, *Ways of Seeing* (New York: Viking Penguin, 1973); John Barrell, *The Dark Side of the Landscape* (New York: Cambridge University Press, 1980); Williams, *The Country and the City;* Denis Cosgrove, *Social Formation and Symbolic Landscape* (London: Croom Helm, 1984).

27. Cosgrove, *Social Formation and Symbolic Landscape* (reprint, with a new foreword, Madison: University of Wisconsin Press, 1998), pp. xv, 28.

28. Margaret FitzSimmons, "The Matter of Nature," *Antipode* 21, no. 2 (1989): 106–20. Some more recent works on the production of nature are Neil Smith, *Uneven Development,* and Bruce Braun and Noel Castree, eds., *Remaking Reality: Nature at the Millennium* (New York: Routledge, 1998). See also Don Mitchell, *The Lie of the Land: Migrant Workers and the California Landscape* (Minneapolis: University of Minnesota Press, 1996), and Henderson, *California and the Fictions of Capital* (New York: Oxford University Press, 1999).

29. James Duncan, *City as Text* (New York: Cambridge University Press, 1990); Tuan, *Topophilia*.

30. See Gillian Rose, *Feminism and Geography* (Cambridge, England: Polity Press, 1993).

31. Michel de Certeau, *The Practice of Everyday Life,* trans. Steven Randall (Berkeley: University of California Press, 1984); Mitchell, *The Lie of the Land.* See also J. B. Jackson, "Jefferson, Thoreau, and After," *Landscape* 15, no. 2 (winter 1965–66): 25–27; reprinted in Jackson, *Landscape in Sight,* pp. 175–82. On the conflict between official and vernacular uses of city streets, see Jackson, "The Discovery of the Street," in *The Necessity for Ruins,* pp. 55–66.

32. On methodological changes and the crisis of representation in sociology and anthropology, see Norman Denzin, *Interpretive Ethnography: Ethnographic Practices for the Twenty-first Century* (Thousand Oaks, Calif.: Sage, 1997). For an example of new methods in geography, see John Paul Jones III, et al., *Thresholds in Feminist Geography: Difference, Methodology, Representation* (Lanham, Md.: Rowman and Littlefield, 1997).

33. See Harvey, *Geography of Difference*.

34. Doreen Massey, "A Global Sense of Place," *Marxism Today,* June 1991, 24–29.

35. The late Michael E. Eliot Hurst, addressing the whole of geography, takes this warning to the limit in "Geography Has neither Existence nor Future," in *The Future of Geography,* ed. R. J. Johnston (New York: Methuen, 1985), pp. 59–91. The title is glib, but the contents bear a fresh look: what has the too easy acceptance of the academic division of labor cost us, in terms of

developing normative social and political theory?

36. For a concise overview and analysis of these issues, see Fred Harris and Lynn A. Curtis, eds., *Locked in the Poorhouse: Cities, Race, and Poverty in the United States* (Lanham, Md.: Rowman and Littlefield, 1998).

37. David M. Smith, "How Far Should We Care? On the Spatial Scope of Beneficence," *Progress in Human Geography* 22 (1998): 15–38. See also Stuart Corbridge, "Marxisms, Modernities, and Moralities: Development Praxis and the Claims of Distant Strangers," *Environment and Planning D: Society and Space* 11 (1993): 449–72.

38. Henry Glassie, *Material Culture* (Bloomington: Indiana University Press, 1999), esp. pp. 72–86.

39. Jackson, "To Pity the Plumage."

40. Arguments about human capability are most famously those of the Nobel Prize–winning economist Amartya Sen. See *Inequality Reexamined* (Oxford: Clarendon Press, 1992) and *Development as Freedom* (New York: Anchor Books, 2000). The key work by Iris Marion Young is *Justice and the Politics of Difference* (Princeton: Princeton University Press, 1990). If there is a social justice "turn" in human geography, as I think there is, the work of David M. Smith is the best place to start: see his *Geography and Social Justice* and *Moral Geographies.*

12. SCHEIN, "NORMATIVE DIMENSIONS OF LANDSCAPE"

I thank Peirce Lewis for introducing me to J.B. Jackson's essays and, as Peirce might say, causing the scales to fall from my eyes. I thank Don Meinig for encouraging me to systematically read J.B. Jackson's essays. I thank them both for lessons in the interpretation of ordinary landscapes.

1. Donald Meinig to Richard Schein, July 25, 1997. See D.W. Meinig "Reading the Landscape: An Appreciation of W.G. Hoskins and J.B. Jackson," in *The Interpretation of Ordinary Landscapes: Geographical Essays,* ed. D.W. Meinig (New York: Oxford University Press, 1979), pp. 195–244. For alternative positions on "looking," see also Gillian Rose, "Geography as a Science of Observation: The Landscape, the Gaze, and Masculinity," in *Nature and Science: Essays in the History of Knowledge,* ed. Felix Driver and Gillian Rose, Historical Geography Research Series, no. 28 (London: RHBNC and QMWC, University of London, 1992), 8–18, and Catherine Nash, "Reclaiming Vision: Looking at Landscape and the Body," *Gender, Place, and Culture* 3, no. 2 (1996): 149–69.

2. D.W. Meinig, "The Beholding Eye: Ten Versions of the Same Scene," in *The Interpretation of Ordinary Landscapes,* ed. Meinig, 33–50; Denis Cosgrove, *Social Formation and Symbolic Landscape* (London: Croom Helm, 1984); Denis Cosgrove, "Prospect, Perspective and the Evolution of the Landscape Idea," *Transactions of the Institute of British Geographers,* new series 10 (1985): 45–62; Jonathan Smith, "The Slightly Different Thing that Is Said:

Writing the Aesthetic Experience," in *Writing Worlds*, ed. Trevor J. Barnes and James S. Duncan (New York: Routledge, 1992), pp. 73–85; Rose, "Geography as a Science"; Nash, "Reclaiming Vision."

3. J.B. Jackson, *Discovering the Vernacular Landscape* (New Haven: Yale University Press, 1984), pp. 147, 150. I am fully aware of the problems involved in making absolute statements about an author's position based on selective quotations, especially when the author in question wrote about landscape in a number of venues for almost half a century. However, I am not trying to make absolute claims about J.B. Jackson. Rather, I am trying to show how at least one of Jackson's long-standing concerns for interpreting ordinary landscapes prefigures contemporary theorizations of the topic in general, and the question of normativity in particular.

4. Helen Lefkowitz Horowitz, "J.B. Jackson and the Discovery of the American Landscape," in Jackson, *Landscape in Sight: Looking at America*, ed. Helen Lefkowitz Horowitz (New Haven: Yale University Press, 1997), pp. xxi–xxii.

5. J.B. Jackson, "Goodbye to Evolution," *Landscape* 13, no. 2 (winter 1963–64): 1–2; emphasis in original.

6. Peirce Lewis, "Axioms for Reading the Landscape: Some Guides to the American Scene," in *The Interpretation of Ordinary Landscapes*, ed. Meinig, pp. 11–32 (quotation on p. 12).

7. See James S. Duncan, "The Superorganic in American Cultural Geography," *Annals of the Association of American Geographers* 70, no. 2 (1980): 181–98; J. Duncan and N. Duncan, "(Re)reading the Landscape," *Environment and Planning D: Society and Space* 6, no. 2 (1988): 117–26.

8. See Cosgrove, "Prospect"; R.H. Schein, "Representing Urban America: Nineteenth-Century Views of Landscape, Space, and Power," *Environment and Planning D: Society and Space* 11, no. 1 (1993): 7–21.

9. See Liz Bondi, "Gender Symbols and Urban Landscape," *Progress in Human Geography* 16, no. 2 (1992): 157–70; Cosgrove, *Social Formation*; Stephen Daniels, "Marxism, Culture, and the Duplicity of Landscape," in *New Models in Geography*, vol. 2, ed. R. Peet and N. Thrift (London: Unwin Hyman, 1989), 196–220; James S. Duncan, *The City as Text: The Politics of Landscape Interpretation in the Kandyan Kingdom* (New York: Cambridge University Press, 1990); Jon Goss, "Disquiet on the Waterfront: Reflections on Nostalgia and Utopia in the Urban Archetypes of Festival Marketplaces," *Urban Geography* 17, no. 3 (1997): 221–47; Judith Kenny, "Climate, Race, and Imperial Authority: The Symbolic Landscape of the British Hill Station in India," *Annals of the Association of American Geographers* 85, no. 4 (1995): 694–714; Paul R. Knox, "The Restless Urban Landscape: Economic and Socio-Cultural Change and the Transformation of Metropolitan Washington, D.C.," *Annals of the Association of American Geographers* 81, no. 2 (1991): 181–209; C.A. Mills, "Life on the Upslope: The Postmodern Landscape of Gentrification," *Environment and Planning D: Society and Space* 6, no. 2 (1988): 169–90; Jan Monk, "Gender in the Landscape: Expressions of Power

and Meaning," in *Inventing Places*, ed. Kay Anderson and Fay Gale (Melbourne: Longman-Cheshire, 1992), 123–38; Catherine Nash, "Remapping the Body/Land: New Cartographies of Identity, Gender, and Landscape in Ireland," in *Writing Women and Space*, ed. Alison Blunt and Gillian Rose (New York: Guilford Press, 1994), 227–50.

10. Michel Foucault, *Power/Knowledge*, ed. Colin Gordon (New York: Pantheon Books, 1980); Michel Foucault, *Discipline and Punish*, trans. Alan Sheridan (New York: Vintage Books, 1979); Michel de Certeau, *The Practice of Everyday Life* (Berkeley: University of California Press, 1979); Pierre Bourdieu, *Outline of a Theory of Practice* (New York: Cambridge University Press, 1977).

11. Richard H. Schein, "The Place of Landscape: A Conceptual Framework for Interpreting an American Scene," *Annals of the Association of American Geographers* 87, no. 4 (1997), 660–80.

12. See Kenneth W. Goings and Raymond A. Mohl, *The New African American Urban History* (Thousand Oaks, Calif.: Sage, 1996).

13. Michael Omi and Howard Winant, *Racial Formation in the United States from the 1960s to the 1990s* (London: Routledge, 1994), 55–56; emphasis in original.

14. Richard H. Schein, "Racialized Landscapes," *The Professional Geographer* (forthcoming).

15. David Delaney, *Race, Place, and the Law 1836–1948* (Austin: University of Texas Press, 1998); Douglas S. Massey and Nancy A. Denton, *American Apartheid* (Cambridge: Harvard University Press, 1993).

16. See Arnold R. Hirsch, *Making the Second Ghetto: Race and Housing in Chicago, 1940–1960* (New York: Cambridge University Press, 1983); Kenneth Jackson, *Crabgrass Frontier: The Suburbanization of the United States* (New York: Oxford University Press, 1985), esp. pp. 190–218; Thomas J. Sugrue, *The Origins of the Urban Crisis: Race and Inequality in Postwar Detroit* (Princeton: Princeton University Press, 1996).

17. Susan M. Roberts, "A Critical Evaluation of the City Lifecycle Idea," *Urban Geography* 12, no. 5 (1991): 431–49.

18. Elliott Rudwick, *Race Riot at East St. Louis, July 2, 1917* (Urbana: University of Illinois Press, 1982).

19. In *Buchanan v. Warley*, the U.S. Supreme Court found a segregation ordinance in Louisville, Kentucky, unconstitutional. See Delaney, *Race, Place and the Law*, pp. 123–24, and Massey and Denton, *American Apartheid*, pp. 187–88.

20. Robert T. Ernst, "Factors of Isolation and Interaction in an All-Black City: Kinloch, Missouri" (Ph.D. diss., University of Florida, 1973); Harold Rose, "The All-Negro Town: Problems and Alternatives," *The Geographical Review* (July 1965): 362–81.

21. D. W. Meinig, "Symbolic Landscapes: Models of American Community," in *The Interpretation of Ordinary Landscapes*, ed. Meinig, pp. 164–93.

22. Eugene McCann, "Race, Protest, and Public Space: Contextualizing Lefebvre in the U.S. City," *Antipode* 31, no. 2 (1999): 163–84; Owen Dwyer,

"White Space" (University of Kentucky, Department of Geography, 1999, photocopy).

23. Richard Ulack, Karl B. Raitz, and Hilary Lambert Hopper, eds., *Lexington and Kentucky's Inner Bluegrass Region,* Pathways in Geography, no. 10 (Indiana, Penn.: National Council for Geographic Education, 1994); John Kellogg, "The Formation of Black Residential Areas in Lexington, Kentucky, 1865–1887," *Journal of Southern History* 48, no. 1 (1982): 21–52.

24. Karl Raitz and Dorn VanDommelen, "Creating the Landscape Symbol Vocabulary for a Regional Image: The Case of the Kentucky Bluegrass," *Landscape Journal* 9, no. 2 (1990): 109–21.

25. J. P. Radford, "Identity and Tradition in the Post–Civil War South," *Journal of Historical Geography* 18, no. 1 (1992): 91–103; H. E. Gulley, "Women and the Lost Cause: Preserving a Confederate Identity in the American Deep South," *Journal of Historical Geography* 19, no. 2 (1993): 125–41.

26. David Harvey, "From Managerialism to Entrepreneurialism: The Transformation in Urban Governance in Late Capitalism," *Geografiska Annaler* 71, B (1989): 3–17; Susan M. Roberts and Richard H. Schein, "The Entrepreneurial City: Fabricating Urban Development in Syracuse, New York," *Professional Geographer* 45, no. 1 (1993): 21–34.

27. Schein, "Racialized Landscapes."

28. In fact, Thoroughbred Park is one site in a mile-long *cordon sanitaire* that completely marks off the East End from the rest of Lexington's downtown. That barrier has been a long time in the making and includes the "urban renewal" of a formerly African American business district into a federally funded inner transportation ring meant to funnel rush-hour traffic more efficiently through the downtown into surrounding suburbs.

29. "For Artist, Park Is Greatest Challenge," *Lexington Herald Leader,* October 28, 1989.

30. Raitz and VanDommelen, "Creating the Landscape Symbol Vocabulary."

31. "A Crowded Field for Opening Day," *Lexington Herald Leader,* April 19, 1992.

32. Daniels, "Marxism."

13. FIEGE, "THE ECOLOGICAL COMMONS IN THE WEST"

The author thanks Janet Ore, Chris Wilson, Paul Groth, and the American Studies Faculty Reading Group at Colorado State University for their help and suggestions.

1. For the property-rights viewpoint, see William Perry Pendley, *War on the West: Government Tyranny on America's Great Frontier* (Washington, D.C.: Regnery Publishing, 1995). For a scholarly assessment, see Jacqueline

Vaughn Switzer, *Green Backlash: The History and Politics of the Environmental Opposition* (Boulder, Colo.: Lynne Rienner Publishers, 1997). The Hutchison quotation is from her foreword to Pendley, *War on the West*, p. xiii.

2. See, for example, Lizabeth Cohen, "From Town Center to Shopping Center," *American Historical Review* 101 (October 1996): 1050–81; Dolores Hayden, "Urban Landscape History," in *Understanding Ordinary Landscapes*, ed. Paul Groth and Todd W. Bressi (New Haven: Yale University Press, 1997); Mary Ryan, *Civic Wars: Democracy and Public Life in America during the Nineteenth Century* (Berkeley: University of California Press, 1997). The latest, most comprehensive, and by far most popular contribution to this debate (albeit one that does not focus on space or landscape) is social scientist Robert D. Putnam's *Bowling Alone: The Collapse and Revival of American Community* (New York: Simon and Schuster, 2000).

3. A discussion of this term as applied to the irrigated landscape of southern Idaho is in Mark Fiege, *Irrigated Eden: The Making of an Agricultural Landscape in the American West* (Seattle: University of Washington Press, 1999), pp. 60–61, 69–73, 79. This essay also builds on the work of environmental historians who have taken a more ecological (as opposed to a more cultural) approach to landscape studies; classic works include William Cronon, *Changes in the Land: Indians, Colonists, and the Ecology of New England* (New York: Hill and Wang, 1983); Richard White, *Land Use, Environment, and Social Change: The Shaping of Island County, Washington* (Seattle: University of Washington Press, 1980); and Donald Worster, *Dust Bowl: The Southern Plains in the 1930s* (New York: Oxford University Press, 1979).

4. Hildegard Binder Johnson, *Order upon the Land: The Rectangular Survey and the Upper Mississippi Country* (New York: Oxford University Press, 1976), and Johnson, "Rational and Ecological Aspects of the Quarter Section: An Example from Minnesota," *Geographical Review* 47 (July 1957): 330–48; J. B. Jackson, "Concluding with Landscapes," in *Discovering the Vernacular Landscape* (New Haven: Yale University Press, 1984), pp. 145–57; Jackson, "The Mobile Home on the Range," in *A Sense of Place, a Sense of Time* (New Haven: Yale University Press, 1994), pp. 51–67; Jackson, "The Discovery of the Street," in *The Necessity for Ruins and Other Topics* (Amherst: University of Massachusetts Press, 1980), pp. 55–66; Edward Soja, *Thirdspace: Journeys to Los Angeles and Other Real-and-Imagined Places* (Cambridge, England: Blackwell Publishers, 1996), esp. pp. 1–23. A recent work that discusses the permeability of private property boundaries is Eric Freyfogle, *Bounded People, Bounded Lands: Envisioning a New Land Ethic* (Washington, D.C.: Island Press, 1998).

5. The literature on common property resources is extensive. For an excellent discussion of the topic generally, see Louis Warren, *The Hunter's Game: Poachers and Conservationists in Twentieth-Century America* (New Haven: Yale University Press, 1997), esp. pp. 1–20, 183 nn. 8 and 9. See also Bonnie J. McCay and James Acheson, eds., *The Question of the Commons: The Culture and Ecology of Communal Resources* (Tucson: Arizona Studies in Human Ecology, 1987).

6. Other scholars have alluded to various sorts of commons coexisting with private property. Samuel Hays describes the problems of air, water, land, and pollution within "the urban commons." See his *Beauty, Health, and Permanence: Environmental Politics in the United States, 1955–1985* (New York: Cambridge University Press, 1987), p. 73. Environmental journalist Michael Pollan describes the genetics of crop plants as "the last great commons in nature." See his "Playing God in the Garden," *New York Times Magazine*, October 25, 1998, p. 92. One of J. B. Jackson's comments about vernacular space is relevant: "We have no legal title to it, but custom, unwritten law tells us we can use it in meeting our daily needs. Vernacular space is to be shared, not exploited or monopolized. It is never a source of wealth or power, it is in the literal sense of the term a common ground, a common place, a common denominator which makes each vernacular neighborhood a miniature commonwealth." See Jackson, "Mobile Home on the Range," 67.

7. Unless otherwise noted, the following examples are drawn from Fiege, *Irrigated Eden*.

8. Renee Guillierie and Sharon Norris, eds., *Serving People and the Land: A History of Idaho's Soil Conservation Movement* (n.p., 1985), p. 12.

9. I heard this phrase from several people while doing research in Idaho in the early 1990s. Women in particular seemed to find it amusing. For a discussion of irrigators' belief that they "own" the river, see Tim Palmer, *The Snake River: Window to the West* (Washington, D.C.: Island Press, 1991), p. 22.

10. "The Noxious Weeds of Pony: Together We Can Make a Difference!" *The Tobacco Root News: A Publication of the Concerned Citizens of Pony,* March 1998, 2.

11. The legal challenge to fees for drainage systems is one example of landowners who opposed public programs in the ecological commons. For another example outside Idaho, see the news item from the Glendale, California, *Farm Bureau Monthly* that was reprinted in *Reclamation Record* 9 (September 1918): 426, which mentioned recalcitrant landowners and suggested that they were unpatriotic. Perhaps the best example of resistance today is the widespread western opposition to the 1973 Endangered Species Act. Clearly, westerners are more accepting of local public authorities destroying pests on private land than they are of federal government officials preserving on the same ground flora and fauna in danger of extinction. The public interest (and the ecological commons) is obvious to them in the first case, but not in the second.

12. B. J. Nickel, "Public Must Help Get Out Information on Fire Ban," *Fort Collins Coloradoan*, August 21, 2000; John Opie, *Ogallala: Water for a Dry Land* (Lincoln: University of Nebraska Press, 1993), pp. 161–96; Charles Wilkinson, *Crossing the Next Meridian: Land, Water, and the Future of the West* (Washington, D.C.: Island Press, 1992), pp. 175–218. For another example, see Jim Yardley, "Houston, Smarting Economically from Smog, Searches for Remedies," *New York Times*, September 24, 2000.

13. Elizabeth Neus, "Quarantine Laws Outdated, More Difficult to Apply," *Fort Collins Coloradoan*, September 4, 2000; "When Parents Say No

to Vaccinations," *New York Times,* January 2, 2001; Philip Fradkin, *A River No More: The Colorado River and the West* (New York: Knopf, 1968; reprint, Berkeley: University of California Press, 1996), pp. 235–341; Matt Crenson, "Study: U.S. Dioxin Travels to Arctic," *Fort Collins Coloradoan,* October 4, 2000 (quote); Philip J. Hilts, "Dioxin in Arctic Circle Is Traced to Sources Far to the South," *New York Times,* October 17, 2000. For other examples, see Philip Brasher, "Imported Lemons Leave Sour Taste for U.S. Growers: Farmers Fear Diseased Fruit Will Get Through," *Fort Collins Coloradoan,* September 4, 2000; Elaine Sciolino, "2015 Outlook: Enough Food, Scarce Water, Porous Borders," *New York Times,* December 18, 2000.

14. SEWELL, "GENDER, IMAGINATION, AND EXPERIENCE"

1. J. B. Jackson, "The Word Itself," in Jackson, *Landscape in Sight: Looking at America,* ed. Helen Lefkowitz Horowitz (New Haven: Yale University Press, 1997), p. 305.

2. Paul Groth, "Frameworks for Cultural Landscape Study," in *Understanding Ordinary Landscapes,* ed. Paul Groth and Todd W. Bressi (New Haven: Yale University Press, 1997), p. 1.

3. Several scholars have worked closely with aspects of this trio. For example, Dell Upton, in works such as "Another City: The Urban Cultural Landscape in the Early Republic," in *Everyday Life in the Early Republic,* ed. Catherine E. Hutchins (Winterthur, Del.: Henry Francis du Pont Winterthur Museum, 1994), pp. 61–118, has explored the relationship between ideological constructs, or imagined landscapes, their physical manifestations in the urban landscape, and the ideology constructed to make sense of the unintended consequences of those physical manifestations. Don Mitchell, in *The Lie of the Land: Migrant Workers and the California Landscape* (Minneapolis: University of Minnesota Press, 1996), addresses the conflicted and complicated relationship between the representations (and imaginations) of California and California as experienced by migrant workers. Rina Swentzell's "Conflicting Landscape Values: The Santa Clara Pueblo and Day School," in *Understanding Ordinary Landscapes,* ed. Groth and Bressi, pp. 56–66, explores the conflicting imaginings of space by Native Americans and the U.S. government. Rhyss Isaac's *The Transformation of Virginia, 1740–1790* (Chapel Hill: University of North Carolina Press, 1982) provides an excellent example of the differing experiences of a landscape for those in different class and race positions. Other works, such as Denis Cosgrove's *Social Formation and Symbolic Landscape* (Madison: University of Wisconsin Press, 1998), explore in detail the ideological and cultural meanings of the idea of landscape. See also Denis Cosgrove and Stephen Daniels, eds., *The Iconography of Landscape: Essays on the Symbolic Representation, Design, and Use of Past Environments* (Cambridge: Cambridge University Press, 1988); Kenneth Olwig, "Sexual Cosmology: Nation and Landscape at the Interstices of Nature and Culture; or, What Does Land-

scape Really Mean?" in *Landscape: Politics and Perspectives,* ed. Barbara Bender (Providence: Berg, 1993), pp. 307–43; and W. T. J. Mitchell, ed., *Landscape and Power* (Chicago: University of Chicago Press, 1994).

4. Gwendolyn Wright's chapter "Victorian Suburbs and the Cult of Domesticity," in *Building the Dream: A Social History of Housing in America* (Cambridge: MIT Press, 1981), provides a detailed examination of the creation of American suburbs and their gendered underpinnings. Marion Roberts, in *Living in a Man-Made World: Gender Assumptions in Modern Housing Design* (London and New York: Routledge, 1991), explores working-class suburbanization in England, including the ideological presuppositions underlying it and its material effects on women's lives. In *Discrimination by Design: A Feminist Critique of the Man-Made Environment* (Urbana: University of Illinois Press, 1992), Leslie Kanes Wiesman critiques suburbia as part of a "spatial caste system" in which women are "confined to and maintain" domestic space that men rule (p. 86). Dolores Hayden provides possibilities for remaking suburbia in *Redesigning the American Dream* (New York: W. W. Norton and Company, 1984).

5. *Trips Around San Francisco* (n.p.: Southern Pacific Company, 1917), p. 11.

6. Ibid., p. 22.

7. Charles Keeler, *San Francisco and Thereabouts* (San Francisco: California Promotion Committee, 1903), p. 40.

8. John J. Conlon, Wells Fargo vice president, quoted in Angel Kwolek-Folland, *Engendering Business* (Baltimore: Johns Hopkins University Press, 1994), p. 166.

9. Ibid., pp. 117–19.

10. Ibid., p. 120.

11. Ibid., p. 123.

12. Quoted in Susan Porter Benson, *Counter Cultures: Saleswomen, Managers, and Customers in American Department Stores, 1890–1940* (Urbana: University of Illinois Press, 1986), p. 76.

13. C. E. Cake, "Arranging Goods to Make the Shoppers Buy," *System* 18 (December 1910): 593, quoted in Benson, *Counter Cultures,* p. 76.

14. Eva Carlin, "'America's Grandest' in California," *Arena* 22 (September 1899): 335, quoted in Benson, *Counter Cultures,* pp. 84–85.

15. *How to Advertise to Men* (n.p.: The System Company, 1912), contrasts selling to women, which uses emotion and desire, with the only successful mode of selling to men, which is logical argument, aimed at convincing buyers that the product will save money and time. The book argues that, unlike a woman, "a man does not buy ALL that he wants. To DESIRE a thing is not to immediately buy it" (p. 10).

16. Paul Dubuisson, "Les Voleuses des Grands Magasins," 1903, quoted in Elaine S. Abelson, *When Ladies Go a-Thieving: Middle-Class Shoplifters in the Victorian Department Store* (Oxford: Oxford University Press, 1989), 46. Women's emotional abandon when faced with seductive displays of wares is also described in several long passages in Emile Zola's *Au Bonheur des Dames* (translated into English as *The Ladies' Paradise*).

17. Keeler, *San Francisco and Thereabouts*, p. 37.

18. Richard M. Hurd, *Principles of City Land Values* (New York: Record and Guide, 1911); Cecil C. Evers, *The Commercial Problem in Buildings* (New York: Record and Guide, 1914).

19. *Trips Around San Francisco*, p. 11.

20. Allan Dunn, *Care-Free San Francisco* (San Francisco: A.M. Robertson, 1912), pp. 19–20.

21. Ibid., p. 19.

22. Fannie McLean, "Campaign of Ed," in McLean Family Papers (BANC MSS C-B 501), the Bancroft Library, University of California, Berkeley.

23. College Equal Suffrage League of Northern California, *Winning Equal Suffrage in California: Reports of Committees of the College Equal Suffrage League of Northern California in the Campaign of 1911* (n.p.: National College Equal Suffrage League, 1913), p. 56.

24. Ibid., p. 80; "Diva Sings for Suffrage," *San Francisco Call*, October 10, 1911, p. 1.

25. Selina Solomons, *How We Won the Vote in California* (San Francisco: New Woman Publishing Co., 1912), p. 55.

26. "Yes, the Lady with the Postals Wants Both Coin and Vote," *San Francisco Call*, October 5, 1911, p. 7.

27. College Equal Suffrage League, *Winning Equal Suffrage*, p. 80.

28. Ibid., pp. 80–81.

29. Ibid., p. 84.

30. Fannie McLean, "Speech to Women's Clubs," in McLean Family Papers, Bancroft Library.

15. MOZINGO, "LAWN CULTURE COMES TO THE CORPORATION"

The preparation of this article was supported by a Harvard University Dumbarton Oaks Fellowship for Studies in Landscape Architecture, a Humanities Research Fellowship of the University of California, Berkeley, and the Beatrix Farrand Fund of the Department of Landscape Architecture and Environmental Planning, University of California, Berkeley. Site visits were funded by a Committee on Research Junior Faculty Grant of the University of California, Berkeley.

1. Richard Walker, "A Theory of Suburbanization: Capitalism and the Construction of Urban Space in the United States," in *Urbanization and Urban Planning in Capitalist Society*, ed. Michael Dear and A.J. Scott (New York: Methuen, 1981), pp. 383–429; John R. Stilgoe, *Borderland: Origins of the American Suburb, 1920–1939* (New Haven: Yale University Press, 1988); and Kenneth T. Jackson, *Crabgrass Frontier* (New York: Oxford University Press, 1985).

2. Alfred Dupont Chandler, Jr., *The Visible Hand: The Managerial Revolution in American Business* (Cambridge: Harvard University Press, 1977),

and Chandler, *Scale and Scope: The Dynamics of Industrial Capitalism* (Cambridge: Harvard University Press, Belknap Press, 1990).

3. J.B. Jackson, "The Popular Yard," *Places* 4, no. 3 (1987): 26, 30.

4. Wayne G. Broehl, *John Deere's Company: The Story of Deere and Company and Its Times* (New York: Doubleday, 1984), pp. 614–15.

5. "Should Management Move to the Country," *Fortune* 46, no. 6 (December 1952): 166.

6. L. Andrew Reinhard and Henry Hofmeister, "New Trends in Office Design," *Architectural Record* 97, no. 3 (March 1945): 99–101; Douglas Lathrop, "New Departures in Office Building Design," *Architectural Record* 102, no. 4 (October 1947): 119–23; Francis Bello, "The City and the Car," *Fortune* 56, no. 4 (October 1957): 192.

7. General Foods, *GF Moving Day and You* (New York: General Foods, 1952).

8. "Should Management Move to the Country," 166.

9. Employees of the former General Foods, now part of Kraft Foods, interviewed by the author, June 1997.

10. "Why Companies Are Fleeing the Cities," *Time*, April 26, 1971, pp. 86–88; Richard Reeves, "Loss of Major Companies Conceded by City Official," *New York Times*, February 5, 1971; J. Roger O'Meara, "Executive Suites in Suburbia," *Conference Board Report* 9, no. 8 (August 1972): 6–16; Herbert E. Meyer, "Why Corporations Are on the Move," *Fortune* 92, no. 5 (May 1976): 252–72.

11. "Offices Move to the Suburbs," *Business Week*, March 17, 1951, p. 82.

12. "Explains Plans of Laboratory," *Newark News*, August 1, 1930.

13. William Story, "Advertising the Site through Good Design," *Landscape Architecture* 49, no. 3 (spring 1959): 144.

14. "For Corporate Life '57," *Newsweek*, September 16, 1957, pp. 114–15; "Building with a Future," *Time*, September 16, 1957, p. 91; "Symposium in a Symbolic Setting," *Life*, October 21, 1957, pp. 49–54.

15. "Should Management Move to the Country," p. 116; O'Meara, "Executive Suites in Suburbia"; Meyer, "Why Corporations Are on the Move."

16. "Should Management Move to the Country," 168.

17. Philip Herrera, "That Manhattan Exodus," *Fortune* 75, no. 6 (June 1967): 144.

18. Reeves, "Loss of Major Companies," 39.

19. Robert Hewitt, quoted in "Administrative Center" video presentation at the Deere and Company Administrative Center, Moline, Illinois, viewed by the author June 1997.

20. Mildred Reed Hall and Edward T. Hall, *The Fourth Dimension in Architecture: The Impact of Building on Behavior* (Santa Fe: Sunstone Press, 1975), pp. 58, 61.

21. Edward H. Laird, "Electronics Park: An Industrial Center for the General Electric Company," *Landscape Architecture* 38, no. 1 (October 1946): 16.

22. Roland Marchand, *Advertising the American Dream: Making the Way for Modernity, 1920–1940* (Berkeley: University of California Press, 1998).

23. Kenneth A. Meade, "The Shortage of Scientific Personnel: What Industry Is Doing About It" (address to the National Association for the Advancement of Science) *Science* 105, no. 2731 (May 1947): 460.

24. "New View of Metals," *Business Week*, August 27, 1955, p. 158.

25. Francis Bello, "The World's Greatest Industrial Laboratory," *Fortune* 58, no. 5 (November 1958): 155.

26. Laird, "Electronics Park," pp. 14–16; "Electronics Park, Syracuse, New York," *Architectural Record* 105, no. 2 (February 1949): 96–103; "Large Corporation Builds a Research Campus in New Jersey," *Architectural Record* 106, no. 4 (October 1949): 108–14; Clifford F. Rassweiler, "The Johns-Manville Research Center Six Years Later," *Architectural Record* 118, no. 3 (September 1955): 222–24.

27. Russell Lynes, "After Hours: The Erosion of Detroit," *Harper's*, January 1960, pp. 24. Lynes is the author of *The Tastemakers* (New York: Grosset and Dunlap, 1949); Peirce Lewis commends him thus: "Nobody has written more perceptively and engagingly about [taste in America] than Russell Lynes." See Peirce Lewis, "American Landscape Tastes," in *Modern Landscape Architecture: A Critical Review*, ed. Marc Treib (Cambridge: MIT Press, 1993), pp. 2–18.

28. Christopher Tunnard and Boris Pushkarev, *Man-Made America: Chaos or Control* (New Haven: Yale University Press, 1964), p. 294.

29. "IBM West Coast Programming Center," *Process Architecture* 85 (October 1989): 74–77.

30. Philip Enquist, Skidmore, Owings and Merrill, interviewed by the author, June 1993.

31. Louise A. Mozingo, "The Corporate Estate in the USA, 1954–64: 'Thoroughly modern in concept, but . . . down to earth and rugged,'" *Studies in the History of Gardens and Designed Landscapes* 20, no. 1 (January–March 2000): 25–55.

32. *The Donald M. Kendall Sculpture Garden* (Harrison, N.Y.: PepsiCo [1997?]); "Weyerhaeuser Corporate Headquarters," *Process Architecture* 85 (October 1989): 44–49; Peter Walker, interview with the author, November 1997.

33. Laurie Olin, "Regionalism and the Practice of Hanna/Olin, Ltd.," in *Regional Garden Design in the United States*, ed. Therese O'Malley and Marc Treib (Washington, D.C.: Dumbarton Oaks, 1995), pp. 243–69; Mildred Schmertz, "Recollection and Invention," *Architectural Record* 176, no. 1 (January 1988): 62–72; Robert Campbell, "Arts and Crafts Spirit Pervades Corporate Offices," *Architecture: AIA Journal* 77, no. 5 (May 1988): 139–43; Robert Campbell, "Intimations of Urbanity in a Bucolic Setting," *Architecture: AIA Journal* 77, no. 1 (January 1988): 72–77; Ellen Posner, "Harmony Not Uniqueness," *Landscape Architecture* 79, no. 4 (May 1989): 43–49; Jory Johnson, "Codex World Headquarters: Regionalism and Invention," *Landscape Architecture* 78, no. 3 (April–May 1991): 155–63; Stephen Kliment, "Rooms with a View," *Architectural Record* 181, no. 11 (November 1993): 80–85.

34. "Wooing White Collars to Suburbia," *Business Week*, July 8, 1967, p. 97.

35. J. Ross McKeever, *Business Parks: Office Parks, Plazas, and Centers* (Washington, D.C.: Urban Land Institute, 1971), p. 18.

36. "The Office Park: A New Concept in Office Space," *Industrial Development and Manufacturers Record* 134, no. 9 (September 1965): 9–13.

37. "Wooing White Collars," 97.

38. McKeever, *Business Parks*, 45–67; "The Office Park," 13–14.

39. "The Office Park," 9–13.

40. McKeever, *Business Parks*, p. 8.

41. National Association of Industrial and Office Parks Education Foundation, *Office Park Development: Comprehensive Examination of Elements of Office Park Development* (Arlington, Va.: National Association of Industrial and Office Parks, 1984), p. 42.

42. Marita Thomas, "Superb Teamwork Forges 'Age-Proof' IBM Center," *Facilities and Management* 82, no. 2 (February 1989): 48–55.

43. David Dillon, "And Two in the Country," *Landscape Architecture* 80, no. 3 (March 1990): 62–63; "IBM Westlake/Southlake," *Process: Architecture* 85 (October 1989): 106–13; "Solana," *Baumeister* 187, no. 4 (April 1990): 32–34; Alan Phillips, *The Best in Science, Office, and Business Park Design* (London: B. T. Batsford, 1993); "Solana, Texas," *Architettura* 36, no. 10 (October 1990): 224–26.

44. Richard Walker, "A Theory of Suburbanization," 391.

45. Gabriel Hauge, "Gabriel Hauge," in *Deere and Company Administrative Center* (Moline, Ill.: Deere and Company, 1964), p. 17.

46. Faye Rice, "Who Scores Best on the Environment," *Fortune* 128, no. 2 (July 1993): 122.

47. J. B. Jackson, "Ghosts at the Door," in Jackson, *Landscape in Sight: Looking at America*, ed. Helen Lefkowitz Horowitz (New Haven: Yale University Press, 1997), p. 113.

16. ROJAS, "STREETS AND YARDS OF EAST LOS ANGELES"

My thanks to Lisa Peattie, Sandra Howell, and Antonia Darder at MIT; in Los Angeles, thanks to my family, the families of Jose Resendez and Easter Celiz, and the residents of Rowan Avenue, Burma Road, and Hendricks Avenue. Thanks also to Paul Groth and Chris Wilson for their editorial assistance with earlier drafts.

1. Gerald D. Suttles, *The Social Order of the Slum: Ethnicity and Territoriality in the Inner City* (Chicago: University of Chicago Press, 1968); Philippe Boudon, *Lived-In Architecture: Le Corbusier's Pessace Revisited* (Cambridge: MIT Press, 1979); Amos Rapoport, *House Form and Culture* (Englewood Cliffs, N.J.: Prentice-Hall, 1969); Oscar Newman, *Defensible Space: Crime Prevention through Urban Design* (New York: Collier Books, 1972); William H. Whyte, *The Social Life of Small Urban Spaces* (Washington, D.C.: Conservation Foundation, 1979). See also Allan Pred, "The Esthetic

Slum," *Landscape* 14, no. 1 (autumn 1964): 16–18; Elliot Liebow, *Tally's Corner: A Study of Negro Streetcorner Men* (Boston: Little, Brown and Company, 1967); Herbert J. Gans, *The Urban Villagers: Group and Class in the Life of Italian-Americans,* updated and expanded (New York: The Free Press, 1982; orig. pub., 1962); and Gans, *The Levittowners: Ways of Life and Politics in a New Suburban Community* (New York: Pantheon Books, 1967).

2. James Rojas, "The Enacted Environment: The Creation of 'Place' by Mexicans and Mexican Americans in East Los Angeles" (master's thesis, Massachusetts Institute of Technology, 1991). On Jackson, see especially J. B. Jackson, *A Sense of Place, a Sense of Time* (New Haven: Yale University Press, 1994). See also Jackson, "Chihuahua as We Might Have Been," *Landscape* 1, no. 1 (spring 1951): 16–24, reprinted in Jackson, *Landscape in Sight: Looking at America,* ed. Helen Lefkowitz Horowitz (New Haven: Yale University Press, 1997), pp. 43–53, and Jackson, "The Discovery of the Street," in *The Necessity for Ruins and Other Topics* (Amherst: University of Massachusetts Press, 1980); Steven A. Yates, ed., *The Essential Landscape: The New Mexico Photographic Survey, with Essays by J. B. Jackson* (Albuquerque: University of New Mexico Press, 1985). See also Daniel D. Arreola and James Curtis, *The Mexican Border Cities: Landscape Anatomy and Place Personality* (Tucson: University of Arizona Press, 1993).

3. In addition to the classic studies already listed, notable ethnographic analyses of the use of open space range from James P. Spradley, *You Owe Yourself a Drunk: An Ethnography of Urban Nomads* (Boston: Little, Brown, 1970), to Ellen Fitzsimmons, *Teach Me: An Ethnography of Adolescent Learning—Cultural Shopping and Student Lore in Urban America* (Latham, Md.: International Scholars Publications, 1999). An example of behavioral insights aimed at design is Clare Cooper Marcus and Wendy Sarkissian, *Housing as if People Mattered: Site Design Guidelines for Medium-Density Family Housing* (Berkeley: University of California Press, 1986).

4. J. B. Jackson, "The Popular Yard," *Places* 4, no. 3 (1987): 26–32 (quotations on p. 29). See also J. B. Jackson's much earlier essay on the front yard, "Ghosts at the Door," *Landscape* 1, no. 2 (autumn 1951): 3–9, reprinted in Jackson, *Landscape in Sight,* 107–17; Melvin Hecht, "The Decline of the Grass Lawn Tradition in Tucson," *Landscape* 19, no. 3 (May 1975): 3–10; Virginia Scott Jenkins, *The Lawn: A History of an American Obsession* (Washington, D.C.: Smithsonian Institution Press, 1994); and Fred E. H. Schroeder, *Front Yard America: The Evolution and Meanings of a Vernacular Domestic Landscape* (Bowling Green, Ohio: Bowling Green State University Popular Press, 1993).

5. See Pamela West, "The Rise and Fall of the American Porch," *Landscape* 20, no. 3 (spring 1976): 42–47.

6. J. B. Jackson, "A Pair of Ideal Landscapes," in Jackson, *Discovering the Vernacular Landscape* (New Haven: Yale University Press, 1984), pp. 9–55; see esp. pp. 13–16.

7. On commercial street life in early-nineteenth-century American cities, see Dell Upton, "The City as Material Culture," in *The Art and Mystery of Historical Archaeology: Essays in Honor of James Deetz,* ed. Anne Elizabeth Yentsch and Mary C. Beaudry (Ann Arbor, Mich.: CRC Press, 1992), pp. 51–74; for controversies on the control of ethnic pushcart vendors in early-twentieth-century New York, see Daniel Bluestone, "The Pushcart Evil," in *The Landscape of Modernity: New York City's Built Environment, 1900–1940,* ed. David Ward and Olivier Zunz (New York: Sage Foundation, 1992), pp. 287–312.

8. On the roots of Los Angeles County boulevards, see Douglas R. Suismann, *Los Angeles Boulevard: Eight X-Rays of the Body Politic,* Forum Publication no. 5 (Los Angeles: Los Angeles Forum for Architecture and Urban Design, 1989), esp. pp. 11–17.

9. The New York City–based Latino architect Miguel Balterra made this observation to me.

10. For basic approaches to New Urbanism, see Alex Krieger and William Lennertz, eds., *Andres Duany and Elizabeth Plater-Zyberk: Towns and Town-Making Principles* (New York: Rizzoli, 1991); Peter Calthorpe, *The Next American Metropolis: Ecology, Community, and the American Dream* (Princeton, N.J.: Princeton Architectural Press, 1993); and Peter Katz, *The New Urbanism: Toward an Architecture of Community* (New York: McGraw-Hill, 1994). A classic study in vernacular urbanism is Robert Venturi, Denise Scott Brown, and Steven Izenour, *Learning from Las Vegas: The Forgotten Symbolism of Architectural Form,* rev. ed. (Cambridge: MIT Press, 1977).

11. See, for instance, J. B. Jackson, "The Sunbelt City: The Modern City, the Strip, and the Civic Center," in Jackson, *The Southern Landscape Tradition in Texas* (Fort Worth: Amon Carter Museum, 1980), pp. 25–36; "Looking into Automobiles," and "Truck City," in Jackson, *A Sense of Place,* pp. 165–70 and 171–85; "The Future of the Vernacular," in *Understanding Ordinary Landscapes,* ed. Paul Groth and Todd W. Bressi (New Haven: Yale University Press, 1997), pp. 145–56; and "The Past and Future Park," in *Denatured Visions: Landscape and Culture in the Twentieth Century,* ed. Stuart Wrede and William Howard Adams (New York: Museum of Modern Art, 1991), pp. 129–34. See also Irwin Altman, *Culture and Environment* (Monterey, Calif.: Brooks-Cole Publishing, 1980), and Lee Shippey, *The Los Angeles Book: Photos by Max Yavno* (Boston: Houghton Mifflin, 1950).

17. SLOANE, "AN AMERICAN HEALTH CARE LANDSCAPE"

I would like to thank Richard Longstreth for sharing materials on Los Angeles mini-malls, Beverlie Conant Sloane for her photographs and research assistance, and Paul Groth and Chris Wilson for their helpful editorial suggestions and for organizing the wonderful conference from which this chapter emerged.

354 I NOTES TO PAGES 293-297

1. J.B. Jackson, "The Future of the Vernacular," in *Understanding Ordinary Landscapes*, ed. Paul Groth and Todd W. Bressi (New Haven: Yale University Press, 1997), pp. 152–53.

2. In "The Almost Perfect Town," *Landscape* 2, no. 1 (spring 1952): 2–8, J.B. Jackson described the mythic Optimo City: "Upstairs are the lawyers, doctors, dentists, insurance firms, the public stenographer, the Farm Bureau. Downstairs are the bank, the prescription drugstore, the newspaper office, and of course Slymaker's Mercantile and the Ranch Cafe" (p. 5). The essay is reprinted in Jackson, *Landscape in Sight: Looking at America*, ed. Helen Lefkowitz Horowitz (New Haven: Yale University Press, 1997), pp. 31–42.

3. On the changing health care environment in the twentieth century, see Rosemary Stevens, *In Sickness and in Wealth: American Hospitals in the Twentieth Century* (New York: Basic Books, 1989); Paul Starr, *The Social Transformation of American Medicine: The Rise of a Sovereign Profession and the Making of a Vast Industry* (New York: Basic Books, 1985); and Roy Porter, *The Greatest Benefit to Mankind: A Medical History of Humanity* (New York: W.W. Norton and Company, 1997).

4. The advertisement, headlined "Designed to Serve the Needs of the Medical Profession," appeared in the *Los Angeles County Medical Association Bulletin*, November 5, 1964, p. 11.

5. David C. Sloane, "Scientific Paragon to Hospital Mall: The Evolving Design of the Hospital, 1885–1994," *Journal of Architectural Education* 48, no. 2 (November 1994): 82–98. See also Allan Brandt and David C. Sloane, "Of Beds and Benches: Building the Modern American Hospital," in *The Architecture of Science*, ed. Peter Galison and Elizabeth Thompson (Cambridge: MIT Press, 1999), pp. 281–308; and David C. Sloane and Beverlie Conant Sloane, *Medicine Moves into the Mall: The Evolving Place of Health Care* (Baltimore: Johns Hopkins University Press, 2002).

6. J.B. Jackson, "The Vernacular City," *Center* 1 (1985): 27–43 (quotations on p. 27); reprinted in Jackson, *Landscape in Sight*, pp. 238–47.

7. Similar trends are visible nationally, especially in the Sun Belt cities and suburbs. I have discovered freestanding "surgicenters" and mini-mall medical facilities in Albany, New York; Houston and Dallas, Texas; Tampa, Florida; and Las Vegas, Nevada. Colleagues have told me about others in Chicago, Philadelphia, and several additional cities and smaller towns.

8. Richard Longstreth, *City Center to Regional Mall: Architecture, the Automobile, and Retailing in Los Angeles, 1920–1950* (Cambridge: MIT Press, 1997), and Longstreth, *The Drive-In, the Supermarket, and the Transformation of Commercial Space in Los Angeles, 1914–1941* (Cambridge: MIT Press, 1999). See also Scott Bottles, *Los Angeles and the Automobile: The Making of the Modern City* (Berkeley and Los Angeles: University of California Press, 1987); Robert Fishman, *Bourgeois Utopias: The Rise and Fall of Suburbia* (New York: Basic Books, 1987); Robert Fogelson, *The Fragmented Metropolis: Los Angeles, 1850–1930* (orig. pub., 1967; reprint, Berkeley and

Los Angeles: University of California Press, 1993); Greg Hise, *Magnetic Los Angeles: Planning the Twentieth-Century Metropolis* (Baltimore: Johns Hopkins University Press, 1997); and Kevin Starr's series on California history, particularly *Material Dreams: Southern California through the 1920s* (New York: Oxford University Press, 1990).

9. Jackson, "The Vernacular City," p. 41.

10. Ibid.

11. Ibid.

12. Longstreth, *City Center to Regional Mall*, esp. pp. 43–55.

13. Ibid. The mini-mall appeared in the popular press in the 1970s and became prevalent in the 1980s. Los Angeles newspaper writers define the mini-mall by its location at a busy commercial intersection, often replacing a closed gasoline station; see James Rainey and Nancy Yoshihara, "Mini-Malls: Life in the Fast Aisle," *Los Angeles Times*, September 7, 1984. I have used a broader definition here. See also Timothy Davis, "The Miracle Mile Revisited: Recycling, Renovation, and Simulation along the Commercial Strip," in *Exploring Everyday Landscapes: Perspectives in Vernacular Architecture*, vol. 7, ed. Annmarie Adams and Sally McMurry (Knoxville: University of Tennessee Press, 1997).

14. Stevens, *In Sickness and in Wealth*, p. 333.

15. David M. Eisenberg et al. discuss sixteen alternative therapies in "Trends in Alternative Medicine Use in the United States, 1990–1997," *Journal of the American Medical Association* 280, no. 18 (November 1998): 1571–72—relaxation techniques, herbal medicine, massage, chiropractic care, spiritual healing by others, megavitamins, self-help groups, imagery, commercial dieting services, folk remedies, lifestyle diet services, energy healing, homeopathy, hypnosis, biofeedback, and acupuncture.

16. For a specific discussion of the eye care industry and a broader look at the changing health care field, see Regina E. Herzlinger, *Market-Driven Health Care: Who Wins, Who Loses in the Transformation of America's Largest Service Industry* (Reading, Mass.: Addison-Wesley, 1997), pp. 29–33.

17. The 1999 telephone book confirmed that hundreds of chiropractors have practices throughout Los Angeles. A look at the 1952 telephone book found around fifty entries, with most situated in small office buildings or in unidentified locations.

18. Herzlinger, *Market-Driven Health Care*, pp. 33–34.

19. An ophthalmologist in the Washington, D.C., suburbs has begun conducting eye surgery at a clinic in a local mall—and providing a viewing screen for passersby to watch the surgery as it is performed. The *New York Times* carried a photograph showing the televised procedures on its front page on August 1, 2000.

20. Construction information comes from a plaque on the building.

21. For one discussion of this issue, see "Beware Unlicensed Clinics," editorial, *Los Angeles Times*, March 2, 1999.

22. A startling example of this fragility is the Highland and Wilshire mini-mall. In the eighteen months between when I first drafted this paper and the final edits, the mini-mall underwent a dramatic round of closures, among them the medical and dental clinics. The acupuncturist and chiropractor survived amid many new businesses. Davis, "The Miracle Mile Revisited," considers the changing landscape of the older commercial strips.

CONTRIBUTORS

GRADY CLAY is a veteran journalist and author who has spent a lifetime specializing in the changing urban environment. He is the author of *Close-Up: How to Read the American City* (1973), *Alleys: A Hidden Resource* (1978), *Right before Your Eyes: Penetrating the Urban Environment* (1987), and *Real Places: An Unconventional Guide to America's Generic Landscape* (1994). He was the first urban-affairs editor for the *Louisville Courier-Journal* and has served as president of the American Society of Planning Officials (now the American Planning Association) and the National Association of Real Estate Editors. For twenty-three years, he was the editor of *Landscape Architecture* magazine. Recipient of the Frederick Law Olmsted Medal from the American Society of Landscape Architects, he currently broadcasts a weekly public radio show in Louisville, *Crossing the American Grain.*

TIMOTHY DAVIS is a historian for the National Park Service's Historic American Engineering Record. He received a Ph.D. in American Studies from the University of Texas at Austin and has written on various aspects of the American landscape, ranging from strip malls and satellite dishes to oil fields, parks, and parkways.

MARK FIEGE is associate professor of history at Colorado State University in Fort Collins, where he teaches courses in U.S., American western, and environmental history. Fiege is author of *Irrigated Eden: The Making of an Agricultural Landscape in the American West* (1999). He is working on an environmental history of the United States.

PAUL GROTH is a cultural landscape historian at the University of California, Berkeley, where he is an associate professor in the Department of Architecture, the Department of Geography, and the American studies program. His book *Living Downtown: The History of Residential Hotels in the United States* (1994) won the J.B. Jackson Award from the American Association of Geographers and the Abbott Lowell Cummings Award from the Vernacular Architecture Forum. He is the coeditor with Todd Bressi of *Understanding Ordinary Landscapes* (1997). He has also published interpretations of urban street grids, parking lots, vernacular parks, and research on the history of workers' cottage districts in the American city.

GEORGE L. HENDERSON teaches at the University of Arizona in Tucson, where he is assistant professor of geography and of comparative cultural and literary studies. His highly regarded first book, *California and the Fictions of Capital* (1999), is a study of how the circulation of agrarian capital shaped bourgeois conceptions of nature, labor, race, and gender. In other published work he has written on ideologies of representation in geography, the new western history, and African American literature. He has been a postdoctoral fellow in American cultural studies at the College of William and Mary, is a board member of the People's Geography Project, and sits on the editorial board of *Antipode*.

HELEN LEFKOWITZ HOROWITZ is Sylvia Dlugasch Bauman professor of American Studies at Smith College, in Northampton, Massachusetts. She is the author of *Culture and the City: Cultural Philanthropy in Chicago from the 1880s to 1917* (1976), *Alma Mater: Design and Experience in the Women's Colleges from Their Nineteenth-Century Beginnings* (1984), *Campus Life: Undergraduate Cultures from the End of the Eighteenth Century to the Present* (1987), *The Power and Passion of M. Carey Thomas* (1994), and coeditor, with Kathy Peiss, of *Love across the Color Line: The Letters of Alice Hanley* (1996). She is the editor of the definitive collection of John Brinckerhoff Jackson's writings, *Landscape in Sight: Looking at America*, completed with Jackson's assistance just before his death, and published in 1997.

PEIRCE LEWIS is professor emeritus in the Department of Geography at Pennsylvania State University, where he also taught in the Honors College and in the American Studies program. His book *New Orleans: The Making of an*

Urban Landscape (1976) remains one of the best one-volume introductions to an American city, and one of the few urban landscape studies that successfully integrates both physical and human geography. Lewis has also written about common houses as footprints of migration and ideas; about Bellefonte, Pennsylvania, as a quintessential small town; and about methods for reading and teaching the cultural landscape. He has been a visiting professor at Michigan State University and at the University of California, Berkeley. He is also a past president of the American Association of Geographers.

JEFFREY W. LIMERICK is an architect living in Boulder, Colorado, and practicing in the Denver region. He holds degrees in architecture from the University of California, Berkeley, and Yale University. Limerick is interested in regionally responsive design and is completing a book called *How to Work with an Architect to Design or Remodel Your Home* for the University Press of Colorado. He is married to Patricia Nelson Limerick, which he reports is quite an adventure.

PATRICIA NELSON LIMERICK is chair of the Board of the Center of the American West and professor of history at the University of Colorado, Boulder. She is the author of *Desert Passages* (1985), *The Legacy of Conquest* (1987), and *Something in the Soil: Legacies and Reckonings in the New West* (2000), and is a contributor to *The Atlas of the New West* (1997) and *The Altered Landscape* (1999). She was introduced to J.B. Jackson by her husband, Jeffrey.

TRACY WALKER MOIR-MCCLEAN is associate professor of architecture and directs the graduate thesis program at the University of Tennessee, Knoxville. Her installation piece and accompanying monograph, *Appalachian Summer Rain Place* (forthcoming), reflect her ongoing interest in landscape, cultural qualities, and the history of region and place as conceptual influences on contemporary architectural design.

LOUISE A. MOZINGO is an associate professor in the Department of Landscape Architecture and Environmental Planning at the University of California, Berkeley, which she joined after practicing as a landscape architect in the Bay Area. Her research and creative work center on three topics: the history of suburban corporate landscapes, the aesthetics of ecological design, and social processes in public landscapes. Her articles have appeared in *Places, Landscape Journal, Journal of the History of Gardens and Designed Landscapes, Landscape Architecture,* and the *Journal of the Society of Architectural Historians.*

JAMES ROJAS holds master of city planning and master of architecture studies degrees from the Massachusetts Institute of Technology. His research on Latino built environments in the United States has appeared in *Places* magazine and the *Los Angeles Times.* A project manager for the Metropolitan Transportation Authority of Los Angeles, Rojas has lectured at universities, colleges, conferences, high schools, and community centers, with a goal of empowering Latinos to understand their environment.

RICHARD H. SCHEIN is associate professor in the Department of Geography and a member of the Committee on Social Theory at the University of Kentucky. He writes about American cultural landscapes, including questions of landscape history, interpretation, representation, and symbolism. He has published articles in the *Annals of the Association of American Geographers, Environment and Planning D: Society and Space,* the *Professional Geographer,* and the *Geographical Review.*

DENISE SCOTT BROWN is a partner in the architecture firm of Venturi, Scott Brown and Associates, known internationally for designs such as the Sainsbury Wing of the National Gallery in London; Wu Hall at Princeton University; the Seattle Art Museum; and the Mielparque Hotel at the Nikko Kirifuri Resort, in Nikko, Japan. She is the author of *Urban Concepts* (1990) and coauthor of the classic *Learning from Las Vegas: The Forgotten Symbolism of Architectural Form* (1977) and *View from the Compidoglio* (1984).

JESSICA SEWELL received her Ph.D. in architecture from the University of California, Berkeley, in 2000, where she has also taught in the Women's Studies and American Studies programs. She is now an assistant professor in the Draper Program at New York University and is the author of the forthcoming book *Gendering the Spaces of Modernity: Women and Public Space in San Francisco, 1890–1915.* She has been a Bancroft Library fellow at Berkeley and a Mellon fellow at the Huntington Library in Los Angeles. Her articles have appeared in *Perspectives in Vernacular Architecture* and in *Metaphysics, Epistemology, and Technology.*

DAVID C. SLOANE is associate professor in the School of Policy, Planning, and Development at the University of Southern California. His research examines issues of urban history and community planning, focusing on evolving cultural landscapes, the health care system, and quality of life in neighborhoods. He is the author of *The Last Great Necessity: Cemeteries in American History* (1991), and coauthor with Beverlie Conant Sloane of *Medicine Moves into the Mall: The Evolving Place of Health Care* (2002).

CHRIS WILSON is the author of *The Myth of Santa Fe: Creating a Modern Regional Tradition* (1997) and *Facing Southwest: The Life and Houses of John Gaw Meem* (2001), and is coauthor of *La Tierra Amarilla: Its History, Archi-*

tecture, and Cultural Landscape (1992). A longtime freelance writer and historic preservation consultant, he was named the J.B. Jackson Professor of Cultural Landscape Studies at the University of New Mexico School of Architecture and Planning in 1999.

GWENDOLYN WRIGHT is professor of architecture, planning, and preservation and professor of history at Columbia University, where she was also the founding director of the Buell Center for Research in American Architecture. She is the author of *Moralism and the Model Home: Domestic Architecture and Cultural Conflict in Chicago, 1873–1913* (1978) and *Building the Dream: A Social History of Housing in America* (1981), among other publications on housing, museum collections, and the practice of architectural history in the United States. Her latest book is *The Politics of Design in French Colonial Urbanism, 1890–1930* (1991).

ILLUSTRATION CREDITS

5.1–5.3 Courtesy of *Landscape,* vol. 15, no. 2, winter 1965–66; vol. 6, no. 2, winter 1956–57; vol. 7, no. 2, winter 1957–58.

5.4–5.5 Photographs by J. B. Jackson, 1973, collection of Chris Wilson. © University of New Mexico.

6.1 Photograph by Peirce Lewis, 1997.

6.2 Photograph by Peirce Lewis, 1977.

6.3–6.7 Photographs by Peirce Lewis, 1998.

6.8 Photograph by Peirce Lewis, 1995.

6.9 Contemporary postcard, c. 1895, collection of Peirce Lewis.

6.10 Contemporary postcard, c. 1905, collection of Peirce Lewis.

6.11 Photograph by Peirce Lewis, 1998.

7.1 Courtesy of the Historical Collections of the New York Academy of Medicine Library.

7.2 From Patrick Geddes, "The Valley in the Town," *Survey,* vol. 54, no. 7, July 1, 1925, p. 398.

7.3 Courtesy of *Landscape,* vol. 7, no. 1, autumn 1957, p. 14.

7.4 J. B. Jackson, untitled travel notebook, January 1–February 25 [?], 1957. Box 2, folder 3, Jackson Collection, MSS 633 BC, Center for Southwest Research, University of New Mexico. © University of New Mexico.

7.5 © *The Courier-Journal* (Louisville; successor of the *Louisville Times*).

7.6–7.7 Photographs by Paul Groth.

8.1–8.2 Photographs by Paul Groth.

8.3 Photograph by J. B. Jackson, collection of Helen Lefkowitz Horowitz. © University of New Mexico.

9.1–9.2 Benjamin R. Whittenburg.

9.3 Richard W. Coleman.

9.4 Tracy Walker Moir-McClean.

9.5 Brandon Pace.

9.6 Stacy L. Andrick.

9.7 Keith Allen.

10.1 Engraving from Marc-Antoine Laugier, *Essai sur l'architecture* (1755; frontispiece).

10.2 Photograph by Bernard Rudofsky, *Architecture without Architects* (New York: Museum of Modern Art, 1964), p. 36.

10.3 Photograph by J. B. Jackson, collection of Paul Groth. © University of New Mexico.

10.4 Photograph by Walter Gropius, *Apollo in the Democracy* (New York: McGraw-Hill, 1958), p. 31.

10.5 April 16, 1997, charrette drawing of Forecourt Houses from Frijoles Village Plan (now Aldea de Santa Fe), Santa Fe, New Mexico, by Duany Plater-Zyberk & Co., Town Planners.

10.6 Drawings by Steven Holl.

10.7 Photograph by Jane Lidz, courtesy of Solomon E. T. C. Architecture and Urban Design, San Francisco, California.

10.8 Lewis W. Hine Collection, Milstein Division of U.S. History, Local History and Genealogy, The New York Public Library, Astor, Lenox and Tilden Foundations.

10.9 Photograph by Bill Owens, from *Suburbia* (San Francisco: Straight Arrow Books, 1973; reprint, New York: Fotofolio, 1999). © Billowens.com.

12.1 Missouri Historical Society Library, St. Louis.

12.2 Richard Gilbreath, Gyula Pauer Center for Cartography and Geographic Information, Department of Geography, University of Kentucky.

12.3–12.4 Missouri Historical Society Library, St. Louis.

12.5–12.7 Photographs by Richard Schein.

13.1 Photograph by Mark Fiege.

13.2 Diagram by Mark Fiege and Joseph M. Gallegos.

13.3 R. W. Stone, United States Geological Survey no. 690.

13.4–13.5 Diagrams by Mark Fiege and Joseph M. Gallegos.

13.6 Idaho State Historical Society no. 73–221.123c.

14.1 *San Francisco: Greetings from California, 1904–1905* (San Francisco: Pacific Art Company, 1904), p. 33.

14.2 The Bancroft Library, University of California, Berkeley.

14.3–14.4 Courtesy of the MetLife Archives.

14.5 *The Art of Decorating* (Chicago: Merchant Record Company, 1906), p. 214.

14.6–14.7 The Bancroft Library, University of California, Berkeley.

14.8 College Equal Suffrage League, *Winning Equal Suffrage in California* (n.p.: National College Equal Suffrage League, 1913), cover.

INDEX

Page references in italic refer to illustrations.

Academics: division of labor by, 339n35; Jackson on, 28–29, 32–34, 75–77, 326nn26,29
Acupuncture, 300–301
Adorno, Theodor, 175
African Americans: ghettos of, 204; landscapes of, 203; of Lexington, 212, 214, 343n28; northward migration of, 206; self-governance, 209; of St. Louis, 204
Agassiz, Louis, 87
Agee, James, 323n4
Agency: everyday forms of, 195; and structure, 15, 17, 181, 217
Aked, Charles F., 251
Albuquerque (New Mexico), cross section of, 331n17
Alluvial fans, 96

"Alpha streets," 127, 331n21
American Can headquarters (Greenwich, Connecticut), 268
American Studies, 180; Jackson on, 35
Anatomy: graphic method of, 111; Vesalius's, 84, 110, 112, 117
Anchorage (Louisville, Kentucky), 124
Anderson, Edgar, 18–19, 317n48
Andrick, Stacy, 156
Angkor (Cambodia), 89, 90
Annals of the Association of American Geographers, 338n23
Annual Fiestas (Taos, New Mexico), 19
Anson, P. G., 321n22
Anthropology: in architectural design, 158; methodological changes in, 339n32

Compositor:	MidAtlantic Books and Journals, Inc.
Text:	10/13 Aldus
Display:	Interstate
Printer/Binder:	Thomson-Shore, Inc.